D0015858

D0015815

The God Problem

The God Problem

EXPRESSING FAITH AND
BEING REASONABLE

ROBERT WUTHNOW

UNIVERSITY OF CALIFORNIA PRESS
Berkeley   Los Angeles   London

University of California Press, one of the most distinguished university presses in the United States, enriches lives around the world by
advancing scholarship in the humanities, social sciences, and natural
sciences. Its activities are supported by the UC Press Foundation and by
philanthropic contributions from individuals and institutions. For more
information, visit www.ucpress.edu.

University of California Press
Berkeley and Los Angeles, California

University of California Press, Ltd.
London, England

© 2012 by The Regents of the University of California

Library of Congress Cataloging-in-Publication Data

Wuthnow, Robert.
    The God problem : expressing faith and being reasonable / Robert Wuthnow.
        p.   cm.
    Includes bibliographical references and index.
    ISBN 978-0-520-27428-0 (cloth)
    1.   Faith and reason—Christianity. I. Title.
    BT50.W88 2012
    212—dc23   2012007438

19 18 17 16 15 14 13 12
10 9 8 7 6 5 4 3 2 1

In keeping with a commitment to support environmentally responsible
and sustainable printing practices, UC Press has printed this book on
Rolland Enviro100, a 100% post-consumer fiber paper that is FSC certified, deinked, processed chlorine-free, and manufactured with renew-
able biogas energy. It is acid-free and EcoLogo certified.

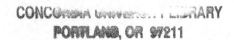
CONCORDIA UNIVERSITY LIBRARY
PORTLAND, OR 97211

Contents

Preface

The message of this book is that we can learn something important about faith by listening closely to the language people use in talking about their faith. One would think we could pretty much take that for granted. But scholarship on American religion has somehow assumed that talk is cheap and for this reason tried to understand faith by focusing on just about everything except what people say about it. Pollsters put their own words in people's mouths by firing questions at them over the telephone and then purport to understand American religion from the 15 percent or so of the people in their sample who actually responded. Historical and ethnographic studies focus on the practice of faith within particular communities. But it is hard to know what people practice unless we also talk to them about the meaning of their faith.

Listening closely to people talking about their faith requires paying attention not only to what they say but also to how they say it. The techniques that facilitate doing this are called discourse analysis. Considerable advances have been made over the past two decades in refining these techniques. The refinement has not come from quantification or computer software as much as from bringing together insights from literary criticism and cognitive science with qualitative methods in the social sciences. Examining religious discourse with these techniques poses new questions and provides new answers about the implicit social norms that shape what people say about their faith and, in turn, why faith flourishes in the presence of those norms.

The evidence demonstrates clearly that expressions of faith in the contemporary United States are powerfully shaped by social norms of reasonableness. When people talk about God, when they pray to God, when they talk about the relationship of God to significant personal and social crises, and when they talk about their own mortality and possibilities of spending eternity in heaven, they talk in specific ways that conform to norms of reasonableness. When evangelical Christians talk about the role of Jesus in their lives, these norms of reasonableness are evident. The same is true in many of the public statements prominent clergy make.

Tacit conformity to these norms of reasonableness is one of the most important clues to the perennial question about America being such a religious nation despite many other features, such as relatively high levels of education, that have always been thought to run against the grain of religion. We manage what are actually very real tensions between faith and reason by shaping our understandings of faith to fit with our understandings of what it means to be reasonable.

Audiences with which I have discussed these claims want to know if I think this adaptation to norms of reasonableness is a good thing or a bad thing. Sometimes the question is framed in terms of assumptions about secularization. Is what we are seeing here evidence that American religion is on a slippery slope toward its possible disappearance, or at least toward capitulating to secularity? Or, short of that, the question is whether my intent is to criticize people of faith for somehow being less devout than they claim to be.

Neither. The secularization question implies having a grasp of long-term historical processes and comparisons among societies over different stages of development. It asks whether norms of reasonableness have become more influential in shaping religion during the long course of history and whether that influence is somehow weakening religion. How anyone could claim to have empirically grounded answers to those questions escapes me. They certainly cannot be answered with the kinds of evidence presented here. Nor can the question of whether this evidence amounts to a criticism of American religion.

It is unfortunate that commentary about American religion has become so charged with normative concerns that these questions have become dominant. The aim here is to observe and describe as dispassionately as possible the specific ways in which some Americans talk about important aspects of their faith. My claim to having unearthed something new or important involves only the idea that the discursive devices we use to express our faith in reasonable ways are often so subtle and so taken for granted that we are unaware of them. In becoming more aware of them, it is up to people themselves to decide whether their implicit understandings are consistent with what they claim to believe.

My argument is critical of the so-called new atheist writers who say religion is so crazy that nobody in their right mind could take it seriously, but I agree with these writers that if religion was as crazy as they say it is, it would indeed be hard to believe. These writers have made a valuable contribution by identifying precisely the kind of religion that most believers distance themselves from when they are given a chance to talk about their faith on their own terms.

A person who wants to be reasonable and regards faith as unreasonable might abandon religion altogether. However, the evidence here suggests that people of faith accommodate rather well, perhaps even easily, to norms of reasonableness. That accommodation reduces the potential conflict. We might even say that it facilitates faith. A person who believes firmly in God and who finds meaning, inspiration, and comfort in that belief can do so without experiencing the sense that this belief is fundamentally incompatible with being a reasonable person.

I do not mean to suggest that all people of faith always conform to norms of reasonableness. Certainly there are believers who relish arguing that their beliefs are not reasonable. They may take pride in having special insights about God or divine revelations that have escaped the minds of ordinary people. Those claims are made often enough that the interesting question is not why they are made but why so many people of faith distance themselves from such claims.

I am indebted to a number of people who assisted valuably with the work that went into this book. Many of the interviews were conducted by Peter Mundey, Steve Offutt, and Karen Myers. Karen Myers also supervised the transcription process and Donna Defrancisco handled many of the administrative tasks. Some of the research emerged as spin-off ideas from projects supported by the Lilly Endowment, the John Templeton Foundation, and Princeton University. Students and colleagues associated with the Center for the Study of Religion were particularly helpful as conversation partners and sounding boards in the development of the ideas. Earlier versions of several chapters were presented at the Religious Research Association meetings, at Yale Divinity School, and at Princeton's Cognitive and Textual Methods seminar.

Introduction

It has become fashionable again in recent years to criticize religion—either as a kind of vestigial superstition that can now be understood in purely naturalistic terms or as something downright reprehensible. The best-known critics include the prominent philosopher Daniel C. Dennett, author of *Breaking the Spell: Religion as a Natural Phenomenon*, and the evolutionary biologist and popular science writer Richard Dawkins, most notably in *The God Delusion*. Works of a more tendentious nature have been written by religious studies graduate student turned neuroscientist Sam Harris, author of *The End of Faith: Religion, Terror, and the Future of Reason*, and by journalist Christopher Hitchens, author of the controversial bestseller *God Is Not Great: How Religion Poisons Everything*. Books taking up related themes include A. C. Grayling's *Against All Gods: Six Polemics on Religion and an Essay on Kindness* and Victor J. Stenger's *God: The Failed Hypothesis: How*

Science Shows That God Does Not Exist. These works vary considerably in tone and in the degree to which they provide supporting evidence and compelling arguments, but they tell a common story: Religion's intellectual foundations are flimsy enough and its social effects are sufficiently dubious that thinking people should be cautious about its claims.[1]

Very little in these books is new. Those of us who call ourselves social scientists have always treated religion as if it were an observable part of the human world and to be studied with the same kind of rigorous, impartial investigation as any other social phenomenon. The roots of our methodological approach can be found in the writings of nineteenth-century thinkers who took a naturalistic view of religion. And it is hardly news to point out that religion has been used to support human sacrifice, war, slavery, mutilation, and all sorts of other atrocities. Even the fact that some of these books have sold well should not be surprising. Mark Twain, Oscar Wilde, H. L. Mencken, Robert Ingersoll, and Madeleine Murray O'Hare all gained notoriety for their negative views of religion. In the post-9/11 world, it is certainly understandable that there is a market for work taking a hard look at the dark side of religion.

However, there is a puzzle. If religion is such a problematic idea, why do so many Americans claim to believe in God? After all, the United States has one of the highest levels of education in the world. The percentages of Americans who attend college, graduate from college, and earn advanced postgraduate degrees have all been rising. Yet there is no evidence that religion is declining.[2] Quite the contrary. It is, if anything, flourishing. Millions of Americans—far more than in any similarly educated country—pray every day. They flock to houses of worship on weekends, watch programs about faith on television, and purchase books about religion—apparently even books that question religion. This is in a nation that expends huge sums every year supporting higher education and funding science. Highly educated Americans continue to believe in God even though they live in a time of unparalleled advances in genomics, neuroscience, and astrophysics. And it is not just that they have yet to read bestsellers casting doubt on religion. These doubts have been around for a long time.

My contention—which I hope to persuade readers of in the course of this book—is that well-educated, thoughtful Americans have found a way of having their cake and eating it too: of affirming their faith while also maintaining their belief in reason. There is no other way to explain the fact that Americans can be as intelligent, thoughtful, and well-educated as they are and believe in God at the same time. The secret does not lie in mental compartmentalization, as critics of American culture sometimes argue, or in a failure of the education system. The coexistence of reason—including reasonable doubt or uncertainty—and faith cannot be attributed to wishful thinking, bad logic, or some mindless, intuitive yearning for divine solace. It has to be taken squarely into account. Many people do entertain doubts, which they have thought seriously about, and yet they also find ways in which to express their faith.

If this juxtaposition of reasonable uncertainty and religious faith is a distinctive characteristic of American culture, it is by no means limited to the United States. Though less evident on as wide a scale, the possibility of expressing a devout commitment to the tenets of religion and at the same time finding ways to avoid sounding like an untutored bigot are common among highly educated and otherwise thoughtful people everywhere. The United States merely provides an extreme case and is thus an interesting laboratory in which to examine how this happens. Is it enough merely to assert, as reasonable people often do, that it is *reasonable* to be religious? Or is it more likely that nearly taken-for-granted habits of thought and speech provide the vehicles through which both doubt and faith are expressed?

The critics of religion are absolutely correct about one thing: There is a God problem. Belief in God is a dubious conviction. There is no getting around it. Nobody can prove that God created the universe or human life, but scientists can offer much evidence about the evolution of life through natural selection. A person who claims to know God's will is likely to be plagued with some doubt about how it is possible to make such an assertion. It is difficult to explain what prayer is or why a person should believe in it, let alone to say whether or not a prayer has been answered. If thoughts of life after death are comforting, they lead readily to the further thought that perhaps they exist only because they are comforting. The casual view that religion is really more about traditions and questions than about beliefs shows only that there are indeed difficulties and that perhaps the persistence of religion lies only in its traditions. Logical proofs for why God must exist or for why God's existence cannot be ruled out are interesting intellectual exercises to which generations of professional philosophers have devoted themselves, but at the end of the day they are not the basis on which thinking people believe in the divine. If the common, decently well-educated person has heard of such proofs, it may be comforting to know that some philosopher or theologian somewhere has thought of one. But that person himself or herself would be unable to repeat it, and there would still be plenty of evidence to raise doubts. The evidence would be from prayers going unanswered, from personal tragedies suffered, from being convinced of the value of science, and from reading about evils perpetrated in the name of religion.

The delicate juggling of reason and faith is accomplished through language. Religion is sometimes considered to be a matter of behavior, such as doing good deeds and participating in worship services. But it is always about language. The cup of water, for the Christian, is to be given in the Lord's name. The worship service is awash in words. In the beginning, the scripture says, was the Word. Talking—out loud or mentally—is how we make sense of our worlds. It is what we do to reconcile ourselves to the conundrums of ordinary life. The substance of belief is language—not some vague intuitive predisposition, but sentences and stories and explanations. Language is not an arbitrary or incidental accompaniment of behavior; it *is* behavior. Talking to ourselves and to others is action, an ongoing stream of action that mediates and shapes the very manner in which we experience the world. This is not to say that everything people think takes shape in particular words and sentences. Language is rather about what is *not* said, as well as what *is* said, and it is shaped by the mental frameworks we learn early in life and come quickly to take for granted. Language is what makes us human. We use it to negotiate our relation to the world and to grapple with the tensions and ambiguities with which life confronts us. It is through language that we turn objects into meanings, people into personalities, and situations into events.

The language of religion is never expressed only in religious texts. These texts are sometimes the source of definitive creeds that become dogma and provide the rallying cries for holy wars and sectarian strife. They are often the material with which scholars work to discern the core teachings of a religion. But the language of religion more often consists of the stories that children learn as their parents read to them or as they attend classes at their parents' churches or synagogues, mosques, or temples. It is reinforced as children intone the words of childhood hymns and as teenagers and adults learn catechisms and hear sermons. It is nevertheless mistaken to imagine that religious language develops only in these ways. Talking about God occurs in conjunction with talking about everything else: cooking dinner, predicting the weather, straightening the covers on one's bed, seeing a dead bird, hearing stories about distant relatives. In these ways, language consists of natural speech and is embodied in everyday discourse. We learn to ask what is being cooked for dinner and not to mention dead birds in that context (even though one is on the menu). It becomes natural to offer predictions about the weather and to come off as a reasonable person who disbelieves in soothsaying. We find ways to talk about a relative who is distant geographically and to distinguish that idea from one who is distant emotionally. Religion is part of these ordinary ways of thinking and talking, not some other realm that demands a language all its own.

Language is the highly adaptable tool we humans use to adjust to vastly different situations. It gives us the capacity to transcend the biological constraints that necessitated a close match between physiological characteristics and the physical environment during the long course of evolution. Language enables imagining and comparing different situations, reflecting about the past, and anticipating future events. I can make up a sentence at almost any moment about something that never happened or that I imagine could happen as well as about something that did happen. And I can pose different interpretations of what did happen, meaning that what happened was partly how I choose to remember and describe it. But language is also influenced by how we think and by how we have come to experience the world. I can make up a silly saying about pigs flying, but something in me knows that pigs do not fly, even though I say it, and I am therefore in need of some other words to help me locate this statement in my knowledge of reality.

This emphasis on language as the key to understanding how people acknowledge uncertainty and express faith is actually quite consistent with the recent work that some interpreters of religion as a naturalistic phenomenon have been doing. Their writing draws heavily on recent research in cognitive anthropology, evolutionary psychology, and linguistics. What they have failed to do—with a few important exceptions—is apply these same insights to questions about the complexities and ambiguities that confront educated people when they talk about God. Instead, the common tactic has been to focus on some recipe version of religious dogma—of the pigs-can-fly variety—and then assume that this is what thoughtful people really believe. This approach is useful up to a point, because there are undoubtedly some people who think and talk this way. However, it would be much more helpful to get real, as it were, by examining the highly supple ways in which language about religion actually works. That is the task of this book.

NOTES

1.   Daniel C. Dennett, *Breaking the Spell: Religion as a Natural Phenomenon* (New York: Penguin, 2006); Richard Dawkins, *The God Delusion* (Boston: Houghton Mifflin, 2006); Sam Harris, *The End of Faith: Religion, Terror, and the Future of Reason* (New York: Norton, 2004); Christopher Hitchens, *God Is Not Great: How Religion Poisons Everything* (New York: Twelve, 2007); A. C. Grayling, *Against All Gods: Six Polemics on Religion and an Essay on Kindness* (London: Oberon, 2007); and Victor J. Stenger, *God: The Failed Hypothesis: How Science Shows That God Does Not Exist* (New York: Prometheus, 2007). Also relevant is Sam Harris, *Letter to a Christian Nation* (New York: Knopf, 2006).
2.   More on this in chapter 1.

ONE Dangerous Dogma

Before turning to a close investigation of the ways in which thoughtful people talk about their faith, we need to step back and consider why the God problem actually is a problem. Our contemporary culture sometimes gives us the false impression that believing in God is not problematic at all, especially because so many people do believe and apparently consider it reasonable to believe. For one thing, our culture is highly relativistic, and so it is not uncommon to hear about people who, for instance, are dedicated scientists *and* devout Christians, and to say to ourselves, "Well, that's their business." Instead of questioning how they can reconcile these beliefs, we just assume they must have their reasons. Similarly, we hear a politician or athlete say that she is asking God's blessing on America or that he is praying for victory, and we somehow determine that these are just figures of speech. Or we fall back on distinctions we have learned somewhere during our long years of schooling

7

and tell ourselves that facts are different from values or that reason is different from faith. These are ways of talking—and will deserve our attention later on—but they do not satisfy the critics who take a skeptical view of religion. The critics have put forth some trenchant arguments about why it actually should be difficult for intelligent, well-educated people in the United States and elsewhere to believe in God.

Much of the recent concern about religion stems from the view that beliefs about God are *irrational*. The kind of rationality with which this criticism is concerned involves using appropriate means to accomplish one's ends. A rational approach to driving a nail involves using a hammer. A rational way of treating an illness is to call a doctor. Asking God to drive the nail or to treat the illness would be irrational because any normal, intelligent person knows there are more effective ways of proceeding. Prayers and other religious incantations do not get the job done, and to think they do is to engage in superstition. In the past, before the advent of scientific medicine, people who held superstitious beliefs could perhaps be excused for these false ways of thinking, critics argue. But in the contemporary world, being superstitious is a sign of stupidity. Thoughtful, educated people should know better. Indeed, the whole purpose of modern science and education has been to develop rational ways of pursuing our goals. If we want to increase the yield of our crops, we experiment with hybrid seed varieties, fertilizer, and irrigation; we do not pray, as people did centuries ago, in hopes that the gods will intervene. This is not to say that thoughtful Americans are always rational about everything they do. We nevertheless strive to find the most effective ways of getting what we want. A person who wants to do well on an exam knows that the rational course of action is to spend time studying. He or she may spend too much time partying, but that is a matter of poor planning and of deflecting one's energies from achieving one's goals. To be irrational would be to assume that partying itself is the correct way to earn good grades. Expecting God to reveal the answers for the exam is similarly irrational. And it strikes us as plain stupid if people think that hexes, magic, and other superstitious activities are going to work.

The criticism that much of what passes for devout faith is irrational has focused especially on prayer. An Internet video entitled "Proving

That Prayer Is Superstition," which has purportedly reached a far larger audience than Dennett, Dawkins, and company, makes this criticism by pointedly likening prayer to asking a lucky horseshoe for favors. A lucky horseshoe has no effect on the outcome when rolling dice, the video explains. Praying would have no effect on the dice, either. "Belief in prayer is a superstition," the narrator observes, "just like the belief in lucky horseshoes." The video continues, arguing that praying for God to cure cancer is similarly superstitious. "Will God reach down and eliminate all the cancerous cells? If you are a normal, intelligent person, you know what will happen. Nothing. This prayer will have no effect whatsoever."[1]

Just to be clear, this criticism taken by itself does not constitute an argument against believing in the *existence* of God. Even the most ardent critics would acknowledge that this is the case. It still might seem rational to believe that God or something God-like exists because there are unknown and perhaps unknowable aspects of the universe. Or it might seem reasonable to believe that God exists because this God offers a person everlasting life in heaven. But those kinds of beliefs have very little to do with the God problem I am describing. God is not a problem only as long as that God steers clear of any active involvement in the world as we know it. The God of an unknowable universe or of life in heaven is a God that can be believed in without imagining that this God intervenes in any way with daily life. This God need not perform miraculous cures, make rain, or assist in winning the lottery. As soon as this God starts messing with the natural order, the God problem comes into play. An educated person will have difficulty believing that God can cause the sun to stand still, virgins to give birth, rain to fall, and diseases to be cured.

A slight variant on the argument that believing in God is an irrational way of achieving one's goals is the idea that God or some other supernatural being is responsible for one's failures. The claim that "the devil made me do it" is one example. Suppose I steal a car, get caught, and at trial explain to the judge that I had been instructed by an evil spirit to commit this felony. The judge might not send me to prison but have me locked up in an insane asylum. At the very least, the court would consider my defense irrational. The same logic applies in less extreme cases. If I am a thoughtful, well-educated person and am having difficulties in my marriage, the rational thing to do is to talk to a friend or seek help from a trained therapist, marriage counselor, or psychiatrist—not to visit an exorcist. If my marriage founders, some part of me may decide that it was God's will, but I would have trouble with the thought that I could have prevented it if I had prayed harder or that God was punishing me for something I had done.

Recent critics of religion have gone a step further than earlier critics in demonstrating that belief in God is very likely to be irrational. The irrationality of believing in God, they argue, is not just a matter of bad logic. There are actually good reasons why a person might hold irrational beliefs about God. Many of these reasons have to do with human evolution. For example, something about the way the human brain has evolved disposes us to look for *agents* as the cause of things. A crop failure prompts us to ask, "Who caused it?" We are also especially inclined to remember stories about *strange* agents: "It was caused by a turtle with a human head." Over the vast expanse of time during which humans evolved, these stories about strange beings gained special staying power. They evolved, the critics argue, into superstitions about God. So it is quite reasonable that humans believe in God. But it is still irrational. Indeed, now that the reasons for those beliefs are understood, it is even more irrational to hold these beliefs, except perhaps as curious relics of the past.[2]

A related criticism that is much broader than the concern about irrationality is the view that beliefs about God are *uninformed*. This criticism is less about superstitious notions of how to get what one wants and more about religious belief simply being naïve. It is concerned with the broader view that an educated person should understand that scriptures were not really divinely inspired, that sacred texts contain errors, and that there are naturalistic explanations for religion itself. People living several centuries ago may have read the biblical story about the world being created in seven days and had little trouble believing that this really happened in that space of time. They may have heard that God created Adam and Eve about 6,000 years ago and figured that was exactly when it happened. A person nowadays with no education might have heard these yarns from a family member and had no reason to question them. A child could learn the story about Noah's ark in Sunday school and think how nice it was that all the animals were saved from the flood. But educated people should have reasons to question all of this. They might still believe in God, and yet they would surely have doubts about many of the things people claim to believe about God. They would certainly disbelieve that the Bible stories should be taken literally. They might have difficulty praying to a God about whom so much false information has been presented. In short, popular concepts of God would be a problem.

Much of Dawkins' work is devoted to demonstrating that religiously inclined people are simply uninformed about science, and especially about scientific arguments that contradict faith or more easily explain natural phenomena. Many of his ideas are directed more at theologians and other apologists—whom he concludes are "often chronically incapable of distinguishing what is true from what they'd like to be true"—than at ordinary readers. He does an excellent job, though, of poking holes in arguments that might be termed resort-to-authority, such as "Well, so-and-so scientist believes in God," or "Pascal settled that a long time ago." He also goes a long way toward making atheism respectable by showing that beliefs about God are unnecessary to support moral arguments and that solace and inspiration can be found elsewhere.[3]

The emphasis on cultural evolution evident in Dawkins and many other critics of religion offers another argument about the difficulties of being well-informed and devoutly religious. In this view, the essence of religion is ritual, which serves as a primitive means of communicating and affirming group loyalty in small, homogenous, local societies, almost like grunts and gestures did before the development of verbal language. But in modern, complex societies these rituals serve less well and indeed are replaced by rational modes of communication. As Jürgen Habermas, one of the leading proponents of this view, observed, "with the development of modern societies, the sacred domain has largely disintegrated, or at least has lost its structure-forming significance."[4] Thus, the incompatibility between devotion to God and functioning as a well-informed citizen has less to do with the knowledge or lack thereof of particular individuals and is more the result of a modernizing process that simply renders religion less meaningful and less socially significant.

There are numerous ways in which being informed can lead a well-educated person to have trouble with standard beliefs about God. Scientific information about evolution or about how big Noah's ark would have had to have been to hold representatives of every species is only one. A thinking person knows that cancer sometimes goes into remission from natural causes. The patient who lives to tell a miracle story about answered prayer has to be considered in relation to the patients who prayed and did not live to tell their story. If a friend says getting a cushy new job was a "miracle," it probably takes only a split second to translate this into something other than an event like somebody being raised from the dead. Being informed means knowing that people kill in the name of God and pray to deities that command human sacrifice. It involves an awareness that the other side is praying to its God for victory and that more than one religion claims to be the only path to divine salvation. If Habermas is right, a thoughtful person would understand that religious rituals are a carryover from an earlier stage of human evolution and that they work better in isolated contexts than for people with cosmopolitan tastes. If nothing else, participating in religious rituals may seem a waste of time compared with devoting oneself to areas of life requiring more specialized knowledge, such as science or medicine. Believers themselves sometimes argue that too much knowledge is a bad thing and affirm that ignorance is the basis of their faith. They disrespect intellectuals or argue that faith must be blind, meaning that it cannot withstand intelligent scrutiny. To a person who values education and reason, people who embrace this kind of blind faith seem to have fallen recently from the proverbial turnip truck.

Dogmatic religion poses special problems in this regard. An adherent of dogmatic religion may be very well versed in the teachings of his or her faith, and yet be closed-minded about everything else. That person is likely to be uninformed about the teachings of other faiths, about the cultural factors that shaped the history of these faiths, or about the arguments of critics. If nothing else, studying the fine points of one's own

dogmatic tradition becomes a higher priority than spending time learning about art, music, or science. The opposite is to be open to new ideas.
"What we respect," Hitchens writes, in describing the critical view of
those he admires, "is free inquiry, open-mindedness, and the pursuit of
ideas for their own sake."[5] This is why atheists have often referred to
themselves as free thinkers. Dogma requires believing in what a person
has been told by a religious leader or in a creed or sacred text. It means
defending wisdom from the past, rather than exploring new ideas. It
stifles intellectual curiosity.

I am not suggesting that a religious person cannot also be an informed
person—and critics of religion generally do not make this argument
either. Saying it is *impossible* to be both is easily refuted by pointing to
Isaac Newton, an example of a religious believer who was clearly well
informed, or to the genomics expert Francis Collins as a current example,
or to many other leaders in their fields who have combined intellectual
curiosity and faith. The point is rather that a thoughtful, well-educated
person has to figure out a way of being informed *and* devout. Otherwise,
the bias in dogma is toward the view that all important knowledge has
been revealed in scripture or can be heard by listening directly to the
voice of God instead of exploring widely in other paths of learning. The
God problem is not unsolvable, but it is a problem. Newton and Collins
had to find ways to pursue higher learning and yet reconcile their faith
with what they learned.

A third, rather different set of criticisms is that beliefs about God
are *antidemocratic* and are for this reason beliefs that educated people
should consider problematic. These criticisms stem from the view that
democracy requires citizens to be able to defend their beliefs through
rational argument and thus be open to the beliefs of others, including
being willing to compromise in service of the common good. Belief in
God is said to be antidemocratic because it leads to arguments that cannot be questioned. In simplest terms, believers assert that God told them
to do something or that something is right. End of story. No debate, no
discussion. And this is especially problematic when people of different
faiths come together, because each group holds its own unique convictions about truth. These convictions are divinely revealed and inviolable,

subject neither to compromise nor to rational explication in terms that other groups can understand.

This argument has had special resonance among political theorists interested in the conditions under which democracy can flourish. Presumably everyone in the United States, Western Europe, Canada, and countries with similar political traditions believes in democracy. A person who has invested considerable time and energy acquiring information and learning how to apply reason to important decisions will be inclined to think that information and learning are especially appropriate to the workings of a democracy. When a religious leader declares that God wants people to vote for a particular political candidate, or when a politician asserts that God told him or her to run for higher office, thinking people are likely to have questions. They may only doubt that God actually spoke. But they may also wonder if faith should be allowed in the political arena. While they might argue that it is fine for a person to hold strange views about God privately, they may feel that it is really better if intelligent people use their brains when thinking about difficult social issues.

This criticism is not about the compatibility or incompatibility of religious traditions and democracy. That is an important question, but different from the one at issue here. It usually focuses on specific countries and asks whether Islam and democracy can coexist in, say, Indonesia, or whether Protestants were correct or incorrect in accusing U.S. Catholics of being antidemocratic during the nineteenth and early twentieth centuries.[6] By and large, the prevalence of religion *and* democracy in many countries, including the United States, would suggest that religion is not inherently antidemocratic. However, the question that critics of religion raise persists. This question, as posed forcefully by political theorist John Rawls, is whether claims about religious truth can be reconciled with the functioning of an effective democracy. They cannot, Rawls argues, because citizens in religiously and culturally pluralistic societies have to agree on freestanding conceptions of justice, rather than ones grounded in different religious traditions. Practically speaking, religion needs to be irrelevant. A person must be able to argue that a particular policy is fair to all and on grounds that all can accept, not because it conforms to the dictates of his or her religion.[7]

It was this concern about the incompatibility of faith and democracy that prompted John Dewey to argue that religion in America would serve the nation better if it abandoned, of all things, its beliefs in the supernatural. Religion as an institution, Dewey argued, contributed many good things, including charitable behavior and a sense of civic responsibility. But devotion to the supernatural established an alternative loyalty that competed with citizenship. The very experiences of life, and especially those aspects deemed to be sacred, were shaped by the doctrines through which they were interpreted. A Christian Scientist and a Lutheran would inevitably experience life differently and appeal to different versions of divine authority to justify their conceptions of the good.[8]

Many arguments have been made on the other side to show that faith and democracy are compatible or can be reconciled.[9] However, these arguments frequently sidestep the fundamental issue of truth being asserted in the name of divine revelation. These claims can be constitutionally bracketed and the more agreeable aspects of religion, such as teachings about good neighborliness, can be emphasized. But when religion encourages people to believe that they speak for God, religion then becomes, in Richard Rorty's memorable phrase, a conversation stopper.[10]

Another set of concerns that is not fully expressed by any of the foregoing is the argument that beliefs about God are *destructive*. This is the idea that religion is actually harmful, either to the individuals who believe in God or to innocent bystanders who do not. It goes beyond the view, for instance, that asking God for help is irrational but unlikely to cause harm.[11] It suggests that religion encourages people to do stupid things that are also dangerous, such as not receiving vaccinations. The list of destructive acts condoned by religion is quite long. The Bible tells of God wiping out whole cities and instructing the chosen people to slaughter their enemies, including women, children, and livestock. The biblical prophets call down divine wrath on false teachers. The psalmist cries out for the Lord's vengeance. The relatively milder teachings of the New Testament condone slavery and tell of people stricken dead for seemingly minor offenses.

Concerns about the destructiveness of religion were less frequently heard during the twentieth century, when atheistic communism and near-atheistic fascism slaughtered millions, but they have returned to the front burner since the September 11, 2001, attacks. Religions that in other eras were thought to be benign or even peaceful are now popularly viewed as promoters of violence. Terrorists engage in religiously motivated holy wars. Suicide bombers imagine themselves being rewarded in paradise for their atrocities. Dogma—whether inspired by the Qur'an or embodied in a fundamentalist Protestant or a Hindu nationalist—is especially to be feared. A thinking person should be repulsed. "People of faith are in their different ways planning your and my destruction," Hitchens warns, "and the destruction of all hard-won human attainments."[12] The language is extreme, and yet it resonates in a world of religiously inspired terrorism. Somewhere a sleeper cell is plotting an attack. Somewhere a religious zealot is planning to assassinate a doctor who performs abortions. The issue is not that only religious people commit atrocities. It is rather that they righteously do so in the name of God.

It is also worth mentioning a particular argument claiming that beliefs about God are *fraudulent*. Fraud goes beyond destructiveness in being intentionally manipulative. It involves deliberate deception. The argument usually focuses on the fraudulent promotion of religion for power or for money. Suppose a gospel preacher asks you to place your hand on the television set, pray, and send him a tenth of your paycheck. The preacher avoids saying directly that you will become rich as a result, but suggests this outcome by showing a picture of a new Hummer and having a believer tell a story about becoming rich. It would be irrational for the viewer to send money; it is fraudulent for the preacher to make such suggestive appeals in the first place. The Internet video I mentioned earlier about prayer makes exactly this point. "What if a minister says, 'God tells you to tithe money to the church,'" the narrator asks. "'If you do, God will answer your prayers.' This is fraud. The minister is lying to you in order to get your money."[13]

The criticism that religion is fraudulent did not have to wait for television hucksters to come on the scene. Nearly two centuries ago, this criticism was at the heart of Karl Marx's concerns about religion. The bourgeoisie, he argued, were all too willing to use religion to oppress the masses. Instead of paying workers a decent wage, the owners of wealth paid clergy to assure workers that they would receive their just rewards in heaven. The criticism has been repeated in numerous versions since then. Religion offers false hope. It encourages people to give their meager earnings to the church instead of feeding their families, and their time to prayer instead of engaging in political protest.

The concern about fraudulent religion is now voiced especially by critics who fear that religion in the United States, the United Kingdom, the Netherlands, and elsewhere is feathering its nest at the expense of taxpayers. Not only are religious organizations exempt from taxes, but now they are often the beneficiaries of earmarks in U.S. congressional funding bills—earmarks totaling more than $300 million, according to one source—including building highways to church colleges, giving federal land to churches, and funding faith-based abstinence programs for teenagers.[14] Why, the critics ask, should thinking people put up with this? Would it not be better policy to spend public money more effectively, either on government programs or in the marketplace?

Saying that belief in God is often associated with irrational, uninformed, undemocratic, destructive, fraudulent behavior is not to imply that nonbelief is free of these ills. The temptation for a believer is to respond by pointing out the irrationality of dogmatic atheists, for example, or the destructiveness of Nazi, Stalinist, and other antireligious regimes. That response may be attractive but is too easy. It misses the point that can be made in terms less extreme than those used by the recent popularizers of antireligious sentiment, and even by many thoughtful people who are themselves favorably inclined toward faith. The very notion of God raises intellectual difficulties. It is not something that can be studied scientifically or proven logically: It conflicts with ordinary ways of thinking about the affairs of daily life. Religious conviction is frequently a source of irrational claims, of divisiveness, and even of violence, or it inspires inexplicable trust and great personal sacrifice.

The recent criticisms of religion are perhaps too easily dismissed in yet another way. The examples of religious irrationality and hatred are typically more representative of some religious groups than others: Protestant fundamentalists more than mainline Protestants, traditional Catholics more than progressive Catholics, ultraconservative Jews more than liberal Jews, radical Islamists more than moderate Muslims, and so on. The culprit clearly is dogma. Yet there is a point in these criticisms that needs to be taken seriously: Nondogmatic religion shares some of the same traits, at least potentially, so that care must be taken to determine the differences. Harris writes, "I have little doubt that liberals and moderates find the eerie certainties of the Christian Right to be as troubling as I do."[15] Yet his argument is not that the Christian Right is the only religion in need of criticism. Moderates and liberals, he suggests, should also be scrutinized. They also pray, expect miracles, defend creeds, and distance themselves from others with different convictions. Do they quietly find faith intellectually problematic? Or have they somehow found a way to transcend these doubts?

In fairness to the critics and to religious people themselves, none of these criticisms imply that it is impossible to be a thinking person and believe in God. But they do make it harder. God is no longer the nice man in the sky who keeps everything going smoothly. God is problematic, an enigma that becomes harder to define and more difficult to view as a source of anything measurable. To believe that God is capable of intervening in the ordinary affairs of human beings is to engage in irrational thinking. God may be God, but not a super-powerful being who disrupts the natural order to supply miracles to people who ask sincerely. Many of the stories in the book purported to be the sacred Word of God simply cannot be true. The rules through which social order is achieved cannot include grandly authoritative revelations from God. A democracy may be able to take account of values embedded in religious traditions, but only as long as those religions are regarded as *traditions*. The vicious potential in religious claims needs to be looked squarely in the face and rejected. So do the self-aggrandizing schemes of religious hucksters.

The point of these recent criticisms is not, at least in the critics' minds, to substitute an antireligious orthodoxy for religious dogma. If what they write is taken at face value, as it should be, their call is largely for critical inquiry focusing on questions that have often been suppressed. The argument is not that religious belief is entirely foolish, at least not so foolish as to cause thinking people to back away from it instinctively. It is rather an argument in favor of open-minded, genuine, no-holds-barred doubt. The call is for intelligent people to acknowledge that religion, like humanity itself, may have evolved through natural causes, and that prayer may be a comforting way of talking to oneself but is not communicating with a sentient being who listens and grants favors to one person and not to the next. The message is that a lot of what religion communicates about God is nothing but raw superstition, which is irrational at best and destructive at worst. There may be ways to redefine religion so that it is about mystery or mysticism or humanitarianism or the ineffable essence of life. But if that is what people really believe, then it is a far cry from the awe and allegiance to an all-powerful being that religion has generally been in the past. For an intelligent, thoughtful person who values reason, God will be a problem.

Suppose, though, that a thoughtful person says to herself, "I believe in God, but not in the dogmatic way that seems to be of concern to these critics of religion. I pray, but I do not imagine that God literally hears me and decides to rejuvenate my friend's amputated leg. It offends me even to think that God is somehow like a lucky horseshoe. Furthermore, I am a well-informed, open-minded person; indeed, I think God made me that way and wants me to use my intellectual faculties to the fullest extent. I live in a democratic society and am happy to discuss social policies in terms that people who do not share my faith can understand. I do not think God has given me a special corner on the truth about social issues, even though there are some about which I care deeply. I do not condone violence in the name of religion or the use of faith to collect money fraudulently." This person is free of all the problems critics associate with religion. And yet, *she too has a God problem*. She has a serious God problem because affirming her faith requires her to find ways to declare that she is not bigoted, dogmatic, stupid, thoughtless, and heartless. She could solve this problem by disavowing religious faith entirely: declaring herself a nonreligious person who does not believe in God and does not pray. Somehow, though, she manages to retain her faith. She may even do this without giving it much thought. Faith seems reasonable to her. She has absorbed a natural language with which to talk to and about God that does not violate her understanding of how a reasonable person thinks and acts. Her God problem involves following a middle path between fanaticism and atheism. She stays the course by drawing on subtle distinctions about certainty and doubt, knowing and unknowing, the natural and the supernatural. Her mental frameworks place God and lucky horseshoes in different categories and apply scientific explanations to some questions and not to others. She somehow differentiates among kinds of faith and kinds of knowledge. Through these distinctions she distances herself from people she regards as religious radicals. She has a language that serves as a grassroots theology. When this language is reinforced by the way her friends talk and by what she reads or sees on television, it works well for her. It does not work all the time, though, or for everyone she knows. There are times when she wonders if there really is a God and times when she does not pray. She is keenly aware that talking to God is different from talking to another person. She finds it puzzling that an invisible entity lacking a body can somehow be expected to talk back. Being a thoughtful person who has learned to think in nonreligious ways about how the world works, her faith is inflected with uncertainty and with the desire to be reasonable.

There is ample evidence that highly educated people who are presumably intelligent and who apparently value open-mindedness and reason do have a problem with God. Consider how different the views of the American public are from the views of highly educated professors at the nation's elite colleges and universities—a special segment of the public that is indeed highly educated and claims to value intelligence and reason. In the general public, where about 25 percent have graduated from college, the overwhelming majority say they believe in God. For example, in a recent Gallup Poll, 86 percent of the public said they believed in God, 8 percent were unsure, and only 6 percent did not believe in God. A *Newsweek* survey found that 91 percent believed in God. A poll for Fox News showed almost the same results: 89 percent said they personally believed in the existence of God. Other polls have yielded additional details. For example, a poll for *Time* magazine revealed that 80 percent of the public believed in "God-inspired miracles." In the same survey, only 4 percent said "recent discoveries and advances in science over the last 10 years or so" had made them less religious. Eighty-one percent said these discoveries had no effect on their views of God and religion, and 14 percent said they had actually become more religious.[16] In contrast to these responses from the general public, the views expressed in surveys among scientists and academics are quite different.

A survey of more than 1,600 scientists and social scientists employed at 21 elite research universities found that only 8 percent of the natural scientists and 10 percent of the social scientists had "no doubts about God's existence." A third (38 and 31 percent, respectively) declared that they did not believe in God. Nearly another third (29 and 31 percent, respectively) said they did not know if there is a God and believed there was no way to find out. In short, a sizable majority were atheists or agnostics. Further differences with the general public were evident in the responses to other questions. Half of these academics said they had no religious affiliation at all, compared to about a seventh of the public who give this response in surveys. Fewer than 10 percent attended religious services regularly—much less than the third to half of the public who attend this often.[17] A separate study of nearly 1,500 college professors spanning twenty disciplinary fields found similar results. From responses to a question about belief in God, the researchers concluded that about 23 percent of the professors were atheists or agnostics—four times as many as in the general population. The study also showed that disbelief ran higher at elite universities than at other institutions. For instance, 37 percent of the faculty at elite doctoral schools reported disbelief in God, compared with only 15 percent at community colleges.[18]

The difficulties educated people have about believing in God are illustrated in other studies that compare Americans who have earned college degrees with Americans who have not been to college. Consider the following: In recent national surveys, those with college degrees were 19 percentage points less likely than those who had not been to college to believe that humans had been created by God, 15 points less likely to say they were sure about God's existence, 14 points less likely to say they ask God for help, 12 points less likely to say they believe that nature was created by God, 11 points less likely to look to God for strength and support, and 10 points less likely to say they feel close to God.[19] The pattern was strikingly consistent: The more education people had, the less likely they were to believe in God.

However, there is a different way to look at the results of these studies. Indeed, the main point I want emphasize is that educated people in the United States somehow manage, for the most part, *to believe in God*. To be sure, they do this less often than Americans who have lower levels of education. And yet in one way or another most of them affirm some faith in God. For example, among Americans who have college degrees, only 11 percent say they do not believe in God or believe there is no way to find out if God does or does not exist. Of the remainder, 52 percent say they have no doubts that God exists, 20 percent say they have some doubts, 4 percent believe sometimes and not at other times, and 13 percent believe in a higher power and are unsure if this is God. Even among those with graduate degrees, only 13 percent give responses indicating that they are atheists or agnostics.

A skeptic might argue that educated Americans believe vaguely that God exists, perhaps as some mysterious and unknowable essence of being, but otherwise have no interaction with this God. That, however, is not what the evidence suggests. Thirty-eight percent of Americans with college degrees say they ask God for help with their daily activities *every day*. Eighty percent of these college-educated Americans say they ask God for help at least once in a while. On another question, three-quarters reported feeling at least somewhat close to God. And on yet another question, more than half said they look to God quite a bit for strength and support.[20]

Questions about prayer are especially interesting. The critics of religion argue that it is irrational to pray because there is no evidence that prayer works. Yet only 12 percent of Americans say they never pray. And among Americans with college degrees, all but 15 percent pray. More than half of college educated Americans (54 percent) claim they pray every day. The pattern that emerges when changes from year to year are examined is also interesting. One would imagine that prayer in the United States, even if common, would be occurring less often than in the past. This is because more and more Americans have been earning college degrees in recent decades, which would suggest that prayer ought to be diminishing if the

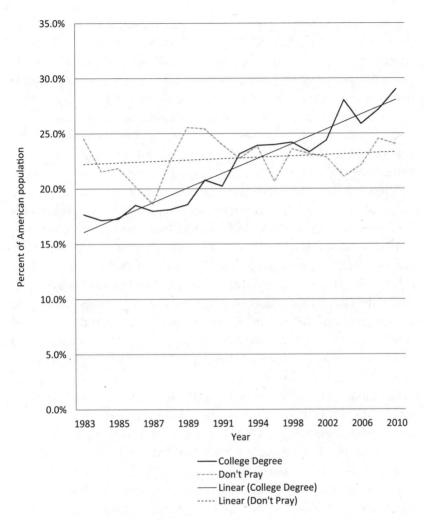

Figure 1.1. Prayer and higher education in the United States.

two are incompatible. However, the evidence on change in prayer over time suggests this is not the case (see fig. 1.1). The trend in higher education over the past quarter century has been steadily upward, but the percentage of Americans who never or rarely pray has remained constant.

The fact that the two lines are further apart in the earlier years than in the later ones implies that higher education and prayer have actually

become *more compatible* during this period. Indeed, if we were to produce a similar chart showing the level of statistical association between
education and prayer for each year, we would see that there has been a
gradually *weakening* negative relationship. In the early 1980s, frequent
prayer was negatively associated with higher education, with a statistical coefficient of −.122, and by 2006, that association had weakened to
−.062. In other words, there was hardly any negative relationship by the
later date, and to the extent that a relationship did remain, it was only
half as strong as in 1983.

These bits and pieces of data from reputable national studies reinforce
the point I made earlier: When it comes to the God problem, Americans
have somehow found a way to have their cake and eat it too. We are a
well-educated society, a culture that values thinking straight and using
our mental faculties, and yet we are also a society in which religious faith
is prevalent. The best-educated among us tilt slightly away from this pattern of devout religious conviction, apparently experiencing some of the
tensions between faith and intellect that the critics argue is there. But this
is only a slight tilt. For the most part, well-educated Americans seem to
have found a way to continue believing in God and praying regularly to
this deity.

One other piece of evidence is worth considering before turning to
some of the arguments that might explain how educated Americans manage to retain their belief in God. This is evidence comparing the United
States with other countries that share the same predominantly Judeo-
Christian religious heritage (see fig. 1.2). In the figure, I have plotted data
from surveys conducted in nearly two dozen countries. The countries
are arranged according to the percentage in each who pray at least once
a week and the percentage of the population who have earned a bachelor's degree or higher. The chart offers a way of seeing if people in better-
educated countries are less likely to pray. Among all the countries, there
is a tendency for this to be the case. For example, Italy and Portugal are
the least-educated of these countries and they also have relatively high
rates of prayer. Israel and Sweden are among the best-educated, and
weekly prayer is quite low in these countries. In addition, the religious
tradition of countries clearly affects frequency of prayer. Italy, Portugal,

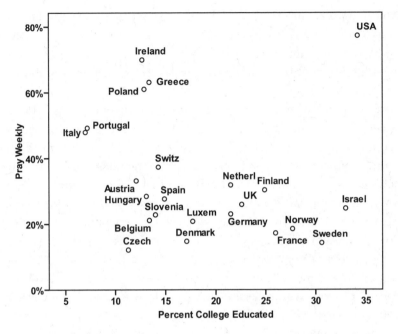

Figure 1.2.   Prayer in 23 countries.

Poland, Ireland, and Greece all have high rates of prayer because of their Catholic or Orthodox traditions. The most striking feature of the chart, though, is the position of the United States. It is the best-educated of all the countries, and yet it also has the highest percentage of people who pray regularly.[21]

How has the United States accomplished this unique balancing act? The cross-country comparisons pose the question forcefully. Why is the United States a country in which higher education and talking to God have been able to coexist? Is it just that the United States is a religious country, as observers often argue? Undoubtedly Americans pray because they are religious, but this observation does not tell us very much. Is there a pattern of American exceptionalism rooted in immigration and religious voluntarism, as historians have shown, that tells the entire story? That may be true, yet it begs the question of how individual

Americans who are relatively well educated manage to resolve the questions about God that have been widely discussed for a long time. Is there perhaps a more interesting story about the ways in which Americans entertain the doubts and uncertainties that cross the minds of thinking people as they pray?

These questions are all the more intriguing, it turns out, because educated Americans do not simply happen to pray and entertain convictions about God in large numbers. They also believe explicitly that there is no contradiction between being educated and being religious. Comparisons between Americans with higher and lower levels of education are again revealing. For instance, in the *Time* magazine survey I mentioned earlier, 74 percent of those with college degrees said scientific advancements do *not* threaten religious beliefs. That was compared with 58 percent among those with no college education. On a question about creation and evolution, the differences were even more pronounced: Sixty-three percent of those with college degrees said it was possible to believe in both, compared with only 35 percent of those with no college education.[22]

The call to understand more clearly how educated Americans reconcile reason and faith has also been an important part of the recent criticisms of religion. Dennett, Harris, and others acknowledge that thoughtful people often believe in God. The implication, these critics argue, is not that everyone should become atheists. It is rather that more attention needs to be paid to what exactly faith means to intelligent people, especially if it does not involve the naïve superstitions that are so easily criticized. Research is needed, not only on the dogmas that have been the focus of most investigations, but also on the departures from dogma.

Several popular arguments about the religious faith of well-educated Americans will spring so readily to readers' minds that we need to mention those briefly, and then set them aside, before moving ahead to more interesting questions about the languages of faith. Some of these arguments have been studied by social scientists and can be dismissed because research does not support them. Some others are plausible, despite a lack of research, and yet fail to get at the complexities of religious belief itself. An argument of the first variety is the notion that the religious involvement of better-educated Americans stems less from faith than from an impulse to join. This idea was more prominent a generation or two ago than it is today, but it is still heard from time to time among casual observers of American culture. It reflects the view of America as a nation of joiners—people who want to fit in and who mostly favor the social life that religious organizations provide, rather than the distinctive teachings of these organizations. Indeed, the argument suggests that well-educated Americans go to church because it is the respectable thing to do, just as serving on committees and belonging to community organizations is, but they do so without believing in much of anything. If this argument were true, it would mean not having to deal with questions of belief at all. But, unfortunately for its proponents, it is not true. To be sure, Americans with college degrees are more likely than Americans who have never been to college to participate in religious services. But among those with college degrees who attend this often, almost everyone believes in God. Clearly, they are not folks who belong without believing. They may very well come up with ways of modifying their beliefs about God, and if so, that again points to the importance of considering more closely their beliefs and the language in which they express their beliefs.[23]

Other arguments tackle the puzzle of educated Americans being religious by focusing on what does or does not happen in institutions of higher learning. Consider again the evidence in figure 1.1 about education and prayer. Why would just as many Americans be praying regularly as in the past if more Americans are earning college degrees? The answer, some would argue, is surely that colleges are failing to do their job. They are turning out good accountants and nurses but failing to instruct students that prayer is irrational. Students come away with their religious beliefs intact, though perhaps compartmentalized from what they know about logic and science. That view would fit pretty well with critics of religion who argue that people would be less religious if only they were confronted more aggressively with logic and science. The fault, according to this interpretation, lies squarely with timid educators. A more benign interpretation could also be given: American higher education has grown in ways that make it less selective and less concerned with the critical questions that might challenge religion. Students enter college, for example, from a broader cross-section of the public, come from families in which religious assumptions have never been examined, and major in subjects that do not challenge these assumptions.

The trouble with this argument is that it assumes that naïve dogmatic religious beliefs have indeed been left intact. There is no middle ground. Students are either fundamentalists or atheists. If they are graduating from college and still praying, they must be fundamentalists. A more subtle interpretation would entertain the possibility that they may have altered how they think about prayer. Even if their accounting instructor never told them that prayer was irrational, they have likely been in an environment in which people talked about prayer in ways that made it seem less irrational. Those would be the languages worth understanding.

The idea that higher education has failed to challenge naïve religious assumptions also finds detractors who argue that faith is actually being encouraged on college campuses. In this view, which is supported by some research, the old antagonism of academics toward religion has been replaced by a new laissez-faire attitude more conducive to frank discussions of faith. Accordingly, students are more open about their spiritual quests, enrollments in religion courses are on the rise, and dorm room discussions abound. The fact that more Americans are graduating from college and still praying would not be surprising to these researchers. It would, however, be all the more important to move past the stereotypic portrayals of superstitious religion and understand how educated Americans are actually talking about God.[24]

Arguments focusing on educational institutions probably give too much weight to these institutions. After all, the four years on average that students spend in college are a short part of their lives. Much has already happened by the time a person enters college. Family, childhood friends, school, and the mass media have all had an impact. Many of these influences continue during and after college. The media especially may be a decisive influence. Consider the fact that many more people pray in the United States than in England or France, despite similarities in education levels in the three countries. Could it be that television and newspapers in the United States are reluctant to speak favorably about the views of atheists? Journalists are perhaps fearful of offending the leaders of religious institutions. They ply political candidates with questions about prayer and church going, and the candidates oblige by saying what they think the public wants to hear. In contrast, criticisms of religion in the other countries have a longer history and are far more acceptable.[25]

There is little doubt that Americans pick up cues about religion from the media. The process is not one-way. Journalists and film producers also report what ordinary people say and mimic the language in which they say it. This is yet another reason to be sensitive to the languages in which faith is expressed. Religion is sometimes as dogmatic as the critics say it is. Television preachers do promise pray-and-get-rich schemes. Mullahs issue fatwahs calling for assassinations. Journalists recount readers' claims of having experienced miracles. And so on. There is enough grist in these accounts to support critics' arguments that faith is indeed irrational, if not downright dangerous. Yet these are the kinds of faiths that people of faith themselves feel compelled at times to distance themselves from and to question. The implication is that there must be something in the language of fanaticism that strikes thoughtful people as wrong. Once again the question of language rises to the surface. If the language of dogmatism does not seem appropriate, then how do people talk about God?

Scholarly discussions of the God problem typically lead in one or another of three directions—and briefly describing these will clarify the perspective I favor. Each of these represents a general orientation that might be taken in trying to understand how thoughtful people in contemporary society deal with questions of faith. One direction basically argues that beliefs in God have been watered down by attempts to deal with criticisms of religion and are thus not as authentic or powerful as they once were or should be. Proponents of this argument usually have a clear, if restricted, view of what authentic religion should be, and they locate that view in ancient religious texts or at some point in the history of the church. They look at contemporary beliefs about God and find to their dismay (although sometimes with rosier interpretations) that things are not what they used to be. A second approach argues that the God problem has not been sufficiently resolved, and that believers would simply abandon their beliefs if they really understood the criticisms. This conclusion perceives quite a bit of power left in religious institutions and is mostly a criticism of the educational system and of educated people for not going far enough in tackling the God problem intelligently. The third approach tries to find some middle ground by granting the critics some but not all of their arguments and by calling on religious people to be more thoughtful.

The first of these approaches will be familiar to readers of Will Herberg's classic work on American religion in the 1950s. Herberg was profoundly impressed by Americans' ability to adapt their faith to the pluralistic, and largely secular, culture in which they lived. We did this, he argued, by making it fashionable to be Protestant, Catholic, or Jewish. To claim one of those three identities was to be an American. Identity, though, trumped conviction. Americans rather enjoyed saying they went to church or synagogue, but were not as serious about their beliefs as their ancestors had been. Faith, Herberg believed, was theologically shallow. It was an unsophisticated faith in faith itself, not dogmatic, and thus not difficult for intelligent people to entertain, but also different from the rigid theism that has troubled most critics of religion.[26]

With greater empirical precision, a similar argument appeared in the 1980s by sociologist James Davison Hunter. From examining the books and articles of evangelical writers and from survey evidence, Hunter argued that even theologically conservative Protestants were adapting their faith in surprising ways to the secular culture in which they lived. God was no longer a wrathful being who demanded righteousness and who inflicted vengeance on evildoers. Jesus was a buddy, an imaginary friend, instead of a divine savior. The Bible was less a story about God and more an instruction book for a happy life. This kind of cognitive bargaining, as Hunter called it, permitted rank-and-file evangelicals to get along with their neighbors and in their jobs. Even students at church-related colleges were learning to adapt.[27]

Hunter's analysis was ingenious. It was one of the few studies at the time to take the language of belief seriously and to suggest that there were ways of resolving the God problem for modern, intelligent people—ways of which they themselves were often unaware. Yet the argument was incomplete. It lacked evidence from rich interviews with religious people themselves and came before much of the recent scholarship on the nuances of language and cultural analysis had developed. There was also an element of nostalgia, a slight hint of a golden age when theological convictions had been more robust, and an implied concern that Christians were somehow on a slippery slope that would result in a loss of faith altogether.

Subsequent work in this vein has generally offered more optimistic conclusions about American religion, including evangelical Protestantism. Evangelical students seem not to have slid further down the slope to perdition. Evangelical adults have managed to maintain their distinctive identity by carping about the immorality of unbelievers, not by lessening their own beliefs. In a book based mostly on his reading of other scholars' in-depth ethnographic work, social scientist Alan Wolfe sought to reassure readers on the secular left that they had nothing to fear from conservative religionists. They were not aligned with the dogmatic Religious Right, Wolfe argued, but a domesticated bunch whose faith had been thoroughly tamed by the live-and-let-live norms of American culture.[28] So convincing was his argument that Daniel Dennett decided these secular religionists hardly fit his definition of religion at all. "They reveal that *revision* of tradition," Dennett wrote, "is often hard to distinguish from outright *rejection*."

But if Dennett was right, the question remained unanswered about how these evangelical Christians, whom he declared not to be representatives of true religion, had actually resolved the God problem. They may have rejected Dennett's idea of a miracle-working big-man in the sky, but they overwhelmingly believed in God and prayed to that God. Hunter was more correct in suggesting that they were engaged in cognitive bargaining than Dennett was in arguing that they had rejected religion. And if Wolfe was right in arguing that they were politically safe adherents of basic democratic principles, an extension of this argument would suggest that they were perhaps equally clever in finding new ways to think about God.

The second approach, which argues that the God problem has not been sufficiently addressed or resolved, is best represented by the recent critics of religion, including Dennett, Dawkins, Harris, and Hitchens. Their approach differs from the one I have just discussed in emphasizing to a much greater degree the difficulties that arise when intelligent people really scrutinize the assumptions involved in prayer, miracles, and other beliefs about God. Herberg, Hunter, Wolfe, and others assume there is a corrosive aspect to American culture that makes it hard for devout believers to live up to their convictions. For instance, the culture places so much emphasis on material goods that a person of faith finds it difficult to be altruistic. Or the relativism of the wider culture encourages believers in one religion to grant the possibility of truth in other religions. Those arguments are quite different from the more trenchant criticism of writers who insist that religion itself is simply a product of human evolution or that the very idea of praying is irrational.

This second approach brings the God problem into much sharper relief and in so doing correctly illustrates that educated people and the institutions instructing them probably have not addressed the logical difficulties in religion as aggressively as they could have. This approach nevertheless suffers from the implicit long-term time frame that comes with the evolutionary perspective it so much values. In this perspective, religion apparently emerged through cultural accidents that occurred over hundreds of thousands, if not millions, of years. Where it is headed in the future, and how long that might take are uncertain. If religion of the dangerous, dogmatic kind has been around this long, it may remain strong for many lifetimes to come. If it has helped humans adapt by encouraging solidarity or giving them hope, it is also likely to continue, but perhaps the raw edges can be modified. Or, in the extreme, once its assumptions are unmasked, once the spell is broken, people will abandon it *en masse*. The black-and-white thinking that pits irrational dogma against enlightened atheism works only if the long evolutionary cycle is truncated, meaning that a point some thousands of years ago is compared with an imaginary point long in the future. But in reality, people live in the present. The God problem is one that they can think about, ignore entirely, or deal with through the various cultural mechanisms currently available. The long-term outcome remains uncertain. A writer who finds religion distasteful can argue that people should reject it, but there is no scholarly basis on which to say that they will. Being true to science requires leaving wishful thinking aside and paying closer attention to what people actually do and say.

The third approach tries to find a middle ground between the first and second approaches. It imagines that religion is more adaptable than scholars assume in either of the other perspectives—adaptable in ways that do not detract from some golden age of authentic religious expression and that do not require it to be abandoned altogether. Some of the writers who represent this third perspective believe religion to be purely cultural and explainable in naturalistic terms, while other scholars believe wholeheartedly that God exists. Which view is taken matters little because the facts on the ground are that religion is a reality, and so are millions of people who believe in God and millions of others who do not. Those realities alone mean that religion not only needs to be understood but also can be subjected to critical inquiry.

The historian Mark A. Noll adopted this third perspective in a widely read critique of what he termed the evangelical mind. Noll, himself a believer, was convinced that evangelical Christians needed to take the created order more seriously and engage it with the rigorous tools of the natural and human sciences. He saw no danger in this proposal, only the possibility of believers leaving behind blind faith for a more thoughtful combination of faith and reason.[29] With quite different theological assumptions, the philosopher of religion Jeffrey Stout took up the problem of religious believers engaging in politics in ways that critics asserted were undemocratic. Stout showed that there was a middle way between authoritative claims based only on divine revelation and arguments that allowed no room at all for such claims. Through a careful analysis of the scholarly debates, he demonstrated that claims of all kinds are nevertheless claims, or statements, and as elements of political discourse can be examined to determine who is making them, how consistent they are, and what their consequences might be.[30] Another example occurs in the writing of constitutional scholars Christopher L. Eisgruber and Lawrence G. Sager, who examine the legal grounds on which arguments about religion can be made. They show that it is neither fraudulent nor dangerous for believers to make arguments about rights and privileges based on religion, but they also demonstrate that these arguments can be compared for consistency and to find further justification for claims focusing on individual human rights and fairness.[31] In each of these examples, the approach is to reject extreme views of religion that by definition require it to be irrational or superstitious and instead to look closely at the real-world complexities of religious expression.

My approach is closest to the last of these three perspectives. It rests on the assumption that religion is here to stay, at least well into the foreseeable future, and that decrying or celebrating some presumably authentic orthodoxy of the past is of little value. Nor is it especially helpful to argue that people would quit believing in God if educational institutions did their job more effectively. The reality is that America is a highly educated society compared to most other parts of the world, and yet most Americans, including the better-educated ones, exhibit high levels of religious activity, including prayer and believing in God. Even though we frequently lament the failures of our educational system, it is an integral part of a society that generally tries to get things done by rational planning, not superstition. The reality also is that many well-educated, well-informed people around the world believe in God or in something resembling God and faithfully practice their religions. We need not assume that thoughtful people are amateur philosophers to see that there is a problem in reconciling God with ordinary life. Believing that prayer can cure terminal illnesses may be illogical, but declaring it illogical, as the recent critics of religion do, is not the end of the story. How people determine that it is worthwhile even though illogical, or why they think it is indeed logical, or why logic is not a consideration uppermost in their minds—those are the questions that merit attention.

Too often, it seems to me, critics and defenders of religion alike emphasize belief and leave it at that. In his treatment of faith, for example, Harris begins with the flat assertion that belief is a lever that "moves almost everything else in a person's life."[32] But of course that is not true. Countless studies have demonstrated that people can hold racist beliefs, for example, and not practice discrimination; hold tolerant beliefs, and be intolerant; believe they are rich, and yet still work; believe with good reason that they are near death, and still live each day as if they were not; and so on. The trouble with beliefs is that they are buried away in people's heads, and for this reason are difficult to observe. Beliefs can be measured in surveys and in psychological experiments. But the difficulty of finding reliable measures of belief makes it possible for writers to make all kinds of flabby assertions about them. People believe in a supernatural being, writers argue, or the devout believe that their prayers are answered. But what does this mean? Arguments about belief in God would be much harder to make if writers had to have evidence for their assertions.

A focus on language has proven to be a better approach. For more than a century, when modern comparative philologists began paying systematic attention to the similarities and differences among languages, and over a much longer period in the work of rhetoricians, language has been recognized as the key to understanding human communication and human culture. Recent advances in linguistics, neuroscience, cognitive anthropology, and cultural sociology have made it possible to say much more about the actual uses of language in verbal and written discourse than ever before. A principal advantage in the study of language is the fact that it is observable. Researchers read or listen to what someone says, paying attention to the style and substance of what is said and observing as well what is assumed and thus left unspoken. Language consists of clusters of words and gestures that convey meaning. It is composed of scripts and repertoires that can be used strategically to communicate to others and to oneself. The words we use provide interpretations of events, imposing schemas of understanding on them, defining categories, and creating order. Language and cognition are closely related. The words we use shape our thoughts, and our ways of thinking influence the words we use. Language is thus flexible but also anchored. We are free to choose what to say, and yet we choose within the constraints established by ordinary categories of thought and by the patterns of speech with which we are familiar.[33]

Language is the key to understanding how thoughtful people resolve the God problem. When people pray, they use words, whether they pray silently or aloud. They also define what they are doing when they pray by using words. The interpretations mediate between their views about God and the ways of thinking that prevail in ordinary life. If a writer only imagines that a person who prays has in mind a super-powerful divine agent who grants wishes the same way a lucky horseshoe does, then that writer needs to get out more, talk to people, and have them describe what they really think. The same is true with other aspects of the God problem. Culture matters. It is insufficient to declare that people believe in God because they want this or that. The reasons people themselves articulate are important.

The central aspect of the God problem that language assists in resolving is the relationship between reasonable uncertainty and faith. It is helpful to think of these terms being balanced on a set of weighing scales like those suspended from the left hand of Lady Justice, the blindfolded Roman goddess who weighs the strength of a case's support and opposition. If the case for uncertainty is weightier, faith erodes and is replaced by serious doubt and unbelief. If the case for faith is too heavy, certainty takes the place of uncertainty and dogmatic assertions about truth are the likely result. The balancing act performed by Lady Justice occurs through the kind of reasoned testimony and deliberation one expects to prevail in a court of law. Keeping uncertainty and faith in balance is seldom so formal or straightforward. The balance is not literally attained by weighing supportive and opposing arguments. It is a function of numerous and largely taken-for-granted language devices through which understandings about uncertainty and faith are expressed.

Uncertainty and faith are better understood as orthogonal than as opposing concepts. The fact that there is more of one does not imply that there will necessarily be less of the other. I can be deeply uncertain about what is going to happen next week or next month and yet have faith that something positive will happen. Or I may have little faith that anything good will happen. If each varies somewhat independently of the other, the two are nevertheless related. For example, when I am almost certain that something is going to happen, I need very little faith that it will happen. There are of course technical aspects of the ways in which uncertainty and faith can be defined that are unnecessary to consider as long as our focus is on the ordinary language people use to construct the relationship between these ideas. Understanding why uncertainty and faith are so important, though, does require thinking for a moment about the broader roles they play in our lives.

Uncertainty and faith are basically about practical knowledge. By practical knowledge I mean the information we use to figure out both in the short and long term what we want to accomplish as individuals and collectively, and how we go about pursuing those goals. Practical knowledge differs in this respect from theoretical knowledge concerned with aspects of the real or imagined world that have little or no bearing on what anybody does. For example, theories of the origin of the universe would likely fall into the category of theoretical knowledge, although some theoretical physicists and metaphysicians might disagree, whereas arguments for or against the sanctity of life would be of greater interest as practical knowledge. Insofar as practical action is involved, some degree of *calculation* is likely to be present. We instantaneously process volumes of information that provide mental calculations about everything from when we should consume our next meal to what the weather will be like tomorrow, to how well a conversation with a friend is going, to the efficacy of plans for starting a family or earning enough to take a vacation. Our calculations tell us that there is a level of uncertainty about our knowledge and that it may or may not make sense to have faith that a particular outcome will occur. We may decide that an outcome is likely or unlikely and that we should or should not have faith in it happening.

However, there is seldom a metric as straightforward as such probabilistic language implies. Instead, the reasonableness of our calculations is something we determine and defend through patterns of speech. We tell ourselves, "I feel lucky today," "I'm an optimistic person," "people who act that way are taking a big risk," "I have it on good authority," "the evidence convinces me," "people have done it this way for a long time," "what's the harm," "nobody knows for sure," "it's a safe bet," and so on. These ways of talking are essentially shorthand summaries of the complex calculations we have performed. What counts as a legitimate statement varies greatly from one context to another. "I feel lucky today" may be an appropriate statement in a casino but is less so from a skilled surgeon about to perform an operation. An actuary can calculate risks covered by an insurance provider with mathematical precision, whereas a risk manager concerned with national security can only predict that the likelihood of a terrorist attack is "elevated." A parent or spouse may think the odds of having cancer are high, but tell her family she has complete faith in the doctors.

The God problem is a special case of the calculations we make all the time about the balance between uncertainty and faith. It differs from other calculations because the calculations are made in the absence of any empirically verifiable knowledge. The existence or nonexistence of God cannot be proven; nor can many other claims about God, including whether God created humans, keeps them alive after they die, or hears prayers. The language of uncertainty and faith is for this reason heavily dependent on religious institutions and the teachings, traditions, and ritual practices of these institutions. Religious institutions encourage people to believe, pray, and place hope in the transcendent in ways that differ from the calculations a person would perform in playing the stock market or roulette. Religious institutions serve as a *speech community* in which special ways of talking occur. Phrases such as "bless me holy father," "we lift our hearts," "Lord we ask," and "turn to verse four" have meaning within these particular settings. A distinctive form of speaking typically demarcates religious speech as well. Prayers, for instance, may be preceded by silence, uttered in a particular cadence, taken verbatim from an authoritative text, and said in a different language (such as Latin or Hebrew). Uncertainty is often addressed explicitly through formal and repetitive affirmations, such as "Lord, we come to you because we know you hear our prayers" or "God, we praise you because you are God." Belief occurs within the religiously instituted speech community through these distinctive linguistic practices. The question of how God is like a lucky horseshoe literally would not arise.[34]

But religious institutions, especially in the contemporary world, are part of the wider culture and society in which they exist, meaning that a Catholic, for instance, thinks and talks about God in ways that the culture provides as well as through church teachings. There is no space dramatically set apart from everyday speech situations by purification rituals and taboo in which God or the spirits of ancestors can speak and be spoken to. The modern religious devotee can pray in the middle of a corporate board meeting, talk about God while peeling potatoes at a soup kitchen, post a prayer request on a website, or read a novel about heaven.[35] Everyday religious language is thus shaped by the larger speech communities in which people participate, including the casual conversational languages used among friends, the languages of generalized information and entertainment produced by the mass media, and the shared languages that make it possible for professionals, public officials, and academics to communicate. Indeed, a mark of being what the critics of religion sometimes refer to as a normal intelligent person is to be a competent speaker within this wider speech community of relatively well-educated, middle-class people. Competence implies being able to communicate with a variety of people from diverse backgrounds and with divergent interests in ways that seem reasonable and that signal shared values and identities (such as being informed, thoughtful, sane, rational, good-natured, and well-intentioned).[36] Competence of this sort is clearly different from the formalized speech on which students of religious ritual in tribal societies have focused.

Contemporary language is adept at providing ways of entertaining complex and even contradictory ideas. Both the syntactical structure of language and the performative aspects of speaking facilitate the communication of meanings that express the subtleties of difference and similarity, knowledge and uncertainty, belief and doubt. Several lines of investigation have illuminated these processes. One example of the adaptability of contemporary language was observed by the anthropologist Basil Bernstein in studying British schoolchildren. Bernstein showed that middle-class children who lived and traveled in more diverse places than working-class children relied more on "elaborated codes" that spelled out in greater detail what was being said because less could be taken for granted in their heterogeneous contacts than in homogeneous settings.[37] Homogeneous local cultures also persist, even among people with cosmopolitan connections, which means that the uses of different codes serve as markers of identity.[38] Switching between elaborated and restricted codes signals distinctions between group members and larger speech communities (as in the case of "y'all" and "all of you").[39] Another example of the adaptability of language was given by the Russian formalist Mikhail Bakhtin, who emphasized heteroglossic speech, in which actors spoke from the standpoint of several different characters and in this way were able to have an internal conversation with themselves or with others that reflected multiple perspectives.[40] For instance, a person might say, "You know, a friend of mine said, 'You're really a devout Christian, aren't you,' but I said, 'No, not really.'" The statement communicates an ambiguous message: The speaker may or may not be a devout Christian depending on which perspective is taken. Multivocality allows a speaker both to give and to take back a message or some aspects of it. A shrug of the shoulders, a wink, an upward inflection at the end of a sentence may accomplish the same mixture of certainty and doubt.[41] As yet another example, the recent work of cognitive anthropologists has shown that language often corresponds with mental schemas learned early in life, such as schemas about the physical world and about differences between animate and inanimate objects. These correspondences reduce complexity but also make possible incongruous statements and metaphoric expressions, such as "time flies" or "I'm feeling down."[42]

In the chapters that follow, I examine the language devices that enable thoughtful responses to questions about prayer and other aspects of how we talk about human relationships with God.[43] The devices provide ways to acknowledge the uncertainties about God that any reasonable person is likely to have and at the same time give expression to the convictions that people of faith claim to hold dear. I argue that a pluralistic speech community has become instantiated in which talking to and about God is widely held to be legitimate by well-educated, well-informed people. The existence of this speech community does not constitute a hegemonic culture in any strict sense of the word, but it does consist of generally shared linguistic practices that offer a great deal of latitude in how people think about God. These are not only modes of talking, but also ways of believing. They largely succeed in making it possible to hold religious convictions that on the surface would appear quite contradictory to established canons of rationality and good sense.

NOTES

1. "Proving That Prayer Is Superstition," online at godisimaginary.com.

2. See especially Dennett, *Breaking the Spell*, 116–152; Dennett's argument is drawn from the path-breaking work of cognitive scientist Pascal Boyer, *Religion Explained: The Evolutionary Origins of Religious Thought* (New York: Basic, 2001).

3. Dawkins, *The God Delusion*, 108.

4. Jürgen Habermas, *The Theory of Communicative Action* (Boston: Beacon, 1987), 196; and for a helpful discussion of the implication of Habermas's argument for understandings of ritual, see David Cheal, "Ritual: Communication in Action," *Sociological Analysis* 53 (1992), 363–174.

5. Hitchens, *God Is Not Great*, 5.

6. On this other debate about religion and democracy in political systems, a particularly useful discussion is found in Alfred Stepan, "Religion, Democracy, and the 'Twin Tolerations,'" *Journal of Democracy* 11 (2000), 37–57.

7. John Rawls, *Political Liberalism* (New York: Columbia University Press, 1993).

8. John Dewey, *A Common Faith* (New Haven: Yale University Press, 1934).

9. These arguments are masterfully reviewed and extended in Patrick Deneen, *Democratic Faith* (Princeton, NJ: Princeton University Press, 2005).

10. Richard Rorty, "Religion as a Conversation Stopper," *Common Knowledge* 3 (1994), 1–6, reprinted in Richard Rorty, *Philosophy and Social Hope* (New York: Penguin, 1999), 168–174.

11. The criticism that religion is irrational is sometimes countered by arguing that people, religious and nonreligious, do irrational things all the time, but that it seldom costs them anything, so they persist. For instance, asking a lucky horseshoe for help on a test takes about a second of one's time and in no way prevents one from studying.

12. Hitchens, *God Is Not Great*, 13.

13. "Proving That Prayer Is Superstition."

14. Diana B. Henriques and Andrew W. Lehren, "Religious Groups Reaping Share of Federal Aid for Pet Projects," *New York Times* (May 13, 2007), online at select.nytimes.com.

15. Harris, *Letter to a Christian Nation*, ix.

16. These surveys are all from national samples of the U.S. adult public, conducted in 2006 and 2007; online at roperweb.ropercenter.uconn.edu.

17. Elaine Howard Ecklund and Christopher P. Scheitle, "Religion among Academic Scientists: Distinctions, Disciplines, and Demographics," *Social*

Problems 54 (2007), 289–307; and Elaine Howard Ecklund, *Science vs. Religion: What Scientists Really Think* (New York: Oxford University Press, 2010).

18.   Neil Gross and Solon Simmons, "How Religious Are America's College and University Professors?" *SSRC Forum* (February 6, 2007), online at religion. ssrc.org. Dawkins, *The God Delusion*, 100–103, discusses some earlier studies, but these were not as rigorous methodologically; curiously, Dawkins uncritically discusses a study by Shermer and Sulloway, which Dennett, *Breaking the Spell*, 320–321, shows was too poorly designed to be credible at all.

19.   These results are from my analysis of results from General Social Surveys conducted between 1998 and 2006 by the National Opinion Research Center at the University of Chicago, comparing respondents with college degrees or higher and respondents with high school diplomas or less on the variables "creation," "god," "naturgod," "cope3," "neargod," and "godhelp." The relationships are all statistically significant at or beyond the .01 level of probability, but are weak to moderate in strength, with negative associations (gammas) of .242, .279, .093, .173, .227, and .161, respectively. Given the ready availability of these data, it is quite surprising that recent critics of religion who take pride in their scientific credentials have made no effort to use them.

20.   Also from General Social Surveys.

21.   The data are from the 2004 European Social Surveys and the 2006 General Social Survey; my analysis of the electronic data files.

22.   My analysis of the electronic data file, *Time*/SRBI Poll (October 4, 2006).

23.   In the General Social Survey data for 2006, 52 percent of those with college degrees and 44 percent of those who had never been to college attended religious services at least once a month. In the 1998 General Social Survey, when a detailed question about belief in God was asked, 91 percent of those who had college degrees and attended religious services at least once a month said they believed in God.

24.   John Schmalzbauer and Kathleen Mahoney, "Religion and Knowledge in the Post-Secular Academy," SSRC Working Papers (2007), online at www .ssrc.org.

25.   Dawkins and Hitchens, for example, comment on differences between England and the United States.

26.   Will Herberg, *Protestant-Catholic-Jew: An Essay in American Religious Sociology* (Chicago: University of Chicago Press, 1955).

27.   James Davison Hunter, *American Evangelicalism: Conservative Religion and the Quandary of Modernity* (New Brunswick, NJ: Rutgers University Press, 1983); James Davison Hunter, *Evangelicalism: The Coming Generation* (Chicago: University of Chicago Press, 1987).

28. Alan Wolfe, *The Transformation of American Religion: How We Actually Practice Our Faith* (New York: Free Press, 2003).

29. Mark A. Noll, *The Scandal of the Evangelical Mind* (Grand Rapids, MI: Eerdmans, 1994).

30. Jeffrey Stout, *Democracy and Tradition* (Princeton, NJ: Princeton University Press, 2003).

31. Christopher L. Eisgruber and Lawrence G. Sager, *Religious Freedom and the Constitution* (Cambridge, MA: Harvard University Press, 2007).

32. Harris, *The End of Faith*, 12.

33. The advantages of language over belief can also be defended in terms of religious practice; see Webb Keane, "Religious Language," *Annual Review of Anthropology* 26 (1997), 47–71.

34. The distinctive authority of ritual speech is perceptively analyzed in J. W. DuBois, "Self-Evidence and Ritual Speech," pp. 313–336 in *Evidentiality: The Linguistic Coding of Epistemology*, edited by Wallace Chafe and Johanna Nichols (Norwood, NJ: Ablex, 1986).

35. The example of talking about God while peeling potatoes is from Courtney Bender, *Heaven's Kitchen: Living Religion at God's Love We Deliver* (Chicago: University of Chicago Press, 2003), which provides an insightful analysis of the many ways in which religious speech mixes with everyday speech.

36. Dell Hymes, "On Communicative Competence," pp. 269–285 in *Sociolinguistics*, edited by J. B. Pride and J. Holmes (Hammondsworth: Penguin, 1972).

37. See especially Basil Bernstein, *Class, Codes and Control*, Vol. 1: *Theoretical Studies Toward a Sociology of Education* (London: Routledge and Kegan Paul, 1971); and A. R. Sadovnik, editor, *Knowledge and Pedagogy: The Sociology of Basil Bernstein* (Norwood, NJ: Ablex, 1995).

38. Wendy Griswold, *Regionalism and the Reading Class* (Chicago: University of Chicago Press, 2007).

39. The deployment of alternating codes to show insider and outsider identities is discussed in Barbara A. Fennell and John Bennett, "Sociolinguistic Concepts and Literary Analysis," *American Speech* 66 (1991), 371–379.

40. M. M. Bakhtin, *The Dialogic Imagination: Four Essays* (Austin: University of Texas Press, 1981), and M. M. Bakhtin, *Speech Genres and Other Late Essays* (Austin: University of Texas Press. 1986); see also Gary Saul Morison and Caryl Emerson, *Mikhail Bakhtin: Creation of a Prosaics* (Stanford, CA: Stanford University Press, 1990), and Maria Shevtsova, "Dialogism in the Novel and Bakhtin's Theory of Culture," *New Literary History* 23 (1992), 747–763.

41.   John J. Gumperz, "Contextualization and Understanding," pp. 229–252 in *Rethinking Context: Language as an Interactive Phenomenon*, edited by Alessandro Duranti and Charles Goodwin (Cambridge: Cambridge University Press, 1992); Alessandro Duranti, "Truth and Intentionality: An Ethnographic Critique," *Cultural Anthropology* 8 (1993), 214–245.

42.   John Tooby and Leda Cosmides, "The Psychological Foundations of Culture," pp. 19–136 in *The Adapted Mind: Evolutionary Psychology and the Generation of Culture*, edited by Jerome H. Barkow, Leda Cosmides, and John Tooby (New York: Oxford University Press, 1992).

43.   The 165 qualitative interviews from which the evidence comes are described in the appendix.

TWO

Talking to God

In her book about evangelical leader Jerry Falwell, anthropologist Susan Harding describes an event that nicely illustrates the peculiarities of contemporary prayer. Needing millions for his fledgling fundamentalist campus in Lynchburg, the television preacher who was soon to become the leading voice of the Religious Right rose early on Monday, September 18, 1978, and drove the 11.3-mile perimeter of Liberty Mountain, praying constantly as he drove. For the next five mornings, he did the same thing, and on the morning of Sunday, September 24, repeated the trip seven times, a total of 79.1 miles, again praying as he circled the mountain. He was literally re-enacting the biblical story of Joshua, whose circling of Jericho caused the enemy's walls to crumble. That September Falwell raised $7 million for his college. Harding writes, "God spoke to him through the story of Jericho as plainly as he . . . had spoken to Joshua that night thousands of years before." God responded graciously to Falwell's earnest prayers. "Jerry's encompassing the mountain that morning was not magical," Harding observes. "His circling was submissive, an act of obedience and sacrifice."[1]

Falwell's Joshua-inspired prayer circuit received little attention beyond the faithful, who gladly learned that their own prayers and small donations had been miraculously amplified. His biographers, Gerald Strober and Ruth Tomczak, included the story in a book Falwell sent in gratitude to loyal supporters, terming the incident a true miracle.[2] Harding's anthropological account sought to demonstrate—with as much sympathy as she could muster—how Falwell and his followers created and lived inside a "storied" world. "The outside, worldly, cynical voice," she wrote, "would say his fund-raising was gimmickry, fleecing, hucksterism, nothing but a con game."[3]

Seven years later, in September 1985, a prayer by fellow televangelist Pat Robertson drew much wider publicity. As Hurricane Gloria approached the Virginia coast where Robertson's broadcasting empire was headquartered, Robertson prayed successfully that the storm would veer away. During the preacher's 1988 bid for the U.S. presidency, an interviewer asked him if the Gloria incident had influenced his decision to run. "It was extremely important," Robertson said, "because I felt, interestingly enough, that if I couldn't move a hurricane, I could hardly move a nation."[4] In another interview, Robertson elaborated, "I knew I could just as easily keep my mouth shut and let the thing hit and not get involved." But, unable to "allow that loss of life," he decided to intervene. "It was, of course, a miracle," he added.[5]

Robertson's intercessory prayer on behalf of Virginia Beach came to be known as the "wacko factor"—which more than anything else doomed his candidacy. "He speaks in tongues, expels demons with shouts of 'Satan be gone!,' cures lung cancer and hemorrhoids," television commentator John McLaughlin charged. "Claiming 'Prophet of God' status, he has called down the divine wrath on his critics."[6] Years later, CBS 60 Minutes commentator Andy Rooney revived the accusation in conjunction with controversy over actor Mel Gibson's film The Passion of the Christ. "I heard from God just the other night," Rooney remarked. "I wish you'd tell your viewers that Pat Robertson and Mel Gibson strike me as wackos. I believe that's one of your current words. They're crazy as bedbugs, another earthly expression."[7]

But if Robertson had crossed the line, millions of Americans seemed in agreement, at least, on the point that miracles can happen. A national poll in 1995 asked Americans if they believed that "miracles are performed by the power of God." Eighty-four percent said they did—75 percent agreed strongly. Only 11 percent thought there was no such thing as miracles. Two years later a poll asked people if they agreed that "even today miracles are performed by the power of God." Eighty-five percent said they did. A more discriminating question in 1998 asked people if they believed in "religious miracles." Nearly half (47 percent) said they definitely did. Another 25 percent said they probably did.

Other studies confirmed widespread belief in miracles. In one poll, 50 percent thought God could bring people back to life who had been declared dead. In that survey, 77 percent thought God or the saints could heal sick people who had been given no chance of survival by medical science. Twenty percent said they had prayed at a shrine or holy place where they believed miracles were performed. In another survey, 80 percent said they believed in "God-inspired miracles."[8]

Whether by prayer or other means, the natural order can be contravened, according to this view—a belief shared by many Americans and non-Americans alike. Prayer can bring rain or stop it, help the home team win, influence the lottery, resolve violence, and end wars. It miraculously heals, cleanses, sparks creativity, and ensures success. Those were apparently the thoughts that inspired David Miller, the mayor of Lubbock, Texas, to declare on a hot July day in 2006 that the city council would adopt a resolution asking the local residents to pray for rain. It had worked before, he said, turning 2004 into the second-wettest year on record. Similar thoughts must have occurred a few months later on the opposite side of the world. "We should all, literally and without any irony, pray for rain over the next six to eight weeks," Australian Prime Minister John Howard said on a national telecast. Others clearly shared the view that prayer could work wonders. "Prayer is a powerful tool," a guest columnist wrote in response to parents' concerns about gang violence in a Michigan town. The trendy website beliefnet.com tantalized readers with "answered prayer" blogs, such as "my prayer to stop smoking was answered right away, the nicotine addiction was gone immediately after I prayed," and "an injury to my knee was spontaneously healed after doctors had given up." It was a view that Daniel Wirth, a medical researcher in New York, took to the bank, promising couples undergoing in vitro fertilization treatment success because an international network of prayer groups was supposedly praying for them.[9]

These are the kinds of beliefs that cause critics of religion to lose sleep at night. But are their worries justified? Is it the case that millions of Americans are on the wacko fringe, praying to a God they believe will redirect hurricanes and rain clouds just because they asked? Are people who otherwise lead rational lives so easily duped by television preachers and fraudulent doctors that they give away hard-earned currency and invest money in questionable schemes? When Americans talk to God, do they hear voices telling them who they should marry, where they should work, and how they should vote?

It is true that unusual dealings with the Almighty have been observed throughout the nation's history. When fits, animal noises, and other strange behavior afflicted the daughters of John Goodwin in 1689, New England preacher Cotton Mather prayed fervently and repeatedly for the departure of the devils that possessed them. In 1823, a 17-year-old prayed to know what he should do with his life, and an angel appeared in his bedroom, telling him that an ancient book written on gold plates— later known as the Book of Mormon—was buried in a nearby hill. In 1903, President William McKinley told an interviewer that he had gone "down on my knees and prayed Almighty God for light and guidance" before annexing the Philippines to "educate the Filipinos, and uplift and civilize and Christianize them." In the 1920s, according to Ronald Reagan biographer Paul Kengor, the future president's mother, Nelle Reagan, "developed a reputation as someone whose prayers were powerful, even to the extent that they might cure the sick," including the miraculous healing of an abscess on the neck of a neighbor's daughter. Reagan himself reportedly prayed frequently, although apparently with less dramatic results.[10]

Unusual dealings of a different sort have proliferated in recent years. One example is a nonprofit organization calling itself the Presidential Prayer Team (PPT), launched in 2001 after the September 11 tragedy by retired Baptist minister Cornell Haan and Scottsdale businessman Bill Hunter. Using the Internet and e-mail, PPT sent out regular messages about news items requiring prayer, and assured its three million members that they were having "an untold impact on America for good and for God." A subsidiary organization called Presidential Prayer Team for Kids published weekly online updates giving young readers "things to pray for this week." The December 1, 2006, edition, for example, asked kids to pray for newly appointed White House Chief of Staff Josh Bolten, briefly summarizing his credentials and asserting, "So you can tell he's a very smart man and a terrific guy to have serving our country!"[11] Another subsidiary, Pray the Vote, encouraged church goers to host "prayer parties" for elected officials and provided informational packets to pastors interested in encouraging their "congregation to pray for righteous leaders to be elected."[12]

Such endeavors notwithstanding, surprisingly little is known about prayer—as it is actually practiced, experienced, and interpreted by ordinary people. In their authoritative examination of the history of prayer, Philip and Carol Zaleski write that scholarship on prayer is a "confusion of tongues."[13] This is partly because prayer itself varies so widely. It can be found in art and music, inscribed on buildings, enacted in dance, turned into great poetry, or just murmured in a brief expletive, "God help me." All can be viewed as attempts to communicate between a human and a divine realm. The confusion also stems from neglect. Countless surveys have asked people how often they pray, but studies seldom probe deeper by examining the texts of informal prayers and asking people to talk about their prayers.

In consequence, much of what is known about prayer comes either from considering the great canonical works of religious traditions or from inquiries into its exotic manifestations. There are the laments and petitions of the Bible and the Qur'an, the Lord's prayer, the Philokalia, the prayers of Bernard of Clairvaux and Teresa of Avila, the Jesus prayer, and countless blessings and incantations. These are occasionally known and sometimes commonly practiced, but by no means exhaustive of how people talk to God. In real life, the more removed from the experiences of better-educated, middle-class Americans a prayer is, the more likely it is to have been studied. The prayer rituals of Native Americans are a source of endless fascination. Glossalalia, faith healing, and serpent handling come in for considerable attention as well.

Amid the profusion of words and deeds that crowd under the umbrella of "prayer," it is easy to miss just how unusual the very idea of prayer is. The assumption that humans can communicate with the divine is like no other. It is an audacious claim, hinged on the notion that some other realm even exists, let alone one that can somehow be entreated or praised. The Zaleskis write that prayer is truly a story about the impossible: "of how we creatures of flesh and blood lay siege to heaven, speak to the Maker of all things, and await, with confidence or hopeful skepticism, a response."[14] It is perhaps the sheer oddity of prayer that encourages people to perform it in one of two ways that writers on the topic argue amount to a basic polarity: highly routinized or completely spontaneous. Examples of the former include most liturgical readings from prayer books and the kinds of bedtime prayers that small children learn to say by heart. The latter are best illustrated by utterances that seem to arise unbidden, such as "God help me" or "Bless you." In both, thought appears to be minimal: The Lord's prayer or the rosary can be recited while thinking about something else entirely, while a brief expletive pops out precisely because something else has happened. The lack of thought makes up for the fact that something quite extraordinary takes place when humans seek to communicate with the divine.

However, this view is incomplete. Insofar as prayer is human, it is also behavior to which we ascribe meaning. It is meaningful because we think about it—puzzle over it, interpret it, find reasons for doing it, and make guesses about what it does to us or for us. This is true of all action, whether it is as simple as brushing one's teeth or as complicated as constructing a building. It is especially true of people—most Americans— who have been taught they must have reasons for what they do. And it is especially true of something as intellectually puzzling as prayer. When the God to whom one prays cannot be seen or heard, talking to that God requires an understanding that goes beyond ordinary conversation. To say that a prayer has been answered involves an interpretation of what such a statement could possibly mean. Even to acknowledge in passing that a prayer heard or recited was a powerful moment necessitates an explanation of why one was moved.

Of course, prayer is learned—in families and houses of worship, through hearing sermons about it, and by listening to the prayers of religious leaders. So it might make sense to argue that there are rather clear understandings of what prayer is and of how it should be interpreted. However, this is often not the case. For one thing, clergy themselves are conflicted. Many have never questioned the value of prayer, but have differing views of it, and others have doubts about its meaning and purpose. And for good reason. They point to biblical examples of doubt. They note that it is human to doubt and that faith is often strengthened in times of uncertainty. Whether people acknowledge doubt or not, how they make sense of prayer is largely of their own design. They pray at home by themselves and sometimes pray with close friends or post prayer requests on websites, and when they pray at their places of worship, their interpretations of what is going on are still formed mostly in private. This means there is variation in how people think about prayer. But it also means that interpretations of prayer are shaped by the general habits of thought—by the everyday language of the wider speech community—that our culture provides.

The hunch I wish to consider in this chapter is that middle-class Americans have found a way to pray that neither violates their basic intellectual integrity nor threatens to be in any way socially disruptive (unlike, for instance, Joshua's entreaty at Jericho). They pray in private and in groups, and, although some Americans do not pray at all, a large number do. Prayer is a meaningful part of their lives, and yet it generally does not imply superstition or faith that God will act in magical ways. This is not to say that Americans' faith is insincere. The point is rather that complex cultural work is going on. Americans have learned how to register an implicit level of uncertainty about what prayer is, how it works, and to whom they are praying. This uncertainty is evident in the language in which prayer is expressed and interpreted. At the same time, prayer points to possibilities beyond ourselves, a layer of reality that transcends what can be known. It enhances life, even though it seldom results in the kinds of supernatural interventions—or "wacko" claims about such interventions—that critics worry about.

Although prayer is popularly understood as simply talking to God, communication with the divine necessitates forming a mental image of who or what is at the other end of the conversation—an image that is informed by ordinary language and experience as much as by theological teachings. It is common for this image to be anthropocentric. Most communication does involve another person, so this is not surprising. However, notions about this divine person being a father, mother, king, lover, priest, or judge help little in understanding how people actually think about God when they pray. The key, it seems, is to imagine God as a powerful and beneficent "other," without turning God into a magical image that insults an educated person's intelligence. In addition, the person talking to God is in some ways a mental image as well—not just a person, but a concept of a person. Then there are often other parties involved, such as a sick or needy person for whom prayer is given. And finally a transaction occurs, as supplicants think about God somehow responding to their prayers. All of these elements of prayer are subject to common uses of language and to interpretation. It is in these interpretations that we can see how middle-class Americans work out a meaningful way of thinking about God. An example will show what I mean.

Marie Pierre is a second-generation American in her mid-twenties who lives in South Florida. Her parents grew up in Haiti, where they spoke Creole, and Marie herself speaks Creole and Spanish as well as English. She is a college graduate—finishing in three years—and currently works as a sales representative for a large financial institution. She doesn't much like her work. The reason is that she is a devout Christian and feels that her job is all about money instead of helping people. She tries to pursue her higher values through her church. She belongs to a conservative evangelical Protestant church that is affiliated with a denomination, but she says the denomination, and even "religion," are less important to her than Christianity itself. She attends worship services weekly and participates in a prayer meeting on Saturdays. She teaches Sunday school, works with the congregation's youth program, and volunteers at a center for disadvantaged families. In brief, she is an extraordinarily active and sincere middle-class American Christian.

Marie is particularly interesting for our purposes because she has a foot in each of two worlds. On the one hand, she is of immigrant stock, coming from a family that struggled economically and had no opportunities for higher education, but was quite religious. Like many Americans who are immigrants or children of immigrants, her ethnic roots are deep, and in her community of origin, people looked to God as a source of hope and comfort. They prayed and expected God to intervene on their behalf. In some instances, the Christianity of Marie's family mixed easily with voudoo, and in others replaced it. On the other hand, Marie is a typical, well-educated, middle-class American. Her college training and her work have placed her in the larger speech community of other middle-class people, and she has learned to think rationally and strategically about how the world works. She budgets her money carefully and when she is ill, goes to the doctor. She scoffs at people who thought Hurricane Katrina was somehow God's punishment. That's just an ignorant view, she says. Katrina came about from natural causes. She believes firmly that hard work is the key to success and that people who break moral rules reap what they sow. She also thinks it is important for people of faith to be educated and knowledgeable about their faith. Straddling two worlds, she illustrates more clearly than some people do the complexities of what it means to pray.

At Marie's church, prayer is an important part of the weekly worship service on Sundays. Being a regular attendee, Marie has no trouble describing the sequence. Near the beginning of the service the pastor gives a broad prayer that covers a range of topics of concern to the congregation and beyond. His prayer includes praise and thanksgiving as well as general petitions for the sick, the needy, the congregation, and the world. Then there is a time for collective prayer, during which people in the congregation pray silently for themselves, utter words of praise and thanksgiving to God, and request various things from God, such as health and protection for their loved ones. A third prayer is for the offering. Following a hymn, a fourth prayer precedes the sermon and asks God to help the listeners receive the word. The service ends with a prayer for people who want to accept Christ and asks God to guide the congregation and be with them as they return to their homes. On the first Sunday of each month, a sixth prayer occurs while the congregation takes communion.

The prayers from week to week are similar enough that they naturally blend into one another and Marie's mind often wanders or is on her own prayer requests instead of on the words being said by the preacher or other members of the congregation. However, one prayer a couple of weeks ago stood out in Marie's memory. "There was this little girl that had, um, um, a cancer, leukemia, she's only seven, in her breast. And she was in chemo, but she wasn't going too well, and they prayed on it, two Sundays before," Marie recalled. Two weeks later the girl returned and was clearly more energetic than she had been before. The congregation thanked God in their prayers. "That was powerful, that was moving, because she was thanking God as well, a seven-year-old girl."

What specifically had the pastor asked God to do or make happen? "Well, she was suffering," Marie explained, "because they put some- thing in her breast to measure the medication and she was hurting so bad. So they asked God to have the doctor to heal the wound and then make it better, and she was throwing up from the chemo, and having, you know, bad diarrhea." God eased the girl's suffering. "She wasn't throwing up as much and then when she finished the chemo, she was, she was very healthy. You wouldn't know that she had cancer or she had a tube in her chest."

Marie remembered almost exactly how the prayer had gone. Speaking in Creole, the pastor said, "Heavenly Father from above us, we thank you for everything you have done for us, for your grace, your mercy and for our forgiveness and please Father, help the doctor. We hand you this little girl, who is suffering for a while, and as she's going through all this chemo. She doesn't understand why she's going through all of that, but you know, please make it—not easy, not easy on her—but make the suffering go as lightly as possible and heal her in the name of our precious Savior Jesus because she wants to serve you. And in the name of God, we pray."

A quick reading of this account, especially by someone from the outside assuming that kooky things happen at evangelical churches, would conclude that the story was about a miraculous healing. The girl was seriously ill. The congregation prayed. God heard their prayers and the girl got better. Or so the church folks believed. End of story. It stood out in Marie's memory because it was dramatic evidence of God's power to heal. Perhaps it also reinforced her own faith and her conviction that spending so much time at the church was worthwhile.

However, that reading of the story is too casual. A closer reading suggests a more nuanced interpretation. On the one hand, the structure of the narrative is clearly a before-and-after tale. Before the congregation prayed, the girl was ill; after the prayer, the girl felt better. In between, God worked. The narrative in this respect conforms to the typical pattern of a religious testimonial: A person is in dire straits, comes to God, and thereafter leads a happier life. In the story, time is also compressed. Marie and presumably the congregation are impressed because they see a girl suffering and then the next time they see her, she is feeling much better. The suddenness of the turnaround conveys the sense that something spectacular has happened, apparently through divine intervention. This may have been how the congregation saw it. On the other hand, the account is not directly about the congregation's reaction, but Marie's interpretation of what happened. She says three things that are especially notable. First, she says that the pastor asked God to have the doctor heal the wound and make it better. Second, she notes that it was "when she finished the chemo" that the girl felt better. And third, she emphasizes that the prayer asked God to make the suffering go as lightly as possible. Although the prayer concludes by asking God to heal the girl, these statements clarify what that means. Healing involves the work of a doctor, chemotherapy, and pain that cannot be escaped but can be lessened.

What does a prayer like this say about Marie's understanding of God? It clearly implies God's existence and approachability. It suggests that God is somehow involved in dramatic and otherwise memorable events. God's work is nevertheless performed largely in ways that do not conflict with ordinary understandings of medicine, disease, and suffering.

There may be an anthropomorphic image of God in Marie's mind. She refers to God twice as a father and recalls that the prayer was given in the name of Jesus. Yet the story is remarkably sparse on explicit or implied details about God. Marie says nothing about God's possible physical manifestations or working in history. The most that can be said from her account is that God is good, "above us," and a possible source of guidance and healing.

It is also worth speculating about why this particular prayer was memorable to Marie. If dramatic healings occurred all the time, the incident would likely have been less memorable, especially because the story was about a girl feeling better after chemo and did not imply that she was necessarily cured of leukemia. The best clue about why it was memorable is probably that the main character was in fact a girl. Marie twice mentions that the girl was only seven years old and twice more refers to her as a "little girl." Perhaps the event was memorable because children usually were not sick or the focus of prayer. She may also have been known to Marie, although it is interesting that the story begins "there was this little girl" and never mentions a name. The girl nevertheless occupies a central place in the narrative. She is small, ill, at the start lacking in energy, and in the prayer lacking in understanding. *She is all the things that God is not.* God's attributes are implied, and can remain unspoken, in contrast to the girl. God is the perfect "other," sizable, powerful, and knowledgeable. By emphasizing certain characteristics of the girl, Marie is able to imply that God has certain characteristics without actually saying explicitly what these are.

This reading of the story is consistent with Marie's way of talking about other prayers at the church and in her personal life. At a recent service, she recalls, someone prayed for the pastor because he was leaving shortly for a trip to Haiti and would be at risk because of the violence there. The prayer asked that the Lord make the pastor "invisible." Like the prayer about healing, there was this small hint of magical or supernatural possibility. However, Marie's interpretation was that this meant praying that the pastor would not be attacked by thieves or gang members while visiting Haiti. Her description of her personal prayers similarly adopts a kind of dual language. For instance, she says she prays any time of day because she knows God is always there. "Even when I'm in my car, I just say God take the wheel." Literally? Not at all. She says it is more like talking out loud, just conversing. "Okay, you see what happened. This wasn't supposed to happen. But tell me what to do. Or, I'm getting frustrated. Show me the light." Just yesterday, she says, "I came home early because I couldn't hold my head up." She said to herself and apparently to God as well, "Okay, I can't take it no more." And then she went to bed. In the morning her headache was gone. "I feel that when I talk to God, he listens."

I have described Marie and what she had to say about prayer in some detail because her remarks show clearly that there is a lot going on when people talk about prayer. She not only prays, but also recalls what she and others have prayed about and in so doing makes sense of prayer— that is, interprets it in ways that correspond with how she understands God, herself, and her relation to God. These interpretations are not sophisticated metaphysical arguments of the kind that might result if she—or a theologian—were asked, what is the meaning of prayer? They are instead built into the selection and arrangement of words. They do not have to be explicated further to seem appropriate as she speaks.

Her words, I contend, also open the door a crack for thinking about the broader puzzle of Americans' ways of coming to terms with God. There is a mingling of languages, including one that directs attention beyond the human realm to a powerful divinity who can perform miracles, heal people, and even make them invisible, and yet a tempering of this language by another that references medicine, sleep, and human frailty. The nuances with which prayer is described provide ways to think about the existence of God and at the same time to stop short of claiming to know very much about God or to avoid having to argue that God acts in ways that a thinking person might question. But how exactly all this works needs to be examined in greater detail.

As a starting point, let us assume that prayer, as popularly understood, is communication—to be sure, unusual—but communication nonetheless. It is composed of language, which in most cases is verbal speech, although it may also include behavioral gestures, such as bowing and genuflecting, and if expressed in language may nevertheless be silent, as when a prayer is spoken only in the heart. As language, prayer is thus accomplished through the use of linguistic devices, and these in turn are associated with cognitive structures or ways of thinking. This much applies to prayer in any context. However, these devices are also shaped by the particular cultural settings in which they appear. In our case, they are informed by American culture. The constraint in contemporary culture is, as I have suggested, to maintain the possibility of believing in and talking to God without seeming to have lost one's senses—that is, to operate in ways that nonreligious people can also understand and in conformity with patterns of thought and speech that pertain in realms other than religion, such as in science, law, business, and daily life.

In what follows, I describe six devices of language that serve as ways of praying and talking about prayer while also expressing some degree of doubt or ambivalence about what prayer is and actually accomplishes: schema alignment, ontological assertion, contingency referents, domain juxtaposition, code switching, and performative competence. For each of the six, I offer examples of how it is applied to prayer within a contemporary cultural setting. I prefer to call these devices in keeping with the idea that these are structures or arrangements in language that accomplish certain communicative tasks, but are not necessarily (or usually) consciously employed. Thus, they are devices rather than "strategies," and to the extent that they are structures within speech itself, they are not "tools." But devices are neither contrived nor trivial. The fact that most of the sentences when we speak and write have nouns and verbs comes naturally. We learn implicit rules of sentence construction early in life. These are very complex rules, as children discover when teachers require them to diagram sentences, but they are also ones that require little thought as we use them. Nor are these devices incidental. They reflect and shape how we interact with the world. My contention is that the devices evident in how we talk about prayer are similarly important. They reveal some very important patterns in how we think about God.[15]

A cultural device that I will call *schema alignment*, drawing on recent work in cognitive psychology, entails a congruence of assumptions about causality between the human and divine realms. It involves thinking and talking about God's actions in ways that align with taken-for-granted notions about human action. For example, moving an object normally requires being physically close enough to push it or pick it up. That is an assumption we take for granted about the human world. Children learn early to understand the causes of certain events in this way: Dropping an object causes it to fall, a stroller moves because someone pushes it, a mother has to be close to spoon food into a child's mouth. But if God is imagined to be distant, perhaps living in a place outside the known universe, then it would seem strange to think of God picking up a person and throwing her across the room. It would seem less strange that God might love that person. Children learn to understand that love can happen at a distance: They hear their mother on the telephone telling them she loves them even though she is at work; their grandmother who lives a thousand miles away loves them. Love at a distance implies a different kind of causality. A person "feels loved" or "feels better" just from being aware that someone far away loves them.

Cognitive psychologist George Mandler defined a schema as an abstract representation of environmental regularities. He had in mind something similar to Kant's idea that "dog" is an abstraction that emerges from and makes sense of a figure we perceive as a four-footed animal within a certain size range and including certain markings and shapes. A schema is a kind of template against which to compare particular perceptions. It implicitly suggests the criteria by which we determine that something is or is not a dog. Considerable research has been conducted by cognitive psychologists over the past quarter century to determine how schemas work. One of the principal conclusions is that schemas entail assumptions about action and the causes of action. For example, dogs and other animals can move themselves. Plants cannot. Neither can rocks. Thus, seeing an animal move implies an assumption that something internal to the animal, such as an instinct or desire, caused it to move, whereas a rock moving implies that some force outside of it caused it to move.[16]

The idea of schemas was applied to the study of prayer in an interesting study conducted by cognitive anthropologist Justin L. Barrett. The study involved students at an evangelical Protestant college in the

Midwest who believed in God but who, Barrett hypothesized, were probably like most educated Americans in drawing on intuitive causal assumptions about how God might work. Barrett conducted a series of experiments in which students read fictitious scenarios involving various dilemmas, such as being stranded somewhere in the South Pacific with a leaky boat and little food or water. The students were then asked to rate the likelihood that they would pray for particular kinds of help from several imaginary deities. The experiments were designed to determine under what conditions the students would invoke what he termed a mechanistic schema and under what other conditions they would invoke a psychological schema. The mechanistic schema involved physical intervention, such as fixing the leaky boat or finding water. The psychological schema involved something mental or emotional, such as nearby islanders understanding one's radio message or the person stranded being able to think more clearly. The experiment showed that students generally preferred praying for psychological interventions. Only when the imaginary deity was described as being close by did they opt for mechanistic interventions. What they were doing, Barrett inferred, was using "intuitive cognition" to provide "inferences regarding what would be reasonable action for God to undertake." Judging from other research, the students usually viewed God as a kind of super human located somewhere "out there." A God out there could not be imagined to act mechanistically. In short, the students were aligning their understandings about prayer and divine action to be consistent with the cognitive schemas they used in ordinary life.[17]

A common criticism of religion is that it necessitates assumptions that are unreasonable in terms of the intuitive understandings of causality that most people take for granted. Praying that God will make a $100 bill appear in one's pocket or instantly heal a serious gunshot wound are examples. The charge that prayer of this kind is unreasonable stems from two assumptions. The first is that there is a clear distinction between "natural" and "supernatural," meaning that schemas are involved. The second is that prayer is to a God that is a powerful supernatural agent, where power implies causality. The way a religious person demonstrates faith, in this view, is to pray that the supernatural agent's power be demonstrated by causing something to happen that would normally occur only through natural causes. By definition, prayer involves a deviation from normal understandings of causality. But Barrett's research challenges this notion. It suggests that reasonable people adjust their causal assumptions about God's power in a way that reduces the tension between their faith and their taken-for-granted ideas about how the world works. They pray, but not for acts that violate assumptions about the mechanics of physical intervention. God is powerful, but more in the sense of being able to influence thoughts or emotions at a distance, like one's grandmother might do.

The wacko factor in Pat Robertson's account of diverting Hurricane Gloria, as critics saw it, was due to a misalignment of schemas. Viewing God as a being located far away, they had trouble imagining God responding to Robertson's plea for mechanistic action. Robertson himself clearly thought of God being located nearby. Falwell's prayer circuit around Liberty Mountain was less problematic, if Harding's interpretation is correct. He did not envision money raining from heaven, but did imagine hearts being moved by people hearing of his obedience to God. Marie Pierre's story illustrates schema alignment insofar as she emphasizes the girl's chemotherapy treatment and God's role in guiding the doctor. In her account, God did not intervene physically to heal the girl, but somehow helped the doctor mentally and emotionally.

Schema alignment frequently takes the form of anthropomorphizing God—imagining that God behaves pretty much like a human person. In another interesting study, Barrett and collaborator Frank C. Keil asked students to complete stories about God and then compared the stories with students' answers to abstract theological questions. Their answers frequently suggested that God acted like a person even though these answers were inconsistent with the students' formal theological views. For example, they said God would finish answering one prayer before helping somebody else, despite believing that God could do many things at once. "At least on one level," the authors concluded, "the problem created by the ontological chasm between humans and the supernatural is solved by ignoring the difference." Schema alignment means living in a world that includes God, but in which the commonsense categories of everyday thought still apply. The God problem is resolved "by creating God in the image of ourselves, and using the constraints of nature and humanity as our basic assumptions for understanding God."[18]

Schema alignment is clearly evident in the ways in which ordinary people pray and talk about prayer. For example, a woman who attends a Disciples of Christ church in Michigan says she has a structured time every day for Bible reading and prayer. "I pray and then I am silent for a while to see what God says to me. I think it's really important that we give him time to answer our concerns rather than just doing all the talking." If she were pressed to explain how it is possible to give God time, she would probably acknowledge that God does not need time. In her everyday thinking, though, God might need some time to think things over and get back to her, or, like a friend, need her to stop talking once in a while and listen.

As another example, a man who has a graduate degree in counseling and guidance and attends an evangelical church in California says he tries to make his daily prayer time "meaningful." His prayers are sometimes meaningful when they deal with dramatic events. For instance, a man in his community recently shot and killed his girlfriend's daughter, so praying for this woman and her grief was meaningful. The event pulled at his heartstrings. However, the clearest contrast between meaningless and meaningful prayer concerns repetitive prayers. He feels these were not very meaningful. The reason? "If I had a friend who, when I went up to him I always said the same thing over and over and over again, what kind of a relationship would you have with that friend? I mean, it would just really get stale." In other words, God is like a human friend. It is not so unusual to be talking to God, after all, because the same rules about being an interesting conversation partner apply.

The distinction between mechanistic and psychological schemas is particularly evident in the following comment by a woman who majored in communications and now attends a suburban Methodist church every Sunday with her husband in Colorado. She prays every day and is confident that her prayers are answered. But she does not ask God for anything that would violate the natural order, such as healing a sick family member. She prays instead that people's stress level will be reduced so they can think better. "I'm not asking God for a gift," she says. "I'm asking for God, not to give people strength, but to give them an idea of what they can do to strengthen themselves."

What distinguishes these anthropomorphisms from literal speech in which God is actually assumed to be like a human person is the degree of reflexivity or self-awareness involved. A Muslim woman, for instance, who includes several supplications in her daily Fajr or dawn prayers says of Allah, "He is in control and if we ask him, he will help us in our situations if we need help." But she also says, "I am praying to the invisible creator. We are so used to saying he, but I don't believe he is a he." Reflexivity is similarly evident in the statement by the man who says rote prayers would be stale. He likens prayer to a conversation with a friend, but is aware that he is offering an illustration, not a statement of fact.

Another form of schema alignment that appears to be quite common distinguishes a natural realm that includes both mechanistic and ordinary psychological processes from a spiritual realm that is defined by religious teachings about God. Schema alignment occurs by associating God's power only with activities within the spiritual realm, thus allowing assumptions about the natural realm to remain intact. Consider the following from an Internet prayer request site: "Please pray for Eric's salvation. Pray God will open the door for Eric to hear and believe the Gospel. Pray that Eric will have the grace and the understanding to believe the word of God." The prayer is for God to cause salvation to occur, something in the spiritual realm that might have other consequences, but those consequences remain unstated. Prayers of this kind typically ask God for "blessings," "peace," "love," "guidance," "light," or "faith." These are appropriate to request because they are understood to be spiritual qualities. A man whose brother had been killed in a motorcycle accident, for example, prayed that God would "shine his light" on the widow and the rest of the family. Another man prayed simply, "I need faith."

A close reading of prayers for health and healing shows that these prayers often ask for spiritual responses from God, rather than for physical cures. "Give your blessing to those who are ill," a woman prayed during a worship service at her church, "to those who carry the worry and fear along with them, to those who heal, or make comfortable, or struggle to find answers for perplexing diseases. May they draw from your well of patience, calm, hope, perseverance, and assurance that you are present with them no matter what the outcome."[19] The request was for God's blessing and presence. Or consider this request posted on an Internet site: "Please offer up prayers for [name withheld] who was just diagnosed with breast cancer and needs the peace of mind of the Holy Spirit to get her through this trying time."

Because the spiritual realm is outside of the known human world, entextualization is often evident in prayers that emphasize spiritual action. It provides words recognizably associated with the spiritual realm. Entextualization involves quoting directly from sacred texts or selecting syntax, rhythm, and words that signal a connection with these texts.[20] The man who prayed, "I need faith," also asked "that all things will work together for the good of all concerned," a loose paraphrase of the biblical passage, "we know that all things work together for good to them that love God," found in Romans 8:28. Or consider the following from a Baptist website: "Pray for the souls closest to Hell that the scales will be removed from their eyes that they may see the Light." Referring to "souls," "Hell," "scales," and "Light" gives the sentence a biblical connotation. An example from an interactive online prayer chain states, "Give Linda the peace and quiet of heart as you unfold your wonderful plan for this family." The cadence and phrasing resemble those of a pastoral prayer or sermon. Prayers for "victory," "open doors," "grace," and "mercy" similarly make use of biblical words to define requested spiritual activities.

These prayers effectively restrict the actions of the deity to be performed within the spiritual realm and according to the petitioner's understanding of spiritual actions that are suitable to the deity. Strictures of this kind illustrate that a deity can still be regarded as a powerful supernatural agent without intervening directly in the natural order. Indeed, an important function of prayer and religious rituals is to *prevent* such intervention. This is especially the case when supernatural intervention can be a source of harm and is the reason dead ancestors that can turn into malicious spirits have their hands and feet tied at burial, are buried with favorite food and jewelry, or are given things to keep them busy (such as threading a needle). Prayers and associated burial practices accomplish schema alignment by keeping the spirits in their place. Contemporary practices that focus on a benevolent deity are less likely to define boundaries for fear of harm than to articulate a spiritual realm that is consistent with intuitive assumptions about natural causes. However, one of the spiritual tasks that a deity can appropriately perform is providing protection from evil. Examples include such petitions as "pull my husband from Satan's reach," "protect my family from the evil one," and "turn our country from its wicked ways."

A second linguistic mechanism that helps people talk to God without seeming to have lost their senses involves affirming the existence of God without necessarily attributing specific actions to God. Ontological questions are concerned with being and existence. *Ontological assertions* about God are statements about God's being, such as theologian Paul Tillich's statement that God can be understood as the "ground of being," or in Judaism, the Shema, which begins, "Hear, O Israel, the Lord our God, the Lord is One."[21] To assert the existence of something is to invoke a schema, and thus to imply assumptions about action (as in the case of a dog running). However, it is possible to make statements that emphasize being without explicitly suggesting action. Prayers are often of this kind. They assert the existence of God without associating any other action with God. God is more of a reality, presence, or being, and less of an agent who engages in action.

Praying in a way that implies God's existence but that does not explicitly suggest divine action avoids the kinds of problems that arise when Pat Robertson claims success in asking God to divert a hurricane. In similar fashion, another galaxy can exist but have few implications for daily life on earth. A fourth dimension can be posited without creating problems for a society located in three-dimensional space. Ontological assertions of a more rudimentary kind are quite common. Take, for example, the assertion that goodness exists. To say this does not imply that goodness will always prevail or that it will be evident in any particular situation. It is an important assertion, but also a rather minimal one that can be posited as an item of faith or by citing a few instances in which goodness seems to have been evident.

Although prayer is popularly understood as a way of asking God to do something (and thus believable only if God responds), many prayers do not take this form at all. Prayers of praise are one example. Consider, for instance, St. Francis of Assisi's "Canticle of the Creatures," which begins, "Most High, all-powerful, all-good Lord, All Praise is Yours, all glory, honor and blessings. To you alone, Most High, do they belong; no mortal lips are worthy to pronounce Your Name." The prayer continues in this vein, asserting the existence of God, and asking for nothing. A member of a Presbyterian church led her congregation in a liturgical prayer with these words, "Gracious and loving God, creator of the universe, ruler of all nations; we bow before you and praise you for the wisdom and breadth of your creative power." The words assert the existence and unique characteristics of God. Prayers of thanksgiving often take a similar form. Instead of thanking God for specific interventions, such as the previously mentioned beliefnet.com prayer about miraculous healing from a smoking addiction, the petitioner thanks God for being God, for the creation, or for "all thy blessings." A man who attends a nondenominational evangelical church in Arizona put it this way: "We typically start with a prayer that acknowledges who God is, a thank you for blessings that He has given and the favor He has shown. And we ask that the Lord will receive all the honor and glory."

Prayers involving ontological assertion frequently emphasize the existence of God by talking about the presence of God. They do not ask God to show up on cue, as it were, but invite the petitioners to become aware of God's presence. This prayer from a guide for Disciples of Christ worship leaders is an example: "O Lord, we come into your presence today giving thanks for all the good gifts you have bestowed upon us— to each of us is given both gifts and calling, and we look now to you to lead us as we offer our gifts to one another in love and rise to the calling we have heard from you. In Christ, we pray."[22] To the extent that action is implied, it is for those who hear the prayer to respond by offering their gifts and rising to their calling.

Private prayers often involve assertions about the existence and presence of God as well. A woman in Texas—a Baptist with a master's degree in psychology—provides an example. She prays for half an hour every morning. "I just acknowledge God," she says, "and give him affirmation of who he is and his presence in me." This alone gives her a sense of "clarity" and "peace within." When she prays sometimes that other people will "come to know the Lord," it is from this reference point. She is expressing her desire that they would also have an awareness of God. She knows her prayers are answered because of the "inner peace" that comes from "knowing that I have had a conversation with God."

Examples also include prayers that imply a slightly more active role for God, but that mostly emphasize the reality of God. An interesting case in point is the refrain, "Lord, hear our prayer," which is spoken by the congregation during worship services in many churches. Taken literally, this phrase suggests that God is a person with ears who may not be paying attention and needs to be asked to take even this minimal action. However, it is probably just as accurate to say that the request affirms the existence of God. As one writer explains, "Intercessory prayer is not a technique for changing God's mind." It is rather "a way in which the events and circumstances are all drawn explicitly into the realm of God's love."[23]

Other formulations call for explicit action on the part of God, and yet the response requested is framed in generic language. Examples include prayers asking for God's help, assistance, guidance, wisdom, and strength. Although these petitions suggest a transaction in which a person talks to God, and God in turn does something that results in a gift passing from the divine realm into the human realm, the request is about something that cannot be measured. It differs from asking a neighbor to come help mow the lawn. That either happens or it does not happen. Whether God provides guidance depends much more on whether the person requesting it perceives it to have happened. In some formulations, the response is in fact associated more with the person than with God. For example, a list of suggested prayers on a church website includes this petition: "Make me aware of Your awesome presence." Another says, "God, help me to wait patiently."

A retired school teacher in Arkansas illustrates a common kind of prayer that asks God to do something, but is largely an affirmation of God's existence. She prays every evening and every morning, usually praying "in my head," as she says, and with a prayer list in mind. She prays "for our family," "for our men serving overseas," "for my friends and acquaintances," and "for our church and our pastors." What exactly does it mean to pray "for" these various people? To pray for them does not always have to be spelled out. It can be as simple as "Lord, I pray for. . . ." Or sometimes it is "Lord, be with. . . ." When she does pray in greater detail, she prays hoping that "God's plan is that they find what they need, because he knows what they need."

An officer in the armed forces who regularly attends an independent Bible church in Oklahoma prays in a similar way. His prayers reflect and emphasize his understanding of the general attributes of God. In his personal prayers each morning, he praises God for forgiveness, asks God for "guidance and blessing on my family," and asks to be "strengthened." As an elder at his church, he sometimes leads the congregation in a time of prayer during the worship service. Recently a member requested prayer for a family member who was undergoing tests for a medical problem. He remembers praying, "Lord, we ask for your blessing on the family, that the doctors and nurses treating her would be guided by your hand."

Ontological assertions are by no means limited to the prayers of well-educated people in advanced industrialized societies. Similar devices appear in prayers and rituals in preindustrial societies, but play a somewhat different role. In those contexts, the invisibility of a spirit or ancestor requires the petitioners to name, describe, and locate that being and to explain in detail how the ritual works and what is expected. These utterances precede asking the deity to perform in some way.[24] The ontological assertions that characterize contemporary prayer in the United States also assert the existence of an invisible deity, but focus more on the presence and general attributes of God than on descriptive details, location, or expectations.

My point in mentioning these ontological assertions in prayers is not to suggest that prayer would somehow be more authentic if it took a different form. These ontological assertions do affirm the existence of God, and those who pray in this way undoubtedly remind themselves of their belief in God. Periodic affirmations are especially important as ways to keep doubts at bay. It is also especially important that these assertions affirm the existence of God without making claims about divine activities that could easily be assailed by skeptics—or inspire doubt among prayer givers themselves.

Contingency referents are a device that makes divine action contingent on human action or circumstances, and thus provides an explanation for apparent failures of the divine. Contingency referents are a kind of warrant or explanation for why something happens or does not happen. We routinely use warrants to account for the behavior of people we know and for our own behavior. Warrants for trust are a good example. The question, why do you trust a particular person, elicits warrants such as he is always there when I need him or she is well trained and really knows her job. But the people we trust are never completely as trustworthy as these warrants imply. He sometimes misses appointments and she sometimes makes mistakes in her job. This is where secondary warrants come into play. Secondary warrants are explanations about the exceptions that seem to contradict our primary warrants. The person who missed an appointment, we might say, missed because I failed to give him the right instructions or because he stopped to help a needy person along the way.[25] The relationships people carry on with God involve similar warrants. Primary warrants assert that God is absolutely trustworthy. Secondary warrants offer explanations for seeming failures. Examples include saying that one had not prayed fervently enough or with enough faith, or that God had answered one's prayers but one did not realize it at the time. The hallmark of a contingency referent in prayer is "if." A person who prays, "God, if you are really there, please help me," explicitly registers both doubt and faith. The commonly included phrase, "if it be your will," provides an out if the hoped for divine answer does not appear.

An important feature of contingency referents is that they stop short of implying that God can somehow be manipulated by human action. This is why Pat Robertson's suggestion that he had caused God to redirect

Hurricane Gloria struck critics as a cultural faux pas. Culturally acceptable constructions are more likely to stress that a person's knowledge of
God is limited. The prayer Marie Pierre recalled placed the little girl in
God's hands. The congregation hoped that God would ease her suffering, but did not claim to know whether this was in God's plan and did
not claim later that their prayers had influenced God. Other formulations suggest that God knew that what a person was praying for actually would have been harmful, so did not answer the way the petitioner
expected, or that God had a higher purpose in mind. "I see things happening," a hospice volunteer began, and then paused. "I see God fulfilling, not necessarily the healing of people I pray for, but their comfort and
peace of mind."

Prayers of submission are a common way of emphasizing contingency. Instead of asking that God perform some action, the supplicant
asks that his or her own behavior and attitudes change. Sometimes such
prayers are expressed in song. An example is the Leonard Cohen lyrics,
"If it be your will/ That I speak no more/ And my voice be still/ As it
was before/ I will speak no more."[26] The lyrics are, of course, reminiscent of the phrase "thy will be done" in the Lord's prayer. However, the
interpretation is neither that God's wrath rain down on earth or that an
army of God be raised up to rid the world of evil, but that humans adapt.
The Archbishop of Canterbury, theologian Rowan Williams, for instance,
says that praying for God's will to be done on earth is a reminder mainly
of the beauty and glory of God's universe. "We human beings unfortunately have a kind of tone deafness about God's will," he says, "we have
to learn to sing in tune with all this."[27]

A variant of this device consists of hints about the impossibility of
humans knowing the mind or will of God. These include largely positive
expressions, such as "I believe" or "I am convinced," which nevertheless subjectivize the claim by making it an article of personal belief, and
less assured phrasings, such as "I wasn't certain" or "I prayed that God
would overcome my unbelief." The writer Anne Lamott provided an
interesting example in an essay explaining her decision in 1999 to write
a novel. She said the idea gradually caught up with her. "I'm almost
sure this is what I'm supposed to do—or I may just be having a massive

nervous breakdown—but not long ago I prayed for knowledge of God's will for me and the power to carry that out, and then next thing I knew, I had come to believe it was time to start a novel." Her choice of words is revealing. Although the implication is that God somehow told her to write the novel, the statement conveys a significant level of doubt. She was almost sure, not completely sure. She may have been suffering a nervous breakdown. She had "come to believe" she should start a novel. "Plus," she added, "I probably also needed the money."[28]

Contingency referents often include a particular kind of schema alignment that credits God with having the same ability to choose that humans do. One explanation for why a person eats a hamburger or takes a walk is that the person simply decided to do so, thus exercising his or her freedom to choose. We sometimes say that the action was willed. Similarly, divine action may be regarded as an expression of divine will. The explanation given for God taking or sparing a life or providing or withholding blessings is that God was freely choosing these actions. Free will becomes the attribute of God that overrides other attributes, such as consistency or mercy. In emphasizing this attribute rather than others, the language about God thus makes it possible to believe that God exists even when prayers seem not to be answered. The interpretation is that God answered, but chose to do so in some other way than the petitioner wished or anticipated.

Contingency referents are especially evident in the conditions petitioners say they themselves must fulfill in order for God to answer their prayers. They have to be patient, in the right frame of mind, quiet, obedient, sincere. If they lacked any of these qualifications, they might miss God's answer because it was subtle, requiring discernment of events and circumstances. Of course, some people say they hear God audibly telling them to turn left at the next intersection, shop at Walmart, buy a new toaster, or vote for a Republican. But audible voices from supernatural beings contradict taken-for-granted assumptions enough that a person can wonder if he or she might be having a nervous breakdown. When God's leading is silent, it becomes contingent on a person's own interpretation. If things do not work out as expected, the interpretation can be blamed instead of God.

Consider what a man in his late thirties who works as an electrical engineer and attends an African Methodist Episcopal church in New York City says about God answering his prayers. The most memorable time, he says, was when he was dating the woman who is now his wife and some difficulties were causing the couple to wonder if they were truly meant for each other. He might have said, "God whispered in my ear one night, 'Marry her!,' and I did." What he actually says is that he "went to God" about it and then worried less about what to do. "It was not until I was willing to let go of the situation that God was able to work." In other words, God's action was contingent on his own. He cites this as an example of a larger lesson he has learned about God and about prayer. Acknowledging that he is "emotional sometimes" and "pig-headed," he says it is usually when he is "broken" and at "wit's end" that he turns things over to God. At that point, "I see him at work."

What is going on here? This is a well-educated, middle-class man who interacts comfortably with people at the large corporation where he works and in his neighborhood. But he is also a person of faith who attends religious services regularly and prays several times every day. In the morning when he is at home, he kneels on a prayer rug in his study. Each evening he prays with his daughter before she goes to sleep. During the day, his prayers are less formal. It may be a silent prayer as he commutes on the train or while sitting at his desk. He says that first of all "I acknowledge who God is." After that he prays for "understanding and wisdom for the things that I do not have a good handle on." This was the pattern when he was praying about his relationship with his wife-to-be and is how he currently prays for himself and for other people. "I acknowledge that I do not know what to pray. I require God to just continue to take control of my life. I pray that I would do the things that please him, you know? I try not to ask for a lot of things. I just try to pray that I get understanding so that I can respond to the needs of others appropriately." He hopes that through his prayers he will be able to somehow more closely reflect God's glory. "Mostly it's about me changing," he says, "and me being better than I am."

This style of praying includes the devices we have considered thus far. Consistent with ideas about schema alignment, the man's prayers do not ask God to speak audibly or to make things happen magically. The principal action that happens is the man changing and better responding to the needs of others. God works the way a good friend might, by being there, even at a distance, and by providing reassurance. The man's acknowledgment of "who God is" in his prayers is an example of ontological assertion. In addition, the contingency referent that is apparently a pattern in his prayer life emphasizes that God is more likely to work if he himself relaxes and lets things work out. In acknowledging that he does not always know what to pray for, he also implies that God might not answer because his prayers have been misguided or inconsistent with God's will. He prays especially for understanding. There is no evidence that he doubts God's existence or fears that his prayers will go unanswered. But neither are there danger zones where these doubts might easily be aroused. In sum, his prayers will be answered *if* an array of particular conditions are met, including figuring out the right things to pray for, letting go of one's desire for control, doing things that please God, and being willing to change.

The idea of being willing to change is similar to another contingency referent that is perhaps expressed most clearly in the saying, "God helps those who help themselves." A Muslim doctor says she believes firmly in the Prophet's teaching that you should ask God for what you need, even if it is a shoelace or some salt. "God is going to provide it," she says. But she adds, "It's not that he's going to give it to me in my hand. I have to struggle to get it." Other people explain that God will help them realize their dreams in life, but only if they work hard, or that God will help them avoid serious illness, but only if they eat right and have regular medical check-ups.

For people who expect truly dramatic results from prayer, contingency referents are especially helpful as explanations for why things do not always turn out as expected. An example is the prayer life of a school teacher who attends a nondenominational Pentecostal church in New Jersey. Over the years, she says, she has learned "you have to be specific when you pray." She means not just praying for guidance and protection, but for a mate, a job, and even a new pair of shoes. Presumably this kind of specificity would get her into cognitive difficulties. What if she asks God for shoes and shoes do not appear? The answer is that shoes might not appear because her prayers include several implicit contingency clauses. The outcome depends on what she means by specific. Just the other day she was in a traffic jam, and she prayed, but she asked God specifically to "relieve this situation without anyone being physically or mentally harmed." Nothing much happened, but that was because God wanted nobody to be harmed. She remembers vividly as a young woman praying for a husband. She got one, but he was not a good husband and they divorced. That taught her to be more specific: Pray for a good husband. She has also learned to pray specifically only for what she needs. She recently prayed for a new pair of heels, only to realize she had forgotten about a pair she already had. She clearly has been disappointed in the responses to some of her prayers, but she does not doubt God as a result; instead, she is trying to fine-tune her prayers in order to be more specific about what she really wants and needs.

For people with less specific expectations about prayer, contingency referents also play an important role. For example, a Catholic who holds a managerial position for a large firm in Maryland says he does not pray for material possessions, but for his loved ones to have "lives that are filled with satisfaction for them." He says he wants them to achieve a kind of "peacefulness and happiness in their existence." That seems vague, compared with asking for new shoes, but it could be a prayer that goes unanswered. What if the loved ones do not experience peace? Is that a reason to question God? No, the man explains. "I'm allowing God to decide what that peace looks like." He adds, "I wish for them to have what God wants them to have."

One could argue that people like this are caught up in rationalizations that prevent them from thinking very seriously about their faith. But that is precisely not what the evidence suggests. What these people doubt, indeed disbelieve, is the existence of a God that can easily be understood. They may liken God to a friend who listens and tries to help, but they believe more deeply that the best response to the question of whether God answers prayer is simply yes. The only thing more they can say is that the answers cannot be predicted, controlled, or understood. In these ways, God is sufficiently other that the usual rules of human interaction do not apply.

The widely held view that God is a spirit provides one of the most powerful contingency referents, namely that a person cannot truly know how God is speaking unless that person himself or herself has developed a high level of spiritual maturity. A Muslim computer scientist who prays regularly puts the idea well when he says that he believes it possible to relate to God personally, but adds, "I am not there yet." He explains, "When you disconnect yourself from worldly things and focus on your own spirit, then the part of you that is not body will connect with God." This view is similar to that of Christians who say they have not properly heard God's answer because they were too busy or who feel they need to spend more time reading the Bible for their prayers to be answered. If their prayers have not been answered as they expected, the fault is not God's, but theirs.

Another device emphasizes transgressions of basic cultural categories, or at least strong contrasts between them, and is thus expressed by the rubric *domain juxtaposition*. Prayer implies that the human realm can somehow communicate with a divine realm. The two realms are necessarily juxtaposed. However, a juxtaposition of this kind must be defined, and doing so involves the construction of a symbolic boundary that both distinguishes the two and brings them together. How this happens has long been a question of interest to social scientists. Drawing on anthropological studies of aboriginal religion in Australia, Émile Durkheim argued that rituals played a key role in distinguishing and juxtaposing the sacred and the profane as cultural categories. Ritual set the sacred apart from everyday life, Durkheim believed, giving it special power.[29] Others, including anthropologists Victor Turner and Mary Douglas, observed that rituals are especially important when the line separating two important cultural categories is unclear. For example, dawn and dusk are times when it is neither day nor night, and for this reason rituals occur during these periods to mark and clarify the transition. Similarly, the passage from youth to adulthood, which occurs gradually, is punctuated with rituals that establish collectively when a youth can be considered an adult.[30]

Prayer is an important part of the rituals that define the relationship between sacred and profane, and prayer often occurs during other

moments of transition, such as at dusk or during ceremonies of confir-
mation and marriage. The words of familiar liturgical prayers clearly
juxtapose the divine realm and the human realm. In the Lord's prayer,
for example, the phrase "thy will be done" is followed by the phrase "on
earth as it is in heaven." The implication is that these two realms should
somehow be in harmony with one another. On the surface, the difference
between the two realms is self-evident. One is infinite, the other finite; one
is a realm of perfection, the other of imperfection, and so on. However,
in reality the difference is often less clear, especially when uncertainty
about the divine is present, and indeed may be considered more as a
continuum, or as a blending of realms, than as two sharply delineated
categories. God being present in all things, imminent, unknown, and
incarnate, and humans having a spiritualized nature and an eternal soul,
suggest the possibilities for overlap. The prayer juxtaposes opposites,
as it were, and thus sharpens the contrast between the two realms. The
language implicitly defines and clarifies assumptions about who God is
by focusing on particular characteristics of the human petitioner.

A member of a nondenominational church in Pennsylvania comments
on the Lord's prayer in a way that illustrates this juxtaposition. He learned
the prayer as a child and now finds that he has to think more about the
words to keep the prayer meaningful. Instead of just praying it, he reads
it and thinks about each phrase. The part about a heavenly father, he
says, reminds him that "we're praying to someone beyond human capa-
bilities, someone who is held in a different position." Clearly, he has in
mind that there are two distinct realms. "Hallowed be thy name" draws
a further contrast. On one side is something "holy and respected." On
the other side would be "a name that's thrown around and has no meaning." He sees other contrasts, too, such as "your will" versus "my will,"
and "being faithful" versus "being tempted."

Although structuralist interpretations of language categories are no
longer as popular as they once were, an important insight that pertains to
domain juxtaposition is the idea of dual mapping, or "double structure,"
as Claude Lévi-Strauss termed it.[31] Dual mapping consists of two pairs
of binary oppositions that are either explicit in language or implied. A
simple example would be the pair of terms *weak* and *strong* mapped onto

human and *God*. The principle of balance in such structures indicates that some of the terms can be implied. Thus, a weak human praying to God implies that God is strong. Durkheim believed a person who communicated with a deity became stronger, but the point here is that the deity also becomes stronger. The deity's strength is shown in contrast with the weakness of the petitioner. Or as the pastor of an evangelical church put it: "God, we're here, we suck, you don't."

Domain juxtaposition is relevant not only to how we organize categories in our minds, but also to how we remember things. Researchers interested in memory have advanced two theories about why some things are more memorable than others. One theory asserts that people remember better those objects and events for which they have some preexisting mental framework. This theory predicts that regular occurrences are easier to recall than irregular ones. For example, informants in one study remembered the names of regular attendees at meetings better than the names of infrequent attendees. They also reported that regular attendees were present at meetings even though they had not been.[32] In everyday life, memory devices often employ this logic, for instance, by associating an oddly spelled name one has not heard before with some familiar object, such as a table or chair. The other theory argues that people remember unusual objects and events precisely because they are unusual. According to this theory, recalling an odd name would likely be made easier by associating it with, say, a pig wearing a red sweater. In an interesting application of this theory to religion, the anthropologists Pascal Boyer and Charles Ramble conducted experiments in France, Gabon, and Nepal asking subjects to recall objects described in narratives about a tour of a fictitious museum. Some of the descriptions conformed easily to ordinary assumptions about daily life (for instance, "pieces of furniture that you can move by pushing them"), while others did not ("pieces of furniture that float in the air if you drop them"). Not surprisingly, subjects were more likely to remember the latter. Boyer and Ramble inferred that religious narratives might be especially memorable because they, too, included such unusual descriptions (for example, a person who is both God and man, a virgin who gives birth, a bush that burns but is not consumed, and so on).[33]

Boyer and Ramble's research might suggest that prayer is especially memorable if it somehow juxtaposes really bizarre ideas, such as talking donkeys and flying pigs. Stories about prayer making it rain or causing people to rise from the dead would also qualify. Juxtaposition of the human and the divine happens in ways that reflect pervasive cultural assumptions. If the human realm is governed by natural laws, then one way of contrasting the divine and human would be to say that the divine contravenes these laws. The idea that humans can be in only one place at a time, while God can be everywhere at once is an example. Similarly, humans can only talk to a few people and think about a few things at a time, whereas the assumption implied when people pray is that God can listen to people all over the world and think about their requests simultaneously. But there may be limits to this kind of juxtaposition. Apparently, as the idea of schema alignment suggests, we find it difficult to imagine that the difference between us and God is that we can only push things around that are close to us, whereas God can do so at a great distance. Another potential difficulty is doubt about our human capacity to understand God. For instance, it may be possible to assert that God can listen to prayers all over the world at once, but much harder to believe it. If so, some other form of juxtaposition may be required.

A way of bringing the human and divine together that may work particularly well in contemporary contexts is to be quite specific about the needs and limits of the human realm and thus leave the characteristics of the divine realm to be implied by the contrast. This device makes it possible to assert the existence of that other realm, but avoids having to say very much about it explicitly. It thus serves to express uncertainty about the supernatural while indicating faith that it exists. The prayer Marie Pierre remembers is a good example. The fact that she twice refers to the person being prayed for as a little girl and twice mentions that the girl was only seven years old poignantly captures the smallness and frailty of the human realm. The girl's suffering and lack of understanding further dramatize what it means to be human. In contrast, the prayer hardly needs to say anything about God, because God is all that the human realm is not. The language points to a God who is large, strong, and knowledgeable but does not say any of this explicitly.

Whether sick or well, children serve usefully as juxtapositions of human weakness against presumptions of divine strength. A man in Pennsylvania recalls a woman in his congregation having the children stand up and then praying for "God's protection and that he'll turn away the bad influences in their lives and make them successful." Another person remembers "there was a young girl murdered" in his city and "in the middle of the worship time praying, the worship leader praying for comfort for that family. She was a ninth grader." Another man says one of the most memorable prayers at his congregation was "this little girl praying." Others describe prayers for sick children and for youth being sent on mission trips. In nearly every case, the person emphasizes something about the size, age, or vulnerability of the children.

Apart from children and the sick, a particularly interesting juxtaposition occurs when people talk about praying for wisdom. It makes sense that people who are well educated and who value education would pray for wisdom. However, wisdom seems to have a special meaning when it comes up as a topic for prayer. It means making informed and thus good decisions, for instance, in choosing a career or performing surgery. It does not refer to decisions the correctness of which can be easily verified at the time, such as picking the right lottery ticket. Wisdom is rather more clearly associated with God, as something that exceeds human knowledge, and thus may be imparted in small, unmeasurable doses. If one thinks of it as an issue of two domains, wisdom is located in the divine realm, and a lack of wisdom is in the human realm. One side has it; the other side needs it. Thinking about it in this way sharpens the contrast. The distinction is further sharpened by the fact that divine wisdom largely remains out of human reach. A woman who attends a nondenominational church in Arkansas puts it well. She prays for wisdom a lot: for herself in raising her children, for her children as they grow, for the doctors treating one of her friends, and for the nation's military and political leaders. The reason she prays this way, she says, is that "God has a plan and I don't know what it is."

In these examples, domain juxtaposition mostly works by implying a contrast between the human and the divine without having to say very specifically what the divine is like. That is a reasonable way to proceed.

Claiming to know exactly what God is or does flies in the face of conventional wisdom.

Code switching involves using words that in context would imply supernatural action, but then changing the terminology to make the meaning of those words metaphorical or ambiguous. The two examples of code switching in Marie Pierre's account are when she says that the congregation asked God to heal the girl and then the girl felt better when the chemo ended, and when she says they prayed to make the pastor invisible, meaning to protect him from gang violence. In both instances, the language changed to render what might have been a straightforward assertion about supernatural intervention into a statement that could be interpreted differently. Anne Lamott's reference to possibly having a nervous breakdown in the context of saying God was leading her to write a novel is another example. The speaker alternates between religious language that refers to divine action and medical or therapeutic language suggesting a more ordinary interpretation of what happened. Another example was given by a man in California—a physicist—who said his prayers do not "fall on deaf ears." He, of course, did not mean that God literally has ears, but as he searched for ways to describe the divine ("who knows how God decides what to do"), this phrase from everyday life sprang to mind.

Code switching is possible when people have been exposed to two distinct languages. Immigrants who have grown up speaking one language and later learned a new one are a common example. People engage in code switching for several reasons. One is simply that the languages to which they are exposed are themselves mixed. It is thus easier to mingle words than to sort them into separate categories. A Chinese speaker telling a friend about a recent meal at the Beijing McDonald's, for example, might say "Big Mac" rather than use a Chinese word for hamburger. A second reason is to maintain an identity that may be threatened or in danger of extinction. Arguably the use of ethnic words helps an ethnic community maintain its identity. A study of naming practices in Los Angeles, for example, showed that highly assimilated Hispanic parents selected English names that were readily translatable into Spanish, such as John (Juan) or Michael (Miguel).[34] A third reason is to express and perhaps even to emphasize ambiguity. An ethnic person may feel herself conflicted about who she is and switch codes to show that she is neither of one group nor of the other but a person who is in between.[35]

Code switching in prayer occurs for all these reasons. There is often a distinctly religious way of talking about God and about prayer that differs from nonreligious speech, and yet the two realms overlap. A person can talk about God and medicine or about God's will and having a nervous breakdown in the same context without having to think at all about possible contradictions. Switching from one code to the other signals different identities and different speech communities, such as the language used in one's congregation and the language one has learned to speak in college classes and to an interviewer conducting research. Mingling two languages also emphasizes ambiguity. It signals doubt as well as faith, and it shows that one is a believer and at the same time a person whose worldview is not strange. Code switching makes it possible to talk to and about God while implicitly acknowledging that God works in multiple and mysterious ways.

One of the more common forms of code switching is between religious language and psychological or therapeutic language (as in Lamott's reference to a nervous breakdown). Prayers commonly ask God for comfort, protection, and inner peace. The words are ambiguous, referring to something spiritual on the one hand, and to ordinary psychological states on the other hand. The language moves back and forth, emphasizing one side of the coin and then the other. An example is an account given by a woman in her twenties who lives in Utah and is a regular participant at one of the Mormon churches in her community. She believes that God has an overarching and often inscrutable plan for the world, so she considers it unproductive to expend time thinking about why specific things happen (they are simply part of the divine plan). But she still tries to discern God's leading in specific situations. She says "the spirit prompts" her sometimes after she prays. That is a religious way of putting it. She adds, "I know the spirit gives me an answer." However, she immediately switches to a psychological or even physiological language and says, "my hands get sweaty and my stomach gets all nervous." That is how she knows the spirit is prompting her. And apparently it is up to her then to decide how to interpret this response. One time she felt this way during a church service and decided the spirit was prompting her to stand up and say something. Another time she felt exactly the same way while talking with her boss about a possible promotion and decided the spirit was telling her not to accept the promotion.

A rather different illustration of code switching is from a Catholic woman in Illinois who works as a registered nurse. When asked if she prays, she says yes, she prays every day. But she adds, "I pray not just prayers." She explains, "It's a way of thinking, an awareness, being meaningful, being present in certain situations, being open to encounters." In this way, prayer is an integral part of her nursing care. "It is just being open and present to them, and just kind of being in tune with them. It is a connection between another individual and your awareness of the spirit between you and the sharing of that."

Code switching in talk about prayer is facilitated, just as code switching between ethnic languages is, by the existence of well-bounded speech communities. A member of a religious community learns a special way of talking about prayer but also learns that this way of talking is more common within the religious community than in other settings. In those other settings, a different language prevails. Consider the response given by a Muslim woman who holds a bachelor's degree in economics and co-manages a successful business when asked if she feels a personal connection with God while praying. "As a scientific, educated mind, I don't think it is true that I relate to God, quote, unquote, on a very personal basis. But I believe it is the spirituality inside you that says, 'This is the God that has created me. He's going to take care of me.'" What is she saying? There are two parts to her—two aspects of her persona that reflect different speech communities. Speaking as an educated mind, she cannot say that she personally relates to God. But switching into her inner spiritual self, she can say that there is indeed a connection.

As these examples illustrate, code switching does not mean that a person is being duplicitous. Nor does it imply an equivalence between two vastly different ways of thinking, such as saying that the Holy Spirit and sweaty hands are the same thing. Rather, it is an act of translation, a way of talking, but also a way of making sense of something that cannot easily be understood. Perhaps a divine spirit mysteriously causes sweaty hands or produces a personal connection with one's creator. Perhaps the divine spirit is what a nurse feels when she is in tune with a patient's needs, or perhaps sweaty hands prompt a person to think and that is how the holy spirit works. The one may be a metaphor for the other, and if so, the difference is significant. Love and a red rose can be compared, and in the comparison there is also a striking contrast, an awareness that love really is not a red rose.

Performative competence is slightly different from the other devices in that it suggests that the appropriate way to assess a prayer is by talking about how it was performed. An example would be saying that a heart-felt prayer is good or especially meaningful because the speaker was sincere. Another example would be saying that a liturgical recitation of the Lord's prayer is good because the exact words of Jesus are being spoken. These ways of talking about prayer suggest that what a person thinks about God may be less important than what the person feels inside while praying or the manner in which the ritual of praying is performed. A competent prayer is one that conforms to these expectations.

The idea of performative competence derives from speech act theory, which suggests that certain utterances can be considered behavior that actually accomplishes something just by being uttered.[36] Promises are the most commonly discussed example. When a couple promises to love and commit their lives to each other during a wedding ceremony, the speech act of promising accomplishes the ceremonial union that takes place. Promises may not be the best example, though, because a promise works only if there is general social agreement that promising means something. Promises during weddings work because the wedding itself is a special occasion for making vows (making the promises uttered quite different from ones the couple may have made in private). Their meaningfulness also depends on whether they can be assumed to reflect the sincere intentions of the persons involved and, to some extent, on expectations about marriages lasting. A better example might be a simple greeting, such as hello. It signals awareness of the other person and shows conformity to certain norms of etiquette, but implies little or nothing about a person's inner state, sincerity, or longer-term commitments.[37] Other examples would include such statements as "I apologize" and "I approve."

Prayer, as speech act, has some aspects of promises and greetings. Like a promise, sincerity typically matters. People are supposed to mean what they say if the prayer is to be meaningful. But unlike a promise, an expectation about long-term commitments or about reciprocity from the other party need not be implied. Prayer is like a greeting in that it shows that a person acknowledges the existence of God and is done in a way that others would recognize as a proper way of praying.

In another series of experiments, Justin L. Barrett showed that sincerity of heart matters under some conditions and does not matter under other conditions. Barrett gave college students stories about fictitious religious rituals and asked them to say whether they thought the rituals would be effective or not. In some of the stories the ritual was being performed for an all-knowing God (which Barrett termed a "smart God"). In the other stories, the God was fallible or limited (a "dumb God"). Because the smart God could see inside people and know their thoughts, the students recognized that intentions would matter. They said the ritual would be more effective if those performing it were sincerely trying to accomplish something. In the other cases, intentions mattered less, but actions mattered more. Students judged rituals more likely to succeed when the participants performed the rituals exactly right.[38]

Barrett's research does not apply directly to real-life prayers but is suggestive. It points to the possibility that people can easily find ways to explain why their prayers may not have been answered. The problem, they can say, was not with God, but because their intentions were insincere or their action was incorrect. For example, Pat Robertson could have explained Hurricane Gloria hitting Virginia Beach, if it had, by saying his heart had not been right, and Jerry Falwell could have said his prayers for college funds went unanswered because he took the wrong road around Liberty Mountain. However, both arguments would suggest a kind of magical manipulation of God that many people would probably consider objectionable. The more likely implication of Barrett's research is simply that people who pray may focus more on how the prayer is performed than on whether or not it is ultimately successful in manipulating God. If they view God as all-knowing, they will worry about what God sees inside them. As a man in Georgia remarked, "I don't think God is impressed with our words; he's impressed with our hearts." If they are less sure that God is looking into their hearts, they may still feel it important to follow a set of rules in performing the prayer.

As these examples suggest, performative competence involves the interpretation of prayer and not just how prayer is actually performed. Sincerity is communicated through words and the display of emotion. A person who sobs, "I really need your blessing, God," is more likely to be regarded as sincere by anyone who hears the prayer than someone who blandly recites, "Lord, hear our prayer." But sincerity is an expression of the relationship between the speaker's inner subjective state and whatever is spoken, and is for this reason unstable and difficult to verify.[39] The speaker, for instance, can say later, "I thought I was sincere, but I was just caught up in the fervor of the moment." If so, the lack of sincerity provides a reason why the prayer may not have been answered. More likely, though, a speaker would assert, "I truly was sincere, so I know God heard me." The speaker would feel no obligation to add that God had or had not responded in some miraculous way. Merely uttering a sincere prayer was enough.

In this sense, prayer is an end in itself. Its purpose is less to extract goods and services from God than to engage in an act that the participants themselves find meaningful or believe is meaningful to God. They assume that there is a God, but what exactly the characteristics of God are matters less than what they do when they pray and how they do it. People can be uncertain that God exists and not feel compelled to resolve those doubts or to speculate about God in ways that go beyond what they feel they know. The act of praying is in itself sufficient. It expresses a faith that goes beyond doubt. It moves them because the person praying is sincere, because emotion is displayed, because the prayer links them to a tradition, or because it demonstrates unity within their congregation or community.

However, what counts as a *competent* performance varies from person to person and in different speech communities. This variation is evident in what people say about the Lord's prayer. Christians respect it because of its historic importance in Christianity and because it is a familiar part of their church services. It is meaningful because of its familiarity. Saying it without thinking about it, though, is problematic, and for this reason people say they work to make it meaningful. For example, a Presbyterian in Connecticut says she recites it almost every day, but she also tries to "personalize" it. She does this by saying a line from the standard prayer and then adding her own words. Interestingly, the words she adds amplify the domain juxtapositions already present in the prayer. After saying "our Father who art in heaven," she adds, "you are mighty, wonderful, and all-knowing." And after saying "on earth as it is in heaven," she elaborates, "make earth as wonderful as heaven." Adding these words sharpens the distinction between how she views herself and how she thinks about God.

What people especially like about the Lord's prayer is the sense of unity it gives them as they recite it. Saying it aloud and in unison at their churches is a ritual of togetherness within the congregation, and the fact that people in other congregations are saying the same words broadens this feeling and elevates it into a kind of spiritual presence. As a Baptist woman in Indiana observes, "It links you all the way back to Jesus and, you know, churches have been doing it ever since, so that's pretty cool." Or as an Episcopalian in Tennessee put it, "We need things that reconnect us to deep places within ourselves, and when you have a prayer that you repeat over and over again, that prayer can connect you to it."

These devices—schema alignment, ontological assertion, contingency referents, domain juxtaposition, code switching, and performative competence—illustrate some of the ways in which thoughtful, educated people in contemporary society pray, and in many cases pray frequently, without getting mired too deeply in intractable questions about the nature of God. They pray using language that avoids superstition. Their prayers occur as affirmations of faith even though the petitioners are unsure what exactly God is and might be hard pressed to say how exactly their prayers are heard or answered. Their interpretations of prayer and their stories about memorable prayers at their congregations and in their personal lives leave uncertainty about God and at the same time affirm God's existence. The words sometimes imply that God is just another person, and yet the language also provides ways of saying directly or indirectly that God clearly is different.

Language devices like these are ways of thinking as well as of speaking. Together, they define and constitute a spiritual realm—a schema set apart from the known, natural world. This is a realm in which God exists and in which God's distinctive characteristics are located. It is alien enough from ordinary life that anthropomorphisms are sometimes invoked to normalize it. But it is also aligned with assumptions about physical and mechanistic aspects of the world by being distinguished from them. Ontological assertions help to define it as an "other" characterized by power, perfection, majesty, holiness, and timelessness. The spiritual realm cannot be fully understood by humans and thus cannot be expected to respond on cue to the prayerful supplications of humans. It is a realm that nevertheless is interlaced with ordinary life and can be communicated with more effectively by cultivating personal spiritual qualities. Being different from ordinary life, this spiritual realm is also defined through juxtaposition with human qualities and through implied contrasts and metaphoric constructions. It can be praised and prayed to in many ways, but sincerity is especially to be valued. The spiritual realm is defined in these ways through language, which in turn is reinforced within religious speech communities.

Nearly all of this is missed by critics of religion who treat the God problem as if it were a puzzle to be understood entirely in terms of the imagined interventions of a powerful supernatural agent into the natural world. In reality, supernatural beings have seldom been conceived of in any culture as entities that can be understood apart from a more complex spiritual realm. Without this larger understanding of a spiritual realm, supernatural agents turn out to be no different from the magical machines described in psychological experiments or the lucky horseshoe to which prayer is likened. As people of faith understand and talk about the spiritual realm, it is populated in some instances with ancestral spirits and saints, or more commonly by characteristics that contrast with the human world, such as strength, comfort, mercy, and love. The line between the natural and supernatural is far less clear than in abstract philosophical treatments. People enter into a spiritual realm when they pray and experience a sense of the sacred that they do not understand and do not expect to respond according to their bidding.

The remarks people make about prayer suggest self-awareness about its ambiguities and complexities. They do not deconstruct the language they use as I have done here, but they recognize that prayer is a difficult topic for thoughtful people. The devices evident in the way they talk to and about God reflect both the implicit messages they have learned from being around others who speak similarly and their own thoughts about what it can possibly mean to communicate with God. The nurse I quoted earlier put it well in remarking that she grew up thinking the idea was to pray really, really hard and God would grant you your wish, but she says, "I don't believe that any more. That's a magical way of thinking." What happens if you pray hard for someone not to die, and they do die? Then "people get mad" at God. "That's not the way it works. At least the way I believe it." Her view is that God is a creative life force and when people pray, they send out positive spiritual energy that is part of this force and unites with it.

A man who attends a Presbyterian church in California expresses a similar idea. "I feel that active communicating with God is of value in itself. Whether you get the bag of gold you ask for isn't the issue." A member of an independent Bible church in Arkansas has a more traditional view of God as a source of comfort and guidance, and yet he prays mostly for "spiritual well-being" and, laughing, says you can always depend on God to say yes, no, or wait. In his view, people need to remember their responsibility to do their part. "If there is an issue between you and someone else," he says, "you need to work that out."

Of course, prayers that ask God to intervene directly and miraculously are not uncommon. "Repair my hernia and the lining of my stomach and esophagus," a man asked Jesus through an online prayer chain. A woman asked that a friend "not get any more blood clots" and meet a "nice compatible companion man." Another woman prayed that God would save her marriage and another, that a friend's custody battle would be resolved. Yet it is important to note that even these prayers are sometimes expressed in language that provides for uncertain outcomes. "I am anxious about my husband's high blood pressure," a woman prayed, adding, "Pray for *that situation*." In response to the woman who prayed about a friend's custody battle, a fellow prayer chain member responded, "Lift [name withheld] so he has peace and comfort in his heart." Another person prayed simply to be reminded that "human suffering is a fact of life."

For many people, prayer is habitual. They pray to greet the morning, to start the day on a positive note, to bring their loved ones' needs to God, to calm their frazzled nerves, or to conclude their day. Prayer is often formulaic, especially at their places of worship, reinforcing familiar beliefs about the existence of God. Yet it is also a topic that requires thoughtful interpretation. Prayer tells people there is something that their rational minds can only partially grasp. Prayer itself is one of those things. It offers assurance, but seldom confers certainty. As a man in Georgia observed, "You pray for safety for your kids and down deep you know they may be safe—and they might not."

NOTES

1. Susan Harding, *The Book of Jerry Falwell: Fundamentalist Language and Politics* (Princeton, NJ: Princeton University Press, 2000), 105–124; quotations are on page 121.

2. Gerald Strober and Ruth Tomczak, *Jerry Falwell: Aflame for God* (Nashville, TN: Thomas Nelson, 1979), 81–82; the Liberty Mountain episode is not mentioned in Dinesh D'Souza, *Falwell: Before the Millennium* (Chicago: Regnery Gateway, 1984).

3. Harding, *The Book of Jerry Falwell*, 124.

4. "Pat Robertson Says Storm Put Him on Path to '88 Bid: Prayer Diverted Hurricane, Robertson Asserted on TV," *Los Angeles Times* (September 17, 1986), 2.

5. Quoted in Jack Nelson, "Robertson Finds Success Means Increased Scrutiny," *Los Angeles Times* (February 14, 1988), 1.

6. Quoted in James M. Wall, "Preacher Pat Must Overcome the 'Wacko Factor,'" *Chicago Tribune* (July 28, 1986), 15.

7. "Rooney on Robertson: TV Preacher Is 'Wacko,'" *Church & State* (April 2004), 15.

8.   People and the Press Poll (October 30, 1995), Values Update Survey (November 17, 1997), General Social Survey (June 19, 1998), PSRA/ Newsweek Poll (April 14, 2000), Time/SRBI Poll (October 4, 2006); available at roperweb.ropercenter.uconn.edu.

9.   "Lubbock, Texas, Plans to Pray for Rain," *United Press International* (July 24, 2006); "Pray for Rain, Urges Howard" (April 22, 2007), online at www.theage.com.au; P. J. Kitchen, "Prayer Has Power to Create Change in Community," *Battle Creek Enquirer* (May 6, 2007), 9A; Paul Harris, "Exposed: Conman's Role in Prayer-Power IVF 'Miracle,'" *Guardian Unlimited* (May 30, 2004), online at observer.guardian.co.uk.

10.   Kenneth Silverman, *The Life and Times of Cotton Mather* (New York: Columbia University Press, 1985), 83–87; Richard Lyman Bushman, *Joseph Smith: Rough Stone Rolling* (New York: Knopf, 2005). The McKinley quote is frequently repeated in conjunction with stories about other U.S. presidents praying, for instance, in Evan Thomas and Andrew Romano, "In God They Trust," *Newsweek* (May 7, 2007), online at www.msnbc.msn.com; the original quote is in General James Rusling, "Interview with President William McKinley," *The Christian Advocate* 22 (January 1903), 17, reprinted in Daniel Schirmer and Stephen Rosskamm Shalom, editors, *The Philippines Reader* (Boston: South End Press, 1987), 22–23; Paul Kengor, *God and Ronald Reagan* (New York: Regan Books, 2004), 12–13.

11.   Online at www.presidentialprayerteam.org.

12.   From information described on www.presidentialprayerteam .org; background on the organization can be found in K. Connie Kang, "Movement Harnesses the Power of Mass Prayer," *Los Angeles Times* (October 4, 2003), B2.

13.   Philip Zaleski and Carol Zaleski, *Prayer: A History* (New York: Houghton Mifflin, 2005), 5.

14.   Zaleski and Zaleski, *Prayer*, 3.

15   An earlier version of some of the material in the following sections originally appeared in my article, "Teach Us to Pray: The Cognitive Power of Domain Violations," *Poetics* 36 (2008), 493–506.

16.   Mandler's definition and appropriation of Kant are discussed in Roy D'Andrade, *The Development of Cognitive Anthropology* (New York: Cambridge University Press, 1995), 122–149. This source also surveys the research literature. Paul DiMaggio, "Culture and Cognition," *Annual Review of Sociology* 23 (1997), 263–287, summarizes some of the broader applications of schema theory to the sociological study of culture.

17.   Justin L. Barrett, "How Ordinary Cognition Informs Petitionary Prayer," *Journal of Cognition and Culture* 1 (2001): 259–269. An overview of

Barrett's larger research conclusions is available in his book, *Why Would Anyone Believe in God?* (Lanham, MD: AltaMira Press, 2004).

18. Justin L. Barrett and Frank C. Keil, "Conceptualizing a Nonnatural Entity: Anthropomorphism in God Concepts," *Cognitive Psychology* 31 (1996), 219–247.

19. Courtesy of Joyce MacKichan Walker, January 22, 2006.

20. On the functions of entextualization, see Richard Bauman and Charles L. Briggs, "Poetics and Performance as Critical Perspectives on Language and Social Life," *Annual Review of Anthropology* 19 (1990), 59–88. Their discussion focuses on the aspects of discourse that permit it to be extracted from its context. My use of the term here is slightly different. Entextualization that suggests an association between a string of discourse and a sacred text serves to detach that string from the intuitive norms about natural causality that pertain in the everyday speech community.

21. Paul Tillich, *The Courage to Be* (New Haven, CT: Yale University Press, 2000), 156.

22. Beth Burton Williams, Smithfield, North Carolina, online at www.weekofcompassion.org.

23. Patrick Eastman, "Lord, Hear Our Prayer" (May 2005), online at www.cliftondiocese.com.

24. Examples are given in Keane, "Religious Language."

25. For a discussion of primary and secondary warrants for trust, see Robert Wuthnow, "Trust as an Aspect of Social Structure," in Jeffrey Alexander, Gary T. Marx, and Christine L. Williams, editors, *Self, Social Structure, and Beliefs: Explorations in Sociology* (Berkeley and Los Angeles: University of California Press, 2004), 145–167.

26. Leonard Cohen, "If It Be Your Will," online at www.azlyrics.com.

27. Rowan Williams, "Reflections on the Lord's Prayer," online at www.bbc.co.uk.

28. Anne Lamott, "Mothers Who Think" (July 22, 1999), online at www.salon.com.

29. Émile Durkheim, *Elementary Forms of the Religious Life* (Glencoe, IL: Free Press, 1915).

30. Mary Douglas, *Purity and Danger: An Analysis of Concepts of Pollution and Taboo* (London: Penguin, 1966); Victor Turner, *The Ritual Process: Structure and Anti-Structure* (New York: Aldine, 1969).

31. Claude Lévi-Strauss, *Structural Anthropology* (New York: Basic Books, 1963), 210.

32. Linton C. Freeman, A. Kimball Romney, and Sue C. Freeman, "Cognitive Structure and Informant Accuracy," *American Anthropologist* 89 (1987),

311–325; some other examples are included in Linton C. Freeman, "Filling in the Blanks: A Theory of Cognitive Categories and the Structure of Social Affiliation," *Social Psychology Quarterly* 55 (1992), 118–127.

33. Pascal Boyer and Charles Ramble, "Cognitive Templates for Religious Concepts: Cross-Cultural Evidence for Recall of Counter-Intuitive Representations," *Cognitive Science* 25 (2001), 535–564.

34. Christina A. Sue and Edward E. Telles, "Assimilation and Gender in Naming," *American Journal of Sociology* 112 (2007), 1383–1415.

35. Several collections that are especially good on code switching in other contexts are the essays in Lesley Milroy and Pieter Muysken, editors, *One Speaker, Two Languages* (New York: Cambridge University Press, 1996) and in Peter Auer, editor, *Code-Switching in Conversation* (New York: Routledge and Kegan Paul, 1998); see also Penelope Gardner-Chloros, *Code-Switching* (Oxford: Blackwell, 2007).

36. J. L. Austin, *How to Do Things with Words*, 2nd ed. (Cambridge, MA: Harvard University Press, 1975).

37. Erving Goffman, *Interaction Ritual: Essays on Face-to-Face Behavior* (New York: Pantheon, 1982).

38. Justin L. Barrett, "Smart Gods, Dumb Gods, and the Role of Social Cognition in Structuring Ritual Intuitions," *Journal of Cognition and Culture* 2 (2002), 183–193.

39. This understanding of sincerity follows Habermas' discussion of truthfulness; see Jürgen Habermas, *The Theory of Communicative Action*, Vol. 2: *Lifeworld and System: A Critique of Functionalist Reason* (Boston: Beacon Press, 1981), especially 72–76; see also Robert Wuthnow, James Davison Hunter, Albert Bergesen, and Edith Kurzweil, *Cultural Analysis: The Work of Peter L. Berger, Mary Douglas, Michel Foucault, and Jürgen Habermas* (London: Routledge and Kegan Paul, 1984), 204–211.

THREE Big Scary Catastrophes

The great Lisbon earthquake of 1755, which destroyed more than three-quarters of the city and killed a third of its population, prompted Voltaire to question how church leaders could possibly make sense of an event that had devastated one of Europe's most religious cities and flattened most of its churches. Even more, it led him to reject the view that God had created the best of all possible worlds for humans to inhabit, declaring, "Oh wretched man, earth-fated to be cursed, Abyss of Plagues, and miseries the worst!"[1] In England, Charles Wesley described the earthquake as the seventh vial of divine wrath predicted in the Book of Revelation.[2] John Wesley argued that the event should in no way be interpreted as only the result of natural causes, for "what is nature itself," he wrote, "but the art of God, or God's method of acting in the material world?"[3] Catastrophes spoke of the sinfulness of humankind and of listeners' need to seek salvation, the Wesleys preached.[4] In Germany, the disaster played an important role in

Immanuel Kant's efforts to develop a scientific theory about earthquakes arising from shifting gas-filled caverns. In the newspaper stories and small pamphlets that spread quickly throughout Europe, writers speculated that the catastrophe was not only divine punishment but also the beginning of the end—of the world or for religious faith.[5]

It is perhaps unsurprising that thoughts about God sprang so readily to mind in 1755 and that accounts focused both on the many who had been punished and on the few who had been spared through the Virgin Mary's miraculous intervention. Catholic Europe remained subject to the Inquisition and all of Europe was semiliterate, with few sources of information and interpretation as readily available as the local clergy. Fears of divine wrath continued as prophetic voices warned of the return of Halley's comet—expected in 1757 or 1758—and became more believable as the Seven Years' War (1756–1763) spread across Europe, resulting in at least a million deaths before it was over. Yet the relevance of these eighteenth-century responses for our time is that they remind us of how common it has been to associate God with disasters and of the need to ask what associations are currently made.

How do thoughtful people in the twenty-first century think about God in relation to large-scale disasters and potentially devastating dangers, such as earthquakes, tsunamis, global hunger, disease, environmental destruction, and terrorist attacks? The world in recent years has experienced no lack of major catastrophes. The Indian Ocean tsunami of December 2004 claimed 230,000 lives. Hurricane Katrina displaced more than a million people from their homes in 2005. Climatologists predict that global warming will increase the severity of hurricanes and floods. Public health officials warn that a flu pandemic may be overdue. Is God still relevant as people ponder these possibilities? Or have these become issues addressed through science, technology, and public policy? If God is somehow relevant, how do people who view God as a mystery and who are somewhat uncertain about how God works or what God is conceive of a connection with major events that are perhaps metaphorically termed acts of God?

Social scientists have long been interested in the connection between religious views and catastrophic events. Anthropological research on tribal societies with little previous exposure to the industrialized world suggested that religious rituals were ways of guarding against drought, floods, and epidemics. The ancient stories handed down from generation to generation told of great upheavals when ancestors had died in large numbers, or been forced to flee, or been spared. It was almost as if religion may have been invented to make sense of these cataclysmic times. In contexts closer to home, social scientists in Europe and the United States saw evidence in historical accounts that people had prayed to escape the Black Death and other outbreaks of disease or had believed that God was punishing them for their sins. It seemed to many of these social scientists that their own times were different. People no longer believed that catastrophes should be interpreted as divine retribution. Acts of God were relabeled as acts of nature. Science was now the proper method for understanding and guarding against these acts. A process of secularization had taken place.

Once again, though, the fact that millions of well-educated people who knew all about science continued to believe in God posed a problem. Was it that these people were on the slippery slope of secularization and had just failed thus far to slip all the way? Were they somehow influenced by affiliating with a religious subculture that rendered ideas about the divine plausible but left it up to each individual to figure out how he or she was to interpret the big scary dangers of contemporary life? Perhaps these otherwise thoughtful people were silent schizophrenics who publicly espoused technological solutions but privately harbored notions about spirits and demons. It was hard to say. But one thing was sure: These were important questions for social scientists to ask. Whatever one's theory about the long sweep of modern history might be, it was imperative to consider how religion connected with people's thoughts about the larger issues that potentially shaped the course of human life and that did in fact spell the difference between life and death for many on the planet today. If religion had some continuing connection, that was worth knowing, perhaps for practical reasons, but especially for what it revealed about the place of religion in society. If religion had no connection, that was equally worth knowing. And somewhere between the extremes of simply being or not being connected was the possibility that the nature of the connection might be worthy of investigation as a lens into the particular complexities of contemporary culture.

The argument I want to consider in this chapter is that thoughtful people who believe in God find ways to think about large-scale catastrophic events that keep God in the picture, so to speak, giving God and their relation to God a continuing position of relevance in world events, and yet that sidesteps the three most common perspectives that social scientists have identified in textbook treatments of religion: God as magician, God as explanation, and God as comforter. There are variations in the specific ways in which this contemporary thinking occurs. Even among college-educated people living in the United States, it is possible to identify a range of views that reflect different exposure to different confessional traditions and greater or lesser degrees of certainty about who or what God is. The differences are interesting because they sometimes play off one another and because they illustrate the considerable latitude that our society offers for coming up with inventive, idiosyncratic religious beliefs. But there are also commonalities in the languages used, in the substance and form of this language, and especially in the adeptness with which it avoids making claims that presuppose much knowledge about God or that implicate God too strongly in natural events.

It will be helpful before considering how people actually talk about God's relation to catastrophic events to review how social scientists have depicted this connection. My claim is not that the social scientists have been wrong. Quite the contrary. The best bet is that the social scientific arguments have generally been squarely on target. They have been formulated from anthropological investigations and historical accounts and in many cases with remarkable knowledge of theology and philosophy. It certainly makes no sense to argue, as a few bold scholars have done in recent years, that the cumulative weight of social scientific inquiry over the past two hundred years can now be dismissed on the basis of polling results. The point rather is that the prevailing social scientific theories have given us some purchase on how religion has addressed big scary issues in the past and in so doing has also identified key tension points between religion and modern culture. It is not unreasonable, therefore, to imagine that thoughtful people living amidst this culture have noticed some of these tensions and have adjusted how they think and talk about God to take account of them.

Social scientists generally assume that people believe in God because they get something out of it. One of the things people may get, or hope to get, is physical help. In ordinary life, physical help may take the form of finding a parking space or getting over a cold. In catastrophic situations, it can be escaping from a flu pandemic or a flood. Apart from physical protection, belief in God provides answers to the questions that arise when terrible things happen, such as why did an earthquake destroy an entire city or why did an innocent child die in a terrorist attack. The answers help people make sense of suffering and injustice. Closely related to these intellectual benefits, belief in God may also serve an emotional role by providing comfort to victims' families and helping others deal with anxiety and fear. These are not the only reasons people believe in God—for instance, belief is also perpetuated by the desire to worship and by the social support people receive from participating in religious organizations—but the physical, intellectual, and emotional functions of belief are among the most important ways in which people bring God into the picture when they think about or experience major disasters.

Looking to God for physical help is most akin to what social scientists have described as magic. For example, a shaman who tells villagers their crops will yield more if they sacrifice a share of the proceeds to God would be considered a practitioner of magic. In early work on the topic, social scientists drew a sharp distinction between magic and religion. Magic was something practiced by individuals or for the benefit of individuals and focused on immediate concrete needs, whereas religion was a collective practice that benefited the group and dealt with achieving broad societal goals (such as "the good life"). Magic was sometimes thought to be a precursor of religion and to include faith in non-personified powers, such as potions and amulets, whereas religion developed later and was organized around belief in one or more supernatural persons.[6] Later work, though, saw magic and religion more as a continuum than as separate categories, and recent scholarship emphasizes the considerable extent to which the two overlap. Research in both premodern and modern societies suggests that magical practices exist within religion as well as apart from it. The similarity between a person who prays to God for a new car and one who throws salt over his shoulder in hopes of getting one is that in both cases some mysterious contravention of natural cause–effect relations is imagined. Instead of working to earn money to buy a car, a person expects God or salt-throwing to make one magically appear.[7]

Social scientists have examined the extent to which expectations about physical benefits that violate natural cause–effect relations continue to be evident in modern contexts. These studies demonstrate that such expectations exist in tension with the dominant culture and suggest some of the ways in which this tension is resolved or minimized. One tension is between rationality and irrationality. For example, a study of Gulf coast fishermen found they commonly believed that bringing women on board a boat was bad luck. The fishermen said they could not explain why this was the case, unlike their belief that the presence of seagulls was a sign of fish, for which they could give a rational explanation. They sometimes distanced themselves from what they understood to be a magical belief by saying they did not really believe it or take it that seriously, even though they practiced it, or that they had heard that other fishermen believed it. Some said the practice did not result in better fishing, but that it reduced their worries that something might go wrong. They felt the same way about such taboos as never whistling on a boat, never bringing a black suitcase on board, and never saying the word alligator on board. They denied being superstitious, but said there was no reason to push their luck. They expressed similar views about the positive value of having a priest bless their boat.[8] The author of the study concluded that the fishermen had to find ways to justify their beliefs because they knew that outsiders and even other fishermen were skeptical about such beliefs. A similar conclusion emerged from a study of Pentecostal church members in Australia who believed in miraculous healing. Through a detailed examination of their stories, the author showed that the storytellers went to some lengths to demonstrate that a miracle actually had taken place. For example, they emphasized that the doctors had made a definitive diagnosis of an illness and pronounced the person incurable, that prayers had been uttered on several occasions and had perhaps not been performed properly or with enough faith at the start, that the prayers were effective, and that the person not only was healed but also gave credit to God.[9]

The view that people believe in God because of the intellectual functions it fulfills is somewhat more complicated than the idea that God mostly serves as a magical source of good fishing, miraculous cures, and other physical benefits. In this view, religious beliefs explain why things happen—especially bad things—and thus are a way to make sense of suffering. Sometimes this explanatory role excuses people from taking responsibility for their own behavior. An example of this use of religion occurred in 2007 when a Romanian prisoner, Mircea Pavel, serving a twenty-year sentence for murder, filed a lawsuit against God, claiming that God allowed him to fall into the clutches of the devil. Needless to say, the court threw out the suit.[10] This was an extreme case, but scholars of religion have long argued that explanations for things that go wrong are one of its important roles.

In Max Weber's *The Protestant Ethic and the Spirit of Capitalism* and in his subsequent work in the comparative study of religion, religious explanations of suffering are of particular interest. Modern religions, Weber argued, exemplify a rational orientation to the world, an outlook that seeks to make sense of the universe and indeed to impose a kind of mental order on adherents' approach to life. The idea that God created the world is an example. However, within a religious framework in which everything is supposed to make sense, those events that have no obvious purpose must be explained. Why the good die young, why children suffer from illnesses, and why earthquakes wipe out entire cities are among the events that demand explanation. Religions include theodicies—explanations of evil—that seek to resolve the question of how a good and merciful God, or indeed how any rational outlook on life, can be reconciled with the reality of suffering and death.[11]

Central to Weber's interest in theodicy was the argument that different explanations for evil serve as motivations for different strategies of action. A study of responses among Christian groups in the United States to the Y2K crisis—the prediction that on January 1, 2000, computers

around the world would malfunction because of inadequate programming to take account of the new date—nicely illustrated this connection
between explanation and action. One response was to view the impend-
ing crisis as a human-caused event with no particular theological significance; to the extent that people wound up without food or electricity, the
church's role was to be a Good Samaritan and try to assist them. A second response interpreted the event through the biblical story of Joseph,
viewing it as part of a divine plan and thus needing to be prepared
to take advantage of the opportunity to engage in evangelism. A few
churches opted for a more extreme interpretation, viewing it in apoca-
lyptic terms as the end of the world or as part of a broader collapse of
civilization. These churches likened themselves to Noah and developed
survivalist plans to protect themselves against the coming catastrophe.
In each case, the theological framework through which the crisis was
interpreted not only helped make sense of it but also told people how to
respond. Notably, the frameworks were specific biblical narratives rather
than general outlooks or worldviews.[12]

In a rather different vein, sociologist Steven Lukes examined the
public debate generated by Hurricane Katrina, asking how it compared
with the discussions of theodicy following the Lisbon earthquake. The
difference, he argued, demonstrated a marked shift in cultural orientations. The response to Lisbon was largely theological and philosophical.
Besides its impact on Voltaire and Kant, it allegedly marked a turning
point in Goethe's thinking, led to the downfall of the Inquisition, encouraged Rousseau's emphasis on natural causes, and inspired apocalyp-
tic thinking in Germany and Italy. In contrast, the response to Katrina
was sociological and political. It focused on questions about emergency
planning, the respective roles of federal and state government agencies,
the potential fallout for particular officials in subsequent elections, and
questions about race and social class. The only evidence Lukes could
find of religion being part of the debate was from a group calling itself
Columbia Christians for Life claiming that similarities between a satellite
image of the hurricane and an ultrasound image of a six-week-old fetus
was sure evidence that God was punishing New Orleans for its abortion
centers. In Lukes' view, the difference was evidence that social scientists'

theories about modernization resulting in religion's declining relevance were true.[13]

Lukes' interpretation is reminiscent of Weber's argument that modernity was displacing theological understandings of evil and of the prominent extension of Weber's ideas by sociologist Peter L. Berger in the 1960s to the contemporary context. The Christian explanation for suffering, evil, and inequality, Berger observed, "has been collapsing along with the overall plausibility of the Christian theodicy—a point, incidentally, that has been seen much more clearly by the antagonists of Christianity than by the Christians themselves."[14] Although Berger's views subsequently shifted in recognition of religion's continuing influence, the idea that old-fashioned explanations of evil either have been or should become irrelevant has remained. In an interesting discussion of the topic, anthropologist Pascal Boyer, for example, observes that "people struck by misfortune strive for an explanation" and that religious stories would seem to provide answers—answers, he says, that are "probably false."[15] And whereas Boyer concedes that people may have a biological need to attribute evil to the gods, philosopher Richard J. Bernstein asserts categorically, "Today, most of us do not think of such terrible natural events as earthquakes, tsunamis, tornadoes, and hurricanes as manifestations of evil."[16] But if that is the case, it raises the interesting question of how the large majority of the American public who believe in God interpret events such as Hurricane Katrina and the Indian Ocean tsunami. Do they think God is indeed irrelevant? Has their thinking shifted from theological to sociological or naturalistic explanations? Or is it necessary to look more closely at how thoughtful people talk about God?

The other argument that has received considerable attention from social scientists is that religious beliefs and practices fulfill an emotional role, especially by providing comfort. This idea has been popularized in recent years by critics of religion. Daniel C. Dennett, for instance, suggests that one of the "favorite purposes or *raisons d'être* for religion" is "to *comfort* us in our suffering and allay our fear of death."[17] Evolutionary biologist Robin Dunbar argues that almost all religions promise their adherents that a supernatural being will assist them through their difficulties. "This," he writes, "undoubtedly introduces a profound sense of comfort in times of adversity."[18] Pascal Boyer, while voicing reservations about theories emphasizing religion's role in coping with anxieties about death, concedes that "the most natural and the most common explanation of religion is [that] religious concepts are *comforting*."[19] Richard Dawkins writes at length about the possibility that "belief in God's existence [is] completely essential to human psychological and emotional well-being." Dawkins does not think it is, but acknowledges that the "strong arms of God" may be consoling, even if they are purely imaginary, and that "people caught up in a terrible disaster, such as an earthquake" may feel comforted by their religious beliefs, even if these beliefs are untrue.[20]

Researchers find that people of faith do in fact look to religion for comfort. An early study based on survey data from a national sample of Episcopalians, for instance, concluded that religious involvement did more to comfort parishioners than it did to propel them toward helping others and supporting programs for social justice. People who lacked family ties and material goods seemed especially to gravitate to the church for the comfort it provided.[21] This finding initiated a line of research that suggested in various ways that people turn to religion when they are deprived of economic success or plagued with anxiety, or that they are especially motivated to participate in religions that offer solace in the face of illness and death. Whether or not these are reasons people themselves would acknowledge was addressed in an interesting national study in which U.S. adults were asked simply whether they agreed or disagreed that "What religion offers me most is comfort in times of trouble and sorrow." Sixty-five percent agreed, while only 15 percent disagreed.[22] In another study, 52 percent of the U.S. public said they "find comfort in my religion or spirituality" every day, and only 10 percent said they never did or almost never did.[23] Other researchers pondered the possibility that belief in God was becoming a kind of therapy, offering more than the traditional words of comfort one might hear at sickbeds and funerals, and claiming to give peace of mind, happiness, personal fulfillment, and heightened self-esteem. One study examined the titles and content of popular religious books and found overwhelming evidence of these themes.[24] Yet there is also evidence that people in the most extreme situations may not be as comforted by their faith as these studies suggest. For example, sociologist Kai T. Erikson concluded from lengthy interviews with people in West Virginia who survived the Buffalo Creek flood that swept through their community in 1972, killing 118 people and leaving more than 4,000 homeless, that "people who sense the hand of God," as many of the residents did, "have many hard questions to ponder, and none of them are very comforting."[25]

The research social scientists have conducted on beliefs about God's physical intervention to prevent disasters, God's place in explanations of catastrophes, and God as a source of comfort amidst these events suggests that believers are likely to make these kinds of connections, but the research also leaves unanswered some of the more interesting questions it has raised. In the literature on magic and religion, it has often been observed that religious leaders express opposition to magic, but the unanswered question is whether that resistance is only against magic that occurs outside the religious domain or whether religious leaders are queasy about magical practices within their own contexts. Certainly there are examples of religious leaders who argue that God can magically intervene to divert hurricanes and cure individuals from cancer. But does God come through so rarely on these requests that religious people feel a need to think about God in other ways? The studies that focus on how people talk about magic and miracles are suggestive, but point to the need for a more extensive examination of such discourse. Similar questions remain unanswered about the beliefs thoughtful people may hold concerning suffering and evil and about God as a source of comfort. The need to explain suffering, if Weber was right, arises not only from the anguish itself but also from the conviction that the universe should make sense. But is that an outlook that people actually hold or is it an imposition of a view more common to theologians and philosophers? Is it possible that God is popularly understood in different ways, perhaps obviating the need to relate suffering to questions about God at all? In similar fashion, the research on religion as a source of comfort suggests only that believers perceive it that way, but does not illuminate much about the content of these beliefs. If they regard God as a source of comfort, do they then feel comforted and, if so, to what extent? Does it bother them if they are not in fact comforted? Are there perhaps reasons why they might not even want to feel comforted?

To see how well-educated, thoughtful people piece together an outlook on large-scale catastrophic events that preserves a space in their thinking for God, I want to consider the words of two speakers. The first is Dr. Rowan Williams, the Archbishop of Canterbury. Williams is particularly interesting because he is one of the world's best-trained theologians and plays an important public role as interpreter of major events through his office as Primate of the Church of England. The second speaker is an ordinary church member living in the American Midwest. She was interviewed as part of the research project from which I have drawn in the previous chapter. Her remarks are especially revealing because she talks at some length about her faith and does so in ways that are seldom captured by journalists or in surveys. These examples will serve as a kind of benchmark against which to consider the language of other speakers.

On January 2, 2005, a few days after the tsunami in the Indian Ocean, Archbishop Williams published an essay in the *Sunday Telegraph* reflecting on his reactions to the devastation. Essays of this kind are part of the archbishop's official public role, along with regular radio broadcasts on the BBC, television and newspaper interviews, speeches to Parliament, and sermons on such state occasions as the queen's birthday and meetings of the Anglican Communion. The archbishop is in these respects the official voice of Christianity in the United Kingdom, and he fulfills a ceremonial role quite different from that of clergy in the United States who speak on behalf of particular faith traditions and special interest groups. At the same time, the relatively low levels of religious participation in the United Kingdom mean that the archbishop speaks, and understands himself to be speaking, to a secular society. The delicate balance involved in representing Christianity to a diverse and skeptical audience is often evident in the archbishop's sermons and speeches. This was especially the case as he reflected on the tsunami.

Personalizing the tragedy, Williams drew attention to photographs of particular individuals suffering the loss of loved ones and homes. "We learned in Canterbury of the death in the Asian disaster of a 14-year old from the King's School, with her mother and grandmother. And because of that, people here experienced what had happened in a different way."

He remembered himself at about the same age, watching the television coverage of another disaster, and the words spoken by another cleric on that occasion: "I have nothing to say that will make sense of this horror today. All I know is that the words in my Bible about God's promise to be alongside us have never lost their meaning for me." No intellectual explanation, however polished, Williams said, could ever make sense to those most deeply affected. Nevertheless, the question had to be asked, "How can you believe in a God who permits suffering on this scale?"

In the brief paragraphs that followed, Williams answered the question this way: First, the world has "a regular order and pattern of its own," including "causes" that "we can chart." Second, God is not a "puppet-master in regard either to human actions or to the processes of the world" and thus cannot be expected to "step in if things are getting dangerous." That traditional view, he said, is "odd" and "dangerous." Third, religious believers may pray for help and healing, but "if they are honest, they don't see prayer as a plea for magical solutions that will make the world totally safe for them and for others." Fourth, "belief has survived," not because of such explanations about divine intervention, but because believers "have learned to be open to a calling or invitation from outside their own resources, a calling to accept God's mercy for themselves and make it real for others." This is a reality, he explained, that believers often relate to in silence and as a habit of the heart. Fifth, faith in God elevates the "immeasurable value, the preciousness, of each life" and in this way makes suffering all the more harrowing. And finally, faith should encourage "passionate engagement with the lives that are left," meaning efforts to assist and change "the situation in whatever— perhaps very small—ways that are open to us."[26]

The points Williams emphasizes are especially interesting because they are clearly positioned between two alternative perspectives: a more traditional or dogmatic interpretation that wants to envision supernatural intervention of some kind, and a skeptical view that cannot see God being relevant at all. Between these extremes, Williams asserts that the natural order functions according to its own causes and effects, and that God does not magically intervene to prevent danger or speak audibly to salve distress, but that God does exist, represents a reality and a resource beyond ourselves, and encourages a view of the preciousness of life that demands human efforts to be of service. These are ways of thinking about God that a thoughtful person who believes in God as a matter of deep conviction and yet regards direct divine intervention as a violation of reason might accept.

The essay is also of interest because of the response it evoked. Representatives of both of the perspectives that the archbishop tried to position himself against responded in ways that further illustrated the differences. The *Sunday Telegraph*, perhaps thinking it had found a story that would appeal to secular readers, carried a separate news story the same day with the headline, "Archbishop of Canterbury: This Has Made Me Question God's Existence." The story further asserted that the archbishop had written that "the Asian tsunami disaster should make all Christians question the existence of God" and that "stock Christian answers to human suffering do not go very far in helping us."[27] In reality, the archbishop's essay said none of these things and Lambeth Palace immediately issued a statement declaring the headline "a misrepresentation of the Archbishop's views" and asserting that "the Archbishop nowhere says that the tsunami causes him to question or doubt the existence of God; rather that the Christian faith does not invite simplistic answers to the problem of human suffering."[28] That response then prompted reactions from other writers who argued that faith *should* provide simplistic answers or at least that the archbishop's views were too difficult to understand. "The archbishop's article in The Sunday Telegraph was an absolute disgrace," a columnist for the paper wrote the next day. "It is no use his being good and thoughtful, if he is unable to communicate his thoughts clearly to the tens of millions of souls in the Anglican Communion who look to him for guidance."[29] In the United States, a writer for the conservative *Baptist Press* summarized the contretemps by calling it "an example of how not to give a Christian answer" and declaring that "the Bible leaves no room for equivocation."[30]

Sympathetic readings, though, suggested that there were points in the archbishop's essay that rang true. A reader in London wrote the *Sunday Telegraph* expressing displeasure with its handling of the matter, commenting in his letter that it makes sense to "examine what faith we have and how best it should be applied" and to question a comforting faith that claims to have "all the answers." Another writer described the archbishop's essay as a "carefully nuanced" and "positive affirmation of faith and hope."[31] In another venue, a blogger offered this observation: Many journalists "recognize [Williams'] obvious intelligence, but they cannot understand how such an intelligent man could possibly be an orthodox Christian believer, so they assume that he must be a covert unbeliever." As a result, they "attempt to construe his public utterances in such a way as to draw out the loss of faith which (they assume) must be lurking somewhere underneath."[32]

This example illustrates the considerations that arise when statements about God and disasters are part of a *public* debate, a point to which I will return toward the end of this chapter. A contrasting example shows that some of the same considerations arise when people speak *privately* about their personal views. The speaker is a woman I will call Mildred Jones. She is a high school teacher in her mid-fifties who lives with her husband (recently retired from teaching) in central Michigan. They live in a quiet suburb not far from the Catholic church they attend nearly every week. Mrs. Jones has a graduate degree in education and is an avid reader who gives knowledgeable answers when asked to talk about such issues of the day as war, poverty, and health care. She has thought a lot about what it means to be a person of faith. Her belief about God is perhaps best expressed when she says, "God is so much bigger than anything we can fathom." She says this, not in response to a direct question about God, but in talking about the Bible and what it may reveal about God's actions in the world. She prefaces her comment by remarking that she is "not a great biblical scholar" and that "Catholics as a rule" have become more scripturally based only since Vatican II. As she continues, it is clear that she has firm convictions about God, but her statement about the Bible in effect creates distance between herself and people she imagines would cite chapter and verse to defend what they think about God. In describing one of her particular beliefs about God, for instance, she says, "I guess my basis for it would not be Scripture." Belief, for her, is personal and somewhat subjective—perhaps evident in how often she uses phrases such as "I guess," "I believe, "I think," and "I don't think"—and yet it is grounded in her "knowledge of existence," as she puts it, and is for this reason a stable aspect of her outlook on life rather than an ephemeral or idiosyncratic opinion.

Another important clue to how she thinks and talks about God is her response when asked how, if at all, her religious faith helps in thinking about big issues in the world, such as hunger, war, and poverty. "I think for me," she begins, "I believe that Jesus is an ideal and though the situations, the causes, and the issues are not replicated in Scripture, basically, I see how he dealt with people, how he dealt with people who were thought to be outside the privileged circle, how he dealt with hypocrisy, how he dealt with his relationship with his God, God the Father, and how he focused on that and got the strength to deal with other issues." She says her faith "influences me a great deal." It is notable that she chooses to talk about Jesus, rather than God the Father, and that Jesus has a relationship with *his* God and dealt with different issues particular to his time and yet serves as an ideal, a role model. She does not say so directly, but implies that the influence of faith in her own thinking is to be concerned about people who are not privileged, to watch out for hypocrisy, and to have a relationship with God that gives strength.

If this interpretation is correct, faith in God gives her fortitude and guidance about general ways of thinking, but does not tell her how to think about particular issues. She says as much: "If I pick one side of an issue, I can find persons who are quote 'faith-filled' Roman Catholics who will pick another side of the issue." What she says next is especially interesting. Although she might have gone ahead to criticize those who take the other side of an issue and who believe they know the mind of God, she says instead, "I guess this is one thing I've become more attuned to and in a sense it gives me some empathy with terrorists." She adds, "Every single one of us believes our interpretation of what God has called us to do is right. That's something God is leaving to us to work out with one another and that, I think, is one of the biggest challenges." This is a remarkably complex, reflexive statement. It acknowledges that beliefs about God are *interpretations* and at the same time says that people think these interpretations are *right*—apparently placing herself in that category ("every single one of us"). And the point is neither to give up one's convictions nor to discredit the other side, but to have empathy and struggle with figuring out how to get along. Her language allows her to express the fact that she is a person who has convictions about God and yet holds these convictions with openness that allows room for interpretation, empathy, and negotiation.

How then does an outlook like this fare against presumably popular notions about God's relationship to big scary disasters? Consider the idea that God is a magician to whom entreaties can be made to prevent disasters. That view would be too simplistic for Mrs. Jones. So how would she talk about God to keep God in the picture and yet avoid turning God into a magician? Part of the answer is implied in her assertion about "something God is leaving to us to work out." Whatever preventive or ameliorative action occurs has to be done by humans. She amplifies this idea in talking about the possibility of pandemic flu—something she says she and her husband have discussed quite often. The most hopeful solution, she says, will be discovering a vaccine. "That will come out of the human brain, cooperation, collaboration." An atheist would likely agree, the only difference being that Mrs. Jones thinks the human brain is part of God's plan. And she prays. But she does not pray for God to intervene miraculously in human affairs. For instance, she is quite concerned about world hunger and actively supports relief and microeconomic development programs through her church and other organizations, so in discussing these concerns, she volunteers that she prays about them. She explains, "My prayer is pretty wordless. I don't compose a paragraph and edit it and pass that on. It's more a question of calling to mind people in that circumstance so that on a day when I get to go out to eat, or on the occasions when I'm actually having to throw something away, I'm calling to mind the people who haven't had a fresh tomato ever, or any kind of fruit, or for whom nutrition is not the issue but satisfying the pangs of hunger." Prayer for her is a matter of *mindfulness*. "I just call to mind the people whom I know cannot even hope to be quote 'full' when it comes to food." Talking to God is not a matter of asking God to step in and prevent people from dying. It is rather a way of reminding herself that she needs to do something to help. When she thinks about God, she thinks about God's concern for the hungry, about humanity's common relation to God and its need to take care of one another. "Regardless of where you find yourself," she says, "regardless of what country you're born into, what color of skin, what economic situation, and regardless of what religious tradition, who your God is, if a God at all, we're all part of the same fabric of God's creation and it is all one, and we are supposed to help one another."

What about the idea that belief in God provides a way of explaining why bad things happen? Being a teacher, Mrs. Jones might be expected to think of God as a teacher who lets things happen to teach people a lesson. Or she might say that her knowledge of God convinces her that the universe makes sense and that good things and bad things happen for a reason. She does in effect have beliefs that serve as a way of making sense of these things. But it is important to look closely at how she talks about these beliefs. When asked if she feels that God has a reason for things like wars and disease, she answers, "As in a lesson? I don't think God deliberately looses the forces of disease. God wouldn't deliberately set forth a pandemic to quote 'teach us a lesson.' I believe it all comes out of an original authorship of the capacity for evil or bad things loosened early on and things will just evolve. And, you know, sometimes in these things we're also given our greatest challenges and successes." Pressed to say more, especially about whether wars and disease are a result of sin, she elaborates: "I believe it's the result of sin in the sense of the first human beings choosing the lesser side of their nature and not the God side of their nature. To me, that just sort of opened up that side of us. So every human being has to deal with the God side of their nature and the lesser side, and some of these things are the result of people pursuing their lesser side."

Read one way, her statement is quite biblical, implying the role of Adam and Eve in bringing evil into the world, and is an expression of the classic dualist or Manichean view about continuing struggle between forces of good and forces of evil. But the fact that she does not actually mention Adam and Eve or the forces of good and evil should not be overlooked. The first human beings remain unspecified and good, and she talks about a God side and a lesser side of our nature and of a capacity for evil or bad things. God does not behave with an intention of teaching or punishing, but as an author who establishes freedom of choice as an essential feature of human nature. Choice is paramount, and yet God remains present on an ongoing basis because it is the God side of their nature that humans choose or reject. *Some* of the wars, illnesses, and other bad things that happen result from humans choosing their lesser nature, but there is no direct correspondence between specific choices and specific consequences, meaning that innocents die in wars and from starvation through no fault of their own and as a result of evil that may have been in the world for a long time. What these assertions accomplish is to say that God is relevant to how one understands good and evil in the world, but not in specific ways that run counter to human freedom or to the complexity of human affairs.

The possibility that God comes into play for Mrs. Jones primarily as a source of comfort also requires a close reading. Her God is not a feel-good God or one who supernaturally channels calm into her heart when she is worried or depressed. She does talk about God in relation to her emotions, but the relationship is multifaceted and puts as much of the responsibility for how to experience her emotions and what to do about them on her as on God. For example, she prefaces her remarks about world hunger by saying that this has been an "emotional" issue for her lately, so praying to be mindful of the hungry is both a consequence of those emotions and a way of focusing them on concrete needs toward which she can be of some assistance through her charitable giving and volunteering. Prayer serves a rather different function when she thinks about war. At the time of her interview, she was quite distraught about the U.S. war in Iraq. She had written to her legislators and only received formulaic letters in return. "It's something I can only pray about," she says. "I'm at a loss as to how to affect change." Praying does not make her feel better about war, but is something she can do. There is a kind of stoicism in her views when she thinks about pain and suffering closer to home. Asked about the possibility of dying from a pandemic or terrorist attack, she does not say it is comforting to know that God will be with her. She says, "If it happens and I die, I die. If it happens and I survive, I want God to give me the grace to not look toward the past but to pick up the pieces and do what needs to be done so that life can go on." The key word is grace, not comfort. The grace she desires is to be able to keep going and to do what needs to be done. It reminds her of two things she learned as a teenager watching her father die of cancer. One was that she was unable to pray for a miraculous cure. Her father was in too much pain. She prayed he would die. The other was that her mother relied on a circle of women from the parish. They prayed together and then they played bridge. She thinks this is how God works. Comfort can come as much from playing bridge as from praying.

No two people are alike. Mrs. Jones' ways of relating God to the big scary aspects of life are uniquely hers, drawn from going to church as a child, attending a parochial school as a teenager, participating actively in her parish, and having conversations with her friends and family about personal struggles and public issues. Yet she is also a reflection of the culture in which she lives. I have discussed her statements about God in some detail because they offer a starting point for considering how thoughtful people in today's world manage to bring God into their thinking about world affairs and yet avoid having to believe in a God that would run afoul of almost everything else they know about life. Mrs. Jones expresses no explicit doubts about God's existence and she thinks of herself as a faithful, faith-filled Catholic. She clearly believes in God, thinks her beliefs are relevant for how she understands large-scale issues, and tries to put her beliefs into practice by going to church, doing volunteer work, and writing letters to her legislators. She has found a way of thinking and talking about God that fits into and influences her outlook on life. God is a creator or author of life whose ways cannot be fully comprehended, but whose principles and desires for humanity can be seen in the example of Jesus and in church teachings about the one-ness of humanity and the need to care for one another. God does not intervene miraculously in human affairs and there are no airtight expla-nations for why bad things happen. It nevertheless makes sense to pray as a way of being mindful of the needy and of getting in touch with the God side of one's nature.

The idea that God miraculously intervenes to spare people from natu-ral disasters and other catastrophes is quite common, both in religious teachings and in popular culture. People pray that their lives and their loved ones will be spared and praise God when their prayers are answered. But these prayers and the assumptions on which they are based are problematic. The same concerns that discourage thoughtful people from praying for a new car or that a life-threatening illness will magically disappear pertain to these instances of divine intervention in larger events. If hundreds or thousands of people are killed, does it really make sense to say that some people were spared because they prayed? A moment's thought shows that either the people who died did not pray (unlikely) or that God chose to kill them anyway. The arguments quickly get into logical quicksand that thoughtful people are likely to steer clear of. But how do they do this? Is it possible to believe that God does respond when people are in danger and yet talk about God in ways that avoid these other questions?

In the weeks following the 2004 Indian Ocean tsunami, stories of God's miraculous intervention flourished in the world's newspapers and news magazines. One was about Daylan Sanders, the director of an orphanage in Sri Lanka, who believed God saved his family and the children under his care. They were eating breakfast when they heard the tsunami coming "like a thousand freight trains." Sanders ordered everyone to jump into his boat. "Something miraculous had to happen if we were going to get out of this alive," he recalled. Just at that moment he remembered a Bible verse: "When the enemy comes in like a flood, the Spirit of the Lord shall raise up a standard against it." He commanded the wave, "In the name of Jesus, stop!" Suddenly the water became sluggish, like something was holding it back. "The only force or power that could have stopped it was the power of God," Sanders believed. Briefly, they were safe, but as they headed into the lagoon, a second wave bore down on them. Sanders ordered the fisherman manning the boat to turn and head directly into the wave. The 15-foot fiberglass boat with 32 people aboard almost went under, but Sanders prayed and again the Lord answered. "The hand of God lifted the boat and He placed us right on top of the wave!" Eventually they made it to safety. Everyone survived.[33]

Few of the stories were this dramatic, but many others emphasized miraculous escapes. At another location in Sri Lanka the pastor of

St. Peter's Church canceled the regular service at his beachfront church building and held an alternative service for his 1,500 parishioners at another location a mile inland. For various reasons the service started late and lasted longer than usual. When the tsunami hit, the parishioners were still at worship. Had they met at their usual location, most would have been killed as St. Peter's was reduced to rubble.[34] Along the Chennai coast in southern India, the historic Santhome Cathedral Basilica narrowly escaped destruction from the rising water. Father Lawrence Raj at the church said it was spared by the "miraculous post of St. Thomas." The post, which stands between the church and the sea, is thought to have come from a fallen tree that, according to legend, St. Thomas moved centuries earlier when Christianity first came to India.[35] In the Indonesian coastal town of Meulaboh, where 80 percent of the villagers died, 400 Christians survived because they were on a hill outside of town where Muslim authorities had directed them to celebrate Christmas.[36] Countless stories of miracles involving individuals— clinging to uprooted trees, beating the odds at sea, discovered days later under crushed buildings—also found their way onto CNN and network broadcasts and were posted on websites and repeated in religious magazines.

But do miracle stories play well in middle America? To my knowledge, the only nationally representative survey in the past decade or so that has asked enough questions about miracles to give a sense of what the public at large believes was a poll of approximately 800 people conducted for *Newsweek* by Princeton Survey Research Associates in April 2000. An overwhelming 87 percent of those polled said they "believe that God performs miracles." Nearly half (48 percent) said they had personally "experienced or witnessed" what they considered to be a miracle. And 71 percent thought "God or the saints" currently performs the kind of miracle that involves "saving people who face death in accidents or natural disasters." Not surprisingly, there was near-consensus among born-again or evangelical Christians that miracles exist. Belief in miracles and preaching about them is common in conservative churches. More than 90 percent of evangelicals agreed that miracles were real and seven in ten had personally experienced or witnessed one. Evangelicals who had graduated from college were just as likely as those who hadn't to believe. Among non-evangelicals, where there was more room to be influenced by other factors, education made more of a difference. For example, 40 percent of those without college degrees had experienced or witnessed a miracle, but only 27 percent of the college graduates had. In short, the study suggested that better-educated people find it harder than less well-educated people to believe in miracles. But there was one surprise: Non-evangelical college graduates were just as likely as non-evangelicals who hadn't graduated to think God miraculously saves people from accidents and natural disasters. Two-thirds (68 percent) felt this way.[37]

This evidence suggests that miracles still spark the imagination even among people whom we might think would be skeptical. In my interviews, several people said they had witnessed or experienced instances of divine intervention. For example, a school administrator whose Florida neighborhood had been hit by Hurricane Dennis in 2005 remembers watching "four of my big oaks a hundred feet from the house fall like dominoes within two minutes. Boom. Boom. Boom. Boom. All of them fell parallel to the house, not towards the house." He asks, "What kept those trees from hitting my house? I think divine intervention." After the storm, another huge tree ("a hundred feet tall") was leaning toward his house. "But God held that tree up for weeks until I could get a cherry picker and get up there and trim that tree." A pediatrician in Missouri who attends a theologically conservative nondenominational church gives a rather different example of divine intervention. Talking about George W. Bush's narrow victory in the 2000 presidential election, she says, "I just felt that God had put him there for a reason. Whether it was the war in Iraq or dealing with the whole war on terror, I think God placed him in this position." She sees a direct parallel with the biblical stories about God's dealings with the kings of Israel. Just as God orchestrated events in those times, God "orchestrated George Bush coming into power to be the leader of our country in a very difficult time. I just see God's hand in it."

These were exceptions, though, rather than the rule. Nobody else mentioned the word "miracle" (and, in fact, neither did these two) and nobody felt that it made much sense to talk about divine intervention as protection against natural disasters. They may well have felt that miracles were possible, but if they did, it was not how they chose to describe God's role. They spoke instead of God being a presence that people could be aware of even as they suffered devastation and died. This was the most common view among interviewees across the theological spectrum. Consider how a woman in her thirties who works for a recording studio in Tennessee and attends a conservative Baptist church thinks of God's role during Hurricane Katrina. She says God sometimes uses natural disasters to "clean house," and she figures she would have been "pretty scared" if she had been facing death there but would have hoped to remember that God was in charge. A Catholic woman in her sixties who lives in Indiana is sure God exists and says God keeps people "in the palm of his hand" during difficult times, but denies that God intervenes directly to cause or to prevent major catastrophes. A man who attends a Presbyterian church in Georgia expresses a similar view. As a career employee of a large disaster relief organization, he has thought a lot about God's role in these events. What comes to mind is the story of the Good Samaritan, who gave help to the person who was hurt, rather than looking only for "technical" explanations. Another man put it this way: "God has chosen not to directly intervene, but has given us the resources to do the job that needs to be done."

At first glance, it may be difficult to understand why interviewees who claim to believe in God and who attend religious services regularly so rarely mention the possibility of miracles when talking about God's role in natural disasters. This silence makes more sense when we consider how miracles are discussed in the popular media to which Americans are so thoroughly exposed. Miracles are mentioned quite often. For example, in the quarter century starting in 1981, the *New York Times* mentioned "miracle" more than 17,000 times. But it was not the case that these were mostly stories about divine intervention. In fact, only 4 percent (about 700) of the stories also mentioned God.[38] Of course, the *New York Times* is hardly where one would go to read about God. News magazines, such as *Time, Newsweek,* and *U.S. News & World Report,* are better for this purpose because their editors do feel more compelled than those at the *New York*

Times to carry stories about religious beliefs and practices at Christmas, Passover and Easter, and a few other occasions. With far fewer pages in their weekly issues than in daily newspapers, these magazines during the same 25-year period mentioned miracles more than 2,100 times. Yet only 21 percent of these stories mentioned God.

The dictionary gives two definitions of miracle: "an extraordinary event manifesting divine intervention in human affairs" and "an extremely outstanding or unusual event, thing, or accomplishment."[39] The second meaning is clearly the one that prevails in the news media. Miracles involve escapes from death, medical intervention, and scientific discoveries. They are rare enough that they appear to be statistical anomalies, and for this reason they are causes for wonder, inspiration, and hope. They demonstrate that unexpected favorable outcomes sometimes do happen, either from perseverance or by sheer luck. A thoughtful person can easily speak of modern miracles, medical miracles, and miraculous escapes without thinking about God at all.

Within religious contexts, though, the matter is rather more complicated because miracles do connote divine intervention. Believers can hardly escape hearing stories about God speaking to Moses in a burning bush or Jesus turning water into wine and raising Lazarus from the dead. In many contexts it is common for preachers to argue that these miraculous interventions can still happen to ordinary people. The story about Daylan Sanders and the tsunami miracle appeared on Pat Robertson's Christian Broadcasting Network, where viewers hear often about miraculous answers to prayer. Research among Christians in Latin America, Africa, and Asia frequently evokes stories about miracles.[40] But in other settings religious leaders themselves urge believers to be cautious about how they seek to interpret miraculous events. "We must speak where the Bible speaks, and be silent where the Scripture is silent," counsels Southern Baptist theologian Albert Mohler Jr.[41] Philip Hefner, a Lutheran theologian, writes that a good deal of what religious people say about miracles is repugnant and perhaps even blasphemous. He recalls hearing a TV evangelist praising God that a Christian motel clerk had seen a vision and stayed home the night an intruder gunned down three other clerks. Apparently God had been powerful enough to save all four but chose only one. It may be better, Hefner suggests, to talk about miracles as unexpected blessings that come in dark times, and not as God contravening the laws of nature.[42] The same call for caution emerged as religious leaders reflected on stories of tsunami miracles. "What makes it seem dubious," a commentator wrote about the Meulobah event, "are all the religious emendations," such as the Christians being spared because they humbled themselves and the Muslims being killed because they refused the Christians' request to celebrate Christmas in the city."[43] Several of our lay interviewees also mentioned clergy telling them how to think about disasters. For example, a Catholic woman remembers "one pastor we had who would always say that others can only know Christ through us." Christ is present to victims of violence or hurricanes, she says, through the people who "come to their aid."

A study of Katrina victims illustrates how people who experience disasters describe God's intervention. The participants, all African Americans in their fifties and sixties, perceived God's power in "unpredictable daily occurrences that solve apparently insoluble problems." They did not think God manipulated nature to spare their lives, but gratefully saw events taking shape in unexpected ways. A woman who slept outside the Superdome for hours said, "Even though we didn't have control of where we were going, I thought God was controlling where I needed to end up. You can't figure out what God's purpose is, but you know the purpose was for you to be here." Another woman remarked, "God was there. He blessed me. My home is safe. A tree could have fell on it or anything. And when I got to the shelter, I was the first one to leave. You see the good Lord removed me from there before I was hurt."[44]

In other settings, people describe miracles as personal experiences that cannot easily be disconfirmed and indeed can be told as a kind of maybe-it-happened-maybe-it-did-not account that illustrates the mysteries of faith. An elderly woman who worked for many years as a college administrator and attends an Episcopal church in New Jersey describes an event like this: As a member of her family lay dying, she remembers "asking God to send angels to be with us and, honestly, there were times when I felt like the room was full of angels from top to bottom." She kept saying to her relative, "Keep your eyes on Jesus," and "the moment he passed the front door of the house flew open, the wind blew through in a fury, the sky was dark like it was going to rain, and then the sun came out." A man who works as an engineer and attends an evangelical church in Texas is more guarded, but says he prays every day and has witnessed times when he felt God was answering his prayers for loved ones who were seriously ill. "People who have cancer are healed, at least temporarily, almost from a miraculous point of view, and situations have turned around that are unexpected."

Accounts like these are often open-ended. People tell them in ways that leave room for interpretation. Were angels really present or did the narrator only feel that they were? Did it matter? Did God decide to end a drying person's life at a particular moment and send a gust of wind to mark the transition? Was the wind a coincidence? The storyteller does not address these questions or provide a definitive summary statement at the end. The logic of the story requires that some things remain unsaid. In the other account, it is notable that the language pertains as closely to the broader dictionary definition of miracles as rare events as to divine intervention. The man says some of the events have been "dramatic" and are "pleasantly unexpected." He too uses ambiguous language. The events could be interpreted *almost* from a miraculous *point of view*.

When terrible tragedies do occur, it is common for people today, just as it probably has been throughout history, to cry out in anguish at the seeming meaninglessness of it all. The simplest expression of this anguish is "why"? A woman who works as a marketing director and attends a Catholic church in Virginia recalls the despair she felt after the 9/11 attacks, feeling the world was going crazy and that war was imminent. "God, why could you let this happen to these wonderful people? Or to any people?" she kept asking. There was no way of making sense of it. Usually people ask these questions to themselves, privately. But disasters prompt public discussions as well. The head of a construction firm who attends an evangelical church in West Virginia remembers after the tsunami that people at his church got together and discussed the theological questions it raised for them. "People were asking where was God? What happened? Why was God not there or was God there?" Discussions of the why questions also occurred in the media. Describing the tsunami as a "cataclysm of biblical proportions," *Newsweek* religion writer Kenneth L. Woodward wrote that people of all faiths were asking "Why us? Why here? Why now?"[45]

These are the classic theodicy questions. Is God in control? If so, how can a powerful and merciful God allow such suffering? Is God punishing the wicked? Teaching humans a lesson? Are there evil forces in the world that God cannot control? There are textbook answers to all these questions. But are the textbook answers really how people think? Or do the traditional explanations exist mostly in the minds of religious leaders who defend them and skeptics who ridicule them? When a loved one dies in an automobile accident, it is hard to be convinced that God somehow caused the accident, let alone imagine that the loved one was being punished for some wrongdoing. It is much easier to examine the accident in terms of natural causes, such as slippery roads or malfunctioning brakes. A thinking person can more easily see that children die of starvation because food is unavailable than argue that there is some supernatural explanation for it all. Yet the natural explanations seem not to have replaced the religious arguments entirely. For people who want to believe that God matters in these situations, the natural-causes arguments are insufficient. Thoughtful people of faith have to find a reasonable way to keep God in the picture. How do they do it?

A standard social science approach to this question would be to conduct a survey or to give a pencil-and-paper test to subjects in a laboratory experiment and ask people to explain some catastrophic event. Was the death and destruction caused by God, an earthquake or flood, people making bad choices about where to live, human indifference, or what? The results would be fairly predictable, but would also leave a puzzle. Consider the following: Shortly after Hurricane Katrina, ABC News conducted a national poll asking people if the event had been a "deliberate act of God." Evangelical Protestants were twice as likely to say it was than were people who defined themselves as nonreligious. That was the predictable part. Predictably, respondents' level of education also mattered. Among those with college educations, only 11 percent attributed hurricanes to God, whereas three times as many did among those who had not been to college.[46] But just a few months earlier a national survey had shown that 78 percent of Americans with college degrees believed in God, while only 4 percent were sure they did not.[47] Hence the puzzle: What did all those educated believers think about the hurricane? If it was not an act of God, what was it? Was God irrelevant? Did God still enter into their thinking about the hurricane, but in some other way?

Had the surveys asked more questions, they probably could have explored whether respondents did or did not believe New Orleans was being punished and whether people wondered why God allows such suffering. But that kind of research tells very little about how people actually piece together ways of thinking that combine the natural and supernatural. It tells nothing about the subtle uses of language and thought that permit people to believe God is somehow involved but in ways that steer clear of difficult assumptions about how God acts. To answer those questions it becomes necessary to shift from the number-crunching mode of standard social science into the less frequently traversed territory of language analysis.

The Rowan Williams and Mildred Jones examples begin to suggest what may be a common way of including God in thoughts about major catastrophes. God is in charge in a general way, having set the universe in motion and having given humans the ability to choose between good and evil. The bad things that happen in the world are because of evil, but not in a one-to-one relationship. Good people suffer too. Knowing that God is in control prevents having to imagine that events are meaningless or spiraling into chaos. Besides this intellectual reassurance, the argument also tells people to put their faith in God on a daily basis. They cannot know exactly what God was doing when something bad happened, but they can trust that God is still present. And they can find strength to do good by being mindful of God. We can treat these statements as a propositional summary of a kind of grassroots theology. How they are put into words, though, requires closer consideration.

The statements themselves are a mixture of ideas that have been around for a long time in the more formalized teachings of deists, who emphasize God's initial role in setting things up, and in dualistic views about the importance of siding with good against the forces of evil. They do keep God in the picture, and yet may be associated more with having a rather vague notion about God than with the kind of biblical understandings shared by people on the conservative end of the theological spectrum. Theological conservatives are more likely to believe that God directly punishes the wicked, intervenes supernaturally, and has plans that can be known and furthered by the righteous.

A man I will call Russ Conklin provides an opportunity to see how a theological conservative might approach these issues. My interpretation of his remarks is that they show how a well-educated, articulate person can hold quite conservative views and still adapt those views so that they do not conflict very much with commonsense notions about how the world works. I do not mean to imply that he is not really as conservative as he thinks. The point rather is that his particular way of framing what he regards as biblical language fits well enough with broader assumptions and ways of speaking that he can avoid arguments that could easily be disconfirmed and deemed superstitious or stupid.

Mr. Conklin is a certified financial analyst for one of the nation's largest brokerage firms. He lives with his wife and children in south Texas not far from the Louisiana border. Now in his mid-forties, he divides his free time between his family and his church. He would probably prefer to be called an "evangelical" or simply a "Christian," which is how he identifies his religion, but his beliefs and practices fall well within the category generally labeled as fundamentalist. The college he attended affirms the "Lordship of Christ" in all realms of life, asserts in its statement of faith that the Bible is "inerrant" and "infallible," and states that those who are not "saved" will be resurrected to "damnation." The church where he teaches Sunday school and serves on the missions committee is a nondenominational Bible church loosely affiliated with a network of independent Baptist congregations and evangelical churches that seeks to honor Christ by preaching the Bible and exhorting its members to Christian discipleship and accountability. He says he is "one of those intolerant Christians who believe that there is only one way to God and that is through Jesus." He is also a social conservative. He prefers Fox News to CNN, thinks the United States' invasion of Iraq was necessary, considers global warming a farce, and regards homosexuality as a sin. He and his wife have eight children.

If one believed what social scientists have written about people like Mr. Conklin, he is probably a knee-jerk believer who rejects the wider world and insulates himself from it by spending all his time at church fellowshipping with kindred spirits. And this view would be correct up to a point. He does think the media are peddling smut and that the public schools are failing to instill moral backbone. He considers Jesus his personal savior and looks forward to living in heaven when he dies. He also thinks earthquakes and floods are signs of the end times described in the Bible and that there may be supernatural—his word—reasons for these events.

Yet he also lives in the same world as everyone else and his ways of talking about God enable him not only to believe but also to avoid climbing too far out on a limb. Consider his view that everything happens according to a divine plan. Here is what he says about the 9/11 attacks: "I see everything in terms of my God is in control and bad things happen. What we call bad things. Nine-eleven is probably a good example. I don't think God was absent on 9/11. I don't think he was surprised by 9/11. I'm not sure he was the direct cause of 9/11, but it didn't happen without him allowing it to happen. So with that in mind, he was there. It was part of the plan." This is a refrain to which he returns again and again. When Hurricane Katrina hit his community, God was in control. When children in poor countries are dying from hunger, God is in control. Despite the moral decay he sees in America, "God is in control; nothing happens apart from his will." When he worries about big scary things happening that might affect his children, "I know God is in control."

This view of divine control and a divine plan is his way of arguing that the world is meaningful. Whether events are good or bad, they are consistent with God's will. In defense of this view, he cites Romans 8:28, as he says, "where it talks about God will cause all things to work together for those who love the Lord and are called according to his purpose." He further refers to the biblical story of Joseph as an illustration of someone who experienced hardship when his brothers sold him into slavery and then was able to do good for his people as Pharaoh's right-hand man.

Mr. Conklin's conclusion is that everything will work out so that even the bad things will eventually accomplish some good purpose. But when taken at face value, that view raises difficult questions. Why did nearly 3,000 people die on 9/11? Why do six million children starve to death every year? What purpose could it possibly serve for Mr. Conklin to die and leave a widow and eight children? Delving too deeply into those questions might cause a thinking person to doubt that there is a God.

In my interviews I was able to identify four ways in which people avoid these questions, all evident on closer inspection of what Mr. Conklin actually says and present in a number of other interviews as well. Each of these is a kind of script or cultural device that makes it possible to believe God exists and is in charge of everything that happens without having to assume that God intervenes specifically and deliberately in particular events. One is to invoke inscrutability. The impossibility of knowing the specifics of God's plans and purpose means not having to ask questions about people dying on 9/11 or children starving. It does more than assert that answers cannot be found; it implies that asking the question is presumptuous. As we have seen in other examples, the inscrutability principle is easily invoked by people who truly regard God as a mystery. It is harder for a theological conservative who believes that God's will is clearly revealed in Scripture and can be discerned in specific situations through prayer. The theological solution is to argue, as Albert Mohler did in writing about the tsunami, that believers should be silent about everything not explicitly discussed in the Bible. So, for instance, if the Bible does not mention the 9/11 attacks, then a believer should say nothing. In practice, this is a hard rule to follow. The grassroots solution, accomplished through conventions of speech, is to assert a lack of knowledge about God, not as a principle, but as a personal attribute: not "this cannot be known," but "I don't know." Although Mr. Conklin is surer of his beliefs than many people, he repeatedly uses phrases such as "I don't know," "I have no idea," and "I feel" or "I guess." At one point he says, "God is bigger than I ever thought he was and unconstrained by my limited thought." This way of personalizing uncertainty applies not only to the reasons God may have had for doing something but also to figuring out what the possible outcomes might be. For instance, after saying that 9/11 was "part of the plan," he suggests several possibilities, such as waking up America and giving people more resolve to combat evil. He does not venture a guess as to which of these God intended.

People with quite different theological views invoke inscrutability too. When asked what God's reasons might be for catastrophes and serious social problems, they disclaim having personal knowledge without waxing eloquent about the philosophical impossibility of knowing. A Methodist school teacher in California says, "I think God has a reason for everything. I just don't know what the reason is. Might never find out. But I'm not going to be one of those people who blame God or put all the responsibility on God." A member of a nondenominational church in Montana muses, "If we could really understand God's mind, we'd be God." An insurance agent in Illinois who attends a black Baptist church says, "I don't know how God is involved in these big events. I just think that he is." A teacher in Minnesota muses, "How can six million Jews die if there's a God? We're always quick to say something is because of God, but I don't want to say God was mad at those people. I just can't buy that. I don't know. I don't know."

The last of these statements illustrates how the inscrutability script can be adapted to imply several different meanings. Here it suggests that something doesn't quite make sense, unlike some of the other statements that imply greater cognitive closure. "I don't know" is a flexible script that can mean "I doubt if anyone knows, and that is okay," or "I haven't figured it out and doubt that I ever will," or "I wish I knew and it bothers me." Consider this response from a young woman who works as a librarian in Oregon: "If it's a matter of God making something happen to teach people a lesson or to kill off a bunch of bad people, I don't know, that just doesn't seem quite right." In her case, "I don't know" means "it doesn't make sense," as indicated by her saying it "doesn't seem quite right." The full interview supports this interpretation. She used to be more religious than she is now. She still thinks God exists and gives people the strength to endure hard times. However, in a revealing phrasing, she says she doesn't "understand the logic" behind religion. In her case, lacking knowledge implies that her thoughts are still in flux. If she finds a way of talking about God that seems right, we might suppose that she will continue to believe, but if she does not, she is tempted, as she says, to think of the universe and life as simply being composed of energy.

Another possible inference to be drawn from the "I don't know" response is "why bother?" Don't things just happen? Throw up one's hands and think about something else. Why pray? Why try to fix problems if what causes them is beyond comprehension? That implication does come through in the frustration people sometimes express when pushed to say more about God's involvement in tragic events. "I don't know" becomes a way of saying, "That's all I have to say." But lacking knowledge of God's reasons is seldom accompanied by assertions that nothing can be done or should be done to ameliorate the actual problems that afflict humanity. The desire for equilibrium that is so often evident in ordinary speech appears to be operative in the way people talk. A deficit of knowledge has to be made up for in some other way. "I don't know about that" has to be followed by "but I do think. . . ." If it is unclear what God may have intended, then it is all the more important that humans take responsibility. Human action substitutes for divine intentions. The school teacher in California puts it this way: "I just have to find a way to act to bring about a solution. I think that's what God wants all of us to do. Contribute to mankind."

A second way of avoiding thorny questions about God's plan is one that might be termed the CEO analogy. A CEO has an overall plan but leaves it to subordinates to work out the details. The subordinates probably do not know what the big plan is and do not need to know. Their job is to do their part, having faith that the top person has things under control. This is another way of saying that God is inscrutable without having to say that God's will cannot be known at all. Subordinates can figure out a meaningful role to play without having to understand the big picture. Their actions make sense because of their faith that a master plan actually exists. God has a plan. God is in charge. The idea of God being in *control*, as Mr. Conklin emphasizes, is especially attractive. It contrasts with the sense inspired by tragedies and other problems that things are out of control. We want things to be in control again. As various interviewees put it, "things seem to be spiraling out of control," "we need to control the natural balance" of the planet, "people want to control their environment," "people are not in control," do something "before things escalate out of control," and so on. Desiring control and feeling that things are out of control makes it reassuring to talk about God being in control.

The idea of a divine CEO with overall responsibility for the universe helps shift attention from large, unanswerable questions about why things happen to considerations about the behavior of people in particular situations. It is as if employees were huddled around the water cooler saying "I don't know what the big boss has in mind, but Jack sure needs to buckle down and work harder." Mr. Conklin provides an illustration in talking about Hurricane Katrina. If the event prompted him to ask why God had allowed it to happen, this question was not uppermost in his mind. What he remembers is the downed power lines and trees and "20-foot tall piles of debris on each side of the road." It was the human response that struck him most vividly. He remembers people looting and he recalls neighbors helping one another. He especially remembers a neighbor of his bringing in ice for anyone who wanted it. If there was a theological point, it is this: Some of the people involved "will do evil" and some "will do good." God was not going to step in and solve problems, but people could be on God's side by doing good or they could be against God by doing evil.

Although the CEO analogy leaves the responsibility for day-to-day decisions in the hands of ordinary people, it also excuses them from having to worry about things that are beyond their control. Those things are in God's hands. The Missouri pediatrician I mentioned earlier believes firmly that God handles the major events that happen in the world. As we saw, God's hand in the Bush presidency is, in her view, an example. For her personally, knowing that God takes care of larger matters reduces her anxiety. "I'm a control freak," she says, "and I like to be in charge of my environment. For a lot of years I tried to be in control and that was very stressful. When I finally acknowledged that God is sovereign and is in charge and there are a lot of things I have no control over, I let those things go and my anxiety diminished remarkably. I'm grateful I've gotten to that point." Notice that it is not so much that God has manipulated events in her life or that God provides an explanation for specific good things or bad things that happen. It is rather that God has helped her adjust her approach to life. As the popular saying has it, she "lets go and lets God."

A third way of dealing with difficult questions about God's intentions is to personalize one's speech. Inserting first-person pronouns is common: Instead of asserting "God is in control," say "*I believe* God is in control." That phrasing leaves open the possibility that I could be wrong or that others might believe differently. There is also a stronger form of personalization. Consider the interesting phrasing of the statement I quoted earlier: "I see everything in terms of my God is in control and bad things happen." Why would someone who believes there is one true God who controls the entire universe say *my God*? The most likely reason for a fundamentalist to say this is to cast an implicit jibe at others who profess belief in God but who are not really saved: my God versus the God of Muslims or liberal Episcopalians. But this mode of personalization also focuses attention on *me* and thus makes it more likely to focus on the immediate personal consequences of some large-scale event than having to ponder its effects on others. Mr. Conklin's remarks about 9/11 segue from speculating that it was a wake-up call for America to this: "I know I have grown in my faith as I thought about what it would have been like to have been on one of those planes." He likes the story of Joseph because he can relate personally to someone who was at the right place at the right time. Things have turned out well for him. He knows bad things could happen, but thus far they have not affected him personally. That makes it easier than to ponder the reasons for mass death in a tsunami. "I particularly like [the story of Joseph]," he says. "It shows me that God is going to take care of me."

This emphasis on the personal effects of God's action is especially evident among people like Mr. Conklin who believe that God is mainly interested in personal salvation, or, as another conservative Christian put it, "redeeming hearts and minds." Listen to what another Gulf Coast resident said about Hurricane Katrina. "Get away from the grandiose effect and get down to the personal level. Ask people, 'Do you think God had a hand in your life? Does God love you and care for you?' And I'll bet you'll find people who say, 'Oh yeah, God got me to the roof before the water swept me through the window and drowned me.' You know, that kind of thing." He adds, "It's usually at a personal level. God [doesn't] get a big kick out of manipulating natural law."

The fourth mode of speaking goes squarely to the problem of explaining bad things despite believing that God is in control. It concerns sin and is a way of deflecting the view that bad things happen because God is punishing people for their sins. That view quickly gets thinking people into logical trouble because it is hard to argue that innocent children who die in wars or good church people who die of cancer are being punished. As the pediatrician in Missouri says about Hurricane Katrina, "It was a natural disaster. Hurricanes happen on a regular basis. If you want to go down the road of saying that every time a hurricane happens, God is punishing somebody, I think that's ridiculous." But unlike people in the past, who, according to social scientists, argued that some were merely damned or were paying for misdeeds in a previous life, the most common explanation in contemporary culture invokes the view that evil has simply been present in the world since the beginning of humankind and thus affects everyone in ways that cannot be directly associated with their own misdeeds or wrongdoing. Mr. Conklin believes that sin is a condition of humanity that nobody this side of heaven can fully escape, even though the faithful are forgiven and expected to combat evil. He does not say much about sin or feel compelled to reconcile its existence with his conviction that God is in control. But the topic surfaces as he muses about millions of children dying of starvation. "Even this hunger is part of God's plan," he says, but he also believes "it is actually a problem of sin." The earth is fertile enough to produce food for everyone, he says. Sin enters the picture, not as a trait of the children starving, but of the powerful. "We have dictators. We have leaders in charge of governments who do not care about the people. War breeds famine. There are evil men trying to help themselves and others are just incompetent."

His argument resembles the beliefs anthropologists have observed in tribal cultures where the high god is pure and evil arises from lesser gods. The more common reading, though, emphasizes the results of human freedom. "God has given human beings this wonderful thing called free will," a Lutheran in Illinois observes. Given the choice, everyone past and present makes selfish, uninformed decisions from time to time, and these decisions cumulatively contribute to the problems the world faces. "We make our own hell" is how one woman put it. "The result is death, destruction, war, plague, and all these other problems," the Lutheran says. A Catholic health administrator says, "To me, it seems like all the bad stuff that happens is kind of us following our own will." A Catholic sister extends the argument even to nature. "God created the universe, I suppose, with the same freedom we human beings have." Earthquakes and volcanoes, she says, occur because nature is free to act without specific intervention from God. In the long term, some good may emerge from short-term ills, but those, like God's purposes, cannot be known. What can be known are efforts in the short term to ameliorate ills.

Let us assume for the moment that emphasizing God's inscrutability, denying that God is in the details, personalizing one's talk about God, and generalizing about sin are common, culturally acceptable ways of avoiding questions about why God may have allowed specific events to happen. If so, we would expect to see variations on these themes in other statements about God's relationship to big scary events. An interesting variant that combines all three is the claim that the problems, not God, are what cannot be understood. Here is an example from a woman who attended a very conservative church-related college and now teaches drama at another college in the Midwest. In summarizing how she approaches big problems in the world, she explains, "I look at them and say, 'I don't understand how to fix it. I don't understand how it started. I don't understand how it continues.' It seems like a large and complex issue. But then I do know that God is greater than all these things." She does not claim to know the mind or will of God, either. But that is not her point. It is rather that the problems are too complex for her to understand. Or at least she does not understand them now. For example, she talks about the possibility of a flu pandemic like the one that happened in 1918. She says, "we would be in God's hands." But, despite the fact that God is very important to her, she does not jump to questions about why God might allow a pandemic and whether or not the deaths would have some purpose. She instead speculates that things could be learned by looking at the 1918 outbreak, that there would be economic consequences, and that the impact would likely be different because of changes in society since 1918. "I am not an expert," she says.

There is a great deal of meaning in her comment. Expertise has become the prerequisite for knowledge. Anyone can have an opinion, but only experts can supply authoritative knowledge. The average non-expert cannot provide knowledge about why a tsunami happens. An ordinary person can have opinions about terrorism and pandemics, but analysis of the causes and possible solutions must be left to those with expertise. "I don't know" is a perfectly legitimate response. This is even more the case when questions arise about God's hand in natural disasters and other catastrophic events. Religious leaders may be the experts who can speak with authoritative knowledge. But God being beyond comprehension means there are no true experts. Religious assertions, beyond general ones about God being in charge, become matters of conjecture. "I don't know" implies that there may be people who do, but those people are more likely to be interested in knowledge that can be proved or disproved than in speculation about God.

As this example illustrates, claiming to have insufficient knowledge is a good way to avoid thorny questions about God. However, it is not the only way. People who are more confident that they have thought through the issues and found satisfactory theological answers also find ways to show that faith is possible without it sounding unreasonable. A good example is a man in his fifties who has a doctorate in nuclear engineering, works as a research scientist at the National Aeronautics and Space Administration (NASA) facility in Florida, and attends a theologically conservative church in the Mennonite tradition. He reads widely and in his spare time participates in an international humanitarian organization that gives him ample opportunity to consider the relationship of God to natural disasters, disease, and environmental issues. His responses to questions about faith are in no way dogmatic, but they exude a great deal of confidence. For example, he says, "I claim to be a follower of Jesus, and Jesus is the role model for what it means to be a Christian, and I see Jesus involved with all kinds of political and secular issues all over the place, and I don't see Jesus being scared of the issues." When asked if he thinks God has a reason for wars and disease, he says, "No, my belief is that sin entered the world, and when we allowed sin to enter the world, then it took on manifestations of all kinds. It's not God's will that sin would enter the world, but we allowed that to happen and we're suffering the consequences." Asked to explain then how God is involved, he says, "God has given us the ability to overcome these events, but there's a fine balance between free will and God's sovereignty, and God has restricted God's sovereignty to allow us to have choice. We have to come willingly to participate with him in overcoming the sin of the world. God is not going to do it on his own."

For this man, Hurricane Katrina is a clear instance in which the problems resulting from human sinfulness are evident both in general and in specific ways. He says, "Hurricane Katrina is a natural phenomenon in the world as we know it, and it cannot be pinpointed to personal, moral sin. It's the way creation is wound up. Now the destruction it produces could be a result of sin." As an example, he points to people purchasing property along the Atlantic and Gulf coasts without regard for the likelihood of hurricanes. "They suffer the consequences of these natural processes because they ignore them." He denies that God was in any way punishing the people of New Orleans. "It's a very complex situation when people disregard the way God wound up the world. We can't take hurricanes or tornadoes lightly." And part of it, he says, is just humanity being "out of sync with the nature of creation."

Another variation on the broader themes in these examples is evident in the language people who do not believe in God use to explain catastrophic events. This language is especially interesting because of the tendency among critics of religion to present caricatures of what people believe that illustrate how far-fetched belief is. But what would happen if a real-life atheist were asked to *imagine* that he or she was a believer? Consider this response given by a young woman who graduated from one of the nation's elite colleges and was working in New York City on September 11, 2001. She says that if she believed in a God and saw suffering in the world she would need to "think that there is some plan"; otherwise, "I would feel like I would turn away from God at that point." She would not want to think that events occurred purely at random or that suffering was "just for the hell of it." So how exactly would she describe a divine plan of this kind? "Sometimes you don't see the bigger picture, right? I know this is a bad analogy, but there are times when I have to do something really bad to my cat and it's simply for his own health. He has no clue. I had to grab him by the neck and stick some awful pill down his mouth. In his mind I'm treating him really awful. He doesn't see the bigger picture. If I believed in God, I would believe that bad things happen for some reason, some larger plan that I am not capable of seeing."

Her language is remarkably similar to how people who do believe in God talk. The analogy with doing something for the cat's benefit may be idiosyncratic, but her view that a believer would want to think God has a plan and that the believer is incapable of understanding that plan are squarely on target. She has either been around believers enough to know how they think or she is inventive enough to imagine a response that gives a place to God and yet denies knowing what God's reasons might be. How she responds when asked what she *truly* thinks is also revealing. She says some bad things happen because of greed, but when it comes to environmental catastrophes and even war or world hunger, she says, "There are certain things that are just the way they are because that's the way they are. Those are the rules of the game and that's just the way they end up being." What is different is that she does not talk about God. What is similar is that the rules of the game and the way things are have a functionally similar place in her understanding to the idea that God is in charge. She too believes in a kind of overarching order that cannot be fully understood. This is not to suggest that the differences are trivial, especially for believers who insist that the divine order is merciful and involves a loving deity who cares about them as persons. It is to suggest a way in which a person who does not believe in God may also construct a sense of order that helps to make sense of catastrophic events.

A final point about God as a source of explanations for big scary events: Even people who are quite devout about their faith generally do not focus a lot of their thinking on questions about why God allowed something to happen. If they were responding to a survey, they would probably say, yes, they had been wondering about such matters. But a survey would not show much about how frequent or intense the wondering had been or what form it had taken. In designing my interviews,

I framed questions about disasters, starvation, terrorism, war, and the like in more general terms and only later asked people specifically how their faith related to these concerns. Mr. Conklin was an example of someone who brought God into the discussion almost immediately, but most people did not. They speculated about whether what they had read in the newspapers or seen on television was credible, and they mostly talked about what they *would do* if some catastrophe occurred, not how they would try to interpret the hand of God. Even when pressed to see if they somehow thought God was involved, they often did not. As one woman remarked when asked if she thought God had a role in Hurricane Katrina, "No, I think it was caused by warm water and other natural conditions in the Gulf." Or in the words of an engineer who was quite concerned about people dying of hunger, the "ultimate reason" is "misappropriated funds," by which he meant money in rich countries being spent on "selfish desires" instead of real needs. This emphasis on natural and human factors is not surprising, but it is further evidence of the extent to which language matters in shaping thoughts. Most of what we read and hear about large-scale events are words about what happened, the conditions and policies that may have contributed to them, and how people responded. Questions about God come up, but less often and in more limited contexts. If the headline says, "religious leaders are asking why . . . ," the rest of the public may rest easier in their faith knowing that these are questions being discussed elsewhere.

As several of the previous examples show, there is a bias to act when faced with danger that moves the discussion from unanswerable "why" questions to more practical "what can we do" considerations. Notice the evolution in this response to a question asking if God has reasons for suffering and other problems in the world. "I want to know why infants die. I want to know what purpose God has for that. I want to know why we can have children who die from cancerous tumors at the age of three or four. Why does God do that? When I get to the pearly gates, I'm going to say to whoever signs me in, 'I have some questions.' And I do. Why do school buses fall over cliffs and kids die?" The man talking is a doctor. He continues, "I have other questions. Why do we have hunger in the world? Why do we have AIDS and it's not being prevented to the full extent?" He mentions Bill Gates and Angelina Jolie trying to help. "I've been in places where food is rotting on docks because the government is not allowing it to be transferred. It's not easy. A good plan needs to be executed." The evolution is from "why" questions that can only be asked in heaven to remarks about the practicalities of what can be done and how to make it work better. As if to drive home the point, he tells a story a few minutes later about a wounded boy who came to the field hospital where he was working as a medical technician during the war in Vietnam. The doctor assured the boy the surgery was simple and he wouldn't die. Ten minutes later the boy was dead. The doctor was distraught, crying, and asking why God had let the boy die. The man telling the story remembered saying to the doctor, "Let's move on and figure out how to prepare. There are other individuals beyond those doors who expect you to help. You've got to be ready."

Underlying the focus on arguments about God's plan and God being in control when bad things happen is an assumption that the "why" questions that accompany these events are pleas for understanding. But they may be pleas for comfort, registered less in the intellect and more in the emotions, a yearning for pain to be eased and anxiety to diminish. One of the women we talked to who had been musing a lot about the devastation of Hurricane Katrina said she doesn't ask whether God caused it or not because she thinks God is there to help people. It comforts her to talk to God, as she does when she boards an airplane, or as she has recently because of the heaviness she feels knowing a co-worker has cancer. For many in middle-class America, the thought of what it must be like to lose one's home in a flood is only an abstraction formed from images they have seen on television. Yet they can imagine the grief that might overcome them if their loved ones died from a flu pandemic or in a terrorist attack. They can describe some of the feelings because they have experienced the deaths of mothers and fathers or spouses and siblings.

The idea that belief in God is widespread because it provides comfort is appealing at one level. We are a society that wants to feel good, and religion may serve, as some have argued, as a cheap form of therapy. Facing possibilities of terrorist strikes and pandemics and knowing that we will all die some day, we have reason to believe in a God who offers peace of mind. But does it really work that way? Are people gullible enough to believe that God will lower their anxiety levels and make them happy? Isn't it more likely that people are more thoughtful about their experiences than this view implies? Real life includes difficulties; otherwise it is not real. We know, as Rowan Williams observes, that bad things make us feel miserable. There is also a strong tendency in our culture to resist being too happy. A person with no worries is a Pollyanna and, for that matter, probably someone who is too laid back to be accomplishing very much. When people talk about being comforted by their faith in God, it becomes necessary to strike a balance. The trick is to acknowledge being comforted without seeming too carefree, and especially without implying that God intervenes directly to calm a person's emotions. How is this done?

From the interview material, my conclusion is that thoughtful people of faith generally distance themselves from any notion that divine comfort happens magically or is a panacea by strongly asserting their identity as ordinary humans who face the same difficulties in their daily lives as everyone else. They do this by asserting, on the one hand, that God exists, is present, watches, and cares, and on the other hand, that they worry, have fears, do not understand God, argue with God, and sometimes do not even like God. These are *humanizing* traits. They display a persona that is in no substantial way removed from the raw realities of the human condition. Statements about God acknowledge that it is comforting to pray and to know that God is in charge. Yet the language often goes out of its way to demonstrate that the person speaking is neither gullible nor free of anxiety. The language distances the speaker from generalities about people of faith and about creedal statements and emphasizes the idiosyncrasies of personal life that are evident in stories about memorable experiences or in recent events involving friends and family. There is a high level of self-awareness or reflexivity in statements about *how* a person prays, feels, acts, or engages in decision making. Both the complexity of thoughts about faith and the mundane character of everyday life are evident.

A high-ranking military officer who had seen combat duty in Somalia illustrates how language about divine comfort accomplishes these humanizing tasks. He is a well-educated man who recently finished a second doctorate and now teaches and consults on national security policy. He and his wife attend services regularly at a conservative Protestant church, and he has no trouble acknowledging that he believes in God. Toward the end of a lengthy interview in which he talked animatedly about a number of current issues, such as terrorism and threats to the environment, it became clear that he had a story he wanted to work into the interview. A question about the Bible gave him an opportunity. "I'm not a theologian," he began, distancing himself from what he regarded as standard church teachings and opening a space to tell about his own views. The story was about five of his friends going out on patrol one night in Somalia and being captured by rebels and brutally murdered. "The Bible thing," as he calls it, "is to love all mankind." But he is unable to do that. It gives him comfort to know that "it's in God's hands." He repeats that phrase three times, quickly asserting it as a kind of litany. And then he talks at length about how he argues with God. The language becomes richer and more personal, placing himself in real time and revealing more of who he is and what he said. He recalls the exact words he said to his pastor: "I've got to talk to you. I'm torn. I'm having trouble. I'm arguing with God right now." Some people from his church were going on a mission trip to Somalia and he was unable to pray for them. His pastor told him he could do it, eventually, "in your own time." "It's complex," the man muses. "It's not easy." And then he continues his own account, including a time when he went for a long walk in the snow. "I was hollering at God." He prayed for the people on the mission trip, but did so grudgingly. "Let me tell you, it was under protest. I had a huge problem with that."

The story was inspired by the very difficult experience of his friends being murdered, and yet it was not so different from the language other people use to demonstrate that life is an emotional roller coaster even for those who find comfort in God. The story affirms and yet largely sets aside the idea that people of faith can be forgiving. The character who comes alive in the story is a person who questions and argues and then muses about those questions and arguments. The tension between this character and God is only partly resolved as the story concludes.

The man prays but does so grudgingly. In his own summation, life is complex.

The insurance agent I mentioned earlier provides another example of humanizing the way in which divine comfort is perceived. Two people who were close to him died from suicide and another died of cancer, all within a few years of one another. He found comfort in his faith, but it is the uniqueness of his personal struggle that dominates his account. "I was pretty angry," he recalls. "It wasn't until I was able to deal with them my way and with the Lord that I got over them. At the time I was pretty angry." Asked what he meant by "my way," he explains, "My way means coming to terms with it. That I didn't play a role in their deaths. That it wasn't my fault. Being able to talk to my wife and people outside my family about it. Finding the resources to talk about it. And then not blaming the man upstairs for it. I had to come to terms with those deaths my way." The account humanizes the event by showing that it was painful and by emphasizing the man's efforts to gain control of his thoughts and feelings. The peace of mind he eventually gained came less from any kind of supernatural intervention than from an adjustment of his views about God. The active verbs connect with him, not with the man upstairs.

In real life, people usually do not have a numeric scale in mind that allows them to say they have been comforted at about a 3, 5, or 7 on a scale of 1 to 10. A response like that, or its verbal equivalent, such as "somewhat," might also imply that a person was lacking in faith. A better approach is to exploit the richness of language to assert both that we are comforted and that we are not. Consider what Mr. Conklin, the fundamentalist in south Texas, says when asked if he ever feels overwhelmed by all the problems in the world. At first, he asserts that he really does not and repeats his conviction that God is in control. But then he acknowledges that things have gone a "little further" than he had imagined, apparently still thinking about the remarks he made to a previous question in which he mentioned abortions, problems in the schools, and "mindless" television watchers and video game players. There would be "hard times," he says, and nobody would be unscathed, but God would help them handle it. Immediately after that reassuring thought, he says, "I guess the biggest worry I would have would be that one of my children would die. I honest to goodness cannot fathom that." He says he wants his kids to "be safe, but it's not like it's a concern." He finishes, "I don't have very many concerns that keep me up at night. I sleep pretty well."

Is he concerned or is he not? Yes and no. Does his faith help? Yes and no. The back-and-forth nature of the response is an apt reflection of the matter. It acknowledges that everything is not well and could be much worse, but that the worries and fears are not overwhelming. A reasonable person would not deny having fears about a child dying, but a reasonable person also acknowledges that on most days children in middle-class America are relatively safe. Mr. Conklin is, without saying so directly, asserting that he does not believe in God only because it comforts him—or even because he hopes to spend eternity with God. He is rather arguing that his belief in God's existence is solid despite whatever happens. There is a foundation of basic assurance about order and structure in the universe and plenty of room to be aware of what could go wrong and at other times to sleep well at night.

We could summarize this way of talking about God and comfort by saying that it displays *ambivalence*. The reality of human life is that it is a mixture of pain and pleasure, and because we know that and have experienced it, we have ambivalent feelings about the search for comfort. On the one hand, we want to avoid pain and experience pleasure; on the other hand, we would feel that life was diminished if we only experienced pleasure, and we would have difficulty believing someone who said they felt happy all the time and never worried. To say that faith in God helps some of the time, but not all of the time, is a statement that affirms one's humanity. It is a statement in defiance of naïveté. It asserts that a believer in God lives in the real world.

A second way of thinking and talking about God's comfort goes a bit further and asserts that belief in God is actually a source of *discomfort* as well as of comfort. Consider what a professor at a large state university in the Midwest who teaches history and attends a Methodist church says when asked if he ever feels overwhelmed by all the problems in the world today. His initial response emphasizes the comfort he feels as a result of believing in God. Like Mr. Conklin, believing that God is in charge of everything gives him hope. He mentions Isaiah's vision of a peaceful kingdom and Jesus' vision of a time when the hungry will be fed. He believes in the idea that the kingdom of God will come and that the world will be transformed, not in any magical way, but in keeping with God's plan. "At the end of the day," he says, "God will set things right. That brings me comfort." But when asked to say more about his feelings, his thoughts turn to the frustration he feels from trying to put his faith into practice. Believing that it is the duty of people who believe in God to help the needy, he has led a team of students on several occasions to do volunteer work. He recalls a trip to New Orleans after Hurricane Katrina. "We gutted and started rebuilding a house. And then we started driving and saw mile after mile after mile of places that hadn't been touched. And later we learned that the house we rebuilt was going to be torn down anyway because of government regulations. That's kind of indicative of the way it feels. You do one little drop and then there's so much more misery. You hear about three thousand children dying every day of preventable diseases. It's just unimaginable."

What telling this story accomplishes is evidence that faith sometimes makes one feel worse instead of better. If a person wanted to feel comforted, it would be better to stay at home than rebuild houses in New Orleans. The story is framed carefully so that it does not draw a strong connection between faith and volunteering or imply a criticism of those who do not volunteer. It expresses the other side of the coin, balancing the somewhat utopian vision of a transformed world in which God sets everything right. The man underscores the point by adding another example that illustrates the same kind of frustration. "You're giving money or your church is doing something, say in Zaire, and then a rebellion breaks out and undoes ten years of good deeds. It gets frustrating. Frustration, anger, sometimes pessimism, hopelessness—all those arise." The story shows a desire to help make things better and an engagement with suffering that leads to frustration. There is comfort in believing that God is in charge but discomfort from the concerns that arise from faith.

A third way in which some of the people we talked to provide nuance to their understanding of God as a source of comfort is to emphasize the *naturalness* of human life. By this, I mean there is an assumption that faith is not an escape from reality but a way of looking it squarely in the face. A theological interpretation would assert that God created humans and the rest of nature, so a person who believes in God should fully appreciate both the desirable and undesirable aspects of life instead of wishing that things were somehow different. A social welfare administrator who studied theology in college and regards himself as a conservative Christian expresses this view when he observes that the Bible presents "an unbelievably honest assessment of suffering." He says his faith involves a "baseline reality" that includes knowing that he will die and that all of his friends and family will die. He believes that the soul lives after death, but does not emphasize that belief as he talks about the basic reality of life. When his grandfather was dying, he prayed that everyone in his family would understand "that this is a reality."

Finally, there are ways of talking about divine comfort that demonstrate both that faith itself has different dimensions and that it is not quite as distinct from everyday life as is sometimes assumed. For example, a devout Catholic woman in her forties who has worked at her parish office and taught at its school recalls how difficult it was when her mother died and she was trying to look after her father while caring for her own children and grieving. Knowing that God was in charge was in her mind, but very much at the back of it, while the support she received from several of the church women was the most helpful. She does not remember reading the Bible being helpful at all, probably because of "Jesus as such a goody goody" not being what she needed at the time. Most helpful of all was having things to do. Balancing her work and family time and making trips to care for her father gave her a role to play. Faith was fine, but doing things got her through the day.

Keeping busy, though, can be more closely related even to reading the Bible than was true for this woman. A shop owner in Nebraska who goes regularly with her husband to the Catholic church in her community loves to work in her garden and finds that planting flowers and watching them grow is comforting when she is mourning the loss of a family member or worrying about a friend. What is going through her mind are words, such as "beauty" and "new life" and the names of flowers. The words also include bits and pieces of the Bible, such as not worrying about what to wear or God caring if a small bird falls from the sky, and a phrase from last week's homily will pass through her mind, such as the blind man calling to Jesus, "Heal me." Faith is not an abstract theory about the supernatural powers of God, but specific words woven into the fabric of her thoughts as she plants flowers.

The criticism to which these ways of talking about God are subject is that they do not—or probably do not—supply religious people with very much in the way of motivation to *do something* about major threats to society and other potentially catastrophic dangers. The most likely source of motivation is the idea that human action is required because God will not somehow solve the problems. However, it may be just as easy for believers to assume that things will work out for the best or that the clouds have silver linings as it is to see the need for concerted efforts. The view that God has a plan for everything seems especially to be a factor in some of our interviewees' thinking about climate change. God has kept the planet in equilibrium thus far, they argue, so we shouldn't worry about a slight rise in temperatures, and if God chooses to destroy the earth, then we will all happily go live in heaven. Stewardship is reduced to recycling and keeping the lakes clean. The emphasis in some of our interviewees' accounts on themselves—their personal escapes from danger on the one hand, and their struggles with anxiety and pain on the other—presents a further barrier to envisioning the need for larger policies and social programs.

If it is true that these ways of talking about God do not impel people to take action, it is also the case that discourse of this kind avoids what social scientists themselves have often criticized as a *functionalist bias* in the received wisdom about religion. In those interpretations, religion was held to exist because it did something that societies needed doing: provide ways of dealing with difficult technological problems, provide intellectual ways of believing that the cosmos made sense, and provide comfort when bad things happened. If the grassroots theologies of thoughtful Americans do little of any of these things, then a different understanding of religion may be needed. That view, which has already been sketched out in non-functionalist approaches, emphasizes that religion is perpetuated and maintained by a host of social mechanisms that cannot be understood in simple functionalist terms. These include religious institutions that have adapted to the social environment and gained enough institutional autonomy to secure resources whether or not they are especially adept at fulfilling society's core functions. Generational transmission and individual habits are important. However, religious beliefs and practices do continuously adapt to the particular societal niches in which they are located. Ways of talking about God are among these modes of adaptation.

The ways of talking I have described in this chapter accomplish one thing: They make it possible to affirm faith that God exists and is relevant to the world while at the same time avoiding the implication that God directly intervenes in human affairs in any tangible way. That is no small feat. On the surface, it would seem that a God who has so little impact on the world is not much of a God at all. Yet it is clear from people's comments about their faith that God is quite real to them, they entertain few doubts about this God, and they find it meaningful to talk to God and about God. They largely avoid talking about miracles in the old-fashioned sense of divine intervention and instead use the word to mean something that can be identified after the fact as a rare and favorable outcome in a problematic situation. The theodicy problem is resolved or avoided by implicitly denying that God purposively plans—and in this sense causes—specific events, especially bad ones that might be interpreted as wrathful or punishing. God is instead inscrutable and functions as a kind of CEO who keeps the universe under control but lets people make their own decisions for good or for ill. Evil results from human action and is sufficiently widespread that no one-to-one relationship exists between the commission of evil and divine punishment. Knowing that God exists is comforting, but does not excuse people from living in the real world and experiencing the same discomforts as everyone else.

Few of the specific words and phrases that people use to make these assertions can accurately be described (as some scholars would) as scripts or repertoires. A script is a set of words that has been verbalized or written down before and then learned by someone who repeats them, much like an actor does in uttering lines from Shakespeare. A repertoire is merely a collection of scripts, such as an orchestra's repertoire of compositions to perform in concert. Close examination of the language people use in these interviews reveals little of anything that could be considered quoted speech (from someone else) or rehearsed speech (from the speaker's own previous usage). Nor is there much duplication from one interview to the next of the same words. Speakers are improvising the specific language, and yet it is not as if they are making up answers to questions about which they have never thought. Instead, the phrasings draw generally from ideas readily available in the wider culture and are tailored by each speaker. The idea that something rare and unexplained happens, that something about the universe is unknown, and that someone is in charge are all examples. None of these ideas is unique to talking about God or requires familiarity with a particular religious tradition to make sense. "Sin" and "evil" come closer to being distinct religious words, but people who are not religious have no difficulty translating them into common language about doing bad things or about greed, selfishness, and the misuse of power. Personalizing speech by telling stories about oneself is, of course, common as well. In short, what people do in relating God to big scary events is to draw on ideas that make sense in any realm of life, not just religion.

To understand how speech about God can be so different from one person to the next in specific wording and yet conform to broad cultural understandings about what is reasonable to say, it is important to recognize that religious speech is and is not *private*. On the one hand, most people hold their religious beliefs as personal convictions. What they say about God is meant to reflect only their own convictions; they do not speak on behalf of a religious institution, for example, the way clergy are expected to do. Apart from participating in an interview for a research study, they may seldom speak about God at all, other than perhaps in very private moments with their closest friends or in a group meeting at their place of worship. On the other hand, there are two significant ways in which talk about God is public. The first is that talking to a stranger as part of an interview being conducted for a university-based research project means speaking in public. Although interviewees usually speak candidly about their opinions and experiences, their remarks are influenced by the desire to appear reasonable. This does not mean that interviewees put on a false self and claim to have answers when they really have doubts. They clearly do not, as the abundance of comments about not knowing and not understanding demonstrates. It does mean that people invoke the cultural norms about reasonable speech that they have learned to apply in other such settings, ranging from classroom and dorm room conversations to interactions at work or witnessed on television. The second way in which religious speech is public is that ordinary people who are not religious professionals are exposed to a great deal of talk about God by religious professionals and by others in positions of authority, including public officials, newscasters, talk show hosts, characters in movies and books, writers, and bloggers. These authoritative public utterances do not dictate exactly what private individuals think and can say, but they do establish a broad range of expectations about what is or is not appropriate to say and sometimes model how to say it.

Amidst the quite diverse remarks about God among our interviewees, it is evident that there are some things they clearly do not feel comfortable saying and do not want to be regarded as believing. These tacit taboos concern violations of what it means to be a reasonable person. One is a taboo against appearing *superstitious*. Superstition appears to connote irrationality or a lack of logic and is often assumed to arise from ignorance, fear, a deep-seated phobia, or other psychological disturbance. Two varieties of superstition are generally excused from these negative sanctions: "just for fun" habits, such as reading fortune cookies or avoiding black cats, and what is more commonly thought of as magic, involving a temporary suspension of disbelief for purposes of entertainment. With these two exceptions, superstition is something that reasonable people are supposed to eschew. Especially in connection with religion, where supernatural acts are part of the tradition, an accusation of superstition can be particularly powerful. For example, one of the skeptics' favorite charges is that religion is nothing more than superstition. And one can find numerous statements by religious leaders arguing that belief in God is not superstitious. Nobody proudly asserts that their belief in God is superstitious. Avoiding the appearance of superstition is thus one of the cultural norms that shape how people talk about God. If they believe in miracles, they talk about them as rare and wonderful outcomes. A person can be "zapped" by God, but if so, must say it in a light-hearted way that conjures up a science fiction image, and more likely uses the word to indicate that this is not what happened.

A second topic that reasonable people try to avoid, as we have seen, is saying that they *blame God* for something bad. This taboo is not as closely associated with colorful examples (about lucky horseshoes, voudoo, and so on) as those about superstition, but it is reinforced by the view that individuals should take responsibility for their actions as much as possible. Outcomes for which individuals cannot take responsibility, such as natural catastrophes, are to be understood as part of a causal process rather than being attributed to anyone in particular. Blaming God imputes evil or mischievous motives to God, contrary to beliefs about the goodness and purity of God. This is probably as true of people who experience disasters personally as it is for those whose lives are less affected. "God is not blamed lightly for the mistakes of men," Kai T. Erikson writes about the deeply religious people who lost their community in the Buffalo Creek flood. "To do so is to risk something very close to blasphemy, not just because it employs the name of the deity too casually, but because it seems to accuse God Himself of a terrible wrong."[48] Blaming God also diverts attention from humans' responsibility to prevent disasters and to seek practical solutions. To accuse someone of blaming God is thus to criticize them for trying to excuse themselves or for being misinformed about their faith. As our interviews show, it is acceptable to say that God has a plan, is in charge, and may even have reasons for events, but relatively uncommon to assert that God intervened directly enough to be blamed.[49]

Another stricture widely evident in contemporary culture is to avoid being overly sanguine, a Pollyanna, or Panglossian. A Panglossian is blind to the facts, naïve about the realities of life. "It is a mania," Voltaire's Candide explains about his companion's optimism, "for saying things are well when one is in hell."[50] The cultural norms establish that it is acceptable to be cautiously optimistic, but not foolishly so. A person who exudes only happy thoughts is too out of touch with reality to be trusted. Especially when advanced by someone who knows better, Panglossian words are credible only to "the weak and the credulous—the feeble-minded, the nice," as one writer has observed recently.[51] Even the fictional character Forrest Gump, whose most telling self-description is "stupid is as stupid does," understands that life is not like a bowl of cherries, but a box of chocolates ("You never know what you're going to get").[52] Thus, the claim that God provides comfort is couched in disclaimers and ambiguity. Divine comfort is not something that magically arrives to quiet one's nerves, like a stiff drink or tranquilizer, but is something that reasonable people say they strive for and view as a threshold of security while experiencing the same difficulties and raw pain as everyone else.

The other norm governing religious speech is of a different order and discourages believers from saying too publicly or too explicitly that they doubt the existence of God. Judging from surveys, this taboo is by no means absolute, but even among college-educated believers, fewer than a quarter of those who believe in God say they have doubts, whereas more than three-quarters say they have no doubts at all.[53] Doubt is especially unacceptable for clergy to voice too openly, or to be perceived as expressing, but among non-clergy it is also more common to hear people say they are unsure what God is like than that they wonder if God exists. If they do acknowledge doubt, it is having had a period of doubt in the past from which they recovered. Doubt is part of a spiritual journey story involving a low point that has ultimately strengthened their faith. Thus, when bad things happen, doubt either does not result or is temporary. A reasonable person is less likely to say that he or she doubted God's existence and more likely to assert a continuing belief in the reality of God, but less certainty about how God acts. "God has a reason; I just don't know what it is" is an appropriate phrasing.

The upshot of these considerations is that language about God's role in big scary events is congruent with the expectations thoughtful people have about how to live and behave in a society that distrusts claims about direct supernatural intervention. Legitimate religious discourse is broadly bounded by the expectation that a reasonable person is not superstitious, unwilling to blame God when things go wrong, and not foolishly optimistic that everything will go right. Within these broad cultural parameters, thoughtful people have wide latitude to think and talk about God as they choose. Although they may seldom articulate their thoughts to other people, their internal conversation with themselves keeps their beliefs intact. It is possible to be a person who has faith and who is neither fanatical nor ridiculously naïve.

NOTES

1. Ben Ray Redman, *The Portable Voltaire* (New York: Viking, 1949), 560.
2. Charles Wesley, *Hymns Occasioned by the Earthquake, March 8, 1750, to Which Is Added an Hymn upon the Pouring Out of the Seventh Vial, Rev. xvi.xvii Occasioned by the Destruction of Lisbon* (Bristol: E. Farley, 1756), 10.
3. John Wesley, "Serious Thoughts on the Late Earthquake in Lisbon, 1755," 7; quoted in Anne M. Bracket, "Theodicy: Where Would a Just God Be if Not in the Earthquake" (July 15, 2001), online at www.wesleyheritagefoundation.org.
4. Robert G. Ingram, "The Trembling Earth in 'God's Herald': Earthquakes, Religion and Public Life in Britain during the 1750s," in *The Lisbon Earthquake of 1755: Representations and Reactions*, edited by Theodore D. D. Braun and John B. Radner (Oxford: SVEC, 2005), 97–115.
5. On newspaper accounts, see Ana Cristina Araujo, "European Public Opinion and the Lisbon Earthquake," *European Review* 14 (2006), 313–119; and Ana Cristina Araujo, "The Lisbon Earthquake of 1755: Public Distress and Political Propaganda," *e-journal of Portuguese History* 4 (2006), online at www.brown.edu/Departments/Portuguese_Brazilian_Studies/ejph.
6. Early works seeking to distinguish magic and religion include Émile Durkheim, *Elementary Forms of the Religious Life* (Glencoe, IL: Free Press, 1915); James G. Frazer, *The Golden Bough*, 2nd ed. (London: Macmillan, 1900); Bronislaw Malinowski, *Magic, Science, and Religion* (Glencoe, IL: Free Press, 1948); and Edward B. Tylor, *Primitive Culture*, 2nd ed. (New York: Holt, 1889). For example, Durkheim notes similarities between the objects to which petitions are made in magic and in religion, but argues that magic is more utilitarian or technical and thus creates a client-type relationship between the supplicant and the magician, much like that between a patient and a physician, whereas religion binds people together in bonds of solidarity and thus creates a moral community or church. Malinowski argues that magic involves an assumption that nature can be mastered and manipulated,

whereas in religion humans humble themselves before nature and confess their impotence in dealing with it.

7. A brief but insightful overview of the shifting perspectives is found in Dorothy Hammond, "Magic: A Problem in Semantics," *American Anthropologist* 72 (1970), 1349–1356.

8. Patrick B. Mullen, "The Function of Magic Folk Belief among Texas Coastal Fishermen," *Journal of American Folklore* 82 (1969), 214–225.

9. Andrew Singleton, "'Your Faith Has Made You Well': The Role of Storytelling in the Experience of Miraculous Healing," *Review of Religious Research* 43 (2001), 121–138.

10. "Some People Blame God for All Their Troubles," *Texarkana Gazette* (July 16, 2007), online at www.texarkanagazette.com.

11. Max Weber, *The Protestant Ethic and the Spirit of Capitalism* (New York: Charles Scribner, 1958); Max Weber, *Economy and Society* (Berkeley and Los Angeles: University of California Press, 1978).

12. Lisa McMinn, "Y2K, the Apocalypse, and Evangelical Christianity: The Role of Eschatological Belief in Church Responses," *Sociology of Religion* 62 (2001), 205–220.

13. Steven Lukes, "Questions about Power: Lessons from the Louisiana Hurricane," Vilhelm Aubert Memorial Lecture, Institutt for Samfunnsforskning, Oslo, Norway, September 22, 2005; online at understandingkatrina.ssrc.org.

14. Peter L. Berger, *The Sacred Canopy: Elements of a Sociological Theory of Religion* (Garden City, NY: Doubleday, 1967), 79. A more recent essay that emphasizes the collapse of religious theodicies is David Morgan and Iain Wildinson, "The Problem of Suffering and the Sociological Task of Theodicy," *European Journal of Social Theory* 4 (2001), 199–214.

15. Pascal Boyer, *Religion Explained: The Evolutionary Origins of Religious Thought* (New York: Basic Books, 2001), 169–170.

16. Richard J. Bernstein, *The Abuse of Evil: The Corruption of Politics and Religion since 9/11* (Oxford: Polity, 2006), 3.

17. Daniel C. Dennett, *Breaking the Spell: Religion as a Natural Phenomenon* (New York: Penguin, 2006), 102–103.

18. Robin Dunbar, *The Human Story: A New History of Mankind's Evolution* (London: Faber & Faber, 2004), 191.

19. Boyer, *Religion Explained*, 204.

20. Richard Dawkins, *The God Delusion* (Boston: Houghton Mifflin, 2006), 353–360.

21. Charles Y. Glock, Benjamin B. Ringer, and Earl R. Babbie, *To Comfort and to Challenge: A Dilemma of the Contemporary Church* (Berkeley and Los

Angeles: University of California Press, 1967); the survey was conducted in 1952.

22.   Margaret M. Poloma and George H. Gallup Jr., *Varieties of Prayer: A Survey Report* (Philadelphia: Trinity Press International, 1991), 110–115. There were five response categories, with "1" labeled "strongly disagree" and "5" labeled "strongly agree"; 42 percent selected "5," 23 percent "4," 20 percent indicated that they neither agreed nor disagreed by selecting "3," 7 percent selected "2," and 8 percent selected "1." The researchers conceptualized the question as a measure of an extrinsic or instrumental approach to religion, similar to saying that one goes to church to be with friends; however, those who looked to religion for comfort did seem to possess some of the characteristics the researchers expected to be associated more with an intrinsic commitment to faith; for instance, "Those who find religion to be a great comfort to them are more likely to be satisfied with their lives, less likely to respond negatively and more likely to respond positively when injured by another, and more likely to be involved in both national and local politics out of a religious concern."

23.   General Social Survey 2004; electronic data file.

24.   James Davison Hunter, "Subjectivization and the New Evangelical Theodicy," *Journal for the Scientific Study of Religion* 21 (1982), 39–47; the study examined 1,609 evangelical mass-market and trade monographs for themes of psychological balance, emotional maturity, self-actualization, mental health, and related topics; the author concluded that the emphasis on these subjective and emotional topics was perhaps taking the place of more traditional teachings about austerity, personal discipline, and expectations for rewards in heaven.

25.   Kai T. Erikson, *Everything in Its Path: Destruction of Community in the Buffalo Creek Flood* (New York: Simon and Schuster, 1976), 170.

26.   Rowan Williams, Archbishop of Canterbury, "Article on the Asian Tsunami for the Sunday Telegraph—Published 2 January 2005," online at www.archbishopofcanterbury.org.

27.   Chris Hastings, Patrick Hennessy, and Sean Rayment, "Archbishop of Canterbury: This Has Made Me Question God's Existence," *Sunday Telegraph* (January 2, 2005), online at www.telegraph.co.uk.

28.   Rowan Williams, Archbishop of Canterbury, "Statement Issued in Response to Sunday Telegraph Story," January 2, 2005, online at www .archbishopofcanterbury.org.

29.   Tom Utley, "Simple English for the Church of England," *Telegraph* (January 3, 2005), online at www.telegraph.co.uk.

30.   R. Albert Mohler Jr., "First-Person: God & the Tsunami (Part 1)," *Baptist Press* (January 4, 2005), online at www.bpnews.net.

31. "What the Archbishop Really Said," *Sunday Telegraph* Letters (January 9, 2005), online at www.telegraph.co.uk.

32. Andrew Conway, "Rowan Williams in the Telegraph" (January 9, 2005), online at www.thinkinganglicans.org.uk.

33. George Thomas, "Riding the Storm Out: A Tsunami Miracle," *CWNews* (January 28, 2005), online at www.cbn.com/cbnnews.

34. Bay Fang, "Finding God in Tragedy," *U.S. News & World Report* (January 24, 2005), 27.

35. "Tsunami Miracle," *Nova et Vetera* (2005), online at www.snopes.com /religion/tsunami.asp.

36. Donald Sensing, "A Tsunami Miracle? Did God Save 400 Christians of Meulaboh?" *One Hand Clapping* (February 23, 2005), online at www .donaldsensing.com.

37. My analysis of weighted data from the survey (unweighted $N = 752$) data obtained from the Roper Center at the University of Connecticut; Princeton Survey Research Associates, *PSRA/Newsweek Poll #2000-12* (April 13–14, 2000), online at roperweb.ropercenter.uconn.edu. Caution is always advised in polls of this nature, which typically have very poor response rates that are only partly compensated for by weighting procedures.

38. The exact numbers of references to "miracle" or "miracles" from January 1, 1981, through December 31, 2006, in the *New York Times* was 17,608, and 716 of these stories also mentioned "God."

39. *Merriam-Webster Collegiate Dictionary*, 2007 edition, online at www.m-w .com.

40. Marleen de Witte, "Altar Media's *Living Word*: Televised Charismatic Christianity in Ghana," *Journal of Religion in Africa* 33 (2003), 172–202, is particularly helpful in this regard, distinguishing "miracle oriented" and "message oriented" ministries; also of interest is Matthew Engelke, "Discontinuity and the Discourse of Conversion," *Journal of Religion in Africa* 34 (2004), 83–109, which examines references to miracles in stories about conversion.

41. Mohler, "First-Person: God & the Tsunami (Part 1)."

42. Philip Hefner, "Why I Don't Believe in Miracles: A Prominent Theologian with a Love for Science Explores the Contradictions of Faith in Divine Intervention," *Newsweek* (May 1, 2000), 61.

43. Sensing, "A Tsunami Miracle?"

44. Erma J. Lawson and Cecelia Thomas, "Wading in the Waters: Spirituality and Older Black Katrina Survivors," *Journal of Health Care for the Poor and Underserved* 18 (2007), 341–353; the study consisted of qualitative interviews with ten survivors; it is unclear if "miracles" was the word participants used

or was the authors' interpretation of what they said; the two verbatim quotes I have included are the ones the authors report.

45. Kenneth L. Woodward, "Countless Souls Cry Out to God," *Newsweek* (January 3, 2005), online at www.msnbc.msn.com.

46. Dalia Sussman, "Poll: Most Say God Not a Factor in Hurricanes," ABC News (October 2, 2005), online at abcnews.go.com. The report indicated that only 8 percent of the 23 percent who saw hurricanes as deliberate acts of God thought they were divine punishment. The response rate was not reported.

47. Pew Religion Center, *Religion and Public Life Survey* (July 2005), electronic data file downloaded from people-press.org/dataarchive; my analysis of the weighted data. The response rate in this survey was below 20 percent.

48. Erikson, *Everything in Its Path*, 178.

49. An example of an accusation that someone had blamed God to excuse his own inaction occurred on September 17, 2005, when a writer for Salon.com observed that President Bush in a speech the day before had "blamed God" for Hurricane Katrina. "The more pertinent question in this case, however, is not why God allowed bad things to happen but why the government did" (Amy Sullivan, "Blame God, Not Me," September 17, 2005, dir.salon.com). The speech in question was given at the Washington National Cathedral during a National Day of Prayer and Remembrance for the Victims of Hurricane Katrina service. What the president actually said is an interesting illustration of how believers talk about God's role while avoiding saying that they blame God: "God's purposes are sometimes impossible to know here on Earth. Yet even as we're humbled by forces we cannot explain, we take comfort in the knowledge that no one is ever stranded beyond God's care." Office of the Press Secretary, "President's Remarks at National Day of Prayer and Remembrance Service" (September 16, 2005), online at www .whitehouse.gov. As examples of religious leaders arguing against blaming God, see Gregory A. Boyd, *Is God to Blame? Moving beyond Pat Answers to the Problem of Evil* (Downers Grove, IL: InterVarsity Press, 2003); and Mark H. Graeser, *Don't Blame God! A Biblical Answer to the Problem of Evil, Sin, and Suffering* (Indianapolis, IN: Christian Educational Services, 1994).

50. Voltaire, *Candide or Optimism*, translated by Robert M. Adams (New York: Norton, 1966), 41–42.

51. Joep P. M. Schrijvers, *The Way of the Rat: A Survival Guide to Office Politics* (London: Cyan Communications, 2004), as quoted in Sam Leith, "From Rat to Biggest Cheese in the Office," *Daily Telegraph* (July 13, 2004), online at www.telegraph.co.uk.

52. Winston Groom, *Forrest Gump* (New York: Washington Square Press, 2002), and more widely known through the Academy Award–winning film by the same title by director Robert Zemeckis and starring Tom Hanks.

53. General Social Survey conducted in 1998, one of the few nationally representative surveys with a respectable response rate that has included a statement about doubt among the response categories; my analysis of responses among respondents who had college or graduate degrees showed that 57 percent chose an option that read, "I know that God exists and I have no doubts about it"; 16 percent said, "While I have doubts, I feel that I do believe in God"; 2 percent said, "I find myself believing in God some of the time but not at others"; 12 percent said, "I don't believe in a personal God but I do believe in a Higher Power of some kind"; 7 percent responded, "I don't know whether there is a God and I don't believe there is any way to find out"; and 5 percent said, "I don't believe in God"; thus, among those who believed in God (73 percent of the total), 22 percent had doubts and 78 percent did not.

FOUR Heaven Is a Wonderful Place

An atheist named Mark wrote to an advice columnist that his marriage was in jeopardy. His wife, a devout Catholic, was desperately anxious that her husband was going to hell. Should he covert for her sake? The advice columnist said he should. Why not, she wrote. "He knows it's not true. He knows it's all a load of piffle." He could go along with the "whole ludicrous farce" with no fear of divine retribution.[1]

The column generated a flurry of comments. One counseled Mark to tell his wife that a heaven full of believers was his idea of hell. An ex-Catholic turned atheist said Mark should stand his ground. Another reader said no self-respecting man should submit to such wifely oppression. To do so was to sacrifice his freedom.

The exchange appeared in Great Britain, where less than a quarter of the public say they definitely believe that heaven exists. It is not uncommon for comments like, "I'm an atheist, thank God" or "I don't believe in heaven; when you snuff it, you just go" to show up in British news-papers. Things are quite different in the United States. Two-thirds of the American public are sure heaven exists and another fifth say they believe it probably does. Only one person in seven thinks it probably does not.[2]

It is true that better-educated people find it harder than other people apparently do to believe in heaven. In one study, only half of college grad-uates said they definitely believed in heaven, compared with 70 percent of those who only finished high school. Among the college graduates, a quarter thought heaven probably did not exist—twice as many as among high school graduates.[3] Nevertheless, belief in some kind of afterlife remains remarkably popular. Despite the dramatic increases in education and the pervasiveness of a secular culture oriented toward material grati-fication, belief in life after death has held steady over the past half century and by some indications may have even risen slightly.[4]

But what exactly do people mean when they say they believe in heaven? Do they imagine themselves walking on streets of gold wear-ing crowns and strumming harps? Do they turn into guardian angels that pay visits to lovelorn friends on earth, as Hollywood depictions would have it? Is heaven "a land that is fairer than day," as the old hymn intones, where loved ones meet on a beautiful shore? Why do thoughtful people think it is sensible to believe in heaven? Why don't they reject it as a load of piffle? Are they driven by some yearning to escape the reality of their own mortality? How do they talk about heaven that makes it all seem reasonable?

In this chapter I want to look closely at statements about heaven to see how they are constructed and what conventions are evident that may prevent these statements from seeming ludicrous to intelligent people. If we merely assume that rational people find it reasonable to believe in heaven, we make things too simple. Of course, we know from countless polls that people do believe, but the polls tell little about the cognitive frameworks through which these beliefs are maintained. Nobody learns to believe in heaven by being told, "It exists, just believe." The beliefs are interlaced with ways of talking about them, with assertions about why something can be said and about who has the right to say it and in what contexts. My argument is that these familiar ways of speaking about heaven make it reasonable to believe in heaven. Statements about heaven are grounded in references to authority, and they include disclaimers and shifts in register that make it possible to avoid saying more than is credible. Talking about heaven is always a delicate matter in this regard. Like talking about God, it requires making assertions that contrast with known realities and at the same time denying that these contrasts are sufficient. Who can be expected to be in heaven and why are especially tricky questions. They reflect values and imply definitions of in-group solidarity, and when these definitions change, as they seem to be doing at present, new reasons for religious commitment are required.

My argument proceeds as follows: I begin by examining two conventional theories about why people believe in heaven and suggest that the evidence, largely from quantitative studies, shows the inadequacy of these theories and points to the need for a cultural approach. I then describe several ways of thinking about culture and argue that expectations about what it means to be reasonable are one of the important constraints that govern how statements about heaven are framed. Next, I show how statements about heaven reveal claims about authority and then consider the structured contrasts evident in these statements. Finally, I examine claims about who is likely to be in heaven and how the apparent inclusivism of these claims leads to alternative reasons being given for participating in contemporary faith communities. The primary evidence comes from qualitative interviews, supplemented by information from clergy, sermons, surveys, and popular publications.[5]

An explanation that social scientists have long entertained holds that people believe in heaven because doing so is a way to find consolation for the miseries, disappointments, uncertainties, and indeed brevity of ordinary life. Karl Marx wrote at times critically and at other times sympathetically of belief in heaven as a reflection of human oppression and a search for solace in a heartless world.[6] Max Weber described disprivileged classes' attraction to beliefs promising compensation in a world to come. "What they cannot claim to be," he wrote, "they replace by the worth of that which they will one day become, to which they will be called in some future life here or hereafter."[7] Sigmund Freud associated belief in an afterlife with a longing for consolation over the physical or psychological loss of one's mother.[8] William James described the desire to believe that human suffering has immortal significance.[9] G. Stanley Hall theorized that belief in the immortality of the soul arose from fear of death as "a consolation prize, precious because it atoned for the supremest of all calamities."[10]

It makes intuitive sense that hope of a perfect, blissful life after death provides consolation for the struggles that humans endure. At Christian funerals, verses from the gospel of John, chapter 14, are often read in which Jesus is reported to have said, "Let not your heart be troubled. Ye believe in God, believe also in Me. In My Father's house are many mansions." Hymns sung at funerals include such refrains as "Goin' home," "Hallelujah we shall rise," "In the sweet bye and bye," and "Shall we gather at the river." In a study of American religious literature of the nineteenth century, historian Ann Douglas found a preponderance of "consolation" themes focusing on the deathbed scenes of children, emphasizing their parents' faith in heaven, and calling on readers to affirm their own belief in a heavenly kingdom. In many of these stories, the glories of heaven were magnified by the raw grief of the bereaved, and those who suffered most were expected to receive the highest rewards in the afterlife.[11] A study of parents of deceased children in the 1970s found that most took comfort in the belief that their child was now in heaven and that they would be reunited in the hereafter.[12] A study of elderly African American women in a low-income Philadelphia neighborhood found that most expected to be rewarded in heaven for their hardships. "Nobody can make me believe that I am not going to heaven," explained one. "I'm just worthy to be there because of how I got through my life."[13] If life gives the downtrodden and bereaved special reason to believe in heaven, others may well know the miseries and fears that lead to a longing for another world. "In the healthiest and most prosperous existence," William James wrote, "how many links of illness, danger, and disaster are always interposed? Unsuspectedly from the bottom of every fountain of pleasure, as the old poet said, something bitter rises up: a touch of nausea, a falling dead of the delight, a whiff of melancholy, things that sound a knell, for fugitive as they may be, they bring a feeling of coming from a deeper region and often have an appalling convincingness."[14]

The notion that belief in heaven can be understood as a consequence of humans' need for consolation, though, is at best insufficient. If this were all that mattered, one of the clearest pieces of evidence in support of it should be rising levels of belief in heaven and an afterlife as people grow older. Aging means being closer to death and more in need of solace about one's passing. It also greatly increases the chances of experiencing the deaths of one's friends and loved ones—presumably raising the need for consoling thoughts about heaven. Yet this is not what the research shows. In a national survey conducted in 2006, for example, 70 percent of respondents in their twenties said they believed in life after death, rising to 74 percent among respondents in their thirties and 76 percent among those in their forties, but then falling to 75 percent among those in their fifties, 71 percent among those in their sixties, and 69 percent among those in their seventies and eighties.[15] A different way of looking at the data also shows no indication of rising belief as people age. When the question about life after death was asked in the early 1970s, 72 percent of respondents in their thirties said they believed, and when the question was asked thirty years later, the cohort who would have been in their thirties three decades earlier and who were now in their sixties gave almost the same response (70 percent said they believed). The same was true when respondents in their forties in the earlier surveys were compared with respondents in their seventies in the later surveys.[16] Surveys asking about belief in heaven generally show few differences among age groups either. For example, a national survey found that 74 percent of people in their seventies and eighties believed in heaven, which was about the same proportion as among respondents in their twenties (72 percent) and lower than among respondents in their thirties (79 percent).[17]

One of the more imaginative tests of the idea that belief in an afterlife is driven by the desire for consolation was developed by economists Corry Azzi and Ronald G. Ehrenberg in an attempt to account for church attendance using economic assumptions about the value of time. Azzi and Ehrenberg argued that people allocate time and goods among religious and secular commodities to maximize lifetime *and* afterlife utility. They further argued that the sole reason for going to church is to increase one's chances of receiving rewards in heaven, and on this basis predicted that church attendance would increase with age and would be greater among women (whose time, they said, contributed less to attaining secular goods) than among men. Although Azzi and Ehrenberg claimed to find some empirical support for their arguments, other studies largely failed to show that church attendance increases with age, or if it does, cannot be explained by rising belief in an afterlife. Nor has the research confirmed the arguments about gender differences and, not surprisingly, this has led other researchers to question the assumptions about time management and why people participate in religious activities.[18]

Another study that suggests the inadequacy of consolation as an approach to understanding beliefs about heaven was a national survey conducted in 1997 by the Gallup Organization for the Nathan Cummings Foundation and the Fetzer Institute. The study focused on spiritual beliefs and the dying process and asked respondents to say what would give them comfort if they were dying. Some of the results suggested that beliefs about heaven were indeed a source of comfort. For example, 87 percent agreed that the following would give them comfort: "believing that death is not the end but a passage" and "believing you will be in the loving presence of God or a higher power." However, the study also revealed that equally large proportions would find comfort in other ways. More than nine in ten said it would give them comfort "believing you will not become a burden to those who love you," "believing that death is a part of the cycle of life," "believing that part of you will live on through your children and descendants if you have any," and "believing that your love for others and their love for you somehow lives on and never dies." Almost as many said they would find comfort from "believing that you have made your mark on the world" and from "believing that you have done your best for your family or loved ones." In sum, an afterlife was only one of many beliefs that people found consoling.[19]

This conclusion is supported by social psychological experiments in which subjects are exposed to stimuli that heighten awareness of their

own mortality. The findings suggest that a "lay epistemology" is acti-
vated that may include thoughts about immortality, but is much broader
and consists mainly of cognitive processes that impose structure on the
world. Subjects find consolation in articulating their personal values, in
seeing sharper differences between categories of people who share their
values and those who do not, and in insisting that the world is benevolent
and just. Heightened mortality salience invokes numerous other ways of
coping as well, such as affirming one's worth, seeking social support,
and looking for immortality through the lives of one's children.[20] Some
research in natural settings even suggests that heightened concerns
about death lead to rising fertility rates. For example, a detailed examination of birth rates in metropolitan counties in Oklahoma showed clear
evidence of rising fertility after the bombing of the Murrah Building in
Oklahoma City in April 1995. While it may have been comforting in the
tragedy's aftermath to believe in heaven, people were finding additional
ways to respond.[21]

Another study found mixed results when seeking to determine if specific views of heaven were influenced by particular needs for different
kinds of consolation. In keeping with the argument that heaven is imagined to provide what has been lacking on earth, the study did find that
lower-income people were more likely to believe that heaven was a paradise of pleasure and delights than were higher-income people. However,
the study did not find that the number of traumatic events (bereavement, divorce, job loss, hospitalization) people had experienced recently
increased their belief in an afterlife. Nor did it find that the recent death
of a spouse increased the likelihood of believing in an afterlife involving
reunion with loved ones.[22]

Perhaps the greatest quandary left unresolved by the consolation
approach comes from considering cross-national differences in beliefs
about heaven. If belief in heaven arises simply from individuals' need
for consolation, there should be few differences from one country to the
next because everyone experiences this need. Or, if anything, people in
lower-income countries should be somewhat more likely to believe
in heaven than in countries providing more opportunities for fulfillment in the present life. However, neither is the case (see Fig. 4.1). Belief
in heaven varies dramatically, ranging from a high of 77 percent in the

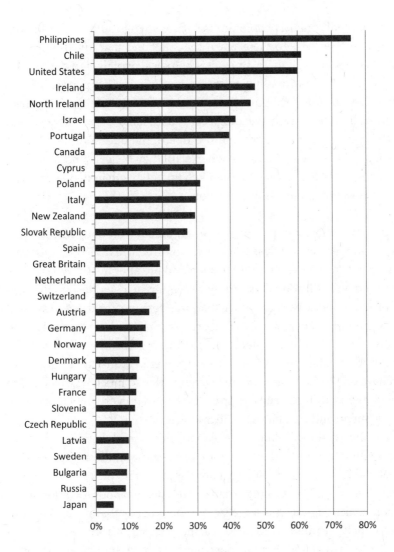

Figure 4.1. Percent of population who definitely believe in heaven.

Philippines to a low of 7 percent in Japan. The United States has one of the highest levels of belief (67 percent), despite its relative affluence. Among other relatively affluent countries, such as Canada, New Zealand, Great Britain, France, Denmark, and Sweden, there are also wide differences in levels of belief.

Undoubtedly many people do find it consoling to think that heaven exists, that they will go there when they die, and that loved ones who have died are already there. But a psychological explanation of this kind goes only so far in providing an understanding of what people believe, who believes, and why. As far as better-educated people are concerned, it may be that they have psychological needs just like everybody else and for this reason believe in heaven. If they do, the question nevertheless remains to be answered about what exactly they believe, and especially why Americans are so much more likely to believe than people in other countries with high levels of education.

As the limitations of psychological arguments become increasingly evident in research studies, scholars have turned to a second approach for understanding beliefs about heaven and life after death. What might be termed an institutional or supply-side approach emphasizes the supply of ideas about heaven rather than the demand for these ideas that might grow out of personal needs. It argues that people believe in heaven mostly because it is in the interest of religious organizations to encourage this belief. This has been an attractive argument because it offers greater purchase on the fact that belief in heaven varies so much from society to society and within societies, despite the fact that everyone faces death, bereavement, and hardships of other kinds.

Like the argument about consolation, this one also makes intuitive sense. Churches and other religious organizations are big promoters of beliefs about heaven, and in many respects they have—or claim to have—a monopoly over authoritative knowledge about the afterlife. In monotheistic religions it is largely from sacred texts that purport to contain divinely inspired words that teachings about heaven derive. These are the texts that religious leaders have claimed special authority to handle, copy, and interpret over the centuries. In the United States and in many other countries, it is common for funerals to be conducted by clergy and for these practitioners to pay hospital visits and make home calls to the bereaved. The supply-side approach further suggests that religious organizations compete with one another, and the ones that offer the clearest assurances of an afterlife will attract the most members. In addition, so the argument goes, religious leaders have a stake in per-suading people that *only faithful members* of their particular organization will go to heaven. That way, people have an incentive to donate time and money to the organization, which in turn makes it possible to pay the clergy's salary, hire missionaries, advertise, and do other things to help the organization grow. The sense of in-group solidarity that results also provides some of the cognitive structure that social psychologists consider important as a hedge against fears of death and other sources of anxiety.

The best evidence that this institutional theory has validity comes from examining the proportions of people in various societies who believe in heaven and comparing them with rates of religious participation in those societies. If it is true that religious organizations promote beliefs about heaven and in turn receive contributions of time and money because of these beliefs, then societies with higher rates of religious participation should also be societies in which more people believe in heaven. This is indeed the case. For example, among the countries listed in figure 4.1, the Philippines, Chile, and the United States rank highest on belief in heaven and they also have the highest percentages who attend religious services nearly every week. Conversely, Japan and Russia are among the lowest on both. Overall, there is a very high statistical correlation among these countries on belief in heaven and religious participation.[23] Of course, the countries included in this list are a small fraction of all countries in the world and have certain biases, such as Russia's history under communism and Japan as one of the few countries from Asia, that might produce these results by virtue of history and tradition more than anything else. However, a larger study that involved surveys with more than 250,000 people in 80 countries also yielded similar results. In this study, where the questions were worded somewhat less precisely, the proportions who said they believed in heaven and the proportions who attended religious services at least once a month also correlated highly.[24]

The notion that religious organizations compete with one another for members by promulgating hopes for an afterlife also finds at least indirect support in some studies. For example, sociologists Andrew Greeley and Michael Hout examined Americans' beliefs in life after death as expressed in national surveys from 1972 to 1998 and were able to estimate changes over a longer period by comparing the views of people in different birth cohorts starting around 1910. They found no change among Protestants and only a slight rise among Catholics, but a dramatic increase in belief in life after death among Jews. They argued that the slight rise among Catholics probably had to do with assimilation among ethnic Catholics and shifts in church teaching, but that the dramatic increase among Jews was evidence that Jews had to compete with Christians by offering otherworldly hope, especially to younger cohorts of Jews. The point was nicely illustrated by a rabbi in Chicago who explained his emphasis on life after death in a funeral sermon to a Catholic priest by asserting, "My people hear about it all the time from your people. So now they expect to hear it from me."[25] The result was consistent with some research among Protestants that, while unconcerned with specific beliefs about heaven, showed that denominations with strict views—ones that presumably limited heavenly rewards to their own members—enjoyed better growth than denominations with less strict views.[26]

This institutional perspective certainly is in need of further research, but its application thus far to beliefs about heaven reveals that it leaves as many questions unanswered as answered. Figure 4.2, which plots data from 80 countries on rates of attendance at religious services and rates of belief that heaven exists, suggests some of what is missing. Despite the fact that countries with higher scores on one have higher scores on the other, the relationship is by no means perfect. On average, the proportions who believe in heaven are considerably higher than the proportions who attend religious services even once a month. If religious organizations are a monopoly force in supplying ideas about heaven, they are not doing a very good job of holding this monopoly. It could be that people believe heaven exists, but do not think they will go there unless they participate in religious services, but, as we shall see later, that is unlikely. A more specific puzzle concerns the points near the left side of the figure and above the diagonal line. One of these is Great Britain, where only 9 percent of those surveyed claim to attend religious services monthly, yet 57 percent believe in heaven. This is a clear example of what British sociologist Grace Davie calls believing without belonging.[27]

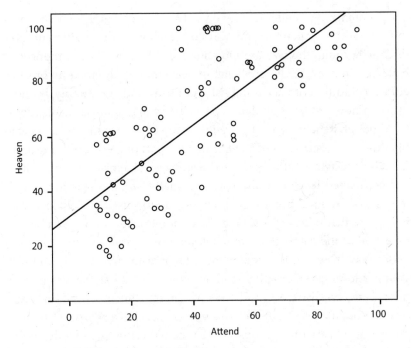

Figure 4.2. Belief in heaven and religious attendance.

Somehow Britons are picking up ideas about heaven without spending much time in church. Other countries exemplifying this pattern include Norway, Iceland, Finland, Taiwan, New Zealand, and Australia. In all of these countries, belief exceeds belonging by a margin of at least two to one. Another puzzle is the cluster of points at the top center of the chart. Almost everyone in these countries believes in heaven, so if the theory about religious competition is correct, these should be highly diverse countries in which religious groups have to compete with one another and thus—like the U.S. Jews in Greeley and Hout's study—encourage more widespread belief in heaven. In reality, these are not pluralistic countries at all. Most of them are monolithically Islamic, including Saudi Arabia, Egypt, Jordan, Morocco, Algeria, Pakistan, Indonesia, and Bangladesh. The one non-Muslim country in this group is Venezuela, which is upwards of 90 percent Roman Catholic. Other puzzles exist as well. For example, religious participation is equally low in Sweden and Denmark, yet belief in heaven is twice as common in Sweden as in Denmark. In Argentina and Mexico, which have quite different rates of church going, the two are indistinguishable in terms of proportions believing in heaven. Clearly belief in heaven is conditioned by broader cultural traditions that distinguish countries and not simply by how much or how little its population participates in religious organizations.

Although it makes sense that religious organizations might compete to offer the best assurances of an afterlife, this part of the supply-side argument is particularly difficult to pin down. The problem is that competition can be defined in almost any way that might suit a researcher's arguments. For example, in the case of Jewish Americans, it could just as well be argued that older Jews saying "Jews don't believe in heaven" was a reflection of the competition they felt between Christians and Jews and was a way in which Jews maintained their distinctiveness. In contrast, younger Jews expressing belief in an afterlife could signal less competition between Christians and Jews. A similar difficulty arises in arguments about the relative attractiveness of conservative or liberal Christian groups. If conservative groups grow, a scholar can argue that they must be championing views about heaven. But if liberal groups grow, a scholar can suggest that they are imitating conservatives. The same ambiguity pertains to the observation that belief in heaven runs high in monolithically Islamic countries. A defender of the competition theory could argue that Muslims' belief is nevertheless conditioned by their sense of competitiveness with the Christian world. The trouble is that competition can be found anywhere it happens to be convenient to find it. Whether it is present or not, the point should be to look at what religious organizations actually teach and how they teach it, not to draw inferences from meager information about percentages and growth rates.

Apart from these questions, the institutional approach runs into several other logical and empirical difficulties. One problem emerges when scholars argue that religious organizations are like entrepreneurs looking to capitalize on new markets. For example, when new religious movements began appearing on the West Coast of the United States and Canada in the 1970s, an explanation was that this was a particularly good niche because church going was low in these areas. But if that is the case, why are there so few aggressive religious groups in Denmark seeking to persuade Danes to believe in heaven? Another difficulty is the view that religious organizations promulgate ideas about heaven that are self-serving in terms of generating resources for those organizations. Yet, as we will see, it is very common for people to believe that everyone goes to heaven, or nearly everyone, and this is true even in countries like the United States, where the institutional argument would suggest that religion is strong because its leaders jealously guard conceptions about who gets into heaven and who does not. It is also the case that religious organizations are not the only sources of ideas about heaven. With as many films and television programs dealing with the topic as there are, one has to question whether religious organizations truly have a monopoly on beliefs about heaven, and if they do, how specifically they maintain this monopoly.

On balance, the institutional approach is most helpful in reminding us that ideas about heaven come from somewhere other than the hearts of individual persons, and are therefore cultural, meaning that they circulate in the wider culture and are reinforced through repetition in social contexts, many of which are religious. Ideas about heaven are produced by religious organizations, but these ideas are also communicated and modified in other venues, such as books, motion pictures, and television. The challenge is to move beyond simple survey questions about the incidence of belief to a more nuanced understanding of what people believe and how they believe it. Religious organizations, I will argue, do have special power when it comes to articulating beliefs about heaven. And yet these beliefs have to be framed in ways that intelligent people find palatable. The ability to do that is key.

Having argued that beliefs about heaven are *cultural* and cannot be understood only in psychological terms as consolation or in institutional terms as the self-interested work of competitive religious leaders, I now have to say more precisely what I mean by cultural. It is true, as critics sometimes argue, that everything is cultural because everything is filtered through our perceptual lenses and language and has meaning only through the interpretations we give it. Trees, money, social classes, physics experiments, babies, footballs, chemicals, smells, sounds are all cultural in this respect, and for this reason it is unhelpful to use the term unless its meaning is further specified. Beliefs about heaven are cultural in the same way that many of these other things are, but these beliefs are also in some ways distinctive. What is most distinctive is that beliefs about heaven only have reality as elements of culture. A football has different meanings in different settings and may be used for different purposes, but it also exists as an object that can be touched, kicked, or thrown no matter what a person's understanding of it may be. Heaven does not exist in the same way. It may exist for the dead in a very tangible way, but for the living, it exists only through the ideas and arguments that have been made about it. Heaven is thoroughly, totally cultural in that respect. In other ways, though, heaven is very much like a football. The meaning of football and the interest in which it is held differs from one society to the next, say, the United States, Great Britain, and Mexico. Its meaning reflects the different cultures of those societies. Beliefs about heaven similarly reflect cultural differences at this level, such as whether a society's culture has been informed by one religion or another or by events that provoked disgust with religion, and by differences in the literacy rates and education levels of societies. One important implication of these broad cultural influences is that beliefs about heaven are likely to be accepted without much questioning as long as these beliefs are part of the society's traditions and as long as people do not feel compelled to make a statement against religion. For instance, in my earlier examples of comments by atheists in British newspapers, disbelief in heaven was a deliberate assertion against the church and against believers. In other cases, it is simply easier for people to say they believe and offer some statement they have heard about heaven or to say they are unsure than to deny believing.

Like football, heaven is cultural in the sense that it is public. People talk about it, read about it, and even see it on television. Of course, they do not see it on television in the same sense that viewers of a football game do. But neither football nor heaven reside entirely in the imagination of a single individual. Both are shaped by public discourse about them. If I had an imaginary friend named Grak that nobody had seen or knew about, that would be different. Confronted with a survey question about whether or not they believed in Grak, people would have no way to respond. Heaven is different. Research among U.S. children shows that by age ten to twelve most have an intense curiosity about the afterlife and many have clear ideas of what heaven may be like.[28] Among adults in the United States, a majority says they have spent a lot of time thinking about what heaven is like and another third have spent some time thinking about it.[29] Younger adults in their twenties and thirties are just as likely to have thought about heaven this much as are older adults in their sixties and seventies.[30] Public conversations about it in the media and among friends influence the likelihood that people will think about heaven and provide them with language in which to think and talk about it. My idea of heaven may differ from yours, but the two ideas will not be totally different. They will have been shaped by songs and sermons we have heard, funerals we have attended, and movies we have seen.

Most relevant to our present concerns is the fact that cultural norms influence what are regarded as acceptable ways of thinking and talking about heaven. Some of these norms involve the metaphors that necessarily come into play when attempting to describe a place or a state of being that is outside the realm of sensory experience. For instance, heaven is usually associated with *up* as a spatial metaphor, more than with down, and a person may feel *uplifted* thinking about heaven, imagine the soul *rising* to heaven, and feeling light or airy. These images are reinforced by common references to the sky as heaven. Other metaphors reflect more specific aspects of the known world. American Plains Indians referred to heaven as the happy hunting ground. Vikings called it Valhalla and imagined a feast of abundant food and drink. Middle-class Americans in the twenty-first century are unlikely to use either of these images.

The cultural norms of particular interest here are norms that prescribe what is acceptable for a reasonable person to think and say about heaven. A reasonable person is not expected to have an airtight logical argument for everything he or she says. Discourse about heaven is different from the norms that are expected to prevail in a courtroom or in a scientific or mathematical paper. Remarks such as "I don't know," "I'd have to think about that," and "my feelings about that" are perfectly acceptable. But a reasonable person is supposed to speak in a way that avoids being branded as a drunk or a fanatic, or being labeled as having the mentality of a small child or someone who is insane. A person who claims to know too much about heaven has to be very careful about what he or she says. A preacher can safely say, "The Book of Revelation gives us a glimpse of what God revealed to John about heaven," but it is quite another thing to say, "I just got back from heaven this morning and it was really swell." Similarly, "I was just talking to Saint Peter yesterday at the pearly gates and he told me" might be part of a joke, but would raise eyebrows if presented as an actual encounter. Subtle differences in phrasing sometimes make all the difference. "It is a city with streets of gold" is less likely to be an acceptable phrasing than "It will be as beautiful as if it were a city with streets of gold."

Talk about heaven can be especially treacherous territory because of its association with death, which, as Peter L. Berger and Thomas Luckmann write, is "the most terrifying threat to the taken-for-granted realities of everyday life." It has to be dealt with, they argue, in a way that gives it meaning in its own right, but that also does not overly burden the assumptions in which day-to-day existence is grounded.[31] A concept of heaven that gives hope of immortality and of rewards or compensation for one's earthly life is a way of satisfying the requirement of giving death meaning. But the added requirement of not challenging the assumptions of ordinary reality must also be met in how death and heaven are described. To say that a person can go back and forth between heaven and this life would especially violate those assumptions. To say that a living person can know very precisely what heaven is like would constitute another such violation.

With these considerations in mind, we can turn to the discourse that people use to express their ideas about heaven and at the same time affirm that they are reasonable persons who think and talk in ways that other reasonable people will understand and accept. To underscore the fact that talk about heaven is part of the shared, public culture in which we live, I will begin with an example from the public domain and after that focus on the less fully public remarks people make about heaven in personal interviews.

On March 7, 2003, a 17-year-old boy in London died after a two-year battle with Hodgkin's lymphoma. He and his family were immigrants from Singapore. At the funeral, where 400 classmates and friends came to pay their respects, mourners spoke of the boy's accomplishments and of their sadness that their prayers for his healing had gone unanswered, as well as of their confidence that he was now with God in heaven. His father recalled the chorus he and his son had sung together during the boy's illness:

Heaven is a wonderful place,
Filled with glory and grace.
I want to see my Saviour's face!
Heaven is a wonderful place.

The words were as vivid in the father's mind and they spoke to him as clearly of heaven as any verses he knew from the Bible. They were words of hope and encouragement to him and his family. That they served in this way is hardly surprising. But these exact words were also part of a shared vocabulary about heaven that was evident in scattered locations all over the world. In Kothara, India, a man in his thirties who had struggled successfully with leprosy only to be diagnosed with cancer was comforted by children he cared for at the leprosy hospital singing his favorite chorus, "Heaven is a wonderful place, filled with glory and grace." In Canada a college student included the same lines in a term paper about heaven. When her grandmother died in Florida, a little girl's parents explained to her that her grandmother had gone to heaven. "Oh," the girl replied, "Heaven is a wonderful place" and proceeded to sing the rest of the song. On the West Coast a young father gave thanks for a new baby and mourned the loss of two others. Sometimes he sings, "Heaven is a wonderful place, filled with . . ." and adds the names of the children he has lost. "My heart is a bit blue . . . longing for that heavenly place where we will be free from the tyranny of time, the pain of separation," a woman in another state writes. Does anyone remember the song, she asks: "Heaven is a wonderful place, filled with glory and grace. I wanna see my Savior's face cause heaven is a wonderful place."[32]

Why would a song like this be so significant that people in such scattered locations would recall the exact words? Clearly it provides consolation. Whenever they may have first learned the song, people remember it and find it comforting as they deal with death, grief, and sadness. But that alone does not tell all of the story. Someone had to produce the song, as the institutional approach reminds us. Unlike so many popular choruses with origins too distant and diverse to trace, this song's history is known. "Heaven Is a Wonderful Place" was composed in 1958 by songwriter O. A. Lambert. By 1971 it was a favorite praise chorus at Calvary Chapel, a nondenominational evangelical church in Costa Mesa, California, founded in the late 1960s by Pastor Chuck Smith. The congregation was an outgrowth of the Jesus Movement then prominent among young people on the West Coast who were dissatisfied with conventional churches. Two years later the chorus appeared in a spiral-bound songbook that eventually sold more than a million copies. In 1980 it appeared on *The Kids Praise Album*, also known as *Kids' Praise! An Explosion of Happiness*, organized by Debby Kerner and Ernie Rettino and produced by Maranatha! Music. The Maranatha label, one of Calvary Chapel's ministries, played an important role in popularizing a new folk-rock style of hymns and worship songs. During the 1980s and 1990s, Calvary Chapel grew to more than 30,000 worshippers at the Costa Mesa site, making it the largest congregation in the United States, and it spun off more than a thousand new congregations at other locations.[33] Thousands of children in these congregations learned the Maranatha songs. The Maranatha label was soon marketed in Christian bookstores and used in Sunday schools and homes across the country. The first *Kids Praise Album* led to other albums with action songs, fun songs, holiday songs, and Sunday school songs, and was part of a growing international enterprise that included original contemporary hymns for all age groups and in several languages.

The institutional history, though, does not illuminate questions about the content of a song's lyrics. What does it mean to say that heaven is a "wonderful place"? Do people in fact think of it as a *place*, whether they know the song or not? Other than the fact that it rhymes, why does the song say that this place is "filled with glory and grace"? Would children have any idea what those words meant? And what about wanting to "see my Saviour's face"? Is it possible for a reasonable person to sing these words and take them seriously? Does it matter if adults recall that the words are part of a children's song? Are they in some way metaphoric, just as lyrics about sweet chariots and gathering at the river may be?

Consider the response of an information technology developer who attends a large evangelical church in Texas when asked what he believes about heaven. "Heaven is a wonderful place, filled with glory and grace." He laughs and the interviewer, who knows the origin of the quote, also laughs. As the interviewer starts to ask for more, the man interrupts, "I guess many mansions. I guess it'll be a happy place and everyone will be God-centric and there will be no crime or hate." He adds, "I understand there won't be marriage," and concludes with a sigh.

As this example suggests, beliefs about heaven involve implicit assertions about the authority that gives one the right to make particular assertions about the topic. Unlike assertions about feeling God's presence, few people regard it as reasonable to make assertions about heaven based on personal experience. Being outside the realm of what they or any of their personal acquaintances have experienced, heaven necessitates other claims. These claims, I shall suggest, reinforce the authority of religious institutions. Quoting from a song that he probably learned in Sunday school and that the interviewer recognizes as a religious song is one way in which this man resorts to religious authority. Quoting the biblical phrase, many mansions, further references religious authority. Although he does not say where his understanding about no marriage in heaven comes from, it is telling that he says "I understand," rather than simply asserting, "There won't be marriage." But to see more clearly how assertions about heaven and implicit references to authority are connected, we need to consider the nature of the question ("what do you believe about heaven?") and what it implies about possible responses. Three aspects of the question are particularly important: the register, the meaning of belief, and the object of belief.

The register of an utterance is the implicit understanding of the speaker about the tone, style, and purpose of what is appropriate to say. Examples include joking, in which something funny or ironic is intended; greetings, in which brief, positive acknowledgment of another person is expected; storytelling, in which a true or fictional set

of utterances follows a narrative pattern of beginning, middle, and ending; and professional speech, in which formal, technical language of the
kind that might characterize a physician's office or scientist's laboratory is used. The appropriate register is a composite of considerations
about the speaker, addressee, their relation, bystanders or other implied
audiences, setting, and frame. The speaker can assume various roles,
such as friend, parent, knowledgeable person, seeker of information,
and supplier of reassurance. The addressee may be a friend, knowledgeable person, person lacking knowledge, and so on. Their relation may
be more or less intimate, more or less equal, and more or less consensual
or characterized by conflict. Bystanders and other possible audiences
include, for example, someone literally sitting within earshot in a restaurant and whose presence may have a monitoring effect on what is
said, or a range of potential or implied listeners, such as additional readers of a written statement (for instance, a will) or the mental presence
of one's reference group, one's mother, or God. The setting is the literal
context in which an exchange takes place, such as in a restaurant, at a
party, in a doctor's office, or by telephone. The frame is the cognitive
or substantive setting that has been established by previous utterances,
such as a discussion of laboratory results preceding a doctor's render-
ing of a diagnosis or words of condolence preceding a question about a
person's emotional state.[34]

The range of appropriate responses to the question about what one
believes about heaven differs considerably depending on the register
involved. A few examples illustrate the range of possibilities. A distraught
child asks a dying parent, what do you believe about heaven? A therapist
asks a client troubled with anxiety about illness and death, what do you
believe about heaven? A guest preacher starts a sermon by asking the congregation, what do you believe about heaven? A journalist asks a famous
writer, what do you believe about God? The same person might be the
dying parent, the therapist's client, a guest preacher, or a famous writer.
The responses would probably differ in length, tone, and content.

The register established in a research interview encourages responses
that are thoughtful, truthful, and personal, while implicitly discouraging
utterances that require intimate knowledge of the speaker or that are

overly self-disclosing or emotional. What a person believes about heaven elicits a response that is arguably less strategic than a dying parent might give a grieving loved one and less candid or emotional than a therapist's client might give. It entails none of the assumptions about knowledge that a sermon does and differs from that of a famous writer in being given anonymously. The response is the kind of statement given to a stranger who is interested in knowing what one has to say. That register encourages utterances that not only say something about the topic at hand, but also demonstrate that a person takes the question seriously, has either thought about it or is willing to think about it on the spot, is able to concede that he or she has not thought about the topic or is uninterested in it, and is stating something that he or she sincerely believes and that reflects his or her experiences and outlook.

The key word in the question is *believe*. Belief implies a lack of certainty. If I know what happened, I do not have to say that I believe something happened; that language applies only if I am unsure what happened. Research among journalists shows that questions are usually framed to elicit answers that can be characterized either as information or as belief. For example, a broadcast journalist who says, "We have Mr. Jones here, an eyewitness to the accident. Mr. Jones, tell us what you saw," is clearly framing the interviewee's response as one of information. In contrast, "Mrs. Smith, based on what you've heard, do you believe the accused is guilty?" asks the interviewee to render an opinion.[35] In certain registers, belief can further be distinguished from opinion. A salesclerk who holds up a blue shirt and a green shirt and asks, "Which one do you like best?" is asking for an opinion. The response could imply that the person's favorite color since childhood is blue, but is just as likely to mean "at this moment" and it depends on how I feel, and could be different in ten minutes. A belief carries more weight. Beliefs are supposed to involve conviction, meaning that a person has thought about them and could give a reason if asked. This is especially the case when beliefs carry value judgments. "I believe candidate X is best for the country" differs in this respect from "I believe candidate X will win."

"What do you believe about heaven?" is a question about something a person presumably has thought about and holds some conviction on. It is not a question about knowledge ("Do you know if heaven exists?") and indeed assumes that knowledge is lacking. An appropriate response can express uncertainty and indicate that one's belief has changed ("I used to believe in heaven, but now I don't"), but unlike in the store clerk example it would be unusual to give a response that seems completely unstable ("Oh, actually, I like the green one better"). Beliefs about heaven may be idiosyncratic, but we expect them to reflect something about a person's thoughts and outlook on life. One empirical indication that this is a reasonable expectation, as I mentioned earlier, is that when asked in a survey if they had tried to imagine what heaven is like, a large share of the U.S. public said they had.[36] In addition, most surveys that ask people whether they do or do not believe in heaven find that relatively few say they don't know and that from survey to survey and from year to year the percentages who say they do believe are fairly stable.

The other key word in the question is *heaven*. The ability to ask about heaven and the nature of the response depend on the degree of cultural proximity between the questioner and the addressee. Clearly, the word has to be part of their shared vocabulary; in addition, cultural distance is likely to evoke a response that reflects that distance. For example, a Muslim or Hindu interviewed in the United States may respond, "We Muslims [or we Hindus] believe such and such," whereas in the example of the evangelical man from Texas, it was possible for him to refer implicitly to religious texts that he imagined the interviewer would understand.[37] The most distinctive aspect of *heaven* is that it has not been experienced by living humans. The assumption that this is the case shapes the range of appropriate responses. "What do you believe about ice cream," as a contrasting example, can legitimately yield responses such as "I've tried it and I like it," "Chocolate is better than vanilla," or "My doctor says I shouldn't eat it." "What do you believe about heaven?" is more like "What do you believe about life in other galaxies?" Personal experience cannot be part of the response. Heaven, though, has the additional feature of being of greater personal relevance. The question is more likely to elicit a thoughtful response because it connects with thoughts of a person's mortality than the question about life in other galaxies does.

These considerations bring us to the question of authority. If belief implies conviction, some reason for that conviction is necessary. An interlocutor might ask, "Why do you believe that?" In the absence of direct questioning, addressees may also feel that they need to supply a reason. They cannot say "heaven is this way because I've experienced it." They can, however, resort to personal experience as a metaphor; for instance, "Heaven must be like being in love." Still, the lack of direct personal experience suggests that authorities other than oneself are likely to be mentioned. An acquaintance who claims to have had a near-death experience and visited heaven might be cited as an authoritative source. A respected figure, such as a scientist or musician, who believes in heaven is another possibility. Yet another, of course, is religion, especially sacred texts and authoritative interpreters of those texts.

Questions about heaven are perhaps uniquely suited to reinforce the authority of religious institutions. This is likely not only in the trivial sense that heaven has more to do with religion than, for example, building bridges does, but also in comparison with other religious topics. A person can argue that prayers are answered, for instance, from personal experience, whereas heaven's existence cannot be. Miracles, angels, ghosts, and God's love can similarly be defended on grounds of personal experience. The authority of religious institutions to make claims about experiences with these supernatural beings, in contrast, is constrained. The reason is that claims about divine intervention allow for humans to have opinions and to disagree. Claims about heaven are almost entirely about a supernatural realm that does not intervene into the human realm. The exceptions are instances of humans claiming to have died and come back to life. Those claims are rare and, as we shall see, are often discounted by believers as reasons to believe in heaven.

It might be argued, of course, that popular culture, such as movies, television shows, books, and music, would be the leading source of authority for talking about heaven. Dozens of movies, including the 1977 box office hit *Oh, God!* starring George Burns and the 1978 film *Heaven Can Wait* starring Warren Beatty and Julie Christie, have focused on heaven, and countless movies and television shows include funeral scenes in which something is said about the departed's continuing existence. Historian

Leigh Schmidt argues that popular culture has long shaped educated Americans' views about spirit worlds, and sociologist Courtney Bender reports evidence from interviews in the Boston area that people piece together novel ideas about reincarnation from metaphysical writings, spiritualists, inspirational fiction, therapeutic and healing practices, and discussions with friends.[38] The opportunities that once made it possible for educated elites to ponder Emerson's ideas about heaven are clearly much wider for a population that can tune in Oprah any weekday afternoon. At the same time, as historian of religion Stephen Prothero has argued, religious illiteracy appears to be rampant in the United States.[39] If few Americans can name the four gospels or recall who Abraham was, they may not know much about the Bible's references to heaven, either. And if that is the case, their ideas may indeed be shaped mostly by what they see at the theater and on television.

Among my interviewees, though, only a few said their ideas came from these popular sources. A saleswoman, age 24, who attends a black Baptist church in Florida, was one of the few. She says that "through movies and stuff" she thinks of heaven as "just the last place you are, where you meet with God." The fact that people seldom mention a movie or television show does not mean that these media have no influence on their ideas about heaven. The "wonderful place" children sing about may conjure up images of beautiful Hollywood types dressed in white and helping themselves to plates of cake and ice cream. However, what scholars of speech registers find in other contexts undoubtedly applies here as well. Fictional representations of heaven do not claim to be factual accounts, any more than jokes about St. Peter and the pearly gates do. A reasonable person who acknowledged thinking of heaven like the one depicted in *All Dogs Go to Heaven* or *The Littlest Angel* would at least have to admit something like "I would like to imagine heaven is the way it was described in the movie. . . ."

In these interviews, a few people nominated themselves as the authority for their views about heaven. This, too, is probably not surprising, given what we know about contemporary culture's emphasis on individual tastes and opinions. For example, one woman described heaven as a place of light and warmth. She said it was definitely this way because a speaker she had heard recently had been dead for ten minutes and had described it this way when he came back to life. She apparently realized that she sounded unreasonable because she went on to explain that she believed the man because he had been recommended by people she trusted and because he was now devoting his life to charitable causes. Yet this account was highly unusual. It was more likely for someone simply to assert his or her authority for speaking about heaven.

One of the clearest examples comes from a woman in her early sixties who works as a teacher and attends a Catholic church in Kentucky. She has strong opinions on a wide range of issues, asserting that she has "read and studied" about one issue or another, that a topic makes her angry, or that a certain view on yet another issue is "absolutely right." Her views about heaven are no different. "I believe in heaven," she says. "I believe strongly that the things that we do here, the things we don't do here, will affect us in the future, meaning for eternity." She mentions hell, saying, "I really believe we send ourselves there by knowing what our call is and then not following it." She explains her view that heaven will include things that have brought joy on earth by saying, "because I believe God is so loving." She concludes that what she thinks is the "gospel according to [her name]." Some of this is just her manner of speaking, but it is instructive that referencing one's own opinions as the source of authority seems to require a particular manner of speaking. One is the use of what scholars of language call intensifiers, such as saying I *really* believe or believe *strongly*. Intensifiers are degree words, such as absolutely, completely, extremely, perfectly, and terribly. A study of intensifiers in television programs suggests that *really* is one of the most popular intensifiers. Its usage appears to help capture the listener's attention and asserts the speaker's authority, confidence, or originality.[40] The other speech device that this speaker employs is reflexivity. By referring to herself (gospel according to me), she at once underscores her authority as the speaker and takes some of the edge off the assertion by deliberately overstating it (she and the interviewer laugh when she says this).

By far the most common source of authority for assertions about heaven is the Bible. People reference the Bible directly and in other instances do so indirectly by quoting from it. An elderly woman who attends a Baptist church in New Jersey says, "All I can say is I just believe what the Bible says, that there is a heaven and some of us will go and there is a hell and some of us will go there." Apparently sensing the need to defend her statement, she adds, "That's what my belief is based on." A Lutheran teacher in Minnesota offers a similar view. "It's in the Bible somewhere that we'll be going to heaven if we believe in Jesus Christ as our savior, and that's what I believe." A college professor who attends an evangelical Protestant church in Oregon appeals even more strongly to the Bible. "Heaven as described in the Bible," he says, "is the place where God himself dwells, and God dwells there with what the Bible calls his saints." After a brief explanation of the Bible's understanding of saints, he continues, "When the Bible describes what heaven is like, it uses words that in our vocabulary bring about a sense of brilliance and radiance and warmth and love and joy."[41]

Without referring specifically to the Bible, others point to it by paraphrasing something Jesus said in the gospels or that Paul or John said elsewhere in the New Testament. The phrasing leaves no question that the source of authority is not the interviewee but someone with divine knowledge. For example, the college professor in Oregon says the Apostle John had a vision of heaven as recorded in the Book of Revelation and, as if John's own apostolic authority might not be enough, explains that "Jesus gives him the revelation." A financial services administrator who goes to a Catholic church in Ohio says, "Jesus said from the cross, he told the other one there, 'You will be in heaven with me.'" A teacher in California who attends a Presbyterian church also cites Jesus as her authority. "Jesus says he'll go and prepare a place there, if it wasn't so I would have told you." She says, "That kind of thing makes me feel that it's real and he's assuring us of that."

In other cases, people do not refer to the Bible by name, but insert words into their responses that are recognizably from the Bible and sufficiently different from normal speech that they might as well have quotation marks around them. For example, a man who attends an evangelical church in Pennsylvania says, "They say in heaven there won't be any crying or pain." An engineer in Kansas says that heaven is "where believers who are sanctified by the blood of Christ" go when they die.

An architect in Illinois asserts that "God is preparing a home where we'll live with him in eternity."

The other authorities cited are usually clergy or religious writers and in some cases more general references to the church. These are mentioned infrequently, but along with the Bible they suggest that organized religion is of considerable importance in shaping opinions about heaven. An Episcopalian who works as a sales representative in Tennessee mentions C. S. Lewis's *Through the Shadowlands* as a book that has given him "glimpses" into what heaven may be like.[42] An attorney in Kansas says his views have been shaped by reading Randy Alcorn's *Heaven*, a bestseller that has been especially popular in evangelical churches.[43] A Presbyterian woman references something her pastor has said about heaven. A lobbyist who attends a Catholic church on the West Coast says heaven "is going to be great," adding that she believes "the Roman Catholic teaching about purgatory" and has read some of the saints' visions of heaven. Another Catholic mentions a "wonderful mission by a priest" at her church who taught that "heaven is where God is and everybody is praising him all the time."

The disclaimers usually take the form of saying that the person—or humans in general—lacks knowledge or understanding or the capacity to describe what heaven is like, despite what the Bible says about it. A journalist in her late thirties who attends a Disciples of Christ church in Colorado puts it this say: "I don't think our brains, I don't think our spirits are capable at really fathoming and grasping a joy and a peace of that magnitude." She is sure heaven exists and she thinks of the description of it in the Book of Revelation, but says it is "hard to imagine" what heaven is really like. A doctor who attends a Mennonite church in Idaho makes almost the same point. "There are depictions in the Bible of incredible beauty and jewels and streets of gold," he says, "but heaven is going to blow us all out of the water because we really have no concept of what it is." Statements like these are different from ones by people who are unsure that heaven exists and doubtful that the biblical descriptions should be taken very seriously. Here, the Bible is still an authoritative source. The point is just that reasonable people understand that heaven is beyond human comprehension. A member of an independent Bible church in Alabama puts it well. "Heaven is a real place," he says, "a place where God is going to be and where we are going to be able to see God face to face." But he adds, "I'm not sure exactly what that is going to be like because we don't understand God very well. I have a hard time thinking we will ever be able to understand God completely because God is so big and we are finite."

On balance, the evidence suggests that heaven is a topic that necessitates an implicit acknowledgment of incomplete information and thus a way of demonstrating that some authoritative source exists for the beliefs one may have about it. In this respect, asking someone what they believe about heaven is like asking what they believe about the theory of relativity. If anything, they would probably say they have no direct knowledge of how it works, but know that Albert Einstein proved that relativity exists. Perhaps they would add that the theory is elegant or a good idea. The need to cite an authority when talking about heaven introduces a bias toward granting authority to the Bible and to other religious sources. People who might be inclined to doubt that everything in the Bible is literally true have no difficulty referencing the Bible as the authoritative source for their beliefs about heaven. It exists because the Bible says it does.

It stands to reason that people would invoke religious authority when talking about heaven, but religious organizations do not automatically exercise control over discourse about heaven. Because it is not used as an invective, "heaven" does not show up in the same range of speech situations that "hell" does, but it is nevertheless a word that appears in many settings that have nothing to do with religion. "Heavenly hash," "heavens to Betsy," and "for heaven's sake" are just a few of the phrases that give other meanings to the word. It appears frequently in newspapers and on television, sometimes with religious connotations, but often in phrases such as "a match made in heaven," "heaven help us," "a little piece of heaven," "heaven forbid," "the heavens above," and "thank heaven."[44] Talk about heaven, though, is different from talk about *beliefs* about heaven, which, as I have suggested, implicitly pose the question of whether or not heaven exists and thus necessitate some authority for one's beliefs. Religious organizations establish a register in which serious talk, as opposed to casual references, about heaven occurs. What a person learns about heaven through a sermon or in a Bible study group is to be taken seriously. Chances are, it would be slightly irreverent in many congregations to say "heavens to Betsy."[45]

The significant extent to which people reference the Bible in making statements about heaven is more surprising than might at first be assumed. In qualitative interviews about a wide range of topics, the Bible seldom comes up unless asked about specifically. Faithful church goers can talk about God, their reasons for going to church, and what they pray about without ever mentioning the Bible. But a question about heaven seems instantly to turn people's thoughts toward something they have heard from or read in the Bible. Perhaps Jesus' statement about his father's house having many mansions stuck in their memory from hearing it at a funeral, or perhaps they heard an especially gripping sermon about the Book of Revelation. They would probably be unable to recall if it was a sermon, a hymn, or a children's chorus. What their words do reveal is that the exact details of what the Bible says about heaven are less important than the fact that it has persuaded them that heaven exists. They can entertain images of beautiful mansions and streets of gold knowing that their minds do not fully comprehend what heaven is like. The images are meant only to suggest that heaven is a wonderful place.

Disclaimers notwithstanding, people have vivid imaginations about what heaven may be like. Indeed, the disclaimers free the imagination. Acknowledging that even the biblical depictions of heaven are inadequate, people invent their own ideas of what a truly wonderful place might be like. In some instances, their imaginations are playfully creative. For example, a business manager who attends an evangelical church in Wisconsin says he hopes heaven has eternal football games and a coffee stand on every corner. But in most cases, the imagination roams less freely. Thoughts about what heaven is like are constrained by culture. A reasonable person can say some things about heaven and not others. Being a person of faith who is also thoughtful and who entertains reasonable doubts requires conforming to these cultural expectations.

Talking about heaven is in many ways similar to talking about God. This is especially so for people, like the man from Alabama, who think of heaven first and foremost as the place where God lives and where they will see God. Just as they do when they pray to God, people imagine what heaven is like by contrasting it with the reality they experience in this life. To show that God is big and powerful, it helps to think about someone praying who is small and weak. Similarly, a person who is old and wrinkled may think of heaven, as one woman did, as a place where people will look young and beautiful, or where they have full heads of hair, as a bald man did. But it is important to be careful in how these remarks are interpreted. A weak person who prays may expect a powerful supernatural being to cross into the natural realm and perform magic to make him or her feel strong. However, close consideration of what people actually say about prayer suggests otherwise. They hope that God will be present or will give wisdom to their doctor or help them realize their own potential.[46] The same is true of remarks about heaven. The point is not that a bald person will really have hair when he gets to heaven. That interpretation leads to the simplistic and, as we have seen, empirically unsupported argument that supply-siders make about heaven being a literal compensation for what people lack on earth. The more credible interpretation is that humans struggle to describe something that they have not experienced and that they believe to be very different from anything they can describe. To accomplish this task reasonably, they do one of two things: They identify some of the things they do not like about their known reality and assert that heaven will not be like that, or they describe some things that are truly wonderful and say that heaven will be even better.

Biblical descriptions of heaven establish the pattern for contrasts with undesirable aspects of human life. "There will be no more death or sorrow or crying or pain, for the old world and its evils are gone forever," the Apostle John declares.[47] Describing heaven as the absence of negatives is a good rhetorical device. Such descriptions can be made without searching for additional words to say what heaven *is*. That which is known to be negative implies that a place without them is better. Death, sorrow, crying, and pain serve well because they are experienced universally. Mention of them occurs frequently in interviewees' remarks. A homemaker who attends an independent Bible church in Illinois refers to "Scripture" and explains, "I don't know what it is going to look like, but I know there will be no more sin and no more tears and no more death and no more night." A man who is still in his thirties and works in construction observes, "Our bodies decay, we get older, and you feel your aches and pains. We'll have new heavenly bodies." A college professor in Ohio says that heaven is a place where people will not "live in dehumanizing, grinding poverty." The head of a nonprofit organization in California observes, "There will be no need for policemen or ambulance drivers, no need for insurance policies or firemen."

Language that describes heaven as more wonderful than the best aspects of lived experience are not as common as the ones I have just mentioned. Perhaps this is because heaven does not come as readily to mind when people are thinking about sex, ice cream, new cars, and nice vacations. As an old Loretta Lynn song observes, "Everybody wants to go to heaven, but nobody wants to die," to which might be added, especially when things are going well. However, people do include some of the pleasures of life among remarks suggesting that heaven will be even better. The joys of love and companionship come especially to mind. A Presbyterian who works as a speech pathologist in Connecticut says it annoys her to think that heaven is a place with streets of gold; she prefers to think of it as not involving space or time but where "everyone loves each other and you're with everyone you ever loved." A waitress in New Hampshire says it will be like "a big ol' party" with everyone you know. Others search for the right words to express the idea that heaven is indescribably wonderful. "Oh, what do I believe about heaven?" a school teacher in Indiana muses. "I believe that we don't have a clue about what it is. Our minds cannot possibly wrap around this, the thought of eternity, the thought of how wonderful it might be, and what it will be like just to be in the presence of God. You know, we try to take the things that we know on earth as the very best things we can think of and say, well that's what heaven is like." A secretary who belongs to a Catholic parish in Ohio says she has been thinking about heaven lately and finds it pleasant to imagine all her loved ones there, but she also believes heaven will be better than that. The picture in her mind is one of "pure light, because God is so much more awesome than anything we could possibly imagine. We will just be absorbed in that pure light."

Among the contrasts that people employ when talking about heaven there are some mixed signals. A person of faith can look forward to heaven, but a reasonable person cannot appear overly confident about his or her knowledge of heaven or seem too eager to get there. Reflexive language occurs frequently. A person makes an assertion about heaven and then follows this assertion with a comment about what he or she has just said. The Indiana school teacher's language is a good example. Starting with "what do I believe about heaven" shows that she is thinking about what she thinks, and then after saying what she thinks, she remarks, "There's just no way that our earthly minds can even begin to wrap around it. If you start thinking about it, it kind of gives you a headache." A military officer who is a member of an evangelical church in Oklahoma provides another example. He says, "The Bible talks about we'll have mansions and streets paved with gold." He adds, "I don't know whether I'll actually be walking down a street of gold or whether that's just talking about a figurative way of doing it." His language communicates that he takes the Bible seriously, but also that he thinks about what the Bible may mean and imagines different interpretations. The language a business manager in Colorado who belongs to a Presbyterian congregation uses is similarly reflexive. He says being with God in heaven is like driving to the Grand Canyon. The closer you get, the more you realize there is a big gap. He feels close to God now, but there is a huge gap between that and actually being with God in heaven. Then, showing that the analogy does not quite satisfy him, he says, "This is probably not a good image."

A way to communicate one's hesitancy about going too quickly to heaven is to express some misgivings about how wonderful it may be. The man I mentioned earlier who regrets thinking there will be no marriage in heaven is an example. Although he believes he will recognize his wife in heaven, it bothers him to imagine no longer being married to her. The Indiana school teacher says, on the one hand, she is "kind of excited to see what it might be like," but, on the other hand, "I'm gonna be bored." A business manager in Pennsylvania looks forward to heaven as a place of "peace," but worries about "how productive I'll be." An office assistant who attends an evangelical church in Illinois is more explicit about the trade-off between this life and the next. "While we do not desire to die and be in heaven," she ventures, "we should certainly look forward to it." She elaborates, "God gave us this life to enjoy and to live, so we should be living it to the fullest, not just sitting in anxious anticipation, on the one hand, but, on the other hand, looking forward to it as a time when we will be with him."

Besides the explicit contrasts involved, talk about heaven often includes shifts of register that communicate implicit messages about the speaker's orientation to the topic. Shifts of register are utterances that are out of place. A doctor who informs a patient that a new medicine may result in "gas" or "passing gas," and then says, "but let me know if you start farting a lot" is shifting the register from the professional medical speech expected in a doctor's office to colloquial speech more common in other settings. A doctor who pronounces a patient dead and then quips to another doctor, "We sent him on to the eternity unit," also illustrates a register shift. A register shift in talk about heaven is nicely illustrated by a Lutheran woman in Minnesota who describes heaven as a spiritual place, as stated in the Bible, where people who believe in Jesus Christ go when they die, and then quips, "I hope it's a really cool place." Cool place is a description a person might give to a bar or a dance club. It is so deliberately colloquial that it is jarring in the context of talk about heaven.

Register shifts are especially evident in interviews with couples. Unlike solo interviews, the couple interviewees listen to each other, pick up on what the other has said, and sometimes deliberately insert a comment that changes the tone of the conversation. For example, a couple who attend an evangelical church in Kansas talk at some length about their very specific beliefs about heaven. The husband says heaven is "where God resides" and "where believers who are sanctified by the blood of Christ" go when they die, adding that believers "live in heaven for eternity with God, Jesus, and other believers." The wife explains that "there is no sin" in heaven, that "things are perfect," and that "it is a beautiful place." Both believe they will meet their loved ones in heaven as long as those loved ones are believers. The wife says she believes she will "know people and recognize people" in heaven. At that point, the husband remarks, "A lot of name tags." He and his wife and the interviewer chuckle.

Shifts of register break the spell. A teacher who ends a stern lecture about getting homework in on time by saying, "And if you don't, I'm going to tie you down and beat the pulp out of you," deliberately inserts a remark that eases the tension. In a serious discussion about people dying and going to be with God, shifts of register are a way to inject humor. By encouraging people to laugh, the shifts change the tone. The absurdity of name tags in heaven suggests by contrast that the more serious part of the conversation has in fact been serious. The remark works in the same way that "No, seriously" after a joke underscores that the previous utterance actually was not serious. The concrete this-worldliness of name tags reinforces that speakers' argument that heaven is actually not concrete or human at all, but spiritual and divine. In addition, the shift accomplished by introducing something clearly out of context communicates that a reasonable person actually does not know what heaven is like and is searching for adequate words. Name tags on heavenly beings who are spirits and who do not have bodies but who somehow recognize one another says, in effect, that the speaker is pointing to something that cannot be described.

Of course, people vary in how confident they are about their views of heaven. The ones who quote the Gospels and the Book of Revelation are often quite certain that heaven exists and have no doubt that they will be there when they die. But the message that comes through more clearly is how even people who believe definitely in heaven feel compelled to express their uncertainty about what it is. Phrases like "hard to fathom," "an unknown place," "not clear," "hard to imagine," and "a total mystery" frequent their comments. Interviewees say the topic is "tough," "difficult," "hard." A man in his sixties who works as an engineer and has attended a Baptist church all his life puts it this way: "I believe there is a place where people go when they die," but he says his training as a scientist and his interest in reading science fiction have left him imagining heaven in different and sometimes conflicting ways. A doctor who attends an independent evangelical church expresses a similar view: "I believe it's a definite place. Whether it is on earth with all evil gone, I don't know. Or whether it's a place in the sky or another planet, I don't know. And I don't have to know. I think it could be any one of those things—a wonderful place on earth, above the earth, or on another planet." His remark that he does not have to know is especially significant. The details about heaven will be known soon enough, he feels as he approaches his eightieth birthday. Meanwhile, the idea that heaven is a wonderful place is sufficient.

If reasonable people are reluctant to say much about what heaven is like, does the same reticence apply to thoughts about who they will see in heaven? "I'm just a poor wayfarin' stranger," the old hymn intones, "there's no sickness, toil, nor sorrow/in that bright world to which I go/I'm going there to see my father/I'm goin' there no more to roam." Another verse says "I'm going there to see my mother." Jokes about heaven frequently mention someone of a particular sect arriving at the pearly gates expecting to find only fellow members of that sect and being surprised to find people from other groups. The man I mentioned earlier who sings "Heaven is a wonderful place filled with," adding the names of his deceased children, expects to see them when he gets to heaven. It is a comforting thought, imagining being reunited with loved ones in heaven. But do people really believe it? Or does their language betray uncertainty?

It has been common in church circles to hear that only Christians— perhaps even only "born again" Christians—can go to heaven. "I am the way, the truth, and the life; no man cometh unto the Father, but by me," Jesus is reported to have said, as recorded in John 14.6, just a few verses after the words about the father's house having many mansions and not letting one's heart be troubled. For born again Christians, it is often comforting to believe that they are certainly going to heaven, and believing that others are not is sometimes a strong inducement to evangelize friends and neighbors and to encourage faithfulness among children and spouses. If reasonable people are uncertain about other aspects of heaven, though, does their language also introduce latitude into these verities?

Whether loved ones, fellow believers, or others, just who will be in heaven is a matter of social boundaries and thus of values and power. In these respects, heaven may be a wonderful place, but it is also a mechanism of social control. As Max Weber recognized, convictions about what must be done to get into heaven can have powerful effects on aspirations about work and money and on definitions of who is elect and who is not. Communities on earth begin to reflect ideas about communities in heaven. Sharply defined demarcations in one map out distinctions in the other. But do these boundaries weaken when people learn to talk about heaven in more nuanced ways? Or does talk about heaven continue to bear the imprint of such ideas?

The question about seeing loved ones in heaven evokes genuine ambivalence, and the best way to understand the language people use is to see it as a way of expressing ambivalence. The contrary values that underlie this ambivalence are not exactly parallel, as in the proverbial example of the donkey standing equidistant between two bales of hay. It is rather an opposition between an instinctual desire and a sense that this desire is too naïve for a thoughtful person to entertain at face value. On the one hand, loved ones are so precious that to imagine them not being in heaven, or being there and not being recognizable, seems incompatible with images of heaven as a wonderful place. On the other hand, the difficulties people communicate when trying to say what heaven is like do seem to inhibit them from asserting without some backtracking that they definitely anticipate a heavenly family reunion. Because the two conflicting thoughts are not mirror opposites, the language involved is typically more nuanced than simple "yes and no" assertions.

Consider the ambivalence expressed by a business manager who attends a large evangelical church in California. When asked if he believes that people meet their loved ones again in heaven after they die, he says, "I think we do, but I don't know if we know those people specifically." He thinks there will be a "happy feeling" in heaven, but is "not sure it exists the way people think it does." To illustrate, he poses the example of a husband and wife who are married for fifty years, and when one dies, the other marries again. Which of the spouses would be reunited in heaven? "I don't know how to explain it," he says, "I don't know if I'm right or wrong or if it's just my opinion." The best he can come up with, he says, is that heaven will involve the same happy feelings people experience with loved ones, but not the actual relationships with those loved ones.

For this man, the struggle is between wanting to be reunited with loved ones ("wanting to say, yeah, I'm going to be in heaven with my mother, father, sister, brother, lost dog, whatever") and not being able to describe how that might happen. The simplest way in which this ambivalence affects the language people use about heaven is to elevate the meaning of *hope*. Religion is all about hope, but hope has many inflections. "My hope is in the Lord who gave Himself for me" is a hymn Christians sing as an affirmation of complete trust that they are saved. "Hope is here, my friends," a pastor preaches, arguing that hope in Christ is the only sure antidote for depression. The refrain, "Hope is on the way," delivered at a political convention, similarly conveys a message of confidence.[48] In contrast, "I sure hope so," uttered by a school child whose mother asks if he or she passed a test, exudes anything but confidence. The hope people express about seeing their loved ones in heaven falls between these extremes. It isn't that they disbelieve in the possibility of this happening. They want it to happen. But their choice of words also conveys uncertainty.

A doctor who attends a Lutheran church in Virginia puts it this way when asked if he believes people meet their loved ones again in heaven after they die: "I'm hoping." In case his meaning is unclear, he adds, "I don't know, but I'm hoping." A Presbyterian who runs a nonprofit organization in Maryland says, "That's a tough one. I don't know. It is hard for me to say yes or no. At times, maybe I think, yes. Or maybe a more correct answer is, I hope so." A Catholic in Colorado who works as an engineer also says, "I hope so," adding, "Is it necessarily [the case] that we meet them? Let's just say I would like to believe so." In these remarks, hope is a one-word way of saying that it would be very nice to see loved ones again in heaven, but too much for a reasonable person to state with certainty, given the sense that heaven implies a wholly different, unknown reality. Other remarks spell out this ambivalence using different words. For example, a computer scientist says "I'm not clear on that" when asked if he thinks people will meet their loved ones in heaven, and then hastens to explain that he would "desire for all my family and friends to go to heaven." A teacher in Indiana who belongs to a Baptist church says she wants to believe that people meet their loved ones in heaven. "I hope to believe," she says. "I hope that's true. I don't know that it's true."[49]

Another language device that helps express ambivalence about meeting loved ones in heaven is distinguishing between *body* and *spirit*. Millions of Christians regularly recite as part of the Apostles' Creed that they believe in "the resurrection of the body and the life everlasting." But that resurrection is more commonly assumed to occur at the last judgment than when a person dies. Death, in this interpretation, marks the separation of body and spirit. A sales representative who attends a Methodist church in New Jersey illustrates the distinction nicely when he asserts, "I've always believed that the people who have left this life go to eternity and that I will see them when I am in heaven with them." Asked how this might be possible, he says it will be a "spiritual recognition." A college professor who describes himself as an evangelical Christian offers a more expansive explanation. Unlike many of his fellow evangelicals, he believes that everyone goes to heaven, not just born again Christians, and so he thinks it is quite likely that people will meet their loved ones in heaven. But he says he has no idea of how that meeting might take place. The only clue, he explains, is to think about the biblical description of Jesus's resurrected body. There was "some kind of continuity" between his earthly body and his new body, but the resurrected body was spiritual, not physical. "He could walk through doors and appear in multiple places at one time." By implication, it is possible to imagine people meeting their loved ones and at the same time deny knowing how this might occur. "Those things," he says, "are beyond my ability to imagine."

Yet another way of addressing the question about loved ones in heaven is to redefine what matters, specifically to narrow the circle so that all that matters is for the individual speaker to get in, or to broaden it so that it doesn't matter that loved ones are there because they will be subsumed within a larger company of saints. A member of a Baptist church in California puts it this way: "I don't know that heaven is going to be like hanging out with your family on a picnic or something. But I don't worry about that. As my mother used to say, 'I don't care what brings you to the campfire as long as you get warm.' All I want to be is in the right spot and get warm." Exactly what he means is unclear, but it appears that his interest is more in knowing that he will be in heaven than in anticipating seeing his loved ones. A Catholic in Texas thinks the "opportunity" to see loved ones may be available, but "it may be that we don't even care at that point [because] everything else is so good." A man who attends a missionary church in Pennsylvania muses about the question a while and asserts that believers would not see friends who were unbelievers, but apparently sensing that this might be a source of discomfort explains, "I don't think [believers] will be saddened by that because they will be beyond that. That won't be a part of their life. You know what I mean?" A Catholic woman in Kentucky finds herself in similarly difficult terrain as she considers what happiness in heaven will be like. She thinks "seeing the face of God will be our ultimate happiness," which implies that "we [do not] have to have our loved ones in heaven to be truly happy in heaven." Yet, considering that thought incomplete, she ventures, "God is so loving" that it is hard to imagine God denying people the joy of seeing their loved ones again in heaven.

The ambivalence expressed in these remarks is not the kind that stems merely from being confronted with a new thought and having to mull it over. None of these interviewees respond, "Hmm, I've never thought about that before." Indeed, it would be odd if they did, given how common it is for people to muse about being reunited with deceased family members.[50] The ambivalence is better understood as tension between using the known to imagine the unknown and believing that the unknown in this case cannot be described this way. On the one hand, facial recognition and physical gratification are among the earliest and most basic associations humans make with feelings of happiness. Ask someone to say what comes to mind when they think about happiness and the responses nearly always include mental images of loved ones, warmth, comfort, and security. If heaven is a happy place, it is difficult not to associate it with the same images. On the other hand, the very idea of heaven requires placing it in a different mental category. It cannot literally mean sitting under a tree on a beautiful summer day enjoying a picnic with one's family. There is no single way in which people learn to express this ambivalence, but the language of heaven dictates that both meanings must be acknowledged.

A different kind of ambivalence occurs in response to questions about who will be allowed entry to heaven and who will not. For those who take the statement about Jesus being the only way literally, there is little doubt that only Christians will be in heaven. Yet that certainty is tempered by not wishing to appear self-assured or bigoted and by the thought that God surely must have ways that are beyond human comprehension. Others are less convinced that heaven is reserved only for followers of Jesus. These differences of belief are important enough that they have long been sources of division within Christendom, and even at present they influence opinions about immigrants and about other religions, as well as views about what kind of nation America should be.[51] But it is important to look closely at the language used to describe and justify beliefs, whatever they may be. The language reveals how people who consider themselves reasonable affirm certain values and at the same time deny having full knowledge of what happens in heaven. The values can be affirmed explicitly, as in the case of asserting that a person must be born again, or they can be implied, such as mentioning that the good deeds someone performs will have lasting rewards. For heaven to be heaven, though, the language must somehow suggest that it is beyond the known reality of human life.

The question of who gets into heaven can be reformulated as a broader question about passage between two vastly different realities. Passage of this kind is always fraught with danger, as Mary Douglas's writing about the cognitive mapping of sacred and profane in tribal societies has emphasized.[52] A person who can cross the boundary separating one realm from the other has special power. The person may be regarded as a shaman or healer or as a source of great wisdom. Beings who transgress boundaries can also be tricksters or demons. The potential benefits of being blessed by saints and angels who can transcend the line between worlds and the fear of perils associated with ghosts and evil spirits who do the same are among the reasons that entry and exit from other realms have to be carefully patrolled. In Christian traditions, the power to cast out demons is reserved for redeemers and exorcists who also have great power. Some interpretations deny that spirits from the other side can penetrate the human world at all. Saints who live in heaven stay there, even though they may be able somehow to help people on earth. They do not literally return as embodied beings. In the Book of Revelation, an angel guards the gates of the heavenly city to prevent unmonitored entry and exit. In *Paradise Lost* it is Satan, the evil one, who persistently trespasses and destroys sacred boundaries and divisions, whereas God circumscribes and restrains the cosmos and himself.[53] Popular culture in our time often refers to Saint Peter and occasionally to Mary as keepers of the door into heaven. Angels live between heaven and earth, as Robert Orsi has suggested in his book on the topic, but typically do not have the same power to grant or deny entry to heaven.[54] They merely assist in the transport of souls, as the 1860 hymn that has experienced renewed popularity among bluegrass vocalists asserts: "Oh, come angel band . . . bear me away on your snowy wings to my immortal home."[55] In contrast, Jesus, as man and God, serves most powerfully as guardian of the gates of heaven. Jesus is popularly understood to have lived first in heaven, then on earth, then in heaven again, and to be both in heaven with God and in the hearts of ordinary believers, as well as the person believers expect to see when their souls go to heaven. In ordinary language, talk about Jesus is a pivotal location for expressions of ambivalence.[56] Believing in Jesus, following Jesus, and seeing Jesus express something that is cherished, and yet some element of doubt, uncertainty, or novelty is often evident as well. Two examples illustrate the tension.

A teacher who attends a Lutheran church near her home in Minnesota looks forward to seeing Jesus in heaven and yet wonders if being a Christian is necessary for this to happen. "I believe there is a heaven," she says. "I believe I'm going there! I believe that I will see Jesus. I can't wait to see what his face looks like. Honest to God, I just can't wait to see what he really looks like." From these remarks, one might assume that Jesus is the central figure in heaven, who makes sure only people who believe in him get in the door. But she continues: "I don't know, this is

really going out on a limb, but I'm not sure that everybody I'm going to
see in heaven is going to be a Christian." She elaborates: "The older I get,
I just think we all have different ideas of heaven, and I'm just not sure
any more if it is reserved for followers of Christ. I'm not sure." She does
not explain why, but her language suggests that the two thoughts are in
tension. For instance, she refrains from suggesting that non-Christians
will be in heaven because God loves everyone or that there may be
ways to experience the love of Christ without believing that Jesus is
God. Instead, she is simply unsure and her lack of certainty puts her out
on a limb.

A nice contrast is evident in the remarks of a professional musician
who attends an evangelical church in neighboring Wisconsin. He, too,
emphasizes seeing the face of Jesus. "What makes it heaven," he says,
"is that I will finally see the face of the Lord. That is my deepest heart's
cry my entire life." He explains that until about five years ago he did not
believe in God, but then realized there was a "big hole" in his life and
that he was "aching" to be with God. He continues in this vein, mentioning stories in the Bible about Jesus returning to earth and affirming again
that he "can't wait" to be with God. Besides the identity of the church he
attends, the language suggests clearly that he is a conservative Christian.
Yet he stops short of saying that only Christians have a place in heaven.
What he does say is "the Bible says, 'If you are right with God, when
you die you will go to be with him.'" He uses the same language in talking about the possibility of seeing loved ones in heaven. "I believe that
people who are right with God, people who want to do God's will, those
will be the only people in heaven." Were he forced to answer a question
on an opinion poll, he would probably say something about the necessity of believing in Jesus. But this is not his choice of language. Being
"right with God" is harder to define. It is a matter of the heart, something
that only God knows.[57]

It might be argued that subtle uses of language like this do not matter at all—or, from a different perspective, that they are symptomatic of
some deep theological shift in popular understandings of salvation. My
point is rather that the language itself is a mode of adaptation to a culture
in which both faith and reason are widely valued. In these two examples,

Jesus is a central figure. The implication is that belief in Jesus matters a great deal, perhaps even as the key to entry into heaven, although that is not stated explicitly. The centrality of Jesus is literally associated with his face. It is as if the chorus, "Heaven is a wonderful place, I want to see my Saviour's face," is the template. Jesus is not so much a gatekeeper as a celebrity. Being close to him, united with him, fulfilled by him is the reward of being in heaven. Reason enters into the language as an acknowledgment of limited information. A reasonable person cannot know for sure who will be admitted to heaven, or if sure, needs to say something about which he or she is not sure. A person may guess that others besides Christians will be present, but that cannot be said without some misgivings, or it may be that only those who are right with God will gain entry, and what exactly that means may be difficult to know.

The doubts that people express about what exactly heaven is like and who exactly will or will not be there are quite different from doubts that what they have heard about heaven is true. Doubts of the former kind reinforce faith. These expressions of uncertainty are ways for people who think of themselves as thoughtful, intelligent persons to maintain their belief in heaven without seeming to be naïve, overly sure about what they know, or too eager to die. When observers of religion argue that faith and doubt go hand in hand, this is the kind of doubt they generally have in mind. It resembles how a reasonable person might talk about the U.S. Declaration of Independence. A person might have no doubts that it exists, but express doubt that he or she fully understands it, would be able to give one definitive view of what it means, or agree with everything that has been written about it. Doubt of the second kind represents a more complete break with faith, and in a society where faith is so common, can be deeply troubling.

Listen to what a man in his late thirties who has been a Southern Baptist all his life says about heaven: "I used to believe it was a very literal place and you had to believe in Jesus to go there. But in about the last two years it has changed so that now I would have to be honest and say I don't know that there is a literal heaven. I'm just not sure about that." When asked what his thoughts about heaven are, he repeats, "I just don't know that it really exists," and says, "I don't know what happens after we die." He then explains how his thinking changed. He recalls a highly publicized case in which an American contractor in the Middle East was kidnapped and eventually killed. "He wasn't a soldier, he wasn't under military contract, or anything like that and it seemed very random. But he was killed anyway and I had always been taught you pray for things and there is God's will and God has a plan. And I thought, gee, if God doesn't hear the prayers of how many hundreds and thousands who were praying for this man, then I don't know that I want to be part of that. It was selfless prayer. It wasn't to get a better parking space. It was just for his basic survival. How can his death be part of God's plan? I don't know that I can believe in something like that."

Paradoxically, this man's crisis of faith stemmed from not having enough doubt at the start. When he began praying for the man who was eventually killed and realized that thousands of other people were praying, he firmly believed that the man's life would be spared. He apparently did not entertain the possibility that God's ways were inscrutable or doubt that his own view of what should happen was correct. The parts of his faith were rationally interconnected. If God is good, and if God hears prayer, then the death of an innocent man for whom many prayers have been offered implies that God either is not good or does not hear prayer. It no longer seemed reasonable to believe in heaven, either. Having lived within a faith community all his life, he now found himself on the outside of that community. He says he no longer prays and has many questions for which he has no answers.

For people who consider it reasonable to believe in heaven, there is also a puzzle about what exactly that implies—to be sure, not as severe as this man's, but important nonetheless. The puzzle is how to think about their faith in ways that encourage active religious commitment rather than only passive contentment. The supply-side theorists' argument, however flawed, is helpful for bringing this puzzle into perspective. As we saw, their view is that religious organizations have to persuade prospective members that only they will go to heaven; otherwise, there is no particular reason to devote time and money to the organization's activities. But if that is the case, it becomes problematic for the survival of religious organizations if people believe that everybody goes to heaven. It may also be problematic if the language of belief suggests that the details about heaven cannot be known or that loved ones will not be recognizable in heaven, or even that heaven is such a wonderful place that absent loved ones will not be missed. The supply-siders are probably wrong in assuming that getting into heaven is the only good reason for being involved in religious organizations. But it clearly is an important reason for some, and for others, attractive reasons of a different kind for being committed to religious organizations probably have to be articulated. In either case, the desire to appear reasonable remains in effect. Reasonable language has to be used to explain why only Christians get into heaven and how that connects with church going. Or reasons that do not seem far-fetched are required to explain why specific faith commitments are important despite the openness of heaven's doors to everyone.

The remarks of a woman who attends an evangelical church on the West Coast are especially helpful for understanding how to convey the reasonableness of a restrictive view of who gets into heaven. She has a graduate degree, works as a college administrator, and clearly has a lot of biblical knowledge at her disposal. When she was in her early twenties, she recalls, God and church were not part of her life. She says, "God was a crutch for weak people who couldn't make decisions on their own and needed excuses." But a few years later, during a low point in her life, she began attending a women's Bible study group, found warmth and acceptance in the group, started to seek God through prayer, and came to experience what she describes as "such peace inside and incredible joy" that she was convinced God exists and loves her. Now, some 25 years later, she says God is the "lover of her soul" and she is certain that Jesus died for her sins. At the little church she attends, which she says is quite conservative theologically, she teaches a class and serves on several committees that bring her to the church at least twice a week and on Sundays. There are a number of reasons she participates—friends, good sermons, gratitude to God, and opportunities to serve. Knowing that she will go to heaven when she dies is one of these reasons. The thought of heaven ("I can't wait to get there") fills her with emotion, just as her sense of God's love does. Yet the view of God as a crutch from earlier in her life keeps her from believing in heaven only because it feels good. Heaven for her is a conviction that she thinks must be grounded in reason.

Her argument for believing in heaven goes something like this: God loves her. She has experienced this love and she associates it with Jesus dying for her sins. Because God is a loving God, God has also provided a peek into heaven through the biblical account in the Book of Revelation. She understands that the description there is inadequate, and she pays little attention to many of the details that are sometimes interpreted to have special meaning. What interests her most is the lamb, symbolizing the Son of God, opening the scroll of final judgment on the world. She sees that as a "perfect picture of grace and justice." This is important to her because, as she says, "If there is anything that people want deep down inside, it is justice. Everybody. God is perfectly just. When he judges at the end of all time, it is with perfect justice in mind." She also thinks God's grace is evident. "He has given us every possible opportunity to make things right with him and to do it his way." She believes that "only those who know Jesus as their personal savior" will be judged favorably. But that is fair because, as she has explained, God's judgments are always gracious and perfectly just.

What further makes it reasonable to think of heaven as a place only for believers is that "the only people, according to God's plan, who get to go to heaven are people who get there God's way." The logic is not self-explanatory. She elaborates with an analogy: "It's kind of like saying to a NASA astronaut who is out in a space shuttle, 'You can come home any old way you want.' That's not true. If that astronaut misses the earth's atmosphere by one percentage in the angle, that space shuttle could skip right off the atmosphere and be gone forever. Or if maybe he is a little too steep, that space shuttle could come in through the atmosphere at such an accelerated rate that it would burn up and never get here. It is not true that you can get there any old way you want. If you are in that space shuttle there is only one way you can get back and you better do it the way the instruction manual tells you to do it. The same is true for heaven." In short, the soul is like a space ship. Both have to operate exactly according to God's plan.

The space ship analogy suggests that there is a right way and a wrong way, which then poses the need to say how one might know the difference. She acknowledges that "religious systems" have different views and argues that they "all contradict one another" and are mutually exclusive, so cannot all be right. The truth, she says, is in the Bible. "I have seen time and again that archeology and history have proven the validity and accuracy of the Bible." The biblical truth is that "someone else has to pay for the penalty for sin if you want your sin wiped away. If you want to pay for it yourself you can, but you can't get to heaven that way." If you do try that, you will be on the road to destruction because "God can't let imperfect people into a perfect heaven. And the only way to become perfect is for the only one who was perfect to give us his perfection."

The final piece of the argument is that "the only way anybody can be in heaven is if we do it God's way because God is the one who established the rules." God's rule about getting into heaven is that "you need to acknowledge that Jesus Christ is my Son who is God fully, completely, and absolutely, who came in the flesh, lived a perfect and sinless life to give you an example, died for your sins because you can't die for your own unless you want to go to hell, and then rose again from the dead to prove absolutely beyond a shadow of doubt that he is God Almighty himself." She concludes: "If you are willing to accept that, receive his forgiveness and follow him, the reward at the other end is that you get to be in heaven."

There are important theological and philosophical claims here. My interest is not to examine those claims or to consider whether each stands up to some logical principles of argumentation. It is rather to emphasize several aspects of the language that is used to communicate why it is reasonable to say that only believers in Jesus go to heaven. Unlike the statements I mentioned earlier about Jesus, this one is, of course, considerably longer. If a person does not convey reason by expressing uncertainty, then it takes quite a lot of effort to do it in another way. There is no single clincher, at least not for this speaker. The argument actually consists of several arguments that reinforce one another and together provide several different ways of arriving at the main conclusion. It involves an assertion about the universal human desire for justice and about God's perfect justice and grace. It further includes an analogy intended to show that there is a right and a wrong way to do things. There is a defense of the Bible in terms of its archeological and historical accuracy. There is an additional argument about God's rules being right simply because God established them. And finally, the argument hinges on a just God being unable to accept imperfection into a perfect heaven and thus requiring people to believe in Jesus as the perfect substitute for their imperfection.

From the inside, anyone familiar with the Christian doctrine of atonement knows that these arguments have long been part of the Christian tradition. However, bracketing that knowledge reveals, first, that the argument involves several layers of complexity, and second, that it is not simply a part of the everyday discourse of ordinary life. The space ship analogy is an attempt at translation into a wider language that anyone might understand. But the recitation soon moves back into a specialized language about information that only a privileged few would have, such as the archeological and historical accuracy of the Bible and what it might mean to "acknowledge," "accept," and "receive" the idea that Jesus is God Almighty. Insider language of this kind requires being part of a religious institution. This is where it is learned and where it comes to be understood.

To return briefly to the supply-side argument about heavenly rewards, the reason a restrictive view of heaven may encourage involvement in a religious organization cannot be understood simply in terms of a naïve economic metric that says the rewards will be greater if the cost is greater. It is rather that participating in a religious organization exposes participants to an elaborate language about heavenly rewards and about how to attain them. The language does not state that going to church every Sunday instead of once a month raises the chances of getting into heaven. Instead, the language suggests that it is reasonable to believe that only Christians go to heaven. The reasons are not self-evident. They require additional arguments and further explication. The more a person participates, the better one becomes at knowing what the language means. The analogies multiply. Some of the arguments are backed up with other arguments. Some of the words are repeated often enough that they no longer need to be explained. There is also enough uncertainty about what it means to accept Jesus that the religious organization can provide tacit answers to that question. Believing in Jesus can be reciting a prayer in one instance, listening to sermons in another, or loving one's neighbor in yet another.

Articulating good reasons for participating in religious organizations is the special task of clergy. They have a professional stake in doing so. The health of their congregations depends on it. Lay members may say, as many do, that they belong to congregations because they enjoy the singing on Sunday mornings or the programs for their children on Sunday evenings. Clergy emphasize these practical reasons for being involved as well. Visitors are encouraged to make new friends and find community at the church. But clergy have by no means given up on arguments about heaven. Lay talk about heaven frequently includes references to religious authority. Clergy reinforce these references. Indeed, the language in which their own arguments about heaven are framed often contrasts with lay remarks by offering stronger claims about the relation between what one does in this life, especially in congregations, and what heaven is like. The arguments affirm conventional biblical teachings about heaven, but they also suggest that a lack of knowledge is to be expected and that it is nevertheless reasonable to be a person of faith.

Consider the remarks of a Presbyterian pastor who has studied the doctrine of the resurrection of the body at great length and spent considerable time thinking about heaven. He says "we are not God" and should not "spend our lives worrying and wondering who is in [heaven] and who is not." Heaven is "the promise that we are not separated from God." He says the biblical teaching that "one day every knee will bow and every tongue confess that Jesus is Lord" may mean that everyone will simply be amazed at the love of God or even that God pardons everyone's sin. In his case, the role of the church is to enact and encourage belief in the promise of not being separated from God. That, he feels, is good news to be "shared through word and deed."

Or consider what the pastor of a nondenominational evangelical church says: "When I think about what I believe as a Christian, I think sometimes either this is really God or I'm really nuts. The idea that God became a human being and then died on a cross and then came back

from the dead and then went up to heaven and then sent a part of himself called the Holy Spirit—all of that, on the surface of things, is pretty
preposterous, so we're just riddled with mystery." He preaches a conservative gospel that emphasizes salvation in Christ, but he also encourages
his members to see that God is ultimately beyond human comprehension. "I don't know how we can worship otherwise," he says.

The pastor of another nondenominational church—this one in the
Pentecostal tradition—says the principal reason for participating at
his congregation is fellowship. He means this in a different sense than
merely making friends, although that is important. Fellowship involves
worship and through that inviting the Spirit into their midst. It is the
"palpable, demonstrable, manifest presence of the Spirit" that attracts
people. That feeling of being in the presence of God, he says, is a glimpse
of heaven on earth. It also moves people to greater selflessness and compassion, he believes.

To recap, I have argued that belief in the existence of heaven poses problems for people who consider themselves reasonable, just as prayer and
assertions about God's role in major disasters do. I do not mean it is
somehow intrinsically and inescapably unreasonable to believe that
heaven exists. Yet the possibility of a reality that is so different from the
reality of this life poses difficulties. It is important to seem reasonable
when talking about heaven, and that cannot be done in the same way
that talking about a new sofa or the evening news can be. Especially
the fact that so many well-educated people in a well-educated country
like the United States believe that heaven exists, despite there being no
concrete evidence that it does, is puzzling, or should be puzzling. True,
it may be comforting to imagine living forever in paradise, and it may
well be the case that religious organizations play a big part in promoting
this belief. But those arguments do not illuminate how people actually
reconcile reason and faith.

Resort to authority is one important way in which reasonable people justify their beliefs about heaven. Despite the fact that movies and
television programs present popular depictions of heaven, and despite
newspapers and newscasts referring to heaven in casual ways, the Bible

and other religious sources remain the most commonly mentioned authorities for beliefs about heaven. Unlike prayers that pose questions about divine intervention in human affairs, heaven remains unknown to all living persons, which perhaps oddly makes it easier for religious authorities' claims to remain credible. Whereas a skeptic can say I prayed and nothing happened, nobody can prove that biblical arguments about heaven are false.

What people think heaven is like cannot be understood as a longing for compensation that somehow makes up for disappointments in this world. Describing something presumed to be good but that nobody has experienced is a challenge in the use of language. Talking about the absence of sorrow and suffering experienced in this life is a good rhetorical device for saying that heaven will be better without actually having to describe it. Asserting that heaven will be better than the most pleasant aspects of worldly life serves similarly, especially if "better" is left unspecified. Heaven as a "wonderful place" filled with "glory" and "grace" is a perfect example.

Talk of heaven is further characterized by assertions of doubt and difficulty, by reflexivity, and by switches of register through which speakers disclaim having more knowledge about heaven than they know is possible. Although heaven is a serious topic, speakers are able through these devices to show that specific knowledge about heaven is provisional.

Much of the talk about heaven shows that people hope to see their loved ones again and for this reason are often concerned that their loved ones are Christians or in other ways will gain entry to heaven. However, the same hedging that characterizes descriptions of heaven is evident. People assert that they are unsure who will be in heaven or that they will recognize who is there. They also suggest that it may not matter because they will simply be enjoying God's presence. These arguments sometimes necessitate religious leaders finding other arguments for being committed to particular faith communities.

Being actively involved in a religious organization does not, as most people see it, literally increase their chances of going to heaven. It is rather that logical arguments about why some people will go to heaven and others will not are complex and require specialized knowledge.

Involvement in religious organizations supplies the language to make those arguments. Although Jesus is often a pivotal figure in these arguments, the language does not always emphasize Jesus as a gatekeeper and judge. It also emphasizes seeing the face of Jesus and the promise of experiencing God's love in heaven.

Behind it all, the language used to describe beliefs about heaven is shaped by the desire to appear reasonable. I have suggested that this desire is evident in expressions of doubt and uncertainty, and in the use of language devices that avoid having to say more about heaven than a reasonable person who has not experienced it would feel comfortable saying. But it is unnecessary to infer that the desire to appear reasonable is in the back of people's minds only from what their language communicates implicitly. A person who violates standard ways of talking can sometimes reveal more than those who conform. Consider what an attorney who believes she has actually communicated with people who have gone to heaven says: "I can't believe I'm telling you all this. You aren't going to use my name, are you? I don't want them to come lock me up!"

NOTES

1.   Virginia Ironside, "Virginia Ironside's Dilemmas," *The Independent* (May 19, 2003).

2.   The figures mentioned in the text are from my analysis of surveys conducted in 1998 by the International Social Survey Programme (ISSP). I refer to other studies later in the chapter, including more recent ones, but the ISSP surveys have the advantage of asking exactly the same question in both Great Britain and the United States and giving respondents four answer options for their belief in heaven: yes, definitely; yes, probably; no, probably not; no, definitely not.

3.   From my analysis of the U.S. data included in the 1998 ISSP study. The percentages who said they definitely believed in heaven, respectively, were: 50 percent among those with completed university degrees, 61 percent among those with some education beyond secondary school, 69 percent among those with high school diplomas, 70 percent among those with incomplete secondary education, 82 percent among those with only primary education, and 93 percent among those with incomplete primary education.

4. On stability and possible increase in belief in life after death, see especially Andrew M. Greeley and Michael Hout, "Americans' Increasing Belief in Life after Death: Religious Competition and Acculturation," *American Sociological Review* 64 (1999), 813–835; and Claude S. Fischer and Michael Hout, *Century of Difference: How America Changed in the Last One Hundred Years* (New York: Russell Sage Foundation, 2007), 208–211; see also Brian Harley and Glenn Firebaugh, "Americans' Belief in an Afterlife: Trends over the Past Two Decades," *Journal for the Scientific Study of Religion* 32 (1993), 269–278.

5. An earlier version of some of the material in the following sections originally appeared in my essay, "Heaven Is a Wonderful Place: The Role of Reasonableness in Religious Discourse," *Review of Religious Research* 52 (2010), 5–20.

6. Karl Marx, "Introduction to A Contribution to the Critique of Hegel's Philosophy of Right," in *Deutsch-Französische Jahrbücher* (February 1844), reprinted in Lewis S. Feuer, editor, *Marx & Engels: Basic Writings on Politics and Philosophy* (New York: Doubleday, 1959), 262–266.

7. Max Weber, *Sociology of Religion*, translated by Ephraim Fischoff (Boston: Beacon, 1963), 106.

8. Freud's arguments have been helpfully interpreted in Diane Jonte-Pace, "At Home in the Uncanny: Freudian Representations of Death, Mothers, and the Afterlife," *Journal of the American Academy of Religion* 64 (1996), 61–88.

9. William James, *The Varieties of Religious Experience* (New York: New American Library, 1958), 122; an insightful secondary source is Ellen Kappy Suckiel, *Heaven's Champion: William James's Philosophy of Religion* (Notre Dame, IN: University of Notre Dame Press, 1996).

10. G. Stanley Hall, "Thanatophobia and Immortality," *American Journal of Psychology* 26 (1915), 550–613; quotation is on page 568.

11. Ann Douglas, "Heaven Our Home: Consolation Literature in the Northern United States, 1830–1880," *American Quarterly* 26 (1974), 496–515.

12. Judith A. Cook and Dale W. Wimberley, "If I Should Die before I Wake: Religious Commitment and Adjustment to the Death of a Child," *Journal for the Scientific Study of Religion* 22 (1983), 222–238.

13. Helen K. Black, "Poverty and Prayer: Spiritual Narratives of Elderly African-American Women," *Review of Religious Research* 40 (1999), 359–374; quotation is on page 365.

14. James, *Varieties of Religious Experience*, 118.

15. General Social Survey 2006, electronic data file; my analysis.

16. My analysis of data from the General Social Survey cumulative data file for 1972–2006, using surveys conducted between 1972 and 1976 and between

2002 and 2006 for the comparisons; 67 percent of respondents in their forties in the earlier surveys said they believed in life after death and 68 percent of respondents in their seventies or eighties in the later surveys said this.

17.   The percentages who said they definitely or probably believed in heaven in the 1998 General Social Survey were 72 percent among those in their twenties, 79 percent among those in their thirties, 78 percent among those in their forties, 80 percent among those in their fifties, 83 percent among those in their sixties, and 74 percent among those in their seventies or eighties; thus, if the oldest group is discounted, it might be argued that there was a slight rise with age in the percentages; however, this was not the case in the 1991 General Social Survey, in which the percentages, respectively, from youngest to oldest age groups were 84, 76, 76, 87, 68, and 77.

18.   Corry Azzi and Ronald Ehrenberg, "Household Allocation of Time and Church Attendance," *Journal of Political Economy* 83 (1975), 27–56; the subsequent studies are discussed in Laurence R. Iannaccone, "Introduction to the Economics of Religion," *Journal of Economic Literature* 36 (1998), 1465–1495; Iannaccone's review is generally sympathetic to Azzi and Ehrenberg's approach and mentions some favorable empirical results, but does not find as much value in this approach as in other applications of economic models.

19.   Spiritual Beliefs and the Dying Process Survey (May 1997), online at roperweb.ropercenter.uconn.edu. The study was conducted by telephone with a randomly selected national sample of 1,200 adults.

20.   A useful article that reports results of several original experiments and reviews much of the literature is Mark J. Landau, Michael Johns, Jeff Greenberg, Tom Pyszczynski, Andy Martens, Jamie L. Goldenberg, and Sheldon Solomon, "A Function of Form: Terror Management and Structuring the Social World," *Journal of Personality and Social Psychology* 87 (2004), 190–210; other studies of particular relevance include J. Arndt, J. Schimel, and J. L. Goldenberg, "Death Can Be Good for Your Health: Fitness Intentions as Proximal and Distal Defense against Mortality Salience," *Journal of Applied Social Psychology* 38 (2003), 1726–1746; M. Dechesne, T. Pyszczynski, J. Arndt, S. Ransom, K. M. Sheldon, and J. Janssen, "Literal and Symbolic Immortality: The Effect of Evidence of Literal Immortality on Self-Esteem Striving in Response to Mortality Salience," *Journal of Personality and Social Psychology* 84 (2003), 722–737; and K. van den Bos and J. Miedema, "Toward Understanding Why Fairness Matters: The Influence of Mortality Salience on Reactions to Procedural Fairness," *Journal of Personality and Social Psychology* 79 (2000), 355–366. A readable introduction to some of this literature is found in Tom Pyszczynski, Sheldon Soloman, and Jeff Greenberg, *In the Wake of 9/11: The Psychology of Terror* (Washington, DC: American Psychological Association, 2003), especially chapter 2.

21. Joseph Lee Rodgers, Craig A. St. John, and Ronnie Coleman, "Did Fertility Go Up after the Oklahoma City Bombing? An Analysis of Births in Metropolitan Counties in Oklahoma, 1990–1999," *Demography* 42 (2005), 675–692; a similar response occurred in South Carolina following Hurricane Hugo, as shown in S. L. Cohan and S. W. Cole, "Life Course Transitions and Natural Disasters: Marriage, Birth, and Divorce Following Hurricane Hugo," *Journal of Family Psychology* 16 (2002), 14–25.

22. Charles P. Flynn and Suzanne R. Kunkel, "Deprivation, Compensation, and Conceptions of an Afterlife," *Sociological Analysis* 48 (1987), 58–72.

23. For all 32 countries surveyed by the ISSP in 1998, the correlation is .879. This figure pertains to countries as the unit of analysis and is between the percentages who believe definitely in heaven and the percentages who attend religious services nearly every week or more often.

24. World Values Surveys, electronic data file; my analysis was based on the surveys conducted between 1995 and 2004; I first derived the percentage for each of the 80 countries who believed in heaven and the percentage who attended religious services at least monthly and then correlated the two; the correlation was .773.

25. Greeley and Hout, "Americans' Increasing Belief in Life after Death"; quotation is on page 813.

26. Laurence R. Iannaccone, "Why Strict Churches Are Strong," *American Journal of Sociology* 99 (1994), 1180–1211.

27. Grace Davie, *Religion in Britain since 1945: Believing without Belonging* (Oxford: Blackwell, 1994).

28. David Heller, *The Children's God* (Chicago: University of Chicago Press, 1986), 54–55.

29. Robert Wuthnow, *All in Sync: How Music and Art Are Revitalizing American Religion* (Berkeley and Los Angeles: University of California Press, 2003), 186.

30. Robert Wuthnow, *After the Baby Boomers: How Twenty- and Thirty-Somethings Are Shaping the Future of American Religion* (Princeton, NJ: Princeton University Press, 2007), 269.

31. Peter L. Berger and Thomas Luckmann, *The Social Construction of Reality: A Treatise in the Sociology of Knowledge* (Garden City, NY: Doubleday, 1966), 101.

32. These are actual stories, all from various Internet blogs and online sites.

33. Information about the growth of Calvary Chapel can be found in Charles Fromm, *Textual Communities and New Song in the Multimedia Age: The Routinization of Charisma in the Jesus Movement* (Ph.D. dissertation, Fuller Theological Seminary, Pasadena, CA, 2006); Donald E. Miller, *Reinventing American Protestantism: Christianity in the New Millennium* (Berkeley and Los

Angeles: University of California Press, 1997); and Scott Thumma and Dave Travis, *Beyond Megachurch Myths: What We Can Learn from America's Largest Churches* (San Francisco: Jossey-Bass, 2007). On Calvary Chapel's and other megachurches' role in producing contemporary music, see Robert Wuthnow, *All in Sync*. In a personal communication, Chuck Fromm, who headed Maranatha! Music during the 1980s and provided some of the historical details, recalls that "Heaven Is a Wonderful Place" was "sung constantly at Bible studies." Often sung in rounds both in Bible study groups and during congregational worship with men's and women's voices alternating, it was adapted for children by leaving the words unchanged but using children as vocalists, adding a crayola cover, and introducing "Psalty" the singing songbook, who needed children to sing with him. Debby Rettino, the voice of Psalty, recalls that the song was sung a lot in early house ministries and home Bible studies in which children were present.

34.   For more on speech registers, see Sandor Hervey, "Registering Registers," *Lingua* 86 (1992), 189–206; Shoichi Iwasaki and Preeya Ingkaphirom Horie, "Creating Speech Register in Thai Conversation," *Language in Society* 29 (2000), 519–554; Anne Burson-Tolpin, "Fracturing the Language of Biomedicine: The Speech Play of U.S. Physicians," *Medical Anthropology Quarterly* 3 (1989), 283–293; Mary Douglas, "The Social Control of Cognition: Some Factors in Joke Perception," *Man* 3 (1968), 361–376; Barbara Kirshenblatt-Gimblett and Joel Sherzer, *Speech Play: Research and Resources for the Study of Linguistic Creativity* (Philadelphia: University of Pennsylvania Press, 1976); and Jean Ure, "Approaches to the Study of Register Range," *International Journal of the Sociology of Language* 35 (1982), 5–23.

35.   See the insightful analysis by Andrew L. Roth, "Social Epistemology in Broadcast News Interviews," *Language in Society* 31 (2002), 355–381.

36.   Wuthnow, *All in Sync*, 186.

37.   The "we Muslims" or "we Hindus" response was in fact quite common among Muslims and Hindus interviewed in several of my research projects.

38.   Leigh Schmidt, *Hearing Things: Religion, Illusion, and the American Enlightenment* (Cambridge, MA: Harvard University Press, 2000); Leigh Schmidt, *Restless Souls: The Making of American Spirituality from Emerson to Oprah* (San Francisco: Harper Collins, 2005); Courtney Bender, "American Reincarnations: What the Many Lives of Past Lives Tell Us about Contemporary Spiritual Practice," *Journal of the American Academy of Religion* 75 (2007), 589–614.

39.   Stephen Prothero, *Religious Literacy: What Every American Needs to Know—And Doesn't* (New York: Harper, 2007).

40. William Labov, "Intensity," in *Meaning, Form and Use in Context: Linguistic Applications*, edited by Deborah Schiffrin (Washington, DC: Georgetown University Press, 1985), 43–70; Rika Ito and Sali Tagliamonte, "*Well* Weird, *Right* Dodgy, *Very* Strange, *Really* Cool: Layering and Recycling in English Intensifiers," *Language in Society* 32 (2003), 257–279.

41. As an indication of the relative prominence of biblical authority, "Bible" appeared 69 times in interviewees' comments about heaven, whereas "movies" appeared only twice.

42. The interviewee may have been referring to C. S. Lewis, *Through the Shadowlands* (Nashville: Fleming H. Revell, 1994) or to Wayne Martindale, *Beyond the Shadowlands: C. S. Lewis on Heaven and Hell* (Wheaton, IL: Crossway Books, 2005); also of relevance is Brian Sibley, *Through the Shadowlands: The Love Story of C. S. Lewis and Joy Davidman* (Nashville: Revell, 2005).

43. Randy Alcorn, *Heaven* (Carol Stream, IL: Tyndale House, 2004).

44. These phrases are all from the *New York Times*, which at the time I wrote this had mentioned heaven more than 15,000 times over a 25-year period.

45. According to Charles Earle Funk, *Heavens to Betsy and Other Curious Sayings* (New York: Harper Collins, 2002), the precise origins of the phrase are unknown, but Funk says it referred neither to Queen Elizabeth nor to Betsy Ross and probably emerged on the American frontier in conjunction with the frontiersman's rifle, which was often called Betsy.

46. This was part of my argument about prayer in chapter 2.

47. Revelation 21:3–4 (Authorized Version).

48. Readers will probably recall this phrase as the refrain of John Edwards' speech to the 2004 Democratic National Convention.

49. Other interviewees pondered whether there was reason to believe they would see their relatives in heaven and rather candidly described hope and something rooted in human longing. For example, a musician whose mother had died within the past year said he hopes to see his mother in heaven. But he thinks "a whole lot of what we think about heaven is the result of human constructs that have developed over the millennia." He thinks there may be a biblical reference suggesting that people will see their loved ones in heaven, but isn't sure. "I don't know," he says, "I've never been [there]. It's a human hope." As another example, a computer scientist says, "The Bible doesn't say that when you die you're going to go up and hug your Grandma. It avoids a lot of that. It's a great unknown." He believes people do see their loved ones, but thinks "we don't really have anything to tell us that."

50. Examples of remarks indicating that the topic of meeting loved ones in heaven is one people have discussed include "It's funny, my husband

and I were just talking about that the other day" and "I've thought about this a whole lot because whenever you are dealing with kids, somebody always asks."

51.   I have examined these differences in some detail in *America and the Challenges of Religious Diversity* (Princeton, NJ: Princeton University Press, 2005).

52.   Mary Douglas, *Purity and Danger* (London: Penguin, 1966).

53.   I am grateful for these insights about *Paradise Lost* for the analysis by C. Herbert Gilliland Jr., "Limitary Patterns in 'Paradise Lost,'" *South Atlantic Bulletin* 43 (1978), 42–48.

54.   Robert Orsi, *Between Heaven and Earth* (Princeton, NJ: Princeton University Press, 2005); popular accounts of angels are included in my book *After Heaven: Spirituality in America since the 1950s* (Berkeley and Los Angeles: University of California Press, 1998).

55.   "Oh, Come, Angel Band," usually attributed to Jefferson Hascall, 1860, and sometimes to William B. Bradbury, 1862; recent versions include those of the Stanley Brothers on the soundtrack of *O Brother, Where Art Thou?* released in 2000 on the Lost Highway label, and the version by Emmylou Harris on *Angel Band*, originally released in 1987 by Warner Brothers.

56.   In the interviews, Jesus was mentioned specifically a total of 65 times.

57.   I picked these two examples because they include similar imagery about Jesus despite somewhat different views about getting into heaven. Many other statements about Jesus in the interviews show people affirming their faith in Jesus and yet seeming to balance the certainty implicit in that faith with assertions about a lack of knowledge, doubt, or uncertainty about the exact nature of heaven. For example, a Methodist in Pennsylvania says, "If you believe in Jesus as the savior, you go to heaven. In terms of what heaven is, that's an interesting thing because I don't know. I'm not sure." A Catholic in Virginia says, "I will get to be with Jesus and people I love who aren't here any more," but as if to balance the suggestion that only believers in Jesus will be there, she adds, "I believe my dogs will be with me." A Catholic in Indiana cites Jesus as her authority on heaven, referring to Jesus saying there are many mansions in his father's house, and then adding, "I don't know if we can translate that to back here. Did he really say mansions?" An evangelical Presbyterian in Massachusetts says heaven "is worth going to because that's where you can have the most satisfying union with God. I believe that believing in Jesus has something to do with heaven. I don't have the time to say who's going to go to heaven and who's not going to."

FIVE Jesus Sets You Free

One of the most memorable ad campaigns of the 1970s focused on the new Datsun 260Z. With dandelion seeds blowing away and a silver sports car visible in the background, the text read, "There's a good life waiting, it's not at all hard to find. Be free." The hook line asserted, "Datsun saves and sets you free."

Released in May 1974, the ad was well suited to the times. The energy crisis following the oil embargo of 1973 drove up gasoline prices 45 percent in little over a year. The new Datsun combined fuel efficiency with the allure of driving on roads with fewer vehicles. The ad was in keeping with the spirit of getting out and getting away that had always been part of Americans' fascination with their automobiles. "Discover a new place, meet new people," it counseled. "Watch dust curl behind you on a country road." The cadence was also profoundly familiar to American church goers. How many times had they heard preachers declare, "Jesus saves, Jesus sets you free"?

The tension between theological understandings of freedom in Christ and popular interpretations of freedom is a particularly interesting topic for exploring the languages Americans use to reconcile faith and reason. On the one hand, theological understandings hold that freedom in Christ is a language describing the spiritual transformation involved in the mystery of God's redemption of humanity. On the other hand, the idea that Jesus sets us free is widely assumed by clergy and lay Christians to have practical implications for everyday life, just as a new Datsun might. These implications may include feeling happier, recovering from an addiction, overcoming guilt, or engaging more freely in altruistic behavior. Ambiguity about what exactly it means to say that Jesus sets you free necessitates talking about it rather carefully, at least if one wants to be understood as a reasonable person. Care must be taken to acknowledge the spiritual mystery implied, but also to draw connections with real-life problems, while stopping short of making untenable claims about the unique pleasures and powers of Christian belief.

Talking reasonably about Christian freedom takes place in the contemporary context against a backdrop of two widely shared ideas in the popular culture. One is that dramatic personal transformations can and often do occur. For instance, many Americans talk of turning points in their lives, moments of realization or insight, experiences of recovery or change, and feelings of being reborn or redeemed. The other is that freedom is highly valued throughout the society and has meanings that have little or nothing to do with religious faith, and yet its connotations are sometimes strikingly consonant with religious language, as the Datsun advertisement illustrates. In consequence, a wide range of claims about Jesus setting people free can be made—from finding true self-fulfillment in Christ to believing that military efforts to promote freedom in other countries are part of God's will. Yet, as we will see, there are limits to what people feel is appropriate to say, and there are distinctive ways of combining the spiritual and the more mundane interpretations. The implicit aim is to communicate in a way that shows one to be a person of faith who values the freeing potential of that faith, while avoiding the appearance of being rash or

naïve. Reasonable people, for instance, report sudden personal transformations that are surprising and uplifting, but they also insist that
these changes involve rational decisions and thorough investments of
time and energy.

The balance of faith and reason associated with freedom in Christ can
be communicated through propositional utterances. For example, a person might assert that "freedom in Christ involves obedience to Christ,"
or express similar ideas through assertions such as "with freedom comes
responsibility," "don't expect miracles," or "God expects people to use
their minds in deciding how to exercise their freedom." Propositional
statements offer straightforward clarifications about where to draw the
line, as it were, between spiritual interpretations and practical applications. For instance, a biblical scholar might explain that the New
Testament contrasts freedom and bondage to illustrate the difference
between godliness and sin, but it does not teach that the early Christians
were to mobilize against slavery. Propositional statements are likely to
be included in popular thinking about freedom and faith because people
hear sermons on these topics, read religious books, and attend classes at
their houses of worship. However, the ways in which thoughtful people
express faith while affirming that they are reasonable individuals seem
equally, if not more, likely to be communicated through implicit patterns
of discourse and thus require paying close attention to the words used
and the connotations they suggest.

A few examples show the wide range of contexts in which ideas about
freedom in Jesus are present in contemporary culture. At a national
gathering of Methodist women, the congregation says in unison, "The
Messiah has come to save us and set us free! It was a virtual riot!
The people wanted to be free!" The liturgist asks, "What freedom from sin
do we seek?" The women respond with readings about sexism, racism,
greed, ignorance, and war, punctuated with cries of "Jesus sets us free."
At the First Christian Church in Mattoon, Illinois, the pastor explains to
his congregation that God's grace through Jesus' death is like an X-Box
game in which you demolish your car, wait a few seconds, and the game
"restores your car to brand new" as if nothing happened. "Grace sets you
free to live for Christ," he says. In a syndicated advice column sponsored

by the Billy Graham Evangelistic Association, a reader in a drug rehabilitation program asks for prayer. The columnist tells the writer to turn to Jesus. "When you invite him into your life, He gives you a new purpose for living." The columnist quotes John 8.36: "If the Son sets you free, you will be free indeed." The pastor of a Chinese church in New Jersey quotes the same verse, adding that it applies not only to drug addicts, gamblers, and alcoholics, but also to people "plagued by an over-attachment to the world, including television." At the Jameson Annex maximum security prison in Sioux Falls, South Dakota, the Prison Lighthouse Fellowship meets for worship under a banner that reads, "If the Son sets you free you will be free indeed." A group of 60 Christians calling itself "Operation Starting Line" visits prisons in Kentucky clad in bright yellow T-shirts. They carry New Testaments emblazoned with "God Sets You Free" on the cover. In Guyana, a young missionary instructs Sunday school children, reading from the same version of the New Testament. One of the most unusual expressions of the idea occurs along the Sunshine Skyway in Florida where 15 motorcyclists go on weekend jaunts for dinner. The group, all members of Church on the Rock (a congregation of 1,500 in Palmetto), calls itself the Unchained Gang, based on the teaching that Jesus sets you free.[1]

These examples suggest that some—perhaps many—Americans think it is reasonable to believe that Jesus sets them free. But making claims about freedom—of the kind that are somehow associated with Jesus— is tricky. If a person believes that "Jesus sets you free," does this mean that people who do not believe in Jesus are not free? Are Jews, Muslims, Hindus, and atheists less free than Christians? Leaving that question aside, suppose a person does believe in Jesus. What kind of freedom is it reasonable to expect? Instant liberation from an addiction? A new start, like a refurbished X-Box car? Feeling better about being in prison? Deliverance from an evil spirit?

For church goers, believing these things might in fact seem so reasonable that the question of *how* they seem reasonable would never come up. But this is why it is helpful to bring the perspective of writers who are deeply skeptical about the reasonableness of religious faith, like Richard Dawkins and Daniel C. Dennett, into the discussion.

The questions Dawkins and company might pose would reflect this skepticism: Isn't it magical thinking to imagine that "accepting Jesus" would suddenly and miraculously free someone from an addiction? Do intelligent people really think there are demons and evil spirits from which they need to be delivered? Or are these elements of a quaint language that needs to be upgraded scientifically? When church goers hear the preacher say they are "free in Christ," does that mean anything to them or has it become an empty ritual? Do American Christians find meaning in these words because they are so used to hearing about freedom in the marketplace and in politics? Are these words potentially dangerous because they encourage Americans to support military aggression in the name of Christian freedom?

Confronted with such questions, Christians who thought of themselves as reasonable people would say, "Of course not." The questions are inappropriate, if not offensive. Dawkins and his fellow travelers do not understand what we really believe. We have a more nuanced understanding of the faith. But the confrontation seldom happens directly. It occurs indirectly through self-monitoring—including the choices people actually make about what and what not to say, and the choices that do not have to be made because of conforming to commonly accepted uses of language. A normal, well-educated American who says "I had a demon living in my body until Jesus freed me of it" has a lot of explaining to do. A person who instead says "I went to AA meetings and gradually started to experience the freedom described in the Bible" comes off as simply a normal person. These are the subtle conventions of thought and speech that make it possible for people to communicate their religious convictions *and* their commitment to being reasonable.

Before examining contemporary descriptions of what it means to be set free by Jesus, it is instructive to look briefly at the history of church teachings on the subject. These teachings were as often topics of dispute as they were matters of consensus, but they show beyond question that ideas about freedom in Christ have always been central to the Christian faith, particularly as part of the doctrine of Christ's substitutionary atonement for human sin. The teachings also interacted with the wider culture and required theologians and other church leaders to formulate language in which to talk about them that reveal some of the same considerations about reasonableness that exist today.

The passage in John 8 in which the statement about being set free occurs is part of a longer discourse in which Jesus tells his listeners that the truth will set them free, to which they reply that they are Abraham's descendants and have never been in bondage to anyone. Jesus then responds that anyone who commits sin is a slave to sin, and says that a slave does not abide in the house forever, but a son does, adding that when the son sets one free, one is free indeed. Paul, in his letter to the Galatians, repeats the idea, saying that followers of Christ are not the children of a bondwoman, but are free, and for this reason should stand fast in the liberty of Christ (Galatians 4:31–5:1).

Christian interpretations of these passages focused on Christ as the atonement for human sin. If humans were enslaved to sin, they could not be united with God because God was perfectly righteous and thus incapable of countenancing sin. This was the meaning of the statement about slaves not abiding in the house forever. Jesus, though, was the sinless son of God and was a permanent inhabitant of God's house. Jesus's death paid for the punishment that human sinners would otherwise incur and thus made them free. Leaders of the early church taught that this interpretation was consistent with Old Testament teachings about an animal sacrificed as a substitute for a man who was condemned to death. It further conformed to teachings about God commanding perfect obedience to divine law, which, if broken, required a sentence of death. To be freed from this divine condemnation, it was necessary to express faith in the atoning sacrifice of Jesus, to repent of one's sins, and to follow the moral life of Christ.

Although there was substantial agreement on the basic doctrine of substitutionary atonement, interpreters found it necessary to clarify its implications. In the teaching of the Apostle Paul, for example, there was great emphasis on God's profound abhorrence of sin, on the one hand, which, on the other hand, showed God's extreme love for humanity in permitting his son to suffer and die in expiation of human sin. The teaching of Peter agrees on these points, but also attaches special emphasis to Christ's suffering as a model for believers who also suffer as a result of their efforts to engage in well-doing. The writer of the letter to the Hebrews stresses Jesus's obedience to God and believers' increased ability similarly to obey God through faith in Christ.

The struggle to experience the freeing effects of Christ in daily life while resisting temptation and seeking to obey God's commandments—memorably described in Paul's letter to the Romans (chapter 7)—was a source of continuing reflection. Augustine pondered these questions not only in reference to personal temptations, but also in drawing distinctions between rules that were to be taken literally and figurative teachings pointing to spiritual realities.[2] Calvin wrote extensively about Christian freedom, on the one hand emphasizing its power to embolden believers' commitment to the dictates of conscience and, on the other hand, arguing against private convictions conducive to a spirit of fanaticism. The political implications of Christian freedom were never far from Calvin's mind. How was it possible to be free in Christ, he asked, and yet be true to biblical teachings about servants and slaves staying in their servile condition? One answer, he observed, was to distinguish between the spiritual liberty of Christ and the temporal life governed by civil authorities. Another was to seek balance in all things, avoiding excess and striving for harmony.[3] In his famous Bible commentary at the start of the eighteenth century, Matthew Henry reminded readers in politically turbulent England and Scotland that freedom in Christ meant having the *power* to withstand evil and the *strength* to resist carnality.[4] Three decades later, Charles Wesley penned a hymn about "amazing love" that would have lasting popularity, including the lines, "Long my imprisoned spirit lay . . . my chains fell off, my heart was free, I rose, went forth, and followed Thee."[5]

In the American context, teachings about freedom in Christ included temporal as well as spiritual applications. Christian liberty meant liberty of conscience expressed in both the right to resist civil authority and the constitutional protection of free exercise of religion. In the early republic, writers sought to balance the various interpretations of being set free in Christ. On the one hand, freedom was a spiritual blessing, a heavenly impulse signifying union with God—"a certain gift for man" in the "manhood of Christ," as one writer put it—the nature of which could not be explained or understood except as part of God's desire to restore human-ity to a perfect state.[6] On the other hand, writers argued that Christ's freedom would have tangible manifestations in even the most mun-dane aspects of ordinary life. Horace Bushnell, for instance, observed that people's hearts would be "in it more fully" when they worked and served others "quickened by the grace of Christ."[7] The biblical references to freedom from bondage naturally inspired applications to the grow-ing debate over slavery as well. Harriet Beecher Stowe, whose views reflected the prevailing theological argument that atonement through Christ offered hope of divine regeneration, associated slavery with the "old covenant" of obedience to the Ten Commandments, whereas the "new covenant" demanded liberty.[8] "The gospel abolished all slavery," New England pastor George Barrell Cheever declared, "and brought in a new and perfect freedom in Christ Jesus."[9] Temperance was another cause for which proponents voiced arguments about Christian freedom. Drunks and saloon keepers who heard the "glad tidings of freedom in Christ" and accepted the "liberty of the Gospel," were said to have lost their appetite for liquor and abandoned their evil ways.[10]

The twentieth century registered conflicting opinions from the start about the meaning of freedom in Christ. The fundamentalist movement emphasized the freedom of those who believed in the literal death and res-urrection of Jesus to enter heaven when they died. The emerging Pentecostal churches associated spiritual freedom with gifts of the Holy Spirit, such as speaking in tongues. Social gospel Christianity stressed the physical deliv-erance of people oppressed by low wages and inadequate housing. Church leaders acknowledged that atonement spoke to a reality beyond human comprehension, but argued that it must have practical consequences as well. A preacher in Chicago put it well in an essay published in 1910: "The preacher tells men that Jesus Christ produces those dynamic conditions in which human life is brought from its lowest registers of vitality to its richest promise and fullest expression of power," he wrote. "And men ask, How? And they cannot well believe until in some measure, at least, the matter is brought livingly home to mind and conscience and heart."[11]

Later arguments continued the discussion of how to think concretely about Jesus setting people free. There was little doubt that Jesus had, in

some manner, come to proclaim freedom. But the challenge lay in specifying how, short of relegating freedom only to the afterlife, people might
expect to experience it from day to day. Writers entertained various possibilities. It could be that freedom in Christ meant being released from mental,
emotional, or spiritual restraints preventing a person from being his or her
"true self." If so, people should somehow function better and perhaps be
happier with themselves. A related thought held that Jesus set people free
to obey his commandments, meaning either to love others more effectively
or to refrain from the kinds of sins described by the Ten Commandments
and elsewhere in the Bible. A person receptive to Jesus's freedom would,
therefore, engage in charitable works, champion the oppressed, and lead a
moral life beyond reproach. An alternative view suggested that freedom in
Christ liberated people from having to abide by the most restrictive biblical
rules. A free Christian would worry less, for instance, about drinking alcohol or attending the theater. There were other views as well; for instance,
if it was truth that made one free, then a free person would seek truth and
experience greater clarity in understanding it.[12]

When being set free by Jesus has practical implications, it becomes
necessary to consider the ways in which these consequences occur—
and especially what constitutes reasonable claims about how, to what
extent, and under what conditions they are expected to occur. Most of
these consequences are, in principle, measurable. For instance, the claim
that a person set free by Jesus is more loving might be examined by
studying charitable giving and volunteering. Whether studies are conducted or not, the *possibility* of measurement is likely to influence the
manner in which claims are made. Knowing that a measurement could
be taken implies that an assertion could be wrong. The claim that freedom in Christ leads people to sin less, for example, could be disproven
if sin were defined as, say, adultery and research showed no differences
between people who felt they had experienced Christ's freedom and
those who had not. A reasonable response might be to argue that studies
showed there were in fact differences. However, being reasonable can
be accomplished much more easily through careful formulations of language. For instance, a speaker might be careful to assert that Jesus sets
people free from feeling guilty about adultery but does not prevent them

from committing it. Or a person wanting to appear reasonable about his or her faith might assert that Christian freedom is a spiritual mystery, and leave it at that, rather than venturing into dangerous speculation about who does or does not commit adultery.

Were it only that freedom in Christ dealt with church teachings, assertions about it would be *protected discourse* occurring only within a speech community over which religious leaders exercise close control. The idea of substitutionary atonement is an example of protected speech. Substitutionary atonement has rich meanings within religious communities. It has virtually no meaning elsewhere. Inside a religious community sermons and lessons can show how Christ's death atoned for human sin and how the language of bondage and freedom makes sense in that context. Behavioral implications can be managed as well—for instance, in explaining that a person is free of sin but may still be tempted to commit adultery. There is little danger that discussions of substitutionary atonement will somehow escape into other settings where different meanings could be inferred. For example, long stretches go by without mention of substitutionary atonement in the *New York Times, Newsweek, Time,* and similar publications.[13]

But freedom in Christ, unlike a rarified phrase like substitutionary atonement, is not protected speech. Assertions about Jesus and freedom interlace with one another in diffuse settings over which religious leaders have little control. This interlacing occurs because religious people want their message to be heard outside of religious settings. As the examples I mentioned earlier illustrate, religious people publish essays in newspapers, hold meetings in prison, and form motorcycle clubs advertising their freedom in Christ. Interlacing also happens because freedom is so widely discussed in contexts other than religion. The same media that seldom mention substitutionary atonement, for instance, print stories every day that mention "freedom."[14] As a result, talk of freedom in Christ picks up some of the same connotations and speech patterns as in these other contexts. To make assertions about freedom in Christ that sound reasonable, therefore, a person has to either go to some lengths to say what the difference is or else follow more general conventions about what can be said without seeming to be fanatical or ridiculous.

Freedom in Christ is by no means an esoteric topic to American Christians. In personal interviews, they talk about it ably and enthusiastically. Most have thought about what it means, heard sermons explicating its centrality to their faith, and pondered how it relates to their daily lives. This is not surprising. Jesus setting people free is a popular theme in inspirational books. If church goers have missed out on sermons about it, they may have heard or sung popular hymns in which it was featured, such as "Out of my bondage, sorrow, and night . . . Into Thy freedom, gladness, and light, Jesus, I come to Thee."[15] They have probably entertained thoughts as well about what it would be like to feel free of worry or to be free of illness and debt.

How people talk about freedom in Christ involves cues about reasonableness especially in reference to assertions about *how* the practical benefits of this freedom come about. Do they happen through direct supernatural intervention, much like miraculous healings? Or are they the result of hard work, perseverance, and rational decisions? Three topics in particular emerge with considerable frequency as people discuss Jesus setting them free: freedom from unwanted feelings, such as worry, guilt, and an inability to forgive oneself; freedom to recover from addictions; and concerns about freedom being a universal divine truth or simply being an American value.

The unwanted feelings that Americans identify when asked to talk about freedom in Christ include worry, anxiety, fear, anger, and guilt. Devout Christians who are actively involved in their churches seldom say they are unfamiliar with the idea of Jesus setting people free. Quite the contrary. In personal interviews, church goers usually talk easily about freedom in Christ and often give examples of why it has been especially relevant to their faith journey. They understand its theological significance, explaining that it involves freedom from sin. In this context, sin is the generic condition of human separation from God, rather than specific transgressions that they themselves may have committed, such as theft or covetousness. They are also quick to point out that freedom in Christ does not entail license to do whatever one wishes. Freedom does, though, affect their daily lives. They claim that it makes them feel better and helps them realize their potential as persons. It releases them especially from long-term feelings and emotional dispositions or habits that have bothered them and in some way held them back.

Freedom from fear is well illustrated by an older woman who attends an Episcopal church in Illinois and was for many years the administrator of a nongovernmental organization in Japan. "Jesus frees us from our sin," she says. "He frees us from ourselves. It's very freeing. The more you know him the freer you are because you realize what he not only has done but also what he does for us on a daily basis. For instance, fear. He has set us free from fear." She illustrates her point by contrasting herself with her mother. "My mother was a very fearful person, so she just worried about everything. Whether money was an issue or not, she worried that there wouldn't be enough money. So I just carried that over into my own life." But it dawned on her that she didn't have to be so fearful and, indeed, was being a bad example to her children by worrying so much. "God has given us life to enjoy," she believes. Jesus has empowered her to believe that.

A welfare administrator who attends a Catholic church in Ohio focuses more on freedom from insecurity. He says "seeking approval from others" is an idol in his life, like the golden calf was in the Old Testament story, and "Jesus wants to free me" from that. Concretely, this means learning to "speak my truth" without being nasty, and then moving on. It is "just a healthy psychological principle, if nothing else." A biotech engineer who belongs to an evangelical church in Kentucky makes a similar point. "On the job we are all given performance reviews and we are all stack ranked to see who gets the biggest raise and the next biggest raise and the smallest raise." When you are truly in Christ, he says, "you are free from all that." A Catholic social worker in New Jersey expresses a related idea more abstractly, referring to people who feel "tormented by shame and guilt." He says having a relationship with God will give them "an emotional lift." A nurse who lives on the West Coast and is an active Lutheran speaks more personally. She recalls being in her early twenties and feeling empty, like she had a hole inside her. "I was always striving, looking, and nothing ever lived up to my expectations. It was a subtlety. I was always left wanting. Most people who knew me wouldn't even have been aware of that. Always left wanting." A few years later she had become involved in her church and was taking her faith more seriously. She realized that the empty feelings were gone. "I no long was left wanting and I then knew, no matter what, I was okay. I was locked in. Things could change all around me. I could experience the worst disaster loss of the world but somehow I would survive. I had confidence. It gave me direction, it allowed me to relax, it gave me peace."

These remarks suggest how Jesus can or does set people free from unwanted feelings. But what makes it seem reasonable to people to make such remarks? Are they so insulated from the rest of the world that they speak a religious language without thinking how it might sound to someone outside their own speech community? Do they believe they are seized by some mysterious supernatural force that produces a chemical transformation in their happiness quotient, like an antidepressant? Did the change happen overnight? Or do they describe the release from emotional bondage in ways that resemble other, less dramatic decisions and accomplishments?

One of the things that reasonable people do is make choices. They do not always make rational choices, at least not if rationality means decisions that achieve desired goals in the most effective and efficient manner (eating too much, spending too much money, and wasting time attest to that). A person can be reasonable, though, without being rational. Claiming to have made a choice demonstrates reasonableness by showing that thought and intention are involved. A person is behaving in the way basic cognitive schemas tell us a person is expected to act, not like a billiard ball that is pushed around by other forces. Even a bad choice shows that a person has volition, could do otherwise, and thus can give an account of the reasons for making the choice.

Accounts of gaining freedom from unwanted feelings through Jesus emphasize personal choice. It is significant that they do because, on the surface, the assertion that "Jesus sets you free" implies that the person involved is merely a passive object in the process. However, actual descriptions of the process are not passive at all. Notice the language the Episcopal woman in Illinois uses. "Some of us choose not to live in that freedom and we keep ourselves tied up with habits or sins." As she discusses fear, she repeats the point. "Some of us choose to live in that fear." Contrasting herself with her mother, she says, "I truly realized that I didn't have to live that way." The realization that her mother emphasized negativity led her to choose a different path. Her motto has become "I choose to look at the good side." The Lutheran nurse has a similar view of freedom. She says it is simply human to be given choices and to make choices. She also thinks God chooses, meaning that God draws connections with different people in different ways.

A business executive who attends a Methodist church in Florida talks about Jesus setting people free in language that further illustrates how choice makes the idea seem reasonable. He says he loves the idea that Jesus sets people free, and to underscore his point he says this is "the most intense type of freedom there is." He then links choice and Christianity this way: "We have freedom of choice and as Christians our choice is we believe Christianity is the basis of choice. It's right down to the gut core of choice. So for me all else is details. To me this is the basic truth." The exact logic (which is murky) is less important than his repeated references to choice and his insistence that choice is basic. The starting point is the assertion that we have freedom of choice. This, as he expresses it, is a reasonable statement. It is, so to speak, common knowledge that everyone has freedom of choice. His emphasis is not on the freedom people may experience after Jesus sets them free, but on the freedom they already have by virtue of being human. That prior freedom is evident as people choose or choose not to believe in Christianity.

When the interviewer asks, "How might the freedom in Christ show up in a person's day-to-day life?" this man continues his emphasis on choice. "The choices [people] make most definitely are so important." To illustrate, he mentions his son and one of his son's friends. "How different their life is now being in the organized church or their love of Christ compared to some of their friends who have decided to make other choices in their lives." The implication is that following Christ is the preferred choice. Then he adds an interesting remark. "On a very personal level, what are we besides our choices in this world? It's got to do with everything." Clearly, it is reasonable to him to emphasize choice.

Closely related to the idea of choosing are claims about having the capacity or ability to choose. The distinction is subtle, but can be illustrated in the following example. Person X chooses to go skiing but no snow falls that winter. Person Y chooses to go skiing but does not know how. Person Z chooses to go skiing and does know how. They all make choices, but only Z has the ability to make a choice that could actually happen. X may know how to ski but does not have the ability to do so because of the weather. Y may have good weather but lacks the relevant skills. In this sense, then, Z would appear to be the most reasonable of the three in being able to claim both to have chosen and to have the ability to exercise that choice.

As people explain it, the freedom Jesus gives them turns out to be very close to having snow and knowing how to ski. The Episcopal woman asserts, "The *ability* to be free is there." She phrases her motto about choosing to look at the good side as something that she is "able to say." A man in North Carolina puts the idea in similar terms. He likens freedom in Christ to "being able to go to a job interview and know that I'm going to be hired for my skills" or "being able to drive across the country on highways knowing that you could drive from one end of the country to the other, and there's going to be a paved road there." Ability is possessing certain talents and enjoying the conditions making it possible to use those talents.

Ability can be natural, as in the case of a person who has an inherited gift for painting or skiing and feels free by virtue of being able to pursue that gift, or it can be cultivated, as might be illustrated by a person who gradually overcomes shyness and learns to be comfortable in social settings. Either meaning—and usually some combination of the two—is a part of conventional ways of speaking about ability. Framing comments about Christian freedom in terms of these understandings of ability is a reasonable way of speaking. Natural ability is evident in the previous comments. Jesus sets people free to discover the ability that is part of their true nature. Cultivated ability is nicely illustrated by a college administrator who attends a conservative evangelical church in Ohio. He defines freedom in Christ as "freedom from your sins." It is very important to him. He describes it as part of coming to "know Jesus Christ" and having

"Jesus Christ living within you." But freedom is not, as he describes it, freeing in the way it might be described in nonreligious settings (such as freedom to gratify one's desires or explore the wild side). Indeed, he asserts in no uncertain terms that he is "not free to break the law, not free to run roughshod and do what you want." Freedom is instead a matter of working hard to cultivate abilities that are pleasing to God. The verbs connote effort: working, striving, not just talking about it, trying, living the fruits of the spirit. The example he gives involves his relationship to his children. Being free in Christ does not mean sitting back, relaxing, and figuring that dads will be dads and kids will be kids. If he thinks this, he does not say it. Instead, freedom in Christ means hard work and the power to engage in that work. Freedom means dying to his naturally sinful self and cultivating a different relationship with his children. The new abilities come as he rethinks the ways he would have reacted in the past. It involves talking with his children about Jesus, reading the Bible, and modeling good behavior. "It can be a daily struggle," he says. "It's daily, constant."

Although this man does not say so directly, the emphasis on culti-vated ability is compatible with feeling freer to be who one really is and even to be spontaneous, rather than only working hard to conform to a set of rules. If pressed, he would probably say that he and his children can have fun together because they know where the boundaries lie. A teacher who attends a Catholic church in Virginia makes the point explic-itly. She has long been attracted to the mystical tradition in Catholicism. "In Catholic mysticism," she observes, "there is a very strong sense of freedom." This mystical freedom, as she understands it, comes from sub-jecting oneself to God. "It isn't New Age freedom where you just go to a mountaintop and you love and stretch and dance or whatever. It is freedom gained through a lot of discipline." She digresses momentarily to mention Thomas Merton as an example and then adds, "I think that kind of freedom emphasizes spontaneity." She thinks this spontaneity results as "God moves you in ways—that are surprising—to deeper and deeper insights."

The other point of emphasis in making it seem reasonable that Jesus frees people is the idea that this freedom comes as part of a process involving effort, rather than happening instantly or automatically. The logic is consistent with another aspect of the basic cognitive schemas we use to make sense of everyday life. We learn not only that a chair moves only if it is pushed, but also that a big chair takes more force to move than a small one, and that it takes longer to move a chair a further distance. The kind of mental arithmetic involved is captured in sayings such as "no pain, no gain," and "Rome wasn't built in a day." Being set free by Jesus is more likely to seem reasonable when it conforms to the same logic. Although the divine power of Jesus is presumed in principle to include instant and dramatic results (such as changing water to wine), the language used to describe actual transformations suggests otherwise.

The idea of growth in one's knowledge of Jesus and relationship to him is one way to slow down the process, as it were, and demonstrate that effort is required to experience the true results of freedom in Christ. The Episcopal woman in Illinois observes that "the more you know him, the freer you are." The realization she experienced of being able to look on the good side was, in her telling, a change, but apparently one that grew as she learned more about Jesus and realized more of what he had done and was doing. A woman who holds an administrative position at a pharmaceuticals company and attends a Presbyterian church in West Virginia provides one of the clearest statements about how freedom in Christ unfolds as a process. In her daily life, she says that Jesus sets her free from worries, by which she means financial worries. She is quite self-conscious about the language she uses, and so she says immediately, "I'm not saying that spiritual belief removes financial problems. It doesn't. But it kind of sets you free from that worry." She then switches registers and quotes the words that calm her as they go through her mind on ordinary days. "Okay, what has to be done today? Here's today, here's what has to be done. How can I best get this done? Do the best that you can for today. Tomorrow is another day." Having emphasized focusing on today, she elaborates, now expressing herself more through the voice of someone giving advice: "The past is past. You can't go back and change it. You can go back and try to apologize if you've hurt someone. But there's not a thing you can do to go back and change that. It's by keeping one foot in the past and then another foot in the future, all you're doing is messing up today. All we have is right now." She says, "That's the freedom it gives me. I just don't worry like I used to worry."

Two aspects of this woman's remarks contribute to the likelihood that she considers them reasonable statements to make about her faith and that listeners in the same cultural setting would agree. The first is that the talking she does to herself and the advice she gives herself are actually little more than the homespun wisdom one might find in self-help books or in advice columns that have nothing to do with religion. A person does not have to believe in Jesus to have heard comments like these before or to believe that there is wisdom in them. The second is that she situates having learned to think in these worry-reducing ways in a larger narrative about growth in her spiritual journey. "If I was to look at my own life," she begins," I would say probably two-thirds of it [did not] set me free. It can be a ball and chain." She recalls the ball and chain being "rules and regs" about what to do to avoid going to hell. "I'm not buying into that any more. I haven't for a while." She now thinks choices are not black or white. "I may not always know what God's will is for me, but I pretty much know what it isn't." She has come to this understanding over a period of time. She now starts her days with a "very simple prayer asking for God to keep my eyes, ears, and mind open to God's will." This is why the homespun advice she gives herself about not worrying is enough. She concludes her narrative with a disclaimer: "Of course I'm older. I don't know how much of it is maturity. I guess a lot of it is, but it's a maturity in faith as well."

It is also notable that the process of learning how to be free from unwanted feelings sometimes involves actual verbal scripts. These are recipes or sayings that people repeat to themselves to assist in overcoming negative feelings. This woman's homespun advice is like a series of utterances that she is able to quote verbatim. The Episcopal woman's motto of looking on the bright side is another example. Yet another illustration is given by a Methodist woman in Ohio who describes herself as a "big worrier" and for this reason says she always tries to think, "I have the Lord on my side. I have done all I can. I'm giving it up to the Lord." She says, "There are a thousand Bible verses that say, 'Do not worry, give it all up to the Lord.'"

Choice, ability, and process are ways of talking that make it seem reasonable to believe that Jesus sets you free. But are thoughtful Christians completely comfortable with the idea, even when it is expressed in these ways? Or does the language they use sometimes suggest otherwise? Consider the language a bank official who attends a Catholic church in Kentucky uses. "I listen to [a fundamentalist pastor on the radio] before I go to my own services, and [they] believe that we are set free, we have a definite goal, a definite way to live our lives, and we don't have to struggle with questions [about] what is right and not right because we know the path we're supposed to follow." Her response puzzles the interviewer, who asks, "You're paraphrasing that in terms of what he preaches about Jesus and freedom. Are you agreeing with that? I mean, does that resonate for you? Does that make sense for you?" She replies, "Yes, I would say so. Yes." Or consider the response of another woman, also a Roman Catholic. She says the Christian emphasis on freedom is a "hard one" and that she could "plug into it" on several levels. She says, "I think it is true that when you live by a set of rules you are free in the sense that you don't have to always go around examining all alternatives." In support of this view, she cites the following: She feels freer at the grocery store when she knows what she wants, she read something by an economist who made this argument, she read an article that people learn better when they start with a few basic principles, and she knows a professor who teaches from only one theoretical perspective for this reason. She laughs about the second two examples, though, and twice uses the phrase "they say" and adds, "I have never seen it." Although she says this view of freedom is "plausible," she then launches into a discussion of an alternative view. In both sets of remarks, the words selected signal some distance or detachment between the speaker and what the speaker says. Although the speaker accepts the view expressed in each case, the view is presented as one with which other speakers might disagree, not as an authoritative source (such as God, the Bible, or science).

Recovery from addiction is a second general category in which people identify connections with the idea of freedom in Christ. Although remarks about freedom from unwanted feelings sometimes refer to sudden or dramatic transformations, they usually focus more on the gradual emergence of new insights or new ways of understanding one's feelings. In contrast, stories of recovery offer greater opportunities to speak of sharp differences between old habits and new ones. The biblical language of bondage resonates with popular uses of words like "enslaved" and "captive" to describe addictions. In the recovery process, Jesus somehow empowers people to break free of drugs, substance abuse, alcohol, smoking, gambling, and so on. There is in fact enough evidence from research studies that religious faith works in these ways—or deters at-risk behavior in the first place—to make accounts of this kind credible. However, the accounts still have to be told in credible ways. From the way people relate them, two aspects of these accounts seem to be important. On the one hand, the narrative suggests that Jesus's role was powerful by showing that the recovery was both dramatic and effective. This characterization is accomplished by contrasting negative aspects of life before recovery with positive aspects thereafter. On the other hand, the recovery process must include reference to the realities of biological dependence, inherited predispositions, the continuing negative influences of peers or the wider society, or other difficulties that make it arduous and never fully complete. These ways of talking are evident both in accounts of actual recovery and in metaphoric references to addiction as illustrations of spiritual freedom in Christ.

A pastoral counselor in Missouri who works with clients seeking to overcome addictions provides a vivid example of the complexity involved in making reasonable statements about the connection between addiction and freedom in Christ. In an opinion column for the local newspaper, he describes the harsh realities, emotional pain, and physical dependence of his clients, observing that "escape is very difficult for the person who is trapped in this deadly way of life." Nevertheless, "AA, NA, CSTAR and myriad other formal and informal treatment programs offer hope." This advice sounds reasonable coming from a trained professional and to anyone who is familiar with addiction. However, the writer continues, almost as an afterthought, "The surest hope for freedom is in Christ," adding, "No matter what has ensnared us, the one who has authority over death itself has the power to free any or all of us."[16] The statement links back to a reference at the start of the essay to Easter, the arrival of spring, budding trees, and Jesus's escape from the grave. Yet it is notable that the text stops short of specifying how belief in Jesus might provide freedom from an addiction or suggesting that it actually would speed the process. The references to Jesus serve as liturgical book-ends, while the action involving addiction and recovery is in a separate domain most explicitly marked by difficulty, struggle, and involvement in Alcoholics Anonymous and other treatment programs. The implica-tion is that faith offers hope, whereas a rational person wanting to escape an addiction seeks treatment.

Because addiction is widely discussed as a contemporary form of bond-age or enslavement, it surfaces in metaphoric ways as well as in literal ways in descriptions of what it means to be set free by Jesus. A homemaker who attends a theologically conservative nondenominational church in Tennessee incorporates addiction into her discussion of Christian free-dom in this way. She begins by asserting that it is "*phenomenal* how differ-ently you see everything" when you have been set free by Jesus. "Once you ask [Jesus] into your heart, it says in the Bible in 2 Corinthians 4:4 that the scales are lifted off the eyes and soul and mind of people." Referring to her own experience, she explains, "When I got saved, it is amazing, I can explain it like somebody coming off of drugs and seeing something, just seeing the world for the first time, in this kaleidoscope of colors or somebody who has smoked for years who finally quit and all of a sud-den could taste food again. That is so like a person getting saved. The grass was greener, the birds were amazing. Life just completely opened up. It's supernatural, it's spiritual, it is absolutely wonderful." She does not think her experience was unique. "Every Christian that I have spoken to that is truly saved has the same experience. Every one of them. It is just wonderful. It changes your life."

There is little doubt about the main theme in this part of her account. It is to show that being set free by Jesus is, as she says, phenomenal, amazing, absolutely wonderful. The reference to drug addiction and smoking is metaphoric. She does not say that she herself was addicted or smoked, but implies that she was not by stating that she "can explain it like somebody coming off drugs." As long as she describes her personal experience as one of wonder and amazement, the description is unassailable. Anyone can wax enthusiastic about something they have experienced. The statement that every Christian she knows has had the same experience, though, bridges into conceptually dangerous territory. A skeptic could say, do you really mean *everyone*, and were their experiences exactly the *same*? Perhaps she realizes that she is in the borderlands of reasonableness, because the discourse immediately shifts gears and focuses on the hardship involved. After stating that her life has been changed, she says, "Now does that mean that life is perfect and that life is bliss forever? No. No. He will carry you for a while and then when he puts you down for you to walk on your own two feet, it is just like a toddler. You walk and you stumble and some people will stumble back into smoking, or pick up the glass and start drinking again." To make the point stronger, she explains, "I mean you choose the narrow road, it's never the wide road where all the crowds are going and everybody is going. It is a tough road; it is a hard road. A lot of people think Christianity is the easiest thing in the world because you just slough it off to your God. It is the hardest walk in your life. You must constantly be seeing him and not doing what you want and not all the pleasures you want in life."

The balance evident in this woman's narrative between spectacular change and slow hard work provides an important clue to understanding why some narratives appear even to the casual listener to be less than fully persuasive. Consider an account given by an American woman who had visited a mission church in Rwanda. During the service, a Rwandan woman stood up and thanked the group for helping repair the roof and windows of her house: "I thank you for everything you've done, but most of all I thank you for your prayers." The American woman witnessed the event as an illustration of the power of Jesus to effect recovery. "This is a woman," she observes, "who is standing in a mud house with no shoes and about eight kids depending on her and no husband because he died in the genocide. There's a conquering awe in daily life because of prayer to Jesus Christ. That allowed her to rise above it all." It might be viewed as an inspiring story, but is clearly incomplete. The human part that emphasizes struggle and difficulty is missing. The Rwandan woman undoubtedly would have supplied that part of the narrative.

The most ambiguous aspect of remarks about freedom to recover from addictions and other problems concerns the role of personal will, or will power. Being set free by Jesus implies that a person now has greater control over his or her will, and for this reason can choose to recover. How exactly knowing Jesus affects the will has long been debated by theologians. In some accounts, there is a mysterious spiritual empowerment effected by the Holy Spirit. In others, the will is strengthened by a shift in perspective as people come to think of themselves as "bond-servants" of Christ instead of as slaves to drugs or alcohol. In still other accounts, knowing Jesus supplies meaning and purpose in life, which in turn makes a person less dependent on drugs. The ambiguity serves a discursive function. It permits speakers to argue reasonably that Jesus does make a difference, without having to be very specific about how that difference occurs. But other ways of describing the will also assist speakers in suggesting how change takes place. These are drawn more from common folk psychology than from theology. One idea plays heavily on up–down metaphors. When a person is feeling down, the goal is to feel up, to stand up, to stand on one's own two feet. If a person has hit bottom, there is no way to go but up. It is this sense of bottoming out that may itself strengthen the will. As a woman in Alabama puts it, "finally the person is desperate to change his heart." Or as a recovering alcoholic recalls, "The whole world caved in on me"; there was "nothing else to live for."[17] Another part of folk wisdom derives more from folk sociology. Drawing on an arithmetic metaphor, it suggests that there is strength in numbers. The idea is that people get by with a little help from their friends, are better able to stand up with that help, and can fall when left without support. The need for support of this kind is evident in the pastor's mention of Alcoholics Anonymous and other self-help groups. Another pastor expresses a similar idea, noting that "receiving advice, help, support, and love" would give someone the "power to overcome" struggles with an addiction. Another example comes from an evangelical woman who observes that freedom in Christ might help someone overcome a drinking problem "if they have a good friend" who is trying to help them. How the will is strengthened is less mysterious if recovery is somehow connected to psychological and social support. As one pastor aptly remarks, Jesus setting someone free from an addiction is "not a magic panacea."

The examples I have given thus far suggest that there is some unease in popular discourse about freedom in Christ. This is not unease in the sense of people doubting that the teaching is meaningful, but a kind of tension that needs to be resolved or a discursive gap that requires closing. Freedom from unwanted feelings implies that these emotions simply disappear or are supernaturally erased, which reasonable speakers balance by emphasizing the ordinary choices, abilities, and processes through which this freedom is gained. Freedom to recover from addictions and other traumas evokes similar discursive unease. Recovery is depicted as dramatic and powerful, but it is also described as slow and heavily contingent on will power. The other source of unease to which I now want to draw attention seems to occur less spontaneously as people talk about spiritual freedom, but puts speakers in need of some complex mental negotiation as soon as it is raised. This is the inherent tension between what Reinhold Niebuhr in broader terms called the relationship of Christ and culture, or, in the more limited context here, between the idea that Jesus sets people free and the idea that freedom is an American value that may or may not signal a connection between spiritual truth and such particular institutions as democracy, free markets, free enterprise, and laws upholding personal freedom. The question is not whether freedom is truly one or the other, but how persons who want to appear reasonable and who recognize the possible connections manage to talk about them.

The link between divine freedom and American values is sometimes dramatically reinforced in political rhetoric. A prominent example was a 2004 Fourth of July speech in Charleston, West Virginia, in which President George W. Bush stated that "freedom is not America's gift to the world; freedom is the Almighty God's gift to each man and woman in this world."[18] It was not the only time the President drew this connection. On other occasions, he described America as a nation of liberators and as the home and defender of freedom, blamed the 9/11 attacks on enemies' hatred of freedom, declared during the Iraq war that freedom was on the march, termed the quest to bring freedom to the rest of the world a calling, observed that God was on the side of freedom, announced that the Almighty believes every person should be free, stated that America has a duty to be the torchbearer of freedom, and asserted that freedom is a birthright that the Creator has written into human nature.[19] At a meeting with journalists in 2007, Bush explained the source of his belief: "I come at it many different ways. Really not primarily from a political science perspective, frankly; it's more of a theological perspective. I do believe there is an Almighty, and I believe a gift of that Almighty to all is freedom. And I will tell you that is a principle that no one can convince me that doesn't exist."[20]

Although President Bush may have given it particular emphasis, the focus in both theology and politics on freedom suggests that in popular culture the one may serve to legitimate the other. Simply put, the argument is that God wants people to be free, spiritual freedom is accomplished by believing in Jesus, and social, cultural, and political freedom is furthered by America. If this is the logic, then people of faith should be able to draw a fairly straightforward connection between their sense of having been set free by Jesus and what they cherish about America. However, responses to President Bush's remarks suggest that the relationships of the Almighty to America's championing of freedom are complicated. For example, columnist Rich Lowry argues that freedom may be a divine gift to everyone, but that its inevitable spread is "flatout wrong." If it is truly inevitable, he asks, "why not spare ourselves all the effort?" Andrew Sullivan, who agrees that the Almighty gives freedom, thinks associating it with political goals is "dangerous, delusional hogwash." Similarly, Ross Douthat observes that "the gift of freedom that Christ promises is far more real than anything else in this world," but calls associating this freedom with universal democracy "utopian."[21] One could argue that these responses are driven by partisan sentiments, and yet they suggest that feeling free in Jesus does not translate directly into support for particular expressions of earthly freedom.

Discovering how rank-and-file Americans talk about freedom in Christ and freedom in America is challenging. For instance, opinions cannot be gauged by asking for reactions to presidential remarks without the responses being influenced greatly by the president's popularity or unpopularity. Apart from partisan politics, the issue is complicated just by the perceived necessity, as we have seen, of speaking carefully about the meanings and implications of freedom in Christ. In our interviews, we approached the topic from two angles, asking first, "In America we value freedom. As people in other countries experience freedom in Christ, do you think they would come to hold some of the same values that we do in America?" Then a follow-up question asked, "By preaching freedom to the rest of the world, we might just be exporting American values. Or maybe freedom is a universal desire. Can you talk a little about that? In what ways is freedom an American value and in what ways is it universal?"

Complicated questions beg for complicated answers, and complexity does characterize the responses. However, it is not so much the fact of complexity that is of interest as its specific content and the manner in which it is framed. The responses reflect different views of America, but reveal a way of championing certain values that is seldom captured in standard discussions of ideology and political legitimation. Consider the views of a man who attends an African Methodist Episcopal church in South Carolina. He thinks the desire to be free is God-given and universal. Nobody is truly free because of sin, he says, but belief in Christ sets us free from sin. "It enables us to live our best lives and be our best selves." This kind of freedom is present in America and is a value Americans should be proud to export. He mentions liberation theology and arguments about self-empowerment and self-determination as examples. However, he also says that the "idea of rugged individualism" as part of the American concept of freedom "is not quite right in a lot of ways." That idea has ill consequences here and should not be exported, especially to contexts in which family and community loyalties remain strong. In short, he thinks some aspects of the American emphasis on freedom are compatible with freedom in Christ and some are not. We might call this selective legitimation or even selective sacralization.

However, there is more in his argument that a summary of what he values and does not value about America reveals. Paying closer attention to the language is required. It is important that the aspect of freedom that he considers not quite right is not actually characterized as freedom. His language switches to slogans at this point: "rugged individualism," "land of the free," "home of the brave," "pull yourself up by your bootstraps," "the American dream." The slogans objectify the ideas and distance them from him. He acknowledges that they have influenced his thinking, but says they were "force fed to me when I was small and painting turkeys and pilgrims." He goes on to say that these notions assume that the individual is in control, but in reality lead to choices that reduce freedom. He says "we really end up enslaving ourselves," and illustrates the point with an example of being "a slave to basketball" when he was in college. The language successfully transforms an aspect of American freedom into the opposite of freedom.

Having offered criticisms of American culture, the expected rhetorical move would be to balance the negative by turning immediately to something positive, just as a teacher might end a critical evaluation of a student's paper by observing that it was enjoyable to read and held promise. In this case, though, more follows than simply an easy rhetorical shift. The language does not turn immediately to assertions about the good kinds of freedom that America exemplifies. If it did, nothing would be said about the connections with spiritual freedom. Instead, the speaker weaves these links into the discourse. "A lot of the choices we make put us in service to something else," he says, anticipating his anecdote about basketball. "Jesus Christ sets us free from the bondage we have to sin, to immorality, to destruction and enables us instead to live our best lives and be our best selves." The contrast is between an apparent freedom involving choices that enslave and a spiritual freedom that is a release from enslavement. Christ "empowers you to live a life which produces and shows fruits of faithfulness and kindness and gentleness and self-control with joy, love, peace—a life which allows you to have your place as God intended you in creation." He restates the point, "So I guess you could say Christ frees us to be our best self." In this framing, the "land of the free, home of the brave" freedom defined by the American dream, therefore, is not only something that he has been "force fed," but also is on the negative side of the contrast he draws between bondage and freedom in Christ.

If there is any doubt about this mapping of the spiritual contrast and the speaker's comments about America, the discourse continues. "People enslave themselves to their job. People enslave themselves to significant others. People enslave themselves to money. People enslave themselves to so many things because that's part of what it is for us to be human." The parallel construction of the sentences reinforces the point: The things that people naturally choose in their freedom are not real freedom at all. "I would say that our idea of rugged individualism and freedom in America is not quite right. It's not right in a lot of ways. It ignores a lot of things that are inherent to the human condition, which is where we get back to the idea of Christ making us truly free and free to be who we were created to be in the first place."

At that point, he digresses to make a point about Eurocentric versus biblical interpretations of Christianity, but soon returns to the point he has just made about how aspects of American culture are inconsistent with freedom in Christ. "We need to stop and look at what we're doing in the things that are culturally American and not actually biblical," he asserts, "versus the things that are biblical, and even take stock of that in light of our inherently individualistic mentality that I was talking about before." The added point here is the need to stop and look. The descriptive language has now become imperative.

The assertions about positive aspects of American freedom come only in conjunction with one more critical remark. He mentions individual salvation ("a personal relationship between you and God through the blood of Christ") and "the conception of rights" as being points of congruence with American versions of freedom, but hastens to add that "I wouldn't expect someone to take on kind of the pure rugged individual, I'm an island, me against the world American mentality, because that's not something extolled in Scripture at all." It is as if the formulaic character of the positive elements ("personal relationship," "rights") requires insertion again of negative slogans.

The truly positive association between freedom in Christ and American freedom comes finally with a prompt from the interviewer asking specifically what might be American and what might be universal. He refers to himself now as an African American and says, "We have people who were enslaved and then they learned of Moses, relating to the slave experience of African Americans." That reference takes him to "Christian influences in abolition," "responses to colonialism in the late twentieth century," and "liberation theology" as examples of "preaching freedom." Unlike the other aspects of American freedom that stood in sharp contrast with spiritual freedom, these now are sacralized through an explicit linkage with Christianity. He describes them as "a very theological conception of freedom" that is "very much a part of Christian faith." Part of the idea, he acknowledges, is "an American freedom," especially "freedom focused self-empowerment and self-determination." But those ideas are tempered by the idea of "doing good works that God wants you to do," rather than being "free to do whatever."

The language this man uses is richer than in many interviews, but for this reason provides a good illustration of the several ways in which people of faith assert that their faith is relevant to questions about freedom in different cultural settings, including America, while drawing distinctions that they believe to be more reasonable than simply expressing a kind of nationalistic equivalence between America and the Almighty. The complexity occurs at three levels. One involves distinguishing some aspects of American freedom that are desirable and some that are not. In a larger sense, this is what thoughtful people are taught to do. The goal is to move past categorical thinking to more nuanced concepts that permit critical distinctions to be drawn. A second involves distinguishing the spiritual understanding of freedom in Christ in sufficient detail from popular understandings of temporal or cultural freedom so that each can be described separately, rather than conflating the two or ignoring one or the other. The third is the ability to map the two sets of contrasting elements onto one another, but to do so without losing sight of the difference between ideas about spiritual freedom and ideas about cultural freedom. For instance, enslavement to one's job is parallel to enslavement to sin, and yet is not the same. Similarly, freedom from slavery and racial discrimination is encouraged by the Christian gospel, but also remains distinct.

A notable feature of discourse that operates at all of these levels is that it does not provide a definitive answer to whether or not the desire for freedom is universal. Indeed, it implies that the question itself is too simple. If the reference is to spiritual freedom, a reasonable answer is that humans everywhere *should* want freedom, but perhaps do not because they are in sin. The answer might also be that *God* wants people to be free, but they are not and will not be because of sin. If the question is framed in purely cultural terms, one answer is that there may be some innate desire for freedom, while another answer is that the desire is present or absent depending on cultural circumstances. These ambiguities nevertheless make it difficult for people of faith to come right out and say that the desire for freedom is *not* universal. To believe that would go against the idea that God has created everyone with this desire, and by implication, possibly that being set free by Jesus may not be what people want. For those who view the latter chiefly as freedom from sin, the logical problem is less severe. People who are free from sin can be happy even if they do not have or even want freedom of worship, speech, association, and so on. As one woman put it, "People have been tortured and exiled and yet in their heart and soul they can still think the way they want to think." However, if freedom from sin means becoming fully human or gaining the ability to be one's true self, those human desires for freedom become more important. How then to say that the desire for freedom is universal without seeming to deny the cultural differences that are so obvious historically and in today's world? People struggle with this.

A Catholic woman who holds an administrative position in the federal government illustrates the difficulty. She thinks freedom in Christ is an important aspect of what it means to be Christian. But she mostly thinks of it in terms of its relevance to her personal life. It helps her detach from concerns that might otherwise drag her down. "When things are going badly," she says to herself, "Well, there's a rhyme and a reason to this, and God's going to get me through it. I'll be a better person for it in the end." When her thoughts turn to freedom on a larger scale, she suggests that a distinction does need to be drawn between the American version of freedom and a more universal view. Yet she acknowledges being unsure of how to describe it. She draws two contrasts. One is between "actual" and "economic" freedom.

Actual freedom, she says, involves "knowledge of Christ" and "caring for others," whereas economic freedom means "freedom to dispose of your money as you wish." The other contrast is between "basic" and "extreme" freedom. Basic freedom is a "basic desire everywhere" and includes freedom of movement and association. Extreme freedom is "the way in which it has been defined in the U.S." It "comes without responsibility." Her conclusion is that the "universal concept" of freedom differs from the "U.S. sense." "Basic freedoms are definitely universal," she says, adding, "I can't define for you what exactly those basic freedoms are."

Interpreted one way, the difficulty this woman has in defining basic freedoms might be taken as an indication, as I implied, that she thinks too much about her own emotional well-being and not enough about larger questions. However, that interpretation fits poorly with the fact that she is highly educated, holds a responsible administrative position in government, and has lived and traveled in several societies where she has been a keen observer of cultural differences. It also is belied by the fact that she actually mentions five specific basic freedoms: "freedom of movement," "freedom of association," "freedom to practice one's faith," "freedom to live one's life according to one's beliefs," and "freedom to protect oneself." She is also quite explicit about the extreme freedom she sees in America: "the least involvement of government as possible," "low taxes," "46 million people without health care," "failure of the government," "losing your health," and a lack of "communal responsibility," "social cohesion," and "equal opportunity." Why then does she seem uncertain about basic freedoms? The key probably lies in the fact that they are "basic." Basic occupies the same place in her discourse as the spiritual concept of freedom in Christ does in others', and in hers as well. Although she gives everyday examples of what this freedom may mean (such as a positive and "kinder and gentler" outlook), she also uses language that resists close definitions. Freedom in Christ is "the deep knowledge of Christ." It means that "your eyes should be firmly focused on heaven." It involves detachment from "material desire," is "achieved by knowing Christ," and it is "very hard to know how it's going to manifest itself in your life." Spiritual freedom and basic freedoms are similar in these respects: They contrast with the surface realities of life and are for this very reason too important to define precisely.

I have argued in this chapter that a common phrase that is so much a part of biblical tradition and repeated so often in religious circles that it becomes thoroughly familiar—a phrase that rolls off the tongue without requiring much thought at all—is part of how reasonable people talk about their faith, not only because it is taken for granted, but also because it is couched in language that makes it seem reasonable. To demonstrate this fact, I have examined in close detail what people say when asked to talk about the teaching that Jesus sets them free. Sensitivity to these nuances of language is gained by starting with thoughts about why the phrase might seem strange or naïve. A skeptic unfamiliar with the phrase would certainly consider it so. Jesus is not physically present, so how is it possible for Jesus to set someone free? How is it possible to be set free if someone is already free? Is supernatural intervention of some kind implied? Is being set free a metaphor, and, if so, what has to be said for the metaphor to make sense?

A brief survey of historical interpretations shows that religious leaders have described freedom in Christ as a spiritual transformation that involves the mystery of divine atonement for human sin *and* as a change that has tangible consequences in ordinary life. However, these consequences are described in ways that vary with temporal circumstances and that also resist being taken too literally. Thus, the condition of being in slavery may be used to illustrate an absence of freedom, but freedom itself may be characterized as emotional fortitude rather than actual emancipation. I suggested that religious communities have sometimes been able to control the more tangible applications of teachings about freedom through the use of relatively distinct religious language (such as substitutionary atonement), but that insulation is difficult when religious teachings are expected to be relevant in wider settings and when these settings themselves include so much language about freedom.

Freedom from unwanted feelings is a popular way to illustrate what it means to be set free by Jesus. The language used to describe these feelings characterizes them as long-term, natural, and somehow entrenched or endemic to the person's approach to life, rather than as short-term or influenced by specific events. Feelings of this kind connote bondage. Freedom involves release from bondage, most obviously as the absence of these feelings. However, it is apparently incongruous for reasonable people to assert that they never have unwanted feelings. The language includes assertions reflecting a kind of folk psychology of ordinary human behavior. Freedom in Christ means having freedom of choice, meaning that people can choose whether or not to enjoy its benefits. In addition, these choices depend on abilities that are shaped both by circumstances and the person. Some of these abilities have to be cultivated. The actual benefits of freedom occur gradually as a person grows and matures. The upshot is that freedom in Christ is neither as mysterious as it might seem nor as sudden or certain. A person who has been set free may choose not to be free, may not recognize his or her ability to choose, and may require some time to develop this ability.

Recovery from addictions provides a language for illustrating dramatic and powerful effects of Jesus setting people free. The before-and-after story draws a sharp contrast between a condition in which a person is enslaved and one in which a person feels liberated. The more desperate the former is depicted as having been, the more wonderful the latter appears. Truncating the path to recovery by describing it as sudden, surprising, or amazing further sharpens the contrast. However, sudden recovery appears to require greater credibility through the addition of qualifiers describing a longer and more arduous process. During this process, the role of freedom in Christ is to animate and empower the person's will. How that happens is left ambiguous, but is understood to involve ordinary human decisions, or is sometimes clarified through metaphors (such as falling and rising) and remarks about social support.

A reasonable response to the question of whether freedom in Christ and freedom American style are congruent or incongruent illustrates the complexities involved in drawing nuanced distinctions within and between the several usages of "freedom." Faith reinforces the conviction that freedom from sin is possible, but reason stops speakers short of equating this freedom with American values, except when those values are more specifically identified. Some of these popular understandings of freedom can actually be desacralized by language that associates them with bad choices, radical individualism, or delusions of control. The language about spiritual freedom, basic freedom, and universal freedom also defies easy categorization. It points to a domain that informs discussions of tangible freedoms but that also represents an ideal that is difficult to describe.

NOTES

1.   United Methodist Women, "If Not Now," online at gbgm-umc.org/umw; Mark Prevo, "Grace—Freedom from the 'Oughtness' of Life," *Journal Gazette* (September 2, 2005), C3; "Give Your Life to God; He'll Help," *Mobile Register* (October 15, 2003), D2; Ian Ma, "Faith: Some Things That Are 'Free' Carry Hidden Price Tags," *Courier News* (August 4, 2005); Jill Callison, "Faith Behind Bars," *Argus Leader* (December 24, 2003), 1A; Frank E. Lockwood, "Operation Starting Line Brings Religious Voice to State's Prisons," *Lexington Herald-Leader* (May 18, 2003), B1; Steve Heisler, "Church Provides Fellowship for Bikers," *Sarasota Herald-Tribune* (August 16, 2007), BM4.

2.   Augustine, *Confessions*, Book 3.

3.   On spiritual and temporal liberty, see especially John Calvin, *Institutes of the Christian Religion*, sections on civil government; and on balance and the avoidance of excess, helpful sources include Gustav E. Mueller, "Calvin's Institutes of the Christian Religion as an Illustration of Christian Thinking," *Journal of the History of Ideas* 4 (1943), 287–300, and Jane Dempsey Douglass, "Christian Freedom: What Calvin Learned at the School of Women," *Church History* 53 (1984), 155–173.

4.   *Matthew Henry's Concise Commentary* (1706), "Commentary on John 8:30–36"; online at www.christnotes.org.

5.   Charles Wesley, "And Can It Be" (1738).

6.   William Carus, *The High-Church Theory of Baptism* (Philadelphia: Collins, 1853), 43.

7.   Horace Bushnell, *Sermons for the New Life* (New York: Charles Scribner, 1858), 12.

8.   The connection between perfectionist theology of the period and Stowe's writing on slavery is usefully examined in Theodore R. Hovet, "Christian Revolution: Harriet Beecher Stowe's Response to Slavery and the Civil War," *The New England Quarterly* 47 (1974), 535–549.

9. George Barrell Cheever, *The Guilt of Slavery and the Crime of Slaveholding, Demonstrated from the Hebrew and Greek Scriptures* (Boston: J. P. Jewett, 1860), xv; the same theme is elaborated in George Barrell Cheever, *God Against Slavery and the Freedom and Duty of the Pulpit to Rebuke It as a Sin Against God* (New York: Joseph H. Ladd, 1857).

10. The quoted phrases are from the *Centennial Temperance Volume: A Memorial of the International Temperance Conference* (New York: National Temperance Society, 1877), 713–714.

11. John J. Martin, "The Nature of the Atonement," *American Journal of Theology* 14 (1910), 382–405; quotation is on page 383.

12. Various meanings of freedom in Christ are identified in Julian N. Hartt, "Christian Freedom Reconsidered: The Case of Kierkegaard," *Harvard Theological Review* 60 (1967), 133–144; and Robert T. Osborn, "Bultmann on Freedom," *Journal of Religion* 42 (1962), 22–33.

13. I checked. Between 1980 and 1987, the *New York Times* did not mention "substitutionary atonement" once, and *Newsweek*, *Time*, and other major news magazines mentioned it only twice. "Atonement," in contrast, was mentioned nearly a thousand times—seldom, however, with references to Christ (the most common references were to the Day of Atonement, to churches with "atonement" in their names, or to books and movies).

14. The same sources over the same period mentioned "freedom" more than 85,000 times.

15. William T. Sleeper, "Jesus, I Come," *Gospel Hymns* (1887).

16. James Regions, "Easter's Arrival Can Provide an Escape from Addiction," *Springfield News-Leader* (April 4, 2007), 9A.

17. Roy Tubbs, "A True Story of an Alcoholic's Deliverance," online at members.aol.com/roy2excel/myhomepage.

18. Vanessa Williams, "Bush Defends Iraq War in W. Va. Visit," *Washington Post* (July 5, 2004), online.

19. Examples can be found at www.whitehouse.gov, including speeches given on September 14, 2001; September 17, 2002; February 10, 2003; May 15, 2003; April 20, 2004; and May 5, 2005.

20. Quoted in Rich Lowry, "A Theology of Freedom," *National Review Online* (July 17, 2007), online at www.nationalreview.com.

21. Quotes are included in Ted Olsen, "Bush's Heresy," *Christianity Today* (July 19, 2007), online edition at www.christianitytoday.com.

SIX Billions of Galaxies

Few topics have brought faith and reason together as squarely or with as much conflict as controversies about science. Especially hotly contested has been the question of whether faith somehow implies views of divine creation or of intelligent design that fundamentally contradict the evidence scientists have gathered about biological evolution. Yet there are many other areas of potential conflict as well. For instance, if there are billions of galaxies in the universe, is it supremely egotistical for humans to think they are somehow uniquely created to have a relationship with God? Or as scientists learn more about the age of the earth and the many species that have inhabited the earth, does not that also cast humans in a different light than the high place they occupy in Scripture? On the one hand, faith and reason seem to be irreconcilably at odds; on the other hand, it is not uncommon to hear people say they have no difficulty reconciling faith and science. If the latter is the case, how is this possible?

Is it because people compartmentalize the two? Or are there cultural devices that facilitate talking about faith and science in reasonable ways?

In seeking perspective on recent controversies about religion and science, one can hardly do better than the wisdom provided by that Bible of guidance and revelation for thoughtful people, the *New York Times*. In its coverage of litigation about the teaching of intelligent design, of school board decisions about evolution, and of policy debates about stem cell research and genetic engineering, the nation's favorite arbiter of educated opinion has documented beyond doubt that questions about the respective roles of science and faith remain of great public interest. What is fascinating about the *New York Times'* coverage is not its reportage or even its editorials, but the letters it chooses to print from readers.

Unsurprisingly, many of the letters speak in favor of science, variously associating it with reason, hard evidence, discovery, and progressive thinking, in contrast with what writers perceive as ludicrous, disheartening, and even dangerous claims made by religious ideologues. A biology teacher from Illinois, for example, accuses religionists of "efforts to deprive millions of American students of the knowledge of how species change." Another writer from Illinois asserts, "As science has yet to prove or disprove the existence of a divine power, and probably never will, I will use my gift of reason, be it from God or evolutionary serendipity, to inform my beliefs and decisions." A scientist from California warns that religious groups could cause American science to be "set back several centuries [and] made the laughingstock of the rest of the world." Other writers note that science is universal, whereas religions are divided among conflicting traditions, and argue that knowledge will never be advanced by religion.[1]

A few readers question whether scientific facts are as firmly established as scientists claim and worry about the moral implications of science, and a handful go so far as to accuse scientists of promoting an agenda of unfettered atheism. A historian from Chicago, for instance, argues that evolutionary scientists "step well beyond science into philosophy and even theology" by asserting "that the theory of evolution leads to materialism without God." Another writer denies that evolution is fact or theory, preferring instead to call it historical interpretation.[2]

But far more interesting are the letters that seek to reconcile science and religion. For example, a reader from Minneapolis writes: "In my view, there is no contradiction between evolution and religion. One explains how, and the other explains why."[3] Alan I. Leshner, Executive Director of the American Association for the Advancement of Science, writes that "Believing in a god and accepting evolution are not inconsistent for many people. But religion should not be substituted for science, or the reverse, since they deal with different domains."[4] A scientist in Los Angeles observes, "Science is a tool for furthering human understanding of the natural world, and as such can co-exist with religion."[5] A reader in New Jersey elaborates: "Science is about the natural, material world; religion is about the supernatural and spiritual. Science operates mainly with numbers; religion with words." He concludes: "In short, they are separate but equal."[6]

This third category of readers presents itself as the defenders of a middle ground threatened as much by the simplistic proponents of science as by the radical claims of religious extremists. Theirs is a both-and rather than an either-or world. And they are in distinguished company. They stand with Albert Einstein, who famously remarked, "Science without religion is lame, religion without science is blind," and with Stephen Jay Gould, who argued that science tells us what the universe is made of while religion deals with ultimate meaning and moral value.[7] They often rise above the fray, so to speak, refusing to opt for the predefined positions presented to them, instead preferring to question the very terms in which the debate has been cast. They are capable of seeing both sides of an argument, of parsing what at first appear to be irreconcilable views and thus transforming black and white into shades of gray.

This is why the both-and arguments are so interesting and important. From a normative perspective, they are the preferred option, or at least abbreviated versions of what we might hope would be a happy way of resolving the seemingly endless tensions between science and religion. Yet, because they are prescriptively attractive, they also warrant closer attention. Standing comfortably on scholarly terrain, it is easier for academics to examine the extreme positions of those on the margins than to scrutinize the assumptions defining the middle. That, however, is what we must do if we are to learn how people of faith who feel inclined to be reasonable about it bring faith and science together.

It has not been especially popular, at least not in my discipline of sociology, for scholars to be interested in studying people who espouse a language of moderation and reason. That language is too much our own to feel the need to examine it. The more common tactic is to start from the supposition that proponents on the religious side of these—and most other—arguments are so downright strange as to deserve most of our attention. Thus, we dig a bit and find that they are really expressing some economic or political grievance that they are too dumb to recognize themselves, or worse, are being led astray by clever political operatives or self-aggrandizing religious leaders. For instance, in *What's the Matter with Kansas?* Thomas Frank, a native of that state who fled to the big time in Chicago, argues that Kansans vote Republican because they are obsessed with keeping evolution out of their schools and putting prayer back in, whereas voting Democrat would be better for their state's economy.[8] Jayhawkers are bargaining away the chance to give their children a better future, he says, by focusing more attention on moral battles than on good jobs and better schools.

Thomas Frank is perhaps not the best example of serious scholarship, since his book is candidly autobiographical and impressionistic. Yet it is worth noting that his work has been warmly embraced in the social science community.[9] A more thoroughly academic example can be found in the work of sociologist Amy Binder, whose book *Contentious Curricula* examines creationist controversies and who has turned her scholarly attention toward the debates about intelligent design.[10] Binder argues that creationists are cleverer than the naïve reader may have supposed. Leaders frame appeals in religious terms when speaking to church groups but downplay this rhetoric when talking to the media or in the courts. They strategically mobilize against school boards rather than against larger governing bodies because it takes fewer resources to do so. It helps when they win elections to these boards. It hurts when school administrators muscle creationists aside with assertions about separation of church and state.

The thrust of such work, perhaps unwittingly, has been to cast the religionists who oppose science in a more favorable light than they may have been viewed previously. They may be rubes and dupes, but if so they are also victims whose interests are not being served by their leaders. The leaders, for their part, may have backwoods ideas, but they are good strategists who know how to take the fight to their enemy. The leaders are especially good at cynically manipulating rhetoric for their self-interested aims. It all makes for good theater—the rhetoric of outsiders pushing their way in, of skirmishes, of combat, of winners and losers. Binder, for instance, in a discussion of intelligent design controversies, writes that her analysis tells "how we have arrived at this particular stage in the battle, and why we should be nearly certain that even if this soldier is defeated . . . the combat will rage on in new uniforms and new discursive artillery."[11] What such colorful rhetoric leaves out are the reasonable people, the more dispassionate souls who can look at the contest from a more nuanced position of neutrality.

It is understandable that scholars focus on what they perceive as deviant behavior. The very idea of a few citizens in out of the way places like Kansas and Dover, Pennsylvania, promoting strange ideas sends journalists and social scientists scurrying to study this quaint phenomenon. It is as if the Amish suddenly ran a candidate for president. What would the world be like if these creationists—whom their own neighbors describe as the laughingstock of the world—succeeded in eliminating science from the curriculum? Perhaps there is something to be learned about the peculiarities of American culture from these strange violators of accepted norms, just as there might be from studying serial killers.

If the goal is to arrive at a better understanding of American religion and culture, it nevertheless seems strange to focus so much attention on the periphery while neglecting the center. The both-and position expressed in thoughtful letters to the editor is held by a large share of the American public. In public opinion polls, this middle ground is favored by a majority or a large minority of the public, depending on the wording of specific questions. A 2006 CBS News survey, for instance, found that 37 percent of the public thought science and religion are "not related to each other in any meaningful way" and 26 percent though they "generally agree with each other," while only 32 percent thought they "generally conflict with each other." A CNN poll a year earlier found almost identical results. And an earlier poll for *Newsweek* showed 68 percent of the public saying "a person [can] believe in both religion and science at the same time," while only 25 percent thought the two "contradict one another."[12]

On the more specific issue of faith and evolution, the both-and position is also the majority view. A CBS News survey conducted in 2005 found that 67 percent of the public believes it is "possible to believe in both God and evolution," while only 29 percent thought this was not possible.[13] Another survey in 2005 asked, "Regardless of what you may personally believe about the origin of biological life, which of the following do you believe should be taught in public schools? Evolution only—evolution says that biological life developed over time from simple substances. Creationism only—creationism says that biological life was directly created by God in its present form at one point in time. Intelligent design only—intelligent design says that biological life is so complex that it required a powerful force or intelligent being to help create it. Or some combination of these?" Fifteen percent opted for only evolution, 21 percent for creationism only, and 5 percent for intelligent design only. In contrast, nearly half (47 percent) said a combination of these should be taught.[14]

The results of an earlier survey analyzed by George Gallup Jr. and D. Michael Lindsay in their book *Surveying the Religious Landscape* are also revealing. When asked in a 1997 Gallup Poll to say which statement came closest to their own views on the origin and development of human beings, 44 percent of the public opted for "God created human beings pretty much in their present form at one time within the last 10,000 years or so"; 10 percent selected the statement "Human beings have developed over millions of years from less advanced forms of life; God had no part in this process"; and 39 percent chose "Human beings have developed over millions of years from less advanced forms of life, but God has guided this process." In their analysis, Gallup and Lindsay compared the responses of different age groups, expecting to find that younger people would be considerably more likely than older people to select the response attributing human development solely to evolution. Contrary to this expectation, younger people were no more likely than older people to opt for the statement focusing on evolution. The largest differences were in the response attributing human development to a combination of evolution and divine guidance. Whereas only 23 percent of those age 65 and older chose this response, 49 percent of those in their 30s and 40s did so.[15] In short, the both-and view seems to be the one gaining in credibility.

The sheer reasonableness of the both-and approach, though, necessarily raises interesting questions. First, why is it that science and religion appear to be in conflict at all? Is it that the antagonists who perpetrate these struggles are less reasonable than everyone else? Is it perhaps true that they are simply duped by their leaders? If it is so sensible to argue that science and religion are simply different, would it not be more likely that conflict between the two would be nonexistent? Pursuing these questions will provide a way of examining afresh why religion and science might not be so easily reconciled, even for reasonable people. Once we have considered these possibilities, though, a different question arises: Why are the conflicts between science and religion as infrequent as they are? This question will take us into the larger terrain of language and culture where we can view the assumptions that undergird the conviction that reasonable people can resolve the differences between science and religion.

The potential for conflict between religion and science is evident from the extent to which the two interact. To understand this interaction, a useful place to begin is the idea social scientists refer to as institutional differentiation. This notion, simply put, is that the various spheres of social life are more distinct and specialized than they were in earlier times when societies were smaller and less complex. For instance, Max Weber argued that one of the important preconditions for the rise of modern capitalism was the separation of paid labor from households. This separation of spheres, Weber suggested, made it possible for labor to be governed with greater attention to rewarding productivity than was the case when workers were also family members.[16] Drawing on Weber and likening social change to the evolution of biological organisms, Talcott Parsons described institutional differentiation as the process through which "a unit, sub-system, or category of units or sub-systems having a single, relatively well-defined place in the society divides into units or systems (usually two) which differ in both structure and functional significance for the wider system."[17] The emergence of modern science in seventeenth-century Europe is typically considered an example of institutional differentiation. Although its rise may have been facilitated by religion, science became an autonomous sphere, capable of setting its own agenda and determining for itself what activities were worth pursuing.[18]

If science and religion are distinct institutions, this separation might be a reason to believe that potential conflict would be overcome by recognizing their differences. These are not merely conceptual differences, such as one of emphasizing the natural or supernatural, but also of social arrangements themselves. Scientific academies do science and religious organizations do religion. Scientists do not preach and preachers are ill-suited to conduct scientific research. Of course it might be objected that greater specialization requires greater interaction across the two spheres—a point Émile Durkheim emphasized in describing the "organic solidarity" that arises from people with different occupations becoming interdependent.[19] Einstein's assertion about science and religion being lame or blind without each other recognizes this interdependence. The two spheres are not only different but also necessary to each other. In this sense, science and religion are not entirely autonomous, but serving different social functions means that they can nevertheless coexist. Thus, as the *New York Times* reader argues, maybe science can tell us how, but religion tells us why.

This argument needs to be examined further, though. A baker and butcher might be mutually dependent, but it is less clear that science and religion bear the same relationship to one another. A better analogy would be two all-purpose delis, one specializing in bread and the other in meat, but both seeking to expand their sandwich business. Science and religion come into conflict because neither stays neatly in its respective sphere. As Gili S. Drori and his co-authors observe in their study of the global expansion of science as a cultural form, "A reasonable way to interpret the long history of conflict between scientific and religious models is to see these institutions as competing on the same ground, rather than operating in different domains."[20]

As science has grown, its autonomy has been compromised by the very fact that it influences more aspects of social life and in turn is dependent on a wider array of social, economic, and political resources. Consider the ways in which science has expanded since its modern origins in the seventeenth century. The patronage that supported Kepler's observatory in Denmark, Galileo's research in Italy, the Royal Society in London, and the French Academy of Sciences in Paris came from royal coffers, the Medici, and other wealthy individuals such as the Dukes of Savoy and Tuscany.[21] Only much later did governments require average citizens to support science through taxes and to expose their children to science in public schools. The advance of science was an act not only of intellectual achievement but also of political displacement. "The three estates of the realm," wrote Don K. Price in his memorable account of this transition, "were the clergy, the nobility, and the burgesses." The privileges of all three were curtailed. "But now," Price observed, "the results of scientific advance have been to require federal support of education and the appropriation of a tithe of the federal budget for research and development, to set up the most powerful and professional military force in history, and to make free competition a minor factor in the relationship to government of some of the major segments of the economy."[22] The implication is that religion and science may well come into conflict, even though they occupy different places in society. A person of faith who feels threatened by science, for example, is still required to pay taxes to support science and may well have children who learn about it at school. Similarly, a scientist may be unable to secure federal funding for stem cell research because religious groups have blocked funding for this purpose. In either case, the parties involved may disagree that science concerns itself only with "how" and religion only with "why."

The idea that science merely describes the natural world, leaving questions about purpose and worth to religion, also too easily denies that conflict will ever arise. The sharp increase in developing nations' founding of government-sponsored science ministries and participation in international scientific organizations illustrates the extent to which being "modern" and "progressive" requires at least a symbolic commitment to science. Being an educated person does not require knowing anything about religion but does involve taking courses in science, passing examinations testing one's familiarity with scientific thinking, and being respectful toward science in one's work and at parties. In these ways, science shapes the cultural norms that serve as standards of self-worth. A person who understands science is not simply more knowledgeable than one who does not, but is likely to be deemed more worthy and deserving of greater self-respect and prestige. Understandings of personal identity and worth are influenced in additional ways by scientific discoveries. The meaning of human personhood is profoundly shaped by how humanity itself is located in an evolutionary chain or an expanding view of nearly infinite galaxies.

For its part, religion may appear in many instances to be in retreat, but it too expands periodically out of its earlier domain. The role of Darwinism in the rise of late-nineteenth-century Protestant fundamentalism is an example. Fundamentalism was as surely an attempt to be scientific as it was an effort to resist science. Millenarian predictions about the fulfillment of biblical prophecies gained popularity as these arguments relied more heavily on numeric calculations and new certainties about the orderly progression of time.[23] Later, during the 1950s, religious organizations drew significantly from the social sciences (especially psychology) and from the expanding mental health movement in developing new and more highly specialized programs of pastoral counseling.[24] This expansion put religion in greater contact with science than if religion had avoided all efforts to deal with health. The more recent emergence of creation *science* and of arguments about intelligent design, borrowing as they do from scientific studies and from critical discussions within the scientific literature, are another such example.[25]

The interaction that results when science and religion expand onto each other's turf is more complex even than an image of competition implies because the boundaries defining the two spheres are themselves matters of negotiation. What Thomas F. Gieryn calls "boundary work" consists of scientists' on-going efforts to create a favorable "public image for science by contrasting it favorably to non-scientific intellectual or technical activities."[26] In Victorian England, for instance, scientists publicly ridiculed church leaders who prayed for God's intervention against the cholera epidemic of 1866, denounced prayer as a form of superstition, and charged the church with standing in the way of scientific progress. Gieryn suggests that religion bashing actually served scientists well, meaning that in a convoluted way religion as an enemy of science is also its friend. Rather that depicting religion as something different from science but useful in its own way, scientists characterized it as pseudoscience based on false empirical claims. That such uses of religion by scientists continue is readily apparent. Writing in the *New York Times*, evolutionary biologist Olivia Judson argues, for instance, that an understanding of evolution is vital to guarding against a flu pandemic and "saving the lives of tens of millions of people." By implication, religionists themselves might be responsible if a flu pandemic occurs. "Let's not strip evolution from the textbooks," she writes, "or banish it from the class, or replace it with ideologies born of wishful thinking. If we do, we might find ourselves facing the consequences of natural selection."[27]

Boundary work suggests conscious and even malicious manipulation of the turf wars between religion and science. It is also the case, though, that boundary questions become important because definitions of "religion" and "science" are themselves vague. For instance, popular assertions about religion often assume that it is readily defined by belief in God or resort in some other way to arguments about the supernatural. Yet scholars of religion seldom define it in those terms. Clifford Geertz's well-worn definition, for example, refers neither to God nor to the supernatural but emphasizes symbols, powerful and long-lasting motivations, and conceptions of a general order of existence.[28] Would that definition not apply equally to some understandings of science?

Recent treatments have challenged Geertz's view for being imprecise and insufficiently connected with social conditions.[29] Yet recent scholarship about the definition of religion emphasizes how contingent it is on these very conditions. The idea of "world religions," as Tomoko Masuzawa has shown, was as much an invention of Western philologists and anthropologists at the height of European imperialism as it was of anything in the regions where these religions were located.[30] Taking the same view a step further, Russell T. McCutcheon argues that scholars of religion continue to construct their subject matter in ways that "obscure the theoretical and methodological modes of its production."[31] If scholars themselves engage in political acts when they conceptualize religion, as McCutcheon suggests, the implication is that scientists, school boards, and journalists do too when they discuss the tensions between religion and science.

Science has come under scrutiny for the same reasons. What counts as scientific fact is by no means dictated only by nature itself. "Scientific activity is not 'about nature,'" Bruno Latour and Steve Woolgar write in their influential ethnographic study of laboratory life, "it is a fierce fight to *construct* reality."[32] They do not mean that scientists falsify their observations or fabricate reality from thin air. They do show through numerous examples how scientific conclusions are influenced by the availability or unavailability of instruments, how powerful teams impose standards that may reduce the ability of other teams to compete, and how tentative statements preclude the possibility of pursuing other reasonable lines of investigation.

Other studies lend weight to the contention that science is not an unambiguous domain that can readily be set apart from considerations about power and culture. A study of the peer review process through which fellowships are allocated, for instance, demonstrates that "originality" is highly valued across disciplines—but how originality is defined varies widely and is not the only criterion used; indeed, peer reviewers frequently resort to language about the *moral* qualities of researchers.[33] Another study draws similar conclusions from examining the discussions of Institutional Review Boards concerning the ethics of research involving human subjects. Although these boards were initiated in response to concerns about unethical behavior on the part of scientists, none of the boards studied included persons professionally trained in ethics. Instead, scientists themselves dominated the boards and focused on editorial minutiae (such as spelling and typos) and judgments about methodological rigor, while seldom talking about ethics at all.[34] Whereas these studies emphasized the social factors influencing science, the biological factors have been examined through fMRI brain imaging studies conducted by neuroscientists. These studies demonstrate more clearly than in the past how higher-order or "top-down" processes of conceptualization override sensory or "bottom-up" information to the point that people with different mental categories actually see the world differently.[35]

The most direct way in which science conflicts with religion is by placing religion itself under the microscope. At least since the Enlightenment, religion has been viewed as a feature of the human world that is as subject to empirical investigation as anything else. Scientific inquiries have focused not only on finding alternatives to religion in other realms (such as medicine), but also on discovering naturalistic explanations for religious behavior itself. As Leigh Eric Schmidt has shown, studies of magnetism, ether, ventriloquism, and hypnosis were all employed to this end.[36]

The implication is that science and religion cannot be compartmentalized as easily into separate and noncompeting domains as some observers would like to think. As long as the two have fuzzy edges, proponents, antagonists, and bystanders in the general public will be able to contest where one domain should end and the other should begin. The likelihood of such contestation increases, moreover, because religion and science are never static. Both struggle to assert themselves as legitimate ways of addressing important issues and thus as legitimate claimants of social resources.

Apart from specific conflicts between religion and science, a second reason to expect controversies about science is the public's ambivalence toward science itself. Consider the fact that of the nine national polls conducted between 1993 and 2001, in all but one a majority of the public agreed that "we depend too much on science and not enough on faith." Or consider the fact that in another national survey 47 percent of college graduates agreed that "we believe too often in science and not enough in feelings and faith" (39 percent of those with graduate degrees agreed).[37] This ambivalence may have little to do with organized religion, but in a society as religious as the United States is, it can be a source of particular tension for people of faith. The ambivalence stems from the high expectations the public attaches to science, on the one hand, and the public's sense, on the other hand, that intuition and emotion are important and, for that matter, scientists may be cold, impractical, egotistical, and irreligious. The latter view is especially evident in public skepticism about science.

Philosopher Paul Ricoeur's phrase, hermeneutics of suspicion, is helpful for understanding the current ambivalence toward science. In Ricoeur's usage, the phrase referred to the critique of religion that one finds in Marx, Nietzsche, and Freud. These masters of suspicion, as Ricoeur termed them, unveiled the illusory character of religion by showing that it concealed political and economic interests.[38] To see reality clearly, one needed to unmask the false perceptions of religion. In our time, this skeptical attitude toward religion has extended to science. Power and privilege most certainly lie with the scientific estate as much today as with religion in the past. The high esteem in which the public holds science and scientists, if polls are to be believed, is tempered with the ambivalence that colors public attitudes toward all elites. Admiration bleeds easily into envy and further into disdain. If a segment of the religious community stands ready to battle science over evolution and genetic engineering, this broader hermeneutics of suspicion is a predisposing factor.

Science is sometimes popularly regarded as the great savior, bringing hope for conquering illnesses and inventing labor-saving technology, but its image has also been tarnished. Critical discussions of science seldom pass up the opportunity to connect it with the development of the atomic bomb. In medical research, the infamous Tuskegee experiment, in which some four hundred poor black men were not told they had syphilis and never treated for it, all in the name of research, is often mentioned. In the social sciences, the experiments conducted by Stanley Milgram, in which subjects were instructed to administer what they presumed to be painful electric shocks to fellow subjects, are characterized as a lesson in depravity. Environmental concerns have also affected public perceptions of science. "Ever since the publication of Rachel Carson's Silent Spring in the 1960s," former National Science Foundation Director Richard C.

Atkinson recalls, "there was a growing feeling abroad that the purity of science . . . was not quite as pure as it had seemed."[39] Although these examples are perhaps unfairly characterized as typical of science, it is not surprising that they raise questions about scientists' values. One of the most common ways in which ordinary people maintain their sense of personal dignity, research has shown, is to depict themselves as having higher moral standards than those above them in the cultural pecking order. Religious commitments often go hand in hand with that sense of moral propriety.[40]

A further contributor to the potential conflict between religion and science is the fact that relatively few scientists are themselves religious (at least in conventional ways). This is a point worth emphasizing because proponents of accommodation between the two cite examples of scientists who believe in God as evidence that science and religion are not contradictory. Francis Collins, a molecular biologist who headed the National Human Genome Research Institute and who is a devout Christian, is a favorite example. "I find my appreciation of science is greatly enriched by religion," Collins has been quoted as saying. "When I discover something about the human genome, I experience a sense of awe at the mystery of life, and say to myself, 'Wow, only God knew before.' It is a profoundly beautiful and moving sensation, which helps me appreciate God and makes science even more rewarding for me."[41] Yet for every quote like this, there are also negative comments, such as Richard Dawkins' remark that religious faith is "one of the world's great evils, comparable to the smallpox virus but harder to eradicate."[42]

Research suggests that pro-religion scientists like Collins are the exception rather than the rule. In a national survey of physicists, chemists, and biologists at elite research universities, only 8 percent said they had no doubts about God's existence, while 38 percent said they did not believe in God and another 29 percent said they did not know if there is a God and believed there was no way to find out. In the same survey, 55 percent said they had no religious affiliation and only 16 percent attended religious services at least once a month.[43] These figures underscore the sharp differences that exist between scientists and the general public, where, for instance, only 7 percent can be regarded as atheists or agnostics.[44] Atheists, moreover, continue to be widely disliked in the general public, eliciting, for instance, indications of social distance more often than any other minority group, including Muslims, Jews, African Americans, and homosexuals.[45] If the public imagines that scientists' personal views influence their scholarship, then perceptions of conflict between religion and science would not be surprising.

Another confounding aspect of the relationship between religion and science is what might be termed the hubris of science. Having considered Einstein's remark about the complementarities of religion and science, it is worth recalling Abraham Heschel's rejoinder: "Hubris, the tragic sin of our time, is the conviction that there exist only laws of nature and technology."[46] Heschel's view is currently echoed in Internet blogs, where this perception of science surfaces freely. "I'm skeptical of scientists and technologists designing animals or genes or drugs or anything else that nature already does perfectly," one blogger remarks. In this blogger's view, scientists are drunk on hubris, in it for the money or their own glory, and sadly incapable of any humility. Annie Dillard, the Pulitzer Prize–winning author of *Pilgrim at Tinker Creek*, which was widely praised for its sensitivity to the complexity of the natural world, identifies hubris among scientists as well. In *For the Time Being*, Dillard adds a theological, cultural, and historical dimension to her reflections. Noting that our time has produced antibiotics, silicon chips, men on the moon, and spliced genes, she asks, "Are not our heightened times the important ones?" She might have added that after eons of evolution suddenly we, through the explorations of science, are now the first ever to have grasped that process. Surely science has taught us so much in the last century that we could not possibly be wrong about what we know. Do we not have good reason to think that our time is especially significant? Her answer: "These times of ours are ordinary times, a slice of life like any other. Who can bear to hear this, or who will consider it?"[47]

Perceptions of scientific hubris are a reminder that cultural disputes with science are not limited to religion. The "two cultures" that C. P. Snow described in the 1950s were not science and religion but science and the humanities or, more specifically, literary intellectuals. Snow argued for greater interaction between science and the humanities, but his remarks about science include criticism. "The scientific culture," he wrote, "is expansive, not restrictive, confident at the roots, the more confident after its bout of Oppenheimerian self-criticism, certain that history is on its side, impatient, intolerant."[48] Snow's concerns continue to be voiced in larger criticisms about the moral fragmentation of a culture in which the can-do attitude of science overwhelms questions about deeper values. Noting contemporary society's assumption "that *every* problem facing mankind is susceptible to technological intervention and control," Roger Kimball writes, for instance, that "the temptation to reduce culture to a reservoir of titillating pastimes is all but irresistible." In this critique, science is not so much the only source of cultural deterioration, but a contributor to the malaise that includes drugs, violence, promiscuity, and an insatiable desire for gratification.[49]

Given the wider ambivalence toward science, it is perhaps surprising that religion is so often singled out as the archenemy of science. Other antagonists could be found in the humanities, in special interest groups, and certainly in the political sphere.[50] But religion appears to conflict with science more often than these other disputants. The reason is arguably that religion and science represent totalistic views of the world, each making absolute claims about the nature of life itself.

With such potential for conflict, the truly interesting question is not why some people view science and faith at odds, but why so many do not. Why are the skirmishes between science and religion relatively rare? Why is it that among the more than 14,000 school districts in the United States, for instance, only a few have had litigation about evolution and intelligent design? What accounts for the fact that most Americans are able to take a both-and approach to science and faith?

Public opinion researchers have long recognized that people give inconsistent responses in surveys without feeling a need to reconcile the apparent contradictions.[51] Anthropologists argue that one of the central features of tribal rituals is their capacity to hold in tension two seemingly opposite beliefs or practices.[52] Cognitive dissonance theory, though no longer as uncritically accepted as it once was, asserts that people adjust their beliefs when asked to perform tasks that deviate from their values.[53]

The common thread is that the mind is malleable and finds ways to create order—or escape having to create order—when tension arises.

Yet the point is not *that* people reconcile themselves to seemingly contradictory beliefs or statements about the world, but *how* they do this. In the case of both-and views about science and religion, resolution does not come by adjusting one's views to be more compatible with *only* science *or* religion. Nor does it involve simply keeping the two apart. The cultural work involved is more complex and, although it includes specific ideas about religion and science, it is also associated with broader ways in which our culture enables us to minimize conflict.

An instructive comparison case is the tension in American culture between individualism and altruism. The two are not mirror opposites, any more than science and religion are, but they do run in opposing directions. Individualism connotes looking out for self-interest, whereas altruism means putting another's needs ahead of one's own. In interviews, altruists who are also individualistic manage the potential conflict by employing discursive devices, one of which is multivocality— literally, speaking through the voice of different characters—saying, for instance, "I help at the soup kitchen one night a week and people there tell me, 'You are really a kind-hearted person,' but I say, 'No, not really. I get a lot out of being here.' I have to admit, though, sometimes I'd rather stay home and relax." Although the remarks are uttered by one person, the different voices permit the complexity to be displayed. The speaker at once affirms that she does engage in helping behavior and is perceived as being altruistic, but also denies being purely altruistic, even while acknowledging that she is making a sacrifice.[54]

A multivocal statement like this is so effortless that its significance is easily missed. The exchange substitutes for taking a single position on whether one is individualistic or altruistic. It depends on flexibility or even decoupling of the various components of one's self—what psychologist Kenneth J. Gergen calls *multiphrenia* or the "splitting of the individual into a multiplicity of self-investments."[55] A multiphrenic person does not say, as Martin Luther did, "Here I stand. I can do no other." Instead, there is a separation of roles and of facets of the self to the point that one can imagine taking several different positions on a topic and engaging in a kind of internal conversation among the proponents of those views. It becomes possible to say, "I heard that Albert Einstein thought it was possible to believe in God and be a scientist, so I suppose if I thought about it more, I might come to the same conclusion, although you could probably persuade me otherwise if we talked long enough."

Examples of multivocality in dealing with questions about science and religion are not hard to find. On October 24, 2005, the U.S. District Court transcript in *Kitzmiller v. Dover Area School District*—the much publicized case in which plaintiffs sued the Dover, Pennsylvania, school board for requiring that criticisms of evolution based on ideas about intelligent design be incorporated into the curriculum—included the following exchange between the plaintiffs' attorney Witold J. Walczak and Professor Stephen Fuller, a sociologist testifying as an expert witness on behalf of the defense:

> Q. Mr. Rothschild asked you, "A theory is not going to graduate into a fact; right?" And the answer was, "Right, exactly, exactly. No, I mean, I do think there is—that the tone of the statement is a little confusing. I mean, so I'm agreeing with Miller [another witness] on that point."
> A. But what I'm agreeing with Miller on is, I can understand why he sort of sees it that way. I wasn't necessarily saying that I had some definitive view about what the statement meant, but rather that I was sympathetic to—you know, I could see where he was coming from in finding this problematic.

Although the attorney persisted in attempting to force Fuller into declaring that he regarded evolution as theory, fact, or some combination of the two, Fuller made it clear that he was merely thinking through the issue and could see it from several different angles.[56]

Negotiating among competing perspectives is strikingly evident in the following example as well. "I do not know whom to believe," a college student writes. "I am handed Bibles on campus and told by pious individuals that God's word is law, only to sit down in class and be handed an excerpt from a scientific journal full of evidence I myself did not collect and which supports a conclusion the foundation of which I am expected to take for granted." His conclusion? "It doesn't matter what you believe, only that you do, because gods and science are divergent approaches to truth that can never be known."[57]

Language that incorporates different voices as a way to reconcile religion and science is consistent with norms of tolerance and respect. Social scientist Alan Wolfe, in *One Nation, After All*, argues that middle-class Americans are remarkably generous toward others who may have profound differences of belief.[58] Wolfe concludes that the so-called culture war, which pits fundamentalists against those with more enlightened views, does not characterize the majority of Americans.[59] The prevailing view, he says, is that we may have our differences, but should abide by the law and treat all views with respect.

In addition to showing respect, multivocality can be a way of indicating that neither science nor religion demand 100 percent commitment. For instance, in arguing that science describes nature while religion deals with questions of meaning and value, a person can in effect point to the limitations of both. Descriptions of nature are incomplete, disappointing, even meaningless, and yet the big questions that religion tries to answer may also be elusive. Thus, concerns about the hubris of science do not take shape as convictions about religion but as unanswered questions about the worth of scientific knowledge. Similarly, doubts about religion remain as uncertainties, rather than translating into a devout faith in science.

In personal interviews, additional ways of negotiating the relationship between religion and science emerge. One in particular differs from the language we have encountered in talk about prayer, tragedy, heaven, and freedom in Christ. In those instances, interviewees find ways to show that much about God is humanly unknown, but few claim not to have thought about the topics. In contrast, the issues raised by science are often less personally relevant, and for this reason easier to acknowledge not having considered. A person can thus avoid perceiving conflict between science and religion by claiming that the topic simply is not worth thinking about. Questions about cosmology provide a vivid example. Scientific discoveries about the solar system and about other galaxies are common fare in science sections of national newspapers and on television programs about science. For more than a decade, astrophysicists have estimated that there are at least 125 billion galaxies in the universe, and probably many more, each with somewhere between 100,000 and a million stars.[60] Technical details aside, the immensity of the universe alone should be reason to ponder its implications for thinking about life on earth. Yet when asked their thoughts about the vastness of the universe, interviewees are sometimes surprisingly candid in acknowledging that they have no opinion. "Oh, I don't think about that," says an insurance executive in Illinois, "I never think about galaxies and planets." An attorney in Virginia asserts, "I don't think about that very often. I mean, the world is a big place, but I don't think about it." A high school teacher in Minnesota expresses a similar view. "My wife and I have laughed about this," he says, "because there's a lot of science that says things like blah, blah, blah, and I'm like, really? So what?"

The reason it is acceptable not to think about cosmology, interviewees say, is that it has no bearing on their personal lives. "I live in today," the insurance executive says. "That doesn't affect me one bit." The attorney explains, "I'm more concerned about the here and now, about what's immediate." The teacher says he just is not "wired" to lie out on a grassy field and be a "scientific wonderer." A business manager in Colorado adds this: "As far as the universe goes, it's something that is not relevant to my daily life."

For some, the point is not simply that they are too busy to ponder questions that have no immediate relevance. It is rather that religious faith itself should, in their view, focus on personal life and not on speculation about the universe. A business manager who attends an evangelical church in Pennsylvania puts it this way. "God has a plan based on allowing me to live in the 1900s and now in this century, and I'm content to pretty much see the world as it has a direct effect on me." A member of a megachurch in California echoes this sentiment: "I just know that God created the world that I live in, and that's really all I worry about." Or as a physician in Arkansas asserts, "I leave the running of the universe to God. I've got enough to do right here."

What these comments convey is trust. They suggest that a person should not feel overwhelmed or insignificant because the universe is vast. At the personal level, life still has meaning. But emphasizing personal relevance can have other connotations as well. It can imply that how one thinks about science (if one does think about it) is really just a matter of perspective after all. A thoughtful young man named Steve who participated in a national study of teenagers, for example, worried that evolution emphasizes self-preservation, which in turn could conflict with universalistic religious notions of morality; and yet he did not worry very deeply about this potential conflict because the ideas were just "fun to think about and kind of interesting, 'cause, I don't know, I don't really let it bother me." He tempers his views about morality and rationality by asserting, "Let each person decide for themselves."[61]

Personalization of this kind fits well with the view that science exists mostly to provide each person with a better life. In a survey conducted for the National Science Foundation, for instance, 86 percent of Americans agreed that "science and technology are making our lives healthier, easier, and more comfortable."[62] Science is in this sense pragmatic. From day to day, it matters less whether science reveals how life evolved or how vast the universe is than that it yields vaccines and new pharmaceuticals. Knowing that humans are a small speck in a nearly infinite universe, or that they share a high proportion of genetic material with other primates, are matters of idle curiosity.

In other cases, especially among people who have spent more time considering the relationship of science and religion, a *possible* option is to argue that science and religion conflict and indeed that science is wrong. In national polls, as many as a quarter of the public say they disbelieve some of what scientists argue. For instance, a 2007 poll showed 28 percent regarded as "definitely false" the view that "human beings developed over millions of years from less advanced forms of life."[63] It is instructive, though, to consider the language that people use to explain *why* they disbelieve the claims of scientists.

One argument says, in effect, that it is important to believe in what we know rather than in what we do not know. This argument is similar to the ones that skeptics of religion make when they assert that science provides knowledge, whereas religion offers only speculation. However, skeptics of science turn it around. What *we* know essentially means what we as Christians know. The head of a construction firm in Pennsylvania provides an example. He is not uneducated—he has a college degree and graduated recently enough that he was exposed to science in the courses he was required to take. However, he attends a small evangelical church and is much more interested in what the Bible says than in what he learned about science. When asked about the vastness of the universe, he says that is "way beyond my reach" and "we have enough to deal with here, just in our lives." The scientific discoveries are not as relevant to his thinking as the fact that "this is where God is working." He explains that "this is where God's working and this is the planet that he's created." Because God is working here on earth, this man focuses his thoughts on what he knows about creation. "You know, starting with Adam and Eve, it's all part of creation. The planets and day and night and water, I think all that was created together." He never says explicitly that he thinks scientists are wrong in arguing that the universe is much older and that human life evolved. He simply argues that it makes sense to him to view it all through the lens of what he knows about God.

This example suggests that it may be difficult for people who disbelieve in science to come right out and say they do. Science carries tremendous authority. People may feel ambivalent about it and think that it oversteps its bounds, but it is hard to deny that it has credence at all. In controversies about creation and evolution, defenders of creation generally do not argue for divine revelation in place of science. They try to use science itself to poke holes in arguments about evolution. In ordinary speech, a similar tactic occurs. Consider this remark: "I don't believe the earth is billions of years old. I studied Genesis this year and I still don't have a total understanding of how old the earth is, but I don't think it's as old as what everybody thinks it is or what the scientists say it is." The speaker is an automobile mechanic who attends a conservative Protestant church in Idaho. His formal education ended in twelfth grade. At first glance, he appears to be voicing unabashed disagreement with scientists. But it is important to note how tentative his remarks are. He follows his assertion about disbelieving the earth is billions of years old by acknowledging that he has not arrived at a firm understanding of the earth's age. His mention of scientists follows the phrase, "what everybody thinks," implying either that he recognizes himself to be in a minority or that it is as much prevailing opinion that he disagrees with as scientists. He adds, "I think that there's no way to prove it otherwise." In short, he does a lot of hedging in stating his disagreement.

Tentativeness about disagreeing too strongly with scientists is evident even in comments about the controversy over evolution. An interesting example comes from an older man who attends a mainline Protestant church in Maryland and for many years was the director of a nonprofit organization. He says God created everything and insists that the idea of evolution "never has bothered me personally." However, he clearly favors the creationist view. He demonstrates this preference without explicitly attacking the other side. He says, "I just happen to believe in the order of Adam and Eve." He also says that "the evolutionists want to say that we evolved from a serpent or apes." Thus, his own belief is softened by its happenstance nature, while the opposing view is a caricature about a snake and held by "evolutionists."

Other language for registering disagreement with evolution adopts a parsing approach. Evolution is credited with being right in most respects, but wrong on a few particulars. The particulars do not discredit the entire theory, but open space for saying that God was somehow involved. A college professor, for example, explains in detail that evolution is essentially a process of random mutation and natural selection and that he agrees with the latter but not the former. "Random mutation—that's complete randomness of the whole process—is the part I simply cannot agree with," he asserts. The reason he disagrees is that randomness is a "violation to a core Christian belief which I hold, which is that human beings are created for a purpose." Yet he goes on to say that "I don't believe God is kind of switching the mutation" and he concludes, "That's my spiel on that." Another example comes from a business manager who attends a Methodist church. He favors intelligent design because "there's a lot of

gaps in the evolution theory" and "some good scientific evidence pointing to some flaws in it." He hesitates to say what those flaws are, though,
acknowledging, "I'm not necessarily, you know, an expert on this."

Language demonstrating that science and faith are *compatible*—that it
is reasonable to take a both-and view—brings God squarely into the
picture, arguing that God had an active hand in creating the universe,
and yet emphasizing that the details of creation are neither known nor
especially important to know. The vastness of the universe serves as a
metaphor for the greatness of God. The more science learns about the
scope and complexity of the galaxies, the more spectacular God's glory
is assumed to be. There is no sense, contrary to what skeptics argue, that
a person could be just as awed thinking that only nature was involved.
The assumption is rather that God simply exists and is reflected in
the natural processes. The reasonable response for the ordinary non-
scientist is to see a connection, not to bracket faith from science, nor to
argue about how exactly the two are connected.

A Catholic who manages a business in California and considers himself reasonably knowledgeable about science reconciles his faith with
science by asserting that God is "large" enough to have done anything,
including creating other planets capable of sustaining life in other galaxies. As far as life on earth is concerned, he says, "Who is to say that it
wasn't God that put his finger in the water and said, I want you to grow
now." He explains, "There are lots of scientific facts that say this is how
we became man and how we evolved. But there's nothing that explains
how life became life."

A Methodist who runs a consulting firm in Michigan and says he
loves to think about galaxies and planets and the possibility of life elsewhere in the universe argues that scientific discoveries do not challenge
his faith at all. They simply show that "God is bigger than anybody
imagines." The Bible, in his view, "was never written to be a science
book." Using the book of Genesis as a scientific explanation of the creation of the world, he says, "is moronic, stupid. It's a poem about the fact
that God is the creator of all. But how he chose to do that, we don't know.
Or when, you know?"

A very similar observation comes from a stockbroker who lives in Mississippi and attends a conservative independent Bible church there. The idea of multiple galaxies, he says, "is a wonderful thing. It makes me know God is bigger than I ever thought he was and is unconstrained by my limit of thought. To me it is just a glorious thing to think that God is that big that he has created all these universes and that he has been here forever and he is going to be here forever." The largeness of the universe reminds him not only of God's power, but also of his own inability to comprehend that power. "Those things are just so big and so above what I could think that they just remind me of how big God is." He adds, "That's the kind of God I want on my side when tough times come."

In each of these remarks, it is as if the speaker envisions a universe that is very large and then imagines that God has to be even larger to have created it. Nobody imagines, for instance, that God may be infinitesimally small, like a compact energy source, and yet powerful enough to create something so large. Nor does anybody speculate that God has to live very far away if the universe is this big. The remarks suggest that skeptics who think of God as a supernatural person living above the clouds somewhere are out of touch. God is a flexible concept that fits easily into discourse about different situations. In this context, size matters. As a member of a nondenominational church in Illinois who works as an architect says, "There is a really big God who no doubt created all of everything." Or as a physician in Idaho explains, she thinks about God's "massiveness" whenever she considers how expansive the universe is.

Besides awe at God's size, the vastness of the universe inspires remarks about God's love. That it does is perhaps surprising, because a massive God that created multiple galaxies would seem too remote to be concerned about specific individuals. Yet the language suggests otherwise. A college professor who attends a mainline Protestant church in Virginia says, "God is concerned about and involves himself with human beings on this planet that is just one little speck of the entire universe. That demonstrates God's love for us." His view resembles that of the man in Mississippi who imagines a massive God coming to his rescue when times are tough. A teacher in Indiana expresses a similar thought: "It just feels nice to be part of such a huge thing and to have a small part in it. God knows we're here and is looking after us and giving us what we need. I find that kind of cool." On the topic of evolution, she explains that what matters is that "God is involved in my day to day life" and, as far as she is concerned, it does not matter "whether the biblical story is literal, whether there are elements of symbolism in it, or whether it is just somebody's story."

These comments are strikingly devoid of easy demarcations between science and religion based on, for instance, facts versus values, knowledge versus faith, or how versus why. Faith and science interpenetrate. But they do so amicably because ordinary speech brackets out the thorny details that plague academics when they try to reconcile the two. Consider how a teacher who attends an evangelical church in Arkansas describes the lack of tension she feels between science and her faith. On the one hand, she thinks there are other planets in the universe capable of sustaining life and imagines that intelligent beings populate these planets. She also accepts as fact that the earth may be billions of years old and that human life evolved over a very long time. On the other hand, she believes God created the universe and has a plan for every living being. She also knows that the Bible describes God creating the world in seven days. But she rejects choosing between evolution and creation. "Evolution is no problem for my faith," she declares. "I believe that whatever got started happened, and how it happened is of no big importance to me." She begins to say more, pauses, and explains, "It's hard for me to separate all this into a hard and fast understanding." Then, restating her belief that God created the world, she concludes, "I accept that and don't take it apart and look at it piece by piece."

Is this the kind of blind faith that worries scientists? Or is she saying that science and faith do not have to be reconciled in fine detail? Assume for the moment that the latter is the case—an assumption that squares readily with the fact that she majored in biology, has taught high school math and science for several decades, and gives thoughtful answers to other questions about current affairs, politics, and religion. Is this not the level of detail that a reasonable person would have at his or her command if asked to talk about science and faith? At some point, the person probably became convinced that the evidence for evolution is compelling, but can no longer cite specifically what that evidence is. The person has also found it meaningful to believe in God as creator and sustainer of life. The reasonable response is to say that, for me personally, the two ideas are merely different.

The other feature of contemporary understandings of religion that contribute to the ease with which people reconcile it with science is the idea that God is ultimately a mystery. Whereas language about creation often leaves room for the unknown, language about mystery specifically applauds it. God is that which science cannot explain. Equally important, God's existence is implied by the logic of discovery itself and by the amazement of the unexpected. Belief in God as mystery does not entail an argument against searching for scientific knowledge. It rather emphasizes that science itself finds knowledge that ordinary humans have difficulty comprehending. Faith serves not so much to fill in the gaps but as an outlook on life that pervades science as well as religion.

A sales representative in Tennessee who attends an Episcopal church says, "Oh, it's a big mystery," when asked about the origins of human life. "It's more mysterious than we as human beings will ever discover. I do believe it's divine." An office assistant who attends a Baptist church in New York has a similar response when asked about the spiritual implications of the vastness of the universe. "We can't comprehend it," she says. "Just like we can't comprehend God. We don't know if God is a he, a she, an it. We can't wrap our heads around that." She says it would not surprise her if God had created the earth as a "speck in the whole, big, humongous picture," and that she just "can't comprehend it at all." A business manager in Texas responds simply, "It's just amazing. It's kind of like, Wow!" He adds, "Only God has it figured out."

The language typically describes mystery in positive terms. Although the unknown can be frightening or overwhelming, the connotation in this context is more often one of excitement at the possibilities for discovery and indeed at opportunities for exercising the imagination. "Isn't it exciting? Just think of the possibilities," a teacher in Minnesota says when asked about the vastness of the universe. A homemaker in Arizona goes a step further. She recalls growing up and wanting firm answers. It scared her not to have strong boundaries around her beliefs. But in middle age she is finding greater freedom in her faith. "I think God is very creative," she says, implying that people of faith should be creative too. "My imagination goes crazy. I wonder how many different planets there might be on earth. Could we break an atom down further?" She muses, "Is there another color we don't know about? How does a bug's mind work?"

A registered nurse in Illinois expresses a similar sense of exhilaration about the intersection of science and faith. At her parish a group of about a dozen people get together on Sunday evenings to discuss books. One they read recently was about cosmology. She says it was especially meaningful because she has long felt a strong connection to the natural universe. One evening she told the group about watching pelicans flying overhead on their way north, tilting for the sun to catch their wings. Another evening she took the group to the edge of town to watch an unusual alignment of the planets. "For me," she says, "this is what God is all about. Not this man up in the sky. Not the Father. It's all of that. It's all of life around us. That's what God is for me."

To sum up, a large majority of the American public believes that science and religion do not conflict and, on the surface, this belief makes sense. As letter writers to newspapers argue, science and religion are different domains, the one dealing with facts and the other with values. I have argued, though, that this way of thinking is too easy. It ignores the fact that science and religion are institutional domains that sometimes expand into what leaders of the other view as their turf. Scientific discoveries pose questions about the meaning and significance of human life, and religious groups are known to argue that particular scientific pursuits (such as stem cell research) violate the sanctity of life. The taxpaying public holds ambivalent views about science that sometimes play into these religious concerns. The potential for conflict between science and religion is sufficiently great that it is actually surprising that overt conflict is not more frequent than it is.

The mitigating factors include technical specialization that discourages religious leaders from claiming scientific expertise and scientists from asserting theological arguments, as well as the public's willingness to embrace science as long as it contributes to technological innovation and medical discovery. In addition, there are ways of talking about science and religion that reduce the perception of conflict. As one example, I mentioned multivocality—the ability to speak from several different points of view and thus to demonstrate the provisionally of one's own perspective.

But, unlike beliefs about such topics as God, prayer, death, and heaven, beliefs about science are for many people less personally relevant. Although they are likely to have taken courses in science if they attended college and may follow the news about scientific discoveries, they feel it is legitimate to not hold opinions about science. There may be life elsewhere in the universe or evolution may have occurred over millions of years, they say, but that has little bearing on their own life. The distance they feel from science allows them to assume that science and religion operate in different spheres. Science is for specialists who largely concern themselves with topics that have little immediate relevance, whereas religion includes daily conversations with God and beliefs that assist in making it through the day.

The idea that science requires opinions only if it is personally relevant does appear to be conducive, in some instances, to negative views of science. These views are reinforced by categorical thinking in the media and from advocacy groups that frames arguments under broad headings and through poignant examples. Language such as "evolution is corrupting morals," "evolutionists believe life has no meaning," "scientists are atheistic," and "evolution doesn't explain this or that fact" are examples.

The more common ways of talking about science and faith emphasize compatibility between the vastness of God and the complexity of the universe. The language does not sort science and faith into separate domains; rather, it brings the two together. If there are billions of galaxies, that implies only that God is immense or that God is especially loving to be interested in humans on one planet in one galaxy. If human life evolved, God surely was involved somehow in the process.

The other point of compatibility is in language emphasizing mystery. Instead of science being described as a body of factual knowledge derived through rigorous empirical observation, it is depicted as an ever-changing series of explorations in which each discovery shows either that previous assumptions were wrong or that more remains to be known. The language describes God in similar ways. God is not the author of definitive knowledge written in Scripture, but a source of awe and wonder. In both science and religion, the appropriate stance toward life is to be surprised.

NOTES

1. "When Politics Mixes with Evolution," *New York Times* (May 13, 2007), A11; "Faith, Reason and a G.O.P. Hopeful," *New York Times* (June 1, 2007), A24; "Can Science and Religion Co-Exist?" *New York Times* (August 24, 2005), A16.

2. "Religion, Science and Our Identity," *New York Times* (October 7, 2005), A28.

3. Julia Williams Robinson, "Religion, Science and Our Identity," *New York Times* (October 7, 2005), 28.

4. "Faith, Reason and a G.O.P. Hopeful."

5. John S. Torday, "Can Science and Religion Co-Exist?" *New York Times* (August 24, 2005), 16.

6. Manfred Weidhorn, "It's Science or Religion," *New York Times* (October 8, 2005), 14.

7. Albert Einstein, "Science, Philosophy and Religion: A Symposium," in *Conference on Science, Philosophy and Religion in Their Relation to the Democratic Way of Life* (New York: Jewish Theological Seminary, 1941); quoted in Gordy Slack, "When Science and Religion Collide or Why Einstein Wasn't an Atheist," *Mother Jones* (November/December 1997), online edition. Stephen Jay Gould, *Rock of Ages* (New York: Ballantine, 1999).

8. Thomas Frank, *What's the Matter with Kansas? How Conservatives Won the Heart of America* (New York: Metropolitan Books, 2004).

9. Embraced as one of the keynote speakers at the American Sociological Association meetings in Philadelphia in August 2004, for example, and at a major conference at New York University.

10. Amy Binder, *Contentious Curricula: Afrocentrism and Creationism in American Public Schools* (Princeton, NJ: Princeton University Press, 2002).

11. Amy Binder, "Gathering Intelligence on 'Intelligent Design': Where Did It Come from, Where Is It Going, and How Do (and Should) Educators,

Scientists, Non-Profit Organizations, and the Media Manage It?" Paper presented at the Center for Arts and Cultural Policy Studies; Princeton University, November 2005.

12. CBS News Poll (April 9, 2006); CNN Poll (September 11, 2005); *Newsweek* Poll (November 4, 1994), available online from roperweb.ropercenter.uconn .edu.

13. CBS News Poll (October 23, 2005), available online through LexisNexis Academic.

14. Center for Public Policy, "Virginia Commonwealth University Life Sciences Survey," (October 24, 2005), available online through LexisNexis Academic.

15. George Gallup Jr. and D. Michael Lindsay, *Surveying the Religious Landscape: Trends in U.S. Beliefs* (Harrisburg, PA: Morehouse, 1999), 36–38.

16. Max Weber, *The Protestant Ethic and the Spirit of Capitalism* (New York: Charles Scribner's Sons, 1958).

17. Talcott Parsons, *Societies: Evolutionary and Comparative Perspectives* (Englewood Cliffs, NJ: Prentice-Hall, 1966), 22.

18. Joseph Ben-David, *The Scientist's Role in Society: A Comparative Study* (Englewood Cliffs, NJ: Prentice-Hall, 1971); Bernard Barber, *Science and the Social Order* (New York: Free Press, 1952).

19. Émile Durkheim, *The Division of Labor in Society* (New York: Free Press, 1915).

20. Gili S. Drori, John W. Meyer, Francisco O. Ramirez, and Evan Schofer, *Science in the Modern World Polity: Institutionalization and Globalization* (Stanford, CA: Stanford University Press, 2003), 9.

21. Robert Wuthnow, *Meaning and Moral Order: Explorations in Cultural Analysis* (Berkeley and Los Angeles: University of California Press, 1987), 279.

22. Don K. Price, *The Scientific Estate* (Cambridge, MA: Harvard University Press, 1965), 18.

23. Richard L. Rogers, "The Role of Elites in Setting Agendas for Public Debate: A Historical Case," in *Vocabularies of Public Life: Empirical Essays in Symbolic Structure*, edited by Robert Wuthnow (London and New York: Routledge, 1992), 234–247.

24. Susan E. Myers-Shirk, "'To Be Fully Human': U.S. Protestant Psychotherapeutic Culture and the Subversion of the Domestic Ideal, 1945–1965," *Journal of Women's History* 12 (Spring 2000), 12–36.

25. Robert Wuthnow, *All in Sync: How Music and Art Are Revitalizing American Religion* (Berkeley and Los Angeles: University of California Press, 2003). I have termed this process selective absorption. Through changes in the wider society that may range from scientific or technological innovations to shifts in the role of government, new needs and opportunities emerge, and

organizations of many kinds, including religion, compete to take advantage of these opportunities. Other examples include the development of family ministries in response to the baby boom after World War II, new faith-based service organizations in response to the Charitable Choice legislation of the 1990s, and religious programs responding to the growing influence of television, the Internet, popular music, and the arts. Selective absorption involves competition not only over ideas, but also about credentials, resources, and who has a legitimate right to make authoritative assertions.

26.   Thomas F. Gieryn, "Boundary-Work and the Demarcation of Science from Non-Science: Strains and Interests in Professional Ideologies of Scientists," *American Sociological Review* 48 (December 1983), 781–795; quotation is on p. 781.

27.   Olivia Judson, "Evolution Is in the Air," *New York Times* (November 6, 2005), 13.

28.   Clifford Geertz, *The Interpretation of Cultures* (New York: Basic Books, 1973), 90.

29.   Talal Asad, *Genealogies of Religion: Discipline and Reasons of Power in Christianity and Islam* (Baltimore: Johns Hopkins University Press, 1993); Nancy Frankenberry and Hans Penner, "Geertz's Long-Lasting Moods, Motivations, and Metaphysical Conceptions," *Journal of Religion* 79 (1999), 617–640; Keven Schilbrack, "Religion, Models of, and Reality: Are We Through with Geertz?" *Journal of the American Academy of Religion* 73 (June 2005), 429–452.

30.   Tomoko Masuzawa, *The Invention of World Religions* (Chicago: University of Chicago Press, 2005). See also the useful discussion of approaches to defining religion in Thomas A. Tweed, "Marking Religion's Boundaries: Constitutive Terms, Orienting Tropes, and Exegetical Fussiness," *History of Religions* 44 (February 2005), 252–276.

31.   Russell T. McCutcheon, *Manufacturing Religion: The Discourse on Sui Generis Religion and the Politics of Nostalgia* (New York: Oxford University Press, 1997), 26.

32.   Bruno Latour and Steve Woolgar, *Laboratory Life: The Construction of Scientific Facts*, rev. ed. (Princeton, NJ: Princeton University Press, 1986), 243.

33.   Joshua Guetzkow, Michele Lamont, and Gregoire Mallard, "What Is Originality in the Humanities and the Social Sciences?" *American Sociological Review* 69 (April 2004), 190–212.

34.   Laura Stark, *Morality in Science: Evaluating Research in the Age of Human Subjects Regulation*. Ph.D. dissertation, Department of Sociology, Princeton University, 2006.

35.   For a general discussion, see Stephen M. Kosslyn, *Psychology: The Brain, the Person, the World* (Boston.: Allyn & Bacon, 2000).

36. Leigh Eric Schmidt, *Hearing Things: Religion, Illusion, and the American Enlightenment* (Cambridge, MA: Harvard University Press, 2002); see also Ann Taves, *Fits, Trances, and Visions* (Princeton, NJ: Princeton University Press, 1999).

37. The nine surveys were conducted by the National Science Foundation as part of its "Public Attitudes Towards and Understanding of Science and Technology Trend Surveys, online at roperweb.ropercenter.uconn.edu; the percentages agreeing in each year were: 1983, 54; 1985, 57; 1988, 52; 1990, 51; 1992, 48; 1995, 52; 1997, 47; 1999, 50; 2001, 50. The other survey was the 2000 General Social Survey, electronic data file (my analysis).

38. Paul Ricoeur, *Freud and Philosophy* (Boston: Beacon, 1970).

39. Richard C. Atkinson, "The Golden Fleece, Science Education, and U.S. Science Policy," *Proceedings of the American Philosophical Society* 143 (September 1999); online at www.ucop.edu.

40. Michele Lamont, *The Dignity of Working Men: Morality and the Boundaries of Race, Class, and Immigration* (Cambridge, MA: Harvard University Press, 2000).

41. Gregg Easterbrook, "Science vs. Religion?" (2000), online at beliefnet.com.

42. Richard Dawkins, "Is Science a Religion?" *The Humanist* (January–February 1997), 26–29; quotation is on page 26.

43. Elaine Howard Ecklund and Christopher P. Scheitle, "Religion among Academic Scientists: Distinctions, Disciplines, and Demographics," *Social Problems* 54 (2007), 289–307; and Elaine Howard Ecklund, *Science vs. Religion: What Scientists Really Think* (New York: Oxford University Press, 2010).

44. Penny Edgell, Joseph Gerteis, and Douglas Hartmann, "Atheists as 'Other': Moral Boundaries and Cultural Membership in American Society," *American Sociological Review* 71 (2006), 211–234.

45. Ibid.

46. Abraham Heschel, "Answer to Einstein," *Conservative Judaism* 55 (Summer 2003), 39–41. I am grateful to Martin Kavka for this source; see his "The Meaning of That Hour: Prophecy, Phenomenology and the Public Sphere in the Early Heschel," in *Religion and Violence in a Secular World: Toward a New Political Theology*, edited by Clayton Crockett (Charlottesville: University of Virginia Press, 2006), 108–136.

47. Annie Dillard, *For the Time Being* (New York: Knopf, 1999), 30.

48. C. P. Snow, "The Two Cultures," *New Statesman* 52 (October 6, 1956), 413–414.

49. Roger Kimball, "The Two Cultures Today," *The New Criterion* 12 (February 1994), online at www.newcriterion.com.

50. For instance, Ronald Reagan's budget director David Stockman did far more damage by eliminating from the National Science Foundation

all science education activities and all funding for the social sciences than any school board decision favoring the teaching of intelligent design is likely to do.

51.   Philip E. Converse, "The Nature of Belief Systems in Mass Publics," in *Ideology and Discontent*, edited by David Apter (New York: Free Press, 1964), 206–261.

52.   Geertz, *Interpretation of Cultures*, 142–169.

53.   Leon Festinger, *A Theory of Cognitive Dissonance* (Evanston, IL: Row and Peterson, 1957); for criticisms, see Charles G. Lord, "Was Cognitive Dissonance Theory a Mistake?" *Psychological Inquiry* 3 (1992), 339–342.

54.   Robert Wuthnow, *Acts of Compassion: Caring for Others and Helping Ourselves* (Princeton, NJ: Princeton University Press, 1991).

55.   Kenneth J. Gergen, *The Saturated Self: Dilemmas of Identity in Contemporary Life* (New York: Basic Books, 1991), 73–74.

56.   United States District Court for the Middle District of Pennsylvania, *Kitzmiller v. Dover Area School District* (October 24, 2005), 8–10.

57.   Chad Wilcox, "Religion, Science Both Require Believer's Faith," *Daily Athenaeum* [West Virginia University] (October 18, 2007).

58.   Alan Wolfe, *One Nation, After All: What Americans Really Think about God, Country, Family, Racism, Welfare, Immigration, Homosexuality, Work, the Right, the Left, and Each Other* (Baltimore: Penguin, 1999). The words in quotes are mine, not from the book, but based on remarks by Professor Wolfe during a personal conversation.

59.   See for instance James Davison Hunter, *Culture Wars: The Struggle to Define America* (New York: Basic Books, 1991).

60.   Besides articles in the mass media, educational materials on the topic are especially interesting; for example, see "In Search of Galaxies," National Aeronautics and Space Administration, Goddard Space Flight Center (2001), online at http://hubblesite.org.

61.   Christian Smith, *Soul Searching: The Religious and Spiritual Lives of American Teenagers* (New York: Oxford University Press, 2005), 96.

62.   National Science Foundation, *Science and Technology: Public Attitudes and Public Understanding* (Washington, DC: Government Printing Office, 2004).

63.   *USA Today* Poll (June 3, 2007), online at roperweb.ropercenter.uconn.edu.

SEVEN

Conclusion

A young pastor struggling to start a church in his basement felt himself surrounded by the forces of Satan. Neighbors told of farmers finding their cattle dead in the fields with organs removed and no sign of tire tracks or blood. A coven nearby was reportedly teaching children to experience demons. An anonymous caller phoned in the middle of the night, threatening his life and the lives of his family. The pastor prayed in anguish. What could he do? A few weeks later, after praying and fasting for three days, he drove to the top of a mountain not far from his home, prayed some more, and received a vision from God. The city would be transformed. There would be a huge, life-giving church on a hill. The man came down from the mountain and with his small band of followers, prayed over a five-gallon bucket of cooking oil, and began walking the sidewalks, blessing the streets block by block, and anointing them with oil.[1]

Prior to his resignation in November 2006 over alleged sexual encounters with a gay prostitute and methamphetamine use, Reverend Ted Haggard was one of the most powerful figures in American religion. His mountaintop vision of 22 years earlier had come true. The city had been transformed. Colorado Springs was the home of his New Life Church, a congregation of 14,000 with a sprawling campus that included its 7,500 seat auditorium, a Bible-themed play land for children, and the World Prayer Center. The city was the home of so many other religious organizations that it was sometimes called the Mecca of the Christian Right. Focus on the Family, the International Bible Society, Navigators, Young Life, Compassion International, Mission of Mercy, and dozens of other organizations located their headquarters there. Haggard was president of the National Association of Evangelicals. He appeared often on CNN, ABC, NBC, and Fox News, was quoted repeatedly in the *New York Times*, and made visits to the White House. *Time* named him one of the 25 most influential evangelical Christians in America.

The story of Haggard's meteoric rise and dramatic fall was widely repeated for a few months as journalists savored the irony and saw in it symptoms of the declining political influence of Christian conservatives. But an earlier incident that drew only passing attention holds even more significance for understanding American religion. In May 2005 Reverend Haggard received word that broadcaster Barbara Walters was planning to visit New Life Church in preparation for an ABC special about life after death to be aired later that year. Eager to make a good impression, Haggard circulated an e-mail to the congregation with advice about how to relate to the media. The e-mail warned against behavior during worship services that "looks too bizarre," such as dancing and jumping. "Worship indicates sincerity," it said, "dancing and jumping looks like excessive emotionalism." The e-mail further cautioned against talking about "the devil, demons, voices speaking to you, God giving you supernatural revelations, etc." Above all, it concluded, "don't be spooky or weird."[2]

An admonition by a leading religious figure against being spooky or weird poses interesting and important questions. An electrical engineer, whose anonymous blog site published Haggard's e-mail, suggested that the church was making an "attempt at faking what actually goes on." Was it? A New Life staff member explained to a Denver journalist that "we weren't trying to shape the experience of the media," but simply suggesting "mind your manners." Meaning what? Another commentator, who thought jumping and dancing in church was perfectly legitimate, accused "uptight secular types" from the media of "putting a damper" on things. For what reason? Journalist Jeff Sharlet, author of an article about the church that had recently appeared in *Harper's*, said he had interviewed a woman at the church who did like to dance during worship and believed in deliverance from demons. "The best things about New Life," Sharlet observed, "are the fog machines and the glow strings and the jumping. That stuff's fun."[3] Was fun the point?

If Sharlet is right, religion is at heart spooky and weird, and any attempt to hide this fact is disingenuous. The truth is that American religion does include, and always has included, the spooky and weird, as well as a notable penchant for reason and respectability. One has only to mention demon possession, exorcisms, hauntings, spiritualists, snake handlers, and talk of Satan, or miraculous healings, spectacular visions of the Virgin Mary, and the imminent return of Christ to understand that religion quite often extends beyond the polite norms of propriety. Sharlet's entertaining *Killing the Buddha: A Heretic's Bible*, with co-author Peter Manseau, provides ample evidence of these eccentricities in stories of cross-dressing terrorists, born-again strippers, cowboy preachers, and other stranger-than-fiction accounts. Is it not the case, Sharlet asks, that American religion is composed of bizarre beliefs and practices, and the mainstream media keep us from seeing it?[4]

In the scholarly literature on religion, there has been no dearth of attention to religious manifestations that deviate from reason and respectability. World rejection, as Max Weber famously termed it, occurs in myriad ways, including magical practices that defy ordinary rationality, charismatic leaders, and prophets who challenge the authority of existing institutions. World rejection also occurs in beliefs that emphasize heaven, mystical withdrawal from secular activities, abstinence from sex, celibacy, civil disobedience, and any number of other acts that set believers apart from the rest of society. Cults and sects typically reject the wider culture in one or more of these ways by, for instance, abandoning the pursuit of material goods, dressing simply, living communally, preparing for the return of Jesus, or seeking to build a utopian society on earth. The scholarly literature also suggests that sects mature, as it were, becoming less at odds with the wider culture as they grow and prosper—an argument that that fits well with New Life Church's apparent progression from feeling besieged by demons and witches to cautioning its members against being spooky and weird.[5]

What popular and scholarly treatments of world-rejecting religion have not dealt with adequately is the tension between faith and reason that continues to exist for practitioners of respectable religions. It is this tension to which Reverend Haggard's advice points. The advice cautions not only against being weird, as the bloggers emphasized, but also against being spooky. Weird involves mannerisms that are simply out of place, such as jumping when others are not jumping or being a born-again prostitute when other prostitutes are not born again. Spooky implies an intrusion into ordinary life from another realm, such as ghosts and goblins, or, as Haggard put it, "voices speaking to you" and "God giving you supernatural revelations." Those are more problematic. Even believers who do not jump or dance are supposed to believe that the supernatural exists, that they can pray to God and receive answers, that miracles happen, that God can work in wondrous ways, that heaven is real, and that Jesus can set them free. These beliefs exist in tension with ordinary assumptions about the everyday world in which supernatural interventions do not occur. It may be especially problematic to talk about them with the media. But the media are not the only source of restraint against appearing spooky and weird. Indeed, the frequency with which stories appear in the media about everything from religious snake handling to prayers for rain to exorcisms suggests that the media are not a restraint at all. It is rather that people of faith are guided by their own desire to be reasonable. To be sure, people sometimes put themselves in contexts in which it is plausible to think and talk in other ways, and thus to pray for magical cures or denounce the influence of demons. But these contexts are never hermetically sealed. Believers usually attend the same schools as everyone else, live in the same neighborhoods, work for the same employers, shop at the same stores, and watch the same television channels. They are influenced by habits of thinking and talking that exist in all of these contexts.

Patterns of thought and speech can best be understood by paying close attention to what people say. Through examining remarks about prayer, tragedies and miracles, heaven, freedom in Christ, and science and faith, I have tried to describe the discourse in which reason is affirmed and faith is expressed. The language devices are too varied to be summarized in a simple catalogue or list, but several patterns that may suggest underlying rules stand out. One is evident in language that avoids saying too precisely what lies beyond the known world. This way of talking appears in discussions of what God is like, how God answers prayer, what God might or might not intend in allowing disasters to happen, what heaven is like, what the spiritual meaning of being set free by Jesus is, and how God may have created the universe. Although it is common for people of faith to assert that God is active or present in all of these contexts, there is a striking reluctance to voice opinions from either the Bible or popular literature and music about the exact nature of the divine. A related language device emphasizes aspects of the known world to supply implicit contrasts with the divine. Characterizing prayer as an activity of the small, weak, powerless, or infirm not only serves to show why a person is praying, but also implies that the being to whom prayer is offered is characterized by the opposite of these traits. Instances in which the boundary between natural and supernatural realms is crossed are especially interesting and problematic. On the one hand, the possibility of such transgressions signals special power, while, on the other hand, it is dangerous to say too much about how divine intervention happens or about how human souls pass into heaven because such claims can be disputed on grounds that a person truly cannot know the ways of God this clearly. Nevertheless, evidence suggests, as cognitive scientists argue, that humans use common mental categories to think about God, and thus think of divine actions affecting physical or mental states in much the same way that human actions do. Discourse about God also involves switches of register and parallel constructions that focus attention on known realities by objectifying these realities. Language about human effort, ability, and choice, as well as formulaic slogans and scripts, are among the devices that accomplish this objectification.

I have suggested that the language used to talk about faith serves the important goal of assisting people not only to express their religious convictions, but also to affirm that they are persons who consider themselves *reasonable*. Having considered numerous examples, we must now return to the question of what exactly being reasonable may mean in this context. It will be helpful to distinguish among three closely related terms: rationality, reason, and reasonableness. The question of whether religion is rational has been so often debated by philosophers, and more recently even by economists, that it is important to emphasize that rationality in that sense is not the issue. Reason comes closer, but is also not quite on target, which is why the somewhat more cumbersome words reasonable and reasonableness are necessary.

Standard definitions of rationality refer to persons who exercise reason and engage in reasonable behavior—thus providing little help in distinguishing more precise usages of the terms. In scholarly usage, rationality refers to arguments that are logically consistent and can be verified or to behavior that is compatible with achieving desired goals. There is a supposition that the rationality of a particular argument or act can be objectively determined by a disinterested observer. This means that different standards of rationality may be present in different contexts, although the aim of philosophical defenses is often to demonstrate that an argument is universally true.[6] A few examples will show what I mean.

The statement "If you drop something, it will fall" is likely to be regarded as a rational assertion in a wide variety of contexts. This is because gravity is assumed to be a universal physical law governing the motion of objects. It can be easily verified by dropping something. People agree that the statement is rational because the action it describes is true. Of course it is not always the case that something falls when dropped: A bird dropped flies away, a feather dropped in an updraft is more likely to rise than to fall, and an object dropped in outer space does not fall. Nevertheless, the statement is one we generally regard as rational because the exceptions can be accounted for and explained. Other statements about the physical world are deemed rational by the same logic. Science examines their validity, shows how and under what conditions they apply, and explains exceptions.

Statements about many other aspects of life, including religion, are often deemed rational or irrational by different criteria, although considerations of logical consistency and congruence with evidence may be included. One criterion emphasizes what might be called pragmatic or utilitarian rationality. A simple example is that if a person feels weak and hungry, a rational act is to eat. A more complex example is a society that wants to avoid violent and irresolvable conflicts and thus considers it more rational to focus on a commonly accepted value, such as fairness, than to bring in claims about divinely revealed truth. In both cases, disinterested observers could agree that the action taken gets the job done, even though they might disagree about other considerations (such as whether the person chose to eat the most nutritious food or whether the divinely revealed truths were really about irresolvable claims). A different criterion focuses on what Jürgen Habermas has termed communicative rationality.[7] According to this criterion, a rational solution to a problem is one that has been arrived at through open, frank discussion among all parties involved (for example, a committee discussing what its goals should be and how to achieve them). Other criteria assess rationality in relation to a prespecified and often formalized code of rules. These may be procedural rules of the kind that specify how a society is to hold an election; legal codes that determine how a police officer should inform citizens of their rights or how a judge should sentence someone convicted of a crime; bureaucratic rules, such as those prescribing how an employee is to be held responsible for behavior within an organization; or traditional rules, such as proscribing a man from marrying his brother's widow because customs or sacred traditions oppose it. Although the criteria differ in these examples, rationality is determined to pertain if an observer can identify the objective rules involved and decide if the behavior conforms to those rules.[8]

Efforts to determine whether religious behavior is rational generally adopt the logic involved in applying one or another of the criteria I have just described. A standard that is prespecified and thus assumed to be objective is set forth by an observer, and the behavior under question is judged accordingly. For example, in an effort to demonstrate that religion is rational, some observers have argued that utilitarian criteria should be the standard by which this determination is made, and therefore seek to show that churches facing competition work harder to solicit donations, that members threatened with hellfire participate more faithfully, and so on.[9] Among writers who take religion seriously, it is more common to apply the logic of communicative rationality, seeking, as theologians and philosophers of religion do, arguments with which they can agree about why humans are interested in transcendence or how various teachings about God fit together to form a coherent world view. Procedural, legal, bureaucratic, and traditional standards of rationality sometimes apply as well. Examples include the rules that religious organizations use to ordain clergy, vote on resolutions, choose bishops, or determine if policies conform with Scripture. Questions about rationality in these examples pertain more to particular religious activities than to broader philosophical considerations of whether religious faith is rational at all.

A common feature of all these criteria for assessing rational behavior is that they are fairly well institutionalized. The criteria are known and generally agreed on within particular contexts because they have been collectively developed and formally applied by the dominant organizations within these contexts. Nobody would imagine it appropriate to apply utilitarian criteria to the soul were it not for the overwhelming preponderance of such thinking in the marketplace and within economic organizations. Theological and philosophical discourse about religion generally takes place among a community of experts who share similar training and who bring familiar assumptions to their debates. Although the arguments may be presented in defense of claims about universal truth, they are posed in ways that depend on the shared language and skills of specialists. The procedural, legal, bureaucratic, and traditional standards against which the rationality of particular religious activities are judged are similarly institutionalized, usually within religious organizations themselves.[10]

What constitutes rationality in these institutionalized contexts can in part be regarded by practitioners as objective knowledge because there is agreement among persons in authority about the relevant criteria. This agreement is reached and maintained partly by bracketing out of consideration assumptions and arguments that do not fit the relevant criteria. For example, a skeptic who argues that praying is like asking a lucky horseshoe to regenerate an amputated limb is introducing assumptions that may be relevant in scientific contexts, but that have been deemed irrelevant in religious contexts. The statement necessarily implies that religion is irrational. In contrast, believers would find nothing irrational about asking the God of the universe to be present and to strengthen them as they seek advice from a doctor. Their way of thinking about prayer makes sense within the religious context with which they are familiar. Or, as another example, consider the claim voiced often in Christian sermons that Jesus was either a liar, a lunatic, or the Son of God. Citing biblical texts, apologists argue that the only rational conclusion is that Jesus was the Son of God because he could not possibly have been a liar or a lunatic. But that argument appears rational only if certain assumptions are made, such as the biblical text being a fully accurate account of what Jesus actually said, liars being intentional about their behavior, the meaning of lunacy being constant over the centuries, and there being no ambiguity raised by Jesus's descriptions of himself as the Son of Man.

My point is not that statements about rational behavior are impossible to defend or that any statement is as rational as any other. It is rather that claims about rationality are based on well-institutionalized rules and assumptions about which there is agreement within particular contexts and that give these claims status as objective and authoritative statements. This is an important consideration because casual remarks about behavior being rational often do not recognize the different criteria by which rationality is judged or the variation in how these criteria are applied in different contexts. The evidence shows otherwise. For example, Bruno Latour and Michael Mulkay's research among scientists shows that presumably rational ways of conducting experiments lead to quite different procedures because different scientists start with different assumptions about what the problem is. Frank Dobbin's research shows that French and British policymakers pursued rational strategies of promoting industrial development in the nineteenth century, but employed quite different understandings of rationality because of different precedents having been established in dealing with railroads earlier in the century. Cristina Mora-Torres shows that prosperity gospel preaching televised by the same religious organization depicts prayer as a rational way of acquiring material goods in Brazil and the United States, but encourages believers to engage in quite different behavior in the two contexts. Other studies show that meanings of rationality vary at different times and places for bioethical debates, environmental policy, and philanthropy. The implication is that assertions about rationality need to be made carefully and with consideration of changing meanings and contexts.[11]

Reasoned behavior can be distinguished from rational behavior. Whereas rational behavior presupposes an objective and institutionalized standard about which there is agreement, reasoned behavior pertains to the fact that an individual, if called on, can supply a reason for his or her behavior. The difference is evident in the following example: Asked why they are in law school, Student A says she wants a comfortable upper-middle-class lifestyle and being an attorney is in demand and pays well; Student B says a yellow bird landed on his shoulder one night while he was sleeping and told him to become a lawyer. A's answer is more likely to be perceived as a rational statement than B's, but in both cases the decision to attend law school is reasoned in the sense that A and B both supply reasons. A's reason appears rational because it conforms to utilitarian criteria widely encouraged in schools, by parents and guidance counselors, and by economists. On the surface, it seems rational, even though for A herself, it might be highly irrational by other criteria (such as having time to cultivate her exceptional talents as a concert pianist). B's answer seems irrational, but only because it is statistically less common than A's. Were B living in a society that took dreams and yellow birds as sources of authoritative wisdom, his reason would seem quite rational.

The question of rationality, though, is not the only or most interesting question in considering reasoned behavior. Indeed, an emphasis on rationality moves too quickly toward conclusions about some reasons being better than others, instead of examining the ways in which reasons are selected, combined, articulated, and deployed. Claims about rationality further focus attention on the assessments of external observers who are assumed to have the authority to make these assessments, rather than on the beliefs and utterances of people themselves. For example, utilitarian arguments about the rationality of religion are made by scholars who claim to find evidence that people are fundamentally driven by the desire to get as much as they can for the least cost, even though the people involved would not think that way and would find it repugnant to be told that they are nothing more than economic maximizers. A focus on reasoned behavior emphasizes the reasons that people themselves give. It emphasizes their thought processes to a greater extent than many arguments about rationality do. Reasons are among the ways that people make sense of their behavior. Reasons provide interpretive explanations that people use in talking to others and to themselves.

Reasons are part of what scholars of culture refer to as accounts.[12] An account is the narrative a person constructs in response to the question, "How did you arrive at the decision you made?" Or, "How did you come to be doing what you do?" Accounts make sense of a decision, act, or event after the fact by describing a starting point sometime prior to the event at issue, a middle that emphasizes particular aspects of the process leading up to the event, and an ending that shows what the event was or what happened after it.[13] Anticipatory accounts take the same narrative form, but start with the present and describe an imagined process that will result in a desired event. For example, a married person might describe the process of falling in love and deciding to be married, or an unmarried person might discuss what it would be like to fall in love and be married. Accounts also differ depending on the purpose for which they are told. For example, Ann Swidler shows how romantic love narratives are used to explain the choice of marital partners, while instrumental or utilitarian narratives are often employed for describing day-to-day relationships between spouses. Swidler observes that accounts are influenced by social institutions, such as the narratives people learn in classes about marriage or in religious organizations, but emphasizes that most people have repertoires that reflect their exposure to different institutions, their own creativity, and the different uses for which their accounts are articulated.[14]

Reasons occur in accounts as responses to why questions such as "Why did you decide to get married right out of college?" or "Why did you marry X instead of Y?" Reasons are more likely to be articulated when behavior is deviant or unusual. A person who marries at age 16 or 45 feels more of a need to give reasons for marrying at that age than someone who marries at an average age. Reasons are often more explicit or elaborate if a conflict of values is present. For instance, in a study of compassionate behavior, I found language that was true both to altruistic values and to the self-interested values that are also widespread in American society.[15] Reasons are sometimes implicit and have to be inferred from what people emphasize or remain silent about. For example, in research on success narratives among immigrants, I observed frequent comments about hard work, but few about assistance from friends.

People make sense of religious beliefs and activities by having reasons for them, and these reasons are a window into the prevailing values of a given time and place. It is instructive, for example, if people in one context say they go to church to prevent crops from failing and children from dying, but in another setting say going to church reduces anxiety. People continue activities for which they have good reasons and abandon activities for which they do not. Having good reasons to believe in God suggests that this belief will continue, whereas having no reasons may be a harbinger of flagging commitment. Naturally, religious authorities hope that the reasons they offer for belief and devotion will be ones that adherents embrace.

What I have referred to as reasonable behavior, or reasonableness, differs from both rational behavior and reasoned behavior. The contrast with rationality is evident in the lucky horseshoe example. People of faith would probably agree that it is irrational to ask a lucky horseshoe to regenerate an amputated limb. But it would not occur to them that praying for strength might be irrational. Praying for strength seems so reasonable that the question would not arise. A reasonable statement conforms well enough with accepted ways of thinking and talking that it seems right. Clearly, someone from another culture who had never heard of praying for strength could ask if this is rational behavior. "What evidence is there that God exists," the person might ask, "and how would one measure this strength?" But in ordinary situations those questions would not come up. Everyday language permits assertions to be made about God, without claiming much knowledge about what God is like, and to use a word like strength as a kind of metaphor for an emotional or mental capacity that cannot and should not be measured. While rationality is generally assumed to involve claims that can be assessed by authorities against some objective standards, reasonableness is conveyed largely through the taken-for-granted conventions of language.[16]

The contrast between reasonableness and reasoned behavior is evident in the same example. Suppose a skeptic asks, "Why do you think praying to God will give you strength?" The believer might offer as reasons, "God promises strength in such and such a verse of the Bible," or "I prayed just yesterday and I definitely felt stronger." Those would be reasons evoked by the question, "Why?" But if the question never came up, no reasons would be needed. It would simply make sense to the person speaking that a statement about God providing strength was reasonable.

Like rational behavior and reasoned behavior, what counts as reasonable behavior depends on the social context in which it occurs. The phrase "thirty is the new twenty," for example, illustrates that many people feel it is reasonable to postpone until they are thirty activities (such as marriage and childrearing) that their parents thought was reasonable to do at age twenty. Or, for example, Americans feel it is reasonable to drive 75 miles per hour on interstate highways, even though gasoline consumption, global warming, and safety considerations might suggest that the enforced limit of 55 miles per hour of a few decades ago was a still more rational alternative. Much of what counts as reasonable behavior is a feature of what other people do. If an implicit consensus emerges that behavior is reasonable, then people assume that it is in fact reasonable. In this respect, reasonableness is the default condition under which explicit reasons may not be needed. Only deviance from the accepted norm requires explanations.

Reasonableness, though, cannot be understood only as going along with the crowd. Solitary motorists notwithstanding, talk is usually an important aspect of human life. Reasonableness involves talking about activities in ways that make them seem reasonable, whether the activity is getting married, making a career choice, or simply selecting a movie. Besides talking audibly with friends and family, we make up stories and engage in silent conversations with ourselves. Talk is especially important in religion. People hear scriptures read and listen to sermons, pay attention to talk about religion on television or in music and films, and talk about it to themselves and their friends. The objects of religious talk depend especially on talk because their existence cannot otherwise be verified. If the reasonableness of other topics, such as weather predictions and definitions of social justice, is, as scholars argue, a function of talk, the reasonableness of religious claims is especially so.

I have suggested that adopting the stance taken by critics of religion helps bring into focus the fact that talk about the supernatural is problematic and thus requires construction in ways that reinforce its reasonableness. The typical middle-class American is not so philosophically wedded to naturalism as to deny the possibility of a supernatural reality. And yet the tacit epistemology of everyday life is quite naturalistic. We do not expect demons to speak, tumors to disappear instantly, or pigs to fly. Nor do we expect God to avert hurricanes or dead people to return from heaven to report what it is like. Yet the vast majority of middle-class Americans believe that God exists, pray fairly often, and claim that miracles can happen. This seeming contradiction poses the question of how people can maintain their faith in quite serious and devout ways and yet live comfortably in a society that implicitly agrees that a lot of what faith might imply simply is not reasonable.

The answer is both simple and complex. In simplest terms, people avoid saying things that are unreasonable and learn to talk in ways that do seem reasonable. The complexity is involved in the content and structure of what passes as reasonable speech. Minimally, reasonable speech established an agreement between a speaker and a listener about what can or cannot be said without becoming incomprehensible or casting the speaker in any of several socially undesirable roles, such as fanatic, bigot, or ignoramus. This implicit compact is not just a matter of being accepted, as might be the case in expressing a controversial view on social issues, but more about being understood. To be understood means that a listener can respond implicitly that the statement uttered by the speaker is intelligible and is the kind of statement that someone in the same general speech community might utter. Saying that God gives a person strength qualifies. Asserting that lucky horseshoes regenerate amputated limbs does not.

The patterns of language that enable reasonable statements about God stem from the fact that being reasonable is expected within most religious communities themselves, and from the reality that religious communities are never insulated from the rest of the society. Ted Haggard illustrates this point. His mountaintop vision could have happened at Sinai instead of in Colorado except for what he actually says. He simply envisioned God blessing his efforts to start a church. He does not say he fell into a trance or heard God speak audibly. The parallel with Moses is only implied. Similarly, the bucket of oil, he says, was his followers' idea, not his, he leaves to the imagination how it was actually used. There is a dual message that might appeal to the magically minded, but that stops short of being spooky. His later e-mail shows awareness of how to speak and behave on camera, but does not cause members to feel they are being asked to engage in deception or to deny their faith.

The language that makes it possible to talk about faith in reasonable ways is sometimes difficult to see because it is so familiar. It reflects basic cognitive schemas that scientists argue develop early in life. The assumption that objects move only when force is applied and that emotional states are different influences how people talk about God's role in their lives. This view of the world makes it easier to talk about God providing hope than magically repairing their car. Facial recognition is another example. The cognitive schema involved forges strong links with basic sentiments of love, security, and trust. These links are undoubtedly associated with the conviction that loved ones will be physically recognizable in heaven, and yet questions arise about their applicability in a spiritual context.

Another language pattern that is almost too familiar to see involves distinguishing better-known from less well-known things, and characterizing the latter in terms of the former. A stranger who comes to town is unknown, but can at least be said to dress differently and talk with an unusual accent. The familiar helps make sense of the strange, but the two are not equated. The same pattern is evident in talk about God. Critics sometimes argue that believers view God in such concrete terms that a supernatural being talks, thinks, and behaves exactly like humans, only in magical ways. In this view, a supernatural being and a lucky horseshoe can indeed be the same thing. But this is not how believers describe God. Other than in words like powerful, righteous, and loving, the language is nonspecific. God's power is implicitly defined through contrasts with human weakness. There is a spiritual realm in which God resides and acts, and this realm differs from the natural world.

An important aspect of what makes ordinary talk reasonable is the ability to back up one's assertions with implied authority. Personal experience works well for this purpose as long as it is truly personal. The easy rejoinder to a skeptic is simply to assert that nobody knows what I experienced but me. The caveat is that personal experience usually has to correspond with understandings of how the physical world operates. Thus, a person can claim to feel deeply moved by the sacred, but not to have been physically transported. If compelling authority from personal experience is lacking, assertions must be hedged with phrases such as I think, I believe, or I feel. These phrases imply that others may legitimately disagree. However, the danger of such phrases is that they reduce convictions to opinions. Thus, intensifiers, such as I really think, I firmly believe, or I strongly feel, are devices that can demonstrate conviction. Although personal experience and personal conviction lend authority to statements about faith, there are also occasions in which experts and sacred texts serve this purpose. Quoting from sermons, citing words from a favorite poem or song, or referring to verses in the Bible are examples.

Scripted speech, though, is more complicated than is sometimes assumed. Scripted speech is by definition from a source other than the speaker and thus signals distance between the statement and the speaker. This distance can either be closed or be increased, depending on how the speaker communicates the statement. "Scientists say," with an air of dismissal, is quite different from "A pastor I really respect says. . . ." "Heaven is a wonderful place" may imply a childish view of heaven that an adult no longer accepts or may indicate that heaven can only be described through music and art. Some formulaic statements, such as "look out for number one," are ways of saying that the speaker regards such views as simplistic or objectionable. Scripted speech also demonstrates that people talk to themselves, such as reciting "look on the bright side" when feeling depressed.

I have also argued that reasonableness is conveyed by speech that is heteroglossic and reflexive. Heteroglossic speech involves more than one voice. Thoughtful people are trained to think about problems from different perspectives and to consider the pros and cons of arguments. One way to do this is to speak with different voices. A person who says "I want to believe that, but my critical mind keeps me from believing" would be an example. Another example would be a person saying, "My mother always said to pray, and I respect her, but my dad was a skeptic and I'm a little like him." Expressing more than one view, even if one view is strongly favored, communicates that a person is not closed-minded. Reflexivity works similarly. An example is "I pray to God and ask him—I don't mean that God is a 'him'—but I do ask for God's blessings." The inserted qualifier indicates that there is a second speaker monitoring what the first speaker says. Thus, the person is not simply speaking, but being thoughtful about what he or she is saying.

Talk about God poses considerations that are different from discourse about most other topics. To talk reasonably about God, Americans find ways to affirm that they believe in God's existence, but at the same time steer clear of assertions that claim too much knowledge of God, or that make God too much like a human person, or that too dramatically contravene standard ways of thinking about the natural world and human behavior. Avoiding being spooky and weird is a consideration that does not arise as acutely in many other settings.

Nevertheless, the tension between saying what one can claim to know and refraining from saying more is a broader quandary that frequently calls for discursive management. Metaphors are a way of managing this tension. The unknown is expressed in terms of the known. Saying that love is like a red rose is an example. Love is difficult to know fully or to express easily, and so a red rose makes the unknown familiar. However, this is not all that metaphors do. God is not understood fully as a human father, and neither is love the same as a red rose. Metaphors express similarities, but also dramatize differences. The concrete element in the pair shows that the less concrete element is harder to describe.

Negative comparisons are also a way of demonstrating a lack of knowledge when such lack is warranted. Talk about prayer, in which the petitioner is described vividly as childlike or small, ill, and needy, is an example. The details about the petitioner show by implication that God is different, and yet what God is does not have to be spelled out. It is a bit like Dorothy's line, "Toto, I've got a feeling we're not in Kansas any more." Kansas is known. Oz is not like Kansas. Or it is like someone struggling to explain a rapturous moment, saying, "It's better than ice cream."

Another quandary involves the normalization of the unusual. Consider a person who is the first in his or her family to go to college. How does a person talk about this behavior? On the one hand, it is undesirable to deny that it is unusual. The person is thrilled at having the opportunity. On the other hand, it has to be brought sufficiently into the experiences of those hearing the story to make sense. What is called for is legitimation or as Clifford Geertz once described it, clothing beliefs with an "aura of facticity."[17] One way is simply to declare, "I'm going to college, and that's it." Be dogmatic about it. But for people who want to seem reasonable, normalization appears to be the preferred strategy. In discourse about faith, statements about the truly amazing acts of God, aspects of living in heaven, and the like, are balanced with assertions that emphasize the normality of ordinary humans. If suddenness is implied on one side of the ledger, then a slow process is mentioned. Seeming effortlessness is balanced by talk of hard work. Utter freedom evokes a discussion of making responsible choices. A mysterious blessing becomes an ability that a person has to cultivate to put into effect. The person going to college might talk in the same ways. "Surprise, I just got accepted. But I've been preparing all my life for this moment and there is a long road ahead of me." The language does no damage to the amazement of the news, but supplies reasons why it is part of ordinary life after all.

In recent approaches to the topic, culture is considered to be decidedly strategic, by which scholars mean that people say pretty much what they need to in order to get what they want. This instrumental view of culture makes sense up to a point. If it is assumed that human action is purposive, there is no reason to think the use of culture should be anything else. But this view leans easily into a more cynical interpretation, which suggests that people really do not have any values, and make things up to fit the circumstances. If culture is mostly a tool kit, the further conclusion is that the use of a hammer or saw is dictated entirely by the job a person wants to get done. But what about the deliberate switches of codes, registers, and voices that appear so often in talk about God? Can these be understood in this way?

If a speaker says God healed someone and then mentions a successful surgical procedure, or claims to have felt visited by the Holy Spirit but may have been having a nervous breakdown, what does this kind of code switching accomplish? Or if a speaker concludes a serious commentary about heaven with a lighthearted remark about wearing name tags, how is that remark to be interpreted? Is it that the tool kit user decided a hammer was not working and switched to a screwdriver? My argument in the cases where these switches have occurred is that they are indeed strategic, but not in the way the deployment of a hammer or screwdriver might suggest. They are better understood as discursive management devices that, consciously or otherwise, communicate uncertainty. They say, in effect, "I don't really know," or "Don't take what I just said too seriously." Especially remarks that are out of place, such as curse words in talking about heaven or humor in talking about tragedies, take the speaker out of frame, as it were. They invite the listener to step back from the conversation and view the dialogue from a different perspective. The speaker shows that it is possible to entertain different thoughts, including doubts, and thus to be regarded as a reasonable person. It is like saying, "That's how I see it."

NOTES

1.   The account of the founding of New Life Church is included in Ted Haggard, *Primary Purpose: Making It Hard for People to Go to Hell from Your City* (Colorado Springs, CO: Charisma House, 1995), 1–20; see also Paul Asay and Dave Philipps, "Haggard's Mecca Materialized, but Vision May Now Be Fading," *Colorado Springs Gazette* (December 32, 2006), A1.

2.   A summary of the main themes of the special can be found in David Bauder, "Barbara Walters Explores Different Beliefs on Life after Death for ABC Special," *Associated Press* (December 18, 2005). The text of Haggard's e-mail was made available as "Ted Haggard: Don't Be Weird," *Non-Prophet* (May 10, 2005), online at http://nonprophet.typepad.com/nonprophet/2005/05/ted_haggard_don.html.

3.   Ibid. Michael Roberts, "The Message: Prophetable," *Westword* (May 26, 2005), online at www.westword.com; "The Lord Works in Mediagenic Ways" (May 11, 2005), online at wonkette.com; "Sharlet on the Email, and Haggard" (May 28, 2005), online at nonprophet.typepad.com.

4.   Jeff Sharlet and Peter Manseau, *Killing the Buddha: A Heretic's Bible* (New York: Free Press, 2004); and Jeff Sharlet, "Remarks," Symposium on Religion and Media, Center for the Study of Religion, Princeton University, October 16, 2007, online at http://www.princeton.edu/csr/.

5.   Hans Gerth and C. Wright Mills, *From Max Weber: Essays in Sociology* (New York: Oxford University Press, 1958), 323–359, is the text in which Weber's thoughts about religious rejection of the world are summarized. Interpreters often suggest that Weber had in mind a four-fold typology of religion, defined by the intersection of inner-worldly and other-worldly orientations and ascetic and mystical perspectives; however, a more accurate reading of Weber shows that aspects of world rejection are characteristic, in his view, of all religions, and exist in tension with the tendency in modern societies toward rationalization of culture. On sects and churches, see especially Ernst Troeltsch, *The Social Teaching of the Christian Churches* (New York: Macmillan, 1931); a valuable discussion of the literature is available in William H. Swatos Jr., "Weber or Troeltsch? Methodology, Syndrome, and the Development of Church-Sect Theory," *Journal for the Scientific Study of Religion* 15 (1976), 129–144.

6. Much of the debate about rationality as it pertains to religion focuses on distinguishing religious truth claims from scientific ones and on refuting arguments suggesting that religion consists of propositions that are relativistic or subjective, or on examining religion within the context of modern epistemology. Some useful sources include Roger Trigg, *Rationality and Religion* (Oxford: Basil Blackwell, 1998); Jürgen Habermas, *Religion and Rationality: Essays on Reason, God, and Modernity* (Cambridge, MA: MIT Press, 2002); and Paul Helm, *Faith with Reason* (New York: Oxford University Press, 2000). My remarks here are, of course, not intended to provide an overview of this literature, but only to indicate briefly how its emphasis differs from the present focus on reasonableness.

7. Jürgen Habermas, *The Theory of Communicative Action: Reason and the Rationalization of Society* (Boston: Beacon Press, 1981).

8. Max Weber, *Economy and Society: An Outline of Interpretive Sociology* (Berkeley and Los Angeles: University of California Press, 1978), remains especially valuable as an outline of the various types of rationality through which claims about social behavior may be authoritatively assessed.

9. Toby Lester, "Oh, Gods!" *Atlantic Monthly* (February 8, 2002), online at www.theatlantic.com, offers some examples of writers who take this utilitarian approach to religion.

10. The relevance of institutions as sources of culture is emphasized in Ann Swidler, *Talk of Love* (Chicago: University of Chicago Press, 2003); and Ronald L. Jepperson and Ann Swidler, "What Properties of Culture Should We Measure?" *Poetics* 22 (1994), 359–371.

11. Bruno Latour and Steve Woolgar, *Laboratory Life: The Construction of Scientific Facts* (Princeton, NJ: Princeton University Press, 1986); Michael Mulkay, *The Embryo Research Debate: Science and the Politics of Reproduction* (New York: Cambridge University Press, 1997); Frank Dobbin, *Forging Industrial Policy: The United States, Britain, and France in the Railway Age* (New York: Cambridge University Press, 1994); John Hyde Evans, *Playing God? Human Genetic Engineering and the Rationalization of Public Bioethical Debate* (Chicago: University of Chicago Press, 2002); Wendy Nelson Espeland, *The Struggle for Water: Politics, Rationality, and Identity in the American Southwest* (Chicago: University of Chicago Press, 1998); G. Cristina Mora-Torres, "Made for TV Prayer: Transnational Pentecostalism and the Representation of Prayer in Religious Television Programming," Princeton University, Center for the Study of Religion, 2007.

12. On accounts, see especially C. Wright Mills, "Situated Actions and Vocabularies of Motive," *American Sociological Review* 5 (1940), 904–913; and Terri L. Orbuch, "People's Accounts Count: The Sociology of Accounts," *Annual Review of Sociology* 23 (1997), 455–478.

13.   A useful review of the literature on narratives is included in Roberto Franzosi, "Narrative Analysis: Or Why (and How) Sociologists Should Be Interested in Narrative," *Annual Review of Sociology* 24 (1998), 517–554.

14.   Swidler, *Talk of Love*.

15.   Robert Wuthnow, *Acts of Compassion: Caring for Others and Helping Ourselves* (Princeton, NJ: Princeton University Press, 1991).

16.   Reasonableness, as I am using the word here, is similar to what some scholars refer to as conventional behavior, or normativity. It is, however, more specific than normativity. Behavior can be normative in a variety of ways: because it is unlawful to do anything else, because no alternative options are available, because it is the most efficient way to achieve goals, because it is virtuous or heroic, and so on. Normativity on grounds of reasonableness connotes that people regard it as behavior that makes sense, shows thoughtfulness or reflection, is at least minimally informed, and can be understood by others who share these values.

17.   Clifford Geertz, *The Interpretation of Cultures* (New York: Basic Books, 1973), 90.

Appendix

The data included in chapters 2, 3, 4, and 6 are from 165 semi-structured qualitative interviews conducted between March 2006 and September 2007 as part of a larger research project concerned with the relationship between social issues and religious beliefs and practices. Respondents were selected through a non-random, multi-start quota design that maximized diversity among denominations and geographic location and included approximately equal numbers of men and women and proportionate representation of African Americans and Latinos. Respondents were identified in four ways: clergy referrals, referrals from other respondents, referrals from respondents in previous studies, and interviewer networks. Four professionally trained interviewers with different networks conducted the interviews. All four were thoroughly familiar with the particularities of the questions asked about religion. One was a male seminary student, one was a male graduate student, and two were women with extensive experience in churches and religious studies.

The interviews were conducted in 32 states and the District of Columbia: 42 of the interviews were in the Northeast, 41 in the South, 43 in the Midwest, and 39 in the West. Half of the interviewees (83) were male and half (82) were female. The median age was 50; the youngest was 18 and the oldest was 86; 27 percent were in their twenties or thirties, 22 percent were in their forties, 24 percent were in their fifties, and 27 percent were in their sixties or older. Thirty-three different religious denominations were represented. A third (34 percent) were evangelical Protestants, 26 percent were mainline Protestants, 8 percent were members of historically black Protestant denominations, 16 percent were Catholics, 7 percent were from "other" denominations (such as Christian Science and Latter-Day Saints), and 8 percent were religiously unaffiliated. Eighty-three percent had graduated from college and 50 percent had some postgraduate education. The interviewees worked in 59 different occupations. The interviews from which the information about freedom in Christ was drawn in chapter 5 were conducted separately among 32 respondents, 23 of whom were female and 9 were male, in 14 different states; all were college graduates, 11 were evangelical Protestants, 10 were mainline Protestant, 2 were members of historically black churches, and 9 were Catholics.

All interviews were conducted with permission of the interviewee according to Institutional Review Board Human Subjects requirements and with the understanding that no names would be disclosed. Interviewers were instructed to ask each question as written and then to probe where needed by asking such additional questions as, "Can you say more?" or "Please connect the dots for me." The interviews were divided into four sections: The first set of questions obtained basic background information (such as age, gender, education level, race, occupation, marital status, and religion); the second section asked general opinions about social issues (such as world hunger, climate change, and morals) and closed with several questions about the relevance of religious faith to these issues; the third section asked about the respondent's congregation (such as size, theological orientation, and typical worship service format), and the fourth section asked specific questions about prayer. All interviews were taped and professionally transcribed. The questions were:

1. For the tape, then, please state your name and spell your last name.
2. Have I explained the purpose of the study and do you give permission to record this interview?
3. Before we begin, I need to fill in some background information; for instance, I will say for the tape that you are [male/female].
4. In what year were you born?
5. So that makes you how old?
6. What was the highest year you completed in school?
7. If any college: Where did you attend college and what was your major?

8. If any post-college: What was your graduate work in?

9. What is your occupation? [If retired, ask what it was.]

10. Are you married?

11. If married, what is your spouse's education?

12. What is your religion?

13. And, for the tape, you live in [name of state].

As I mentioned, the first set of questions is about some major issues facing our world. These are complex issues. I'm not looking for right or wrong answers, just your thoughts and feelings.

1. One issue is world hunger. If the statistics are right, close to a billion people are malnourished and about 6 million children die annually from hunger. In your view, is there anything that can be done about this, or is this just the way the world is?

2. Put it in your own words for me. What are your thoughts about world hunger?

3. What kinds of feelings do you have inside when you think about world hunger?

4. Can you describe those feelings for me?

5. When you think about world hunger, is there anything that makes you feel hopeful?

6. If yes, what is that and why does it make you feel hopeful?

7. So, does world hunger mostly make you feel depressed, or is it just something you know about but you don't think about it that much?

8. Another issue is the environment. Scientists tell us that global warming could bring an end to life as we know it. Do you think the scientists are right?

9. Why or why not?

10. Tell me what your own understanding of global warming is.

11. Just how serious do you think global warming is?

12. Is it likely, in your view, that a lot of coastal areas could be flooded in the future and that there might be famines and dust storms?

13. How much does global warming worry you as you think about the world's future?

14. Can you describe your level of worry to me?

15. Shifting to another issue, a lot of people are concerned about "moral" problems: crime, child abuse, families breaking up, greed among corporate leaders, corruption government, drug use, you name it. What are some of the moral issues that worry you the most?

16. Give me a specific example, maybe a story you've heard about, that would illustrate this problem?

17. Do you think morals in our society are getting worse?

18. If yes: What are some of the reasons that morals are getting worse?

19. If no: Why don't you think they are getting worse?

20. Here is another issue: It is easy to feel overwhelmed by all the problems in the world. Do you ever feel that way?

21. If yes: Tell me about those feelings. What are they like?

22. If no: Is that because you don't think the problems are that serious, or you don't think about them, or what?

23. People also feel overwhelmed sometimes when they think about the vastness of the universe. There could be billions of galaxies and billions of planets. How does that make you feel?

24. We are one planet among billions of planets. Connect the dots for me. What does that imply?

25. For all we know, the earth may be billions of years old, but human life is fairly recent. What are your thoughts about that?

26. Do you think humanity will continue to occupy the earth indefinitely, or do you think humanity will be terminated at some point?

27. Just give me your thoughts.

Let's turn, then, to the second set of topics.

1. Tell me again what your religion is?

2. Are you currently involved in a congregation?

3. About how often do you attend worship services?

4. If any, what other activities are you involved in at your congregation, such as teaching, serving on committees, singing in the choir, or participating in a fellowship group?

5. Are you pretty happy with the congregation?

6. If yes: What do you like most about it?

7. If no: What don't you like about it?

8. How would you describe the congregation theologically—is it pretty conservative, middle-of-the-road, progressive, or what?

9. Do the issues we have been talking about—such as hunger, the environment, war, and disease—get discussed very much at your congregation?

10. If yes: Give me an example of something specific. What was discussed, who was discussing it, and what did they say?

11. If no: So where do you get information about these issues? Is it mostly from television, or where?

12. To be honest, these issues are pretty scary—global warming, nuclear war, a major epidemic, moral decay, the end of humanity. Would you agree that they are scary?

13. "Scary" was my word. How would you put it in your words?

14. When you think about these big issues, how does your faith help, or does it?

15. If yes: Give me a few sentences.

16. If no: Your faith doesn't help? Why not?

17. What do you believe about heaven?

18. Do you believe that people meet their loved ones again in heaven after they die?

19. Tell me what you believe about that.

20. Just a few more questions: About how often do you pray? That is, not just asking a blessing at meals, but actually spending some time praying to God about something?

21. When you pray, what do you pray about?

22. What would be something specific that you prayed about recently?

23. Do you pray for any of the big global issues we were talking about earlier?

24. If yes: Which ones?

25. If yes: What exactly do you ask for when you pray about these issues?

26. Do you feel that your prayers are answered?

27. If yes: What makes you feel that they are answered?

28. At the worship services you attend, am I correct in assuming that prayers are included?

29. Is there just one prayer or are there several prayers during the service?

30. I'd like you to describe the prayer or prayers for me, if you can, for a typical service. When during the service do they occur, who says the prayer, and what sorts of things are included in the prayers?

31. Think now about a recent service you attended. Can you tell me one thing in specific that somebody prayed about?

32. If you can, repeat the words that were used or give me a sense of the prayer.

33. What was the context? That is, why was this prayer included in the service?

34. Now, whether it was recent or not recent, can you recall some prayer during a worship service that has stood out in your memory?

35. Tell me about it. What was said and what were the circumstances?

36. Why has that prayer been memorable for you?

37. Some prayers are included over and over in worship services. For instance, the Lord's prayer is said every Sunday at some churches. How do you feel about that? Is it still meaningful, or does it become too routine to be meaningful?

38. Why is it meaningful to you, if it is?

39. My last question is this: If your congregation was going to do a better job of addressing some of the big global issues we talked about, what could it do?

40. That is all. Was there anything you wanted to go back to and perhaps say more about?

Thank you very much.

Selected Bibliography

Alcorn, Randy. *Heaven*. Carol Stream, IL: Tyndale House, 2004.

Araujo, Ana Cristina. "European Public Opinion and the Lisbon Earthquake." *European Review* 14 (2006): 313–319.

Arndt, J., J. Schimel, and L. Goldenberg. "Death Can Be Good for Your Health: Fitness Intentions as Proximal and Distal Defense against Mortality Salience." *Journal of Applied Social Psychology* 38 (2003): 1726–1746.

Asad, Talal. *Genealogies of Religion: Discipline and Reasons of Power in Christianity and Islam*. Baltimore: Johns Hopkins University Press, 1993.

Auer, Peter, ed. *Code-Switching in Conversation: Language, Interaction and Identity*. New York: Routledge and Kegan Paul, 1998.

Austin, J. L. *How to Do Things with Words*, 2nd ed. Cambridge, MA: Harvard University Press, 1975.

Azzi, Corry, and Ronald Ehrenberg. "Household Allocation of Time and Church Attendance." *Journal of Political Economy* 83 (1975): 27–56.

Bakhtin, M. M. *The Dialogic Imagination: Four Essays*. Austin: University of Texas Press, 1981.

———. *Speech Genres and Other Late Essays*. Austin: University of Texas Press, 1986.

Barber, Bernard. *Science and the Social Order*. New York: Free Press, 1952.

Barrett, Justin L. "How Ordinary Cognition Informs Petitionary Prayer." *Journal of Cognition and Culture* 1 (2001): 259–269.

———. "Smart Gods, Dumb Gods, and the Role of Social Cognition in Structuring Ritual Intuitions." *Journal of Cognition and Culture* 2 (2002): 183–193.

———. *Why Would Anyone Believe in God?* Lanham, MD: AltaMira Press, 2004.

Barrett, Justin L., and Frank C. Keil. "Conceptualizing a Nonnatural Entity: Anthropomorphism in God Concepts." *Cognitive Psychology* 31 (1996): 219–247.

Bauman, Richard, and Charles L. Briggs. "Poetics and Performance as Critical Perspectives on Language and Social Life." *Annual Review of Anthropology* 19 (1990): 59–88.

Ben-David, Joseph. *The Scientist's Role in Society: A Comparative Study*. Englewood Cliffs, NJ: Prentice-Hall, 1971.

Bender, Courtney. "American Reincarnations: What the Many Lives of Past Lives Tell Us about Contemporary Spiritual Practice." *Journal of the American Academy of Religion* 75 (2007): 589–614.

———. *Heaven's Kitchen: Living Religion at God's Love We Deliver*. Chicago: University of Chicago Press, 2003.

Berger, Peter L. *The Sacred Canopy: Elements of a Sociological Theory of Religion*. Garden City, NY: Doubleday, 1967.

Berger, Peter L., and Thomas Luckmann. *The Social Construction of Reality: A Treatise in the Sociology of Knowledge*. Garden City, NY: Doubleday, 1966.

Bernstein, Basil. *Class, Codes and Control*, Vol. 1: *Theoretical Studies toward a Sociology of Education*. London: Routledge and Kegan Paul, 1971.

Bernstein, Richard J. *The Abuse of Evil: The Corruption of Politics and Religion since 9/11*. Oxford: Polity, 2006.

Binder, Amy. *Contentious Curricula: Afrocentrism and Creationism in American Public Schools*. Princeton, NJ: Princeton University Press, 2002.

Black, Helen K. "Poverty and Prayer: Spiritual Narratives of Elderly African-American Women." *Review of Religious Research* 40 (1999): 359–374.

Boyd, Gregory. *Is God to Blame? Moving Beyond Pat Answers to the Problem of Evil*. Gowners Grove, IL: InterVarsity Press, 2003.

Boyer, Pascal. *Religion Explained: The Evolutionary Origins of Religious Thought*. New York: Basic, 2001.

Boyer, Pascal, and Charles Ramble. "Cognitive Templates for Religious Concepts: Cross-Cultural Evidence for Recall of Counter-Intuitive Representations." *Cognitive Science* 25 (2001): 525–564.

Burson-Tolpin, Anne. "Fracturing the Language of Biomedicine: The Speech Play of U.S. Physicians." *Medical Anthropology Quarterly* 3 (1989): 283–293.

Bushman, Richard Lyman. *Joseph Smith: Rough Stone Rolling.* New York: Knopf, 2005.

Bushnell, Horace. *Sermons for the New Life.* New York: Charles Scribner, 1858.

Carus, William. *The High-Church Theory of Baptism.* Philadelphia: Collins, 1853.

Cheal, David. "Ritual: Communication in Action." *Sociological Analysis* 53 (1992): 363–374.

Cheever, George Barrell. *God against Slavery and the Freedom and Duty of the Pulpit to Rebuke It as a Sin against God.* New York: Joseph H. Ladd, 1857.

———. *The Guilt of Slavery and the Crime of Slaveholding Demonstrated from the Hebrew and Greek Scriptures.* Boston: J. P. Jewett, 1860.

Cohan, S. L., and S. W. Cole. "Life Course Transitions and Natural Disasters: Marriage, Birth, and Divorce Following Hurricane Hugo." *Journal of Family Psychology* 16 (2002): 14–25.

Converse, Philip E. "The Nature of Belief Systems in Mass Publics." Pp. 206–261 in *Ideology and Discontent,* edited by David Apter. New York: Free Press, 1964.

Cook, Judith A., and Dale W. Wimberley. "If I Should Die before I Wake: Religious Commitment and Adjustment to the Death of a Child." *Journal for the Scientific Study of Religion* 22 (1983): 222–238.

D'Andrade, Roy. *The Development of Cognitive Anthropology.* New York: Cambridge University Press, 1995.

Davie, Grace. *Religion in Britain since 1945: Believing without Belonging.* Oxford: Blackwell, 1994.

Dawkins, Richard. *The God Delusion.* Boston: Houghton Mifflin, 2006.

———. "Is Science a Religion?" *The Humanist* (January–February 1997): 26–29.

de Witte, Marleen. "Altar Media's *Living Word*: Televised Charismatic Christianity in Ghana." *Journal of Religion in Africa* 33 (2003): 172–202.

Dechesne, M., T. Pyszczynski, J. Arndt, S. Random, K. M. Sheldon, and J. Janssen. "Literal and Symbolic Immortality: The Effect of Evidence of Literal Immortality on Self-Esteem Striving in Response to Mortality Salience." *Journal of Personality and Social Psychology* 84 (2003): 722–737.

Deneen, Patrick. *Democratic Faith.* Princeton, NJ: Princeton University Press, 2005.

Dennett, Daniel C. *Breaking the Spell: Religion as a Natural Phenomenon.* New York: Penguin, 2006.

Dewey, John. *A Common Faith.* New Haven, CT: Yale University Press, 1934.

Dillard, Annie. *For the Time Being.* New York: Knopf, 1999.

DiMaggio, Paul. "Culture and Cognition." *Annual Review of Sociology* 23 (1997): 263–287.

Dobbin, Frank. *Forging Industrial Policy: The United States, Britain, and France in the Railway Age.* New York: Cambridge University Press, 1994.

Douglas, Ann. "Heaven Our Home: Consolation Literature in the Northern United States, 1830–1880." *American Quarterly* 26 (1974): 496–515.

Douglas, Mary. *Purity and Danger: An Analysis of Concepts of Pollution and Taboo.* London: Penguin, 1966.

———. "The Social Control of Cognition: Some Factors in Joke Perception." *Man* 3 (1968): 361–376.

Douglass, Jane Dempsey. "Christian Freedom: What Calvin Learned at the School of Women." *Church History* 53 (1984): 155–173.

Drori, Gili S., John W. Meyer, Francisco O. Ramirez, and Evan Schofer. *Science in the Modern World Polity: Institutionalization and Globalization.* Stanford, CA: Stanford University Press, 2003.

D'Sousa, Dinesh. *Falwell: Before the Millennium.* Chicago: Regnery Gateway, 1984.

DuBois, J. W. "Self-Evidence and Ritual Speech." Pp. 313–336 in *Evidentiality: The Linguistic Coding of Epistemology,* edited by Wallace Chafe and Johanna Nichols. Norwood, NJ: Ablex, 1986.

Dunbar, Robin. *The Human Story: A New History of Mankind's Evolution.* London: Faber & Faber, 2004.

Duranti, Alessandro. "Truth and Intentionality." *Cultural Anthropology* 8 (1993): 214–245.

Durkheim, Emile. *The Division of Labor in Society.* New York: Free Press, 1915.

———. *Elementary Forms of the Religious Life.* Glencoe, IL: Free Press, 1915.

Ecklund, Elaine Howard. *Science vs. Religion: What Scientists Really Think.* New York: Oxford University Press.

——— and Christopher P. Scheitle. "Religion among Academic Scientists: Distinctions, Disciplines, and Demographics." *Social Problems* 54 (2007): 289–307.

Edgell, Penny, and Douglas Hartmann. "Atheists as 'Other': Moral Boundaries and Cultural Membership in American Society." *American Sociological Review* 71 (2006): 211–234.

Eisgruber, Christopher L., and Lawrence G. Sager. *Religious Freedom and the Constitution.* Cambridge, MA: Harvard University Press, 2007.

Engelke, Matthew. "Discontinuity and the Discourse of Conversion." *Journal of Religion in Africa* 34 (2004): 83–109.

Erikson, Kai T. *Everything in Its Path: Destruction of Community in the Buffalo Creek Flood.* New York: Simon and Schuster, 1976.

Espeland, Wendy Nelson. *The Struggle for Water: Politics, Rationality, and Identity in the American Southwest.* Chicago: University of Chicago Press, 1998.

Evans, John Hyde. *Playing God? Human Genetic Engineering and the Rationalization of Public Bioethical Debate*. Chicago: University of Chicago Press, 2002.

Fennell, Barbara A., and John Bennett. "Sociolinguistic Concepts and Literary Analysis." *American Speech* 66 (1991): 371–379.

Festinger, Leon. *A Theory of Cognitive Dissonance*. Evanston, IL: Row and Peterson, 1957.

Feuer, Lewis S., ed. *Marx & Engels: Basic Writings on Politics and Philosophy*. New York: Doubleday, 1959.

Fischer, Claude S., and Michael Hout. *Century of Difference: How America Changed in the Last One Hundred Years*. New York: Russell Sage Foundation, 2007.

Flynn, Charles P., and Suzanne R. Kunkel. "Deprivation, Compensation, and Conceptions of an Afterlife." *Sociological Analysis* 48 (1987): 58–72.

Frank, Thomas. *What's the Matter with Kansas? How Conservatives Won the Heart of America*. New York: Metropolitan Books, 2004.

Frankenberry, Nancy, and Hans Penner. "Geertz's Long-Lasting Moods, Motivations, and Metaphysical Conceptions." *Journal of Religion* 79 (1999): 617–640.

Franzosi, Roberto. "Narrative Analysis: Or Why (and How) Sociologists Should Be Interested in Narrative." *Annual Review of Sociology* 24 (1998): 517–554.

Frazer, James G. *The Golden Bough*, 2nd ed. London: Macmillan, 1900.

Freeman, Linton C. "Filling in the Blanks: A Theory of Cognitive Categories and the Structure of Social Affiliation." *Social Psychology Quarterly* 55 (1992): 118–127.

Freeman, Linton C., A. Kimball Komney, and Sue C. Freeman. "Cognitive Structure and Informant Accuracy." *American Anthropologist* 89 (1987): 311–325.

Fromm, Charles. *Textual Communities and New Song in the Multimedia Age: The Routinization of Charisma in the Jesus Movement*. Ph.D. dissertation, Fuller Theological Seminary, Pasadena, CA, 2006.

Funk, Charles Earle. *Heavens to Betsy and Other Curious Sayings*. New York: Harper Collins, 2002.

Gallup, George, Jr., and Michael Lindsay. *Surveying the Religious Landscape: Trends in U.S. Beliefs*. Harrisburg, PA: Morehouse, 1999.

Gardner-Chloros, Penelope. *Code-Switching*. Oxford: Blackwell, 2007.

Geertz, Clifford. *The Interpretation of Cultures*. New York: Basic Books, 1973.

Gergen, Kenneth J. *The Saturated Self: Dilemmas of Identity in Contemporary Life*. New York: Basic Books, 1991.

Gerth, Hans, and C. Wright Mills. *From Max Weber: Essays in Sociology*. New York: Oxford University Press, 1958.

Gieryn, Thomas F. "Boundary-Work and the Demarcation of Science from Non-Science: Strains and Interests in Professional Ideologies of Scientists." *American Sociological Review* 48 (1983): 781–795.

Gilliland, C. Herbert, Jr. "Limitary Patterns in 'Paradise Lost.'" *South Atlantic Bulletin* 43 (1978): 42–48.

Glock, Charles Y., Benjamin B. Ringer, and Earl R. Babbie. *To Comfort and to Challenge: A Dilemma of the Contemporary Church*. Berkeley and Los Angeles: University of California Press, 1967.

Goffman, Erving. *Interaction Ritual: Essays on Face-to-Face Behavior*. New York: Pantheon, 1982.

Gould, Stephen Jay. *Rock of Ages*. New York: Ballantine, 1999.

Graeser, Mark H. *Don't Blame God! A Biblical Answer to the Problem of Evil, Sin, and Suffering*. Indianapolis, IN: Christian Educational Services, 1994.

Grayling, A. C. *Against All Gods: Six Polemics on Religion and an Essay on Kindness*. London: Oberon, 2007.

Greeley, Andrew M., and Michael Hout. "Americans' Increasing Belief in Life after Death: Religious Competition and Acculturation." *American Sociological Review* 64 (1999): 813–835.

Griswold, Wendy. *Regionalism and the Reading Class*. Chicago: University of Chicago Press, 2007.

Groom, Winston. *Forrest Gump*. New York: Washington Square Press, 2002.

Guetzkow, Joshua, Michele Lamont, and Gregoire Mallard. "What Is Originality in the Humanities and the Social Sciences?" *American Sociological Review* 69 (2004): 190–212.

Gumperz, John J. "Contextualization and Understanding." Pp. 229–252 in *Rethinking Context: Language as an Interactive Phenomenon*, edited by Alessandro Duranti and Charles Goodwin. Cambridge: Cambridge University Press, 1992.

Habermas, Jürgen. *Religion and Rationality: Essays on Reason, God, and Modernity*. Cambridge, MA: MIT Press, 2002.

———. *The Theory of Communicative Action*. Boston: Beacon, 1987.

———. *The Theory of Communicative Action*, Vol. 2: *Lifeworld and System: A Critique of Functionalist Reason*. Boston: Beacon Press, 1981.

Haggard, Ted. *Primary Purpose: Making It Hard for People to Go to Hell from Your City*. Colorado Springs, CO: Charisma House, 1995.

Hall, G. Stanley. "Thanatophobia and Immortality." *American Journal of Psychology* 26 (1915): 560–613.

Hammond, Dorothy. "Magic: A Problem in Semantics." *American Anthropologist* 72 (1970): 1349–1356.

Harding, Susan. *The Book of Jerry Falwell: Fundamentalist Language and Politics*. Princeton, NJ: Princeton University Press, 2000.

Harley, Brian, and Glenn Firebaugh. "Americans' Belief in an Afterlife: Trends over the Past Two Decades." *Journal for the Scientific Study of Religion* 32 (1993): 269–278.

Harris, Sam. *The End of Faith: Religion, Terror, and the Future of Reason*. New York: Norton, 2004.

———. *Letter to a Christian Nation*. New York: Knopf, 2006.

Hartt, Julian N. "Christian Freedom Reconsidered: The Case of Kierkegaard." *Harvard Theological Review* 60 (1967): 133–144.

Heller, David. *The Children's God*. Chicago: University of Chicago Press, 1986.

Helm, Paul. *Faith with Reason*. New York: Oxford University, 2000.

Herberg, Will. *Protestant-Catholic-Jew: An Essay in American Religious Sociology*. Chicago: University of Chicago Press, 1955.

Hervey, Sandor. "Registering Registers." *Lingua* 86 (1992): 189–206.

Heschel, Abraham. "Answer to Einstein." *Conservative Judaism* 55 (2003): 39–41.

Hitchens, Christopher. *God Is Not Great: How Religion Poisons Everything*. New York: Twelve, 2007.

Hovet, Theodore R. "Christian Revolution: Harriet Beecher Stowe's Response to Slavery and the Civil War." *The New England Quarterly* 47 (1974): 535–549.

Hunter, James Davison. *American Evangelicalism: Conservative Religion and the Quandary of Modernity*. New Brunswick, NJ: Rutgers University Press, 1983.

———. *Culture Wars: The Struggle to Define America*. New York: Basic Books, 1991.

———. *Evangelicalism: The Coming Generation*. Chicago: University of Chicago Press, 1987.

———. "Subjectivization and the New Evangelical Theodicy." *Journal for the Scientific Study of Religion* 21 (1982): 39–47.

Hymes, Dell. "On Communicative Competence." Pp. 269–285 in *Sociolinguistics*, edited by J. B. Pride and J. Holmes. Hammondsworth: Penguin, 1972.

Iannaccone, Laurence R. "Introduction to the Economics of Religion." *Journal of Economic Literature* 36 (1998): 1465–1495.

———. "Why Strict Churches Are Strong." *American Journal of Sociology* 99 (1994): 1180–1211.

Ingram, Robert G. "The Trembling Earth in 'God's Herald': Earthquakes, Religion and Public Life in Britain During the 1750s." Pp. 97–115 in *The Lisbon Earthquake of 1755: Representations and Reactions*, edited by Theodore D. D. Braun and John B. Radner. Oxford: SVEC, 2005.

Ito, Rika, and Sali Tagliamonte. "*Well* Weird, *Right* Dodgy, *Very* Strange, *Really* Cool: Layering and Recycling in English Intensifiers." *Language in Society* 32 (2003): 257–279.

Iwasaki, Shoichi, and Preeya Ingkaphirom Horie. "Creating Speech Register in Thai Conversation." *Language in Society* 29 (2000): 519–554.

James, William. *The Varieties of Religious Experience.* New York: New American Library, 1958.

Jepperson, Ronald L., and Ann Swidler. "What Properties of Culture Should We Measure." *Poetics* 22 (1994): 359–371.

Jonte-Pace, Diane. "At Home in the Uncanny: Freudian Representations of Death, Mothers, and the Afterlife." *Journal of the American Academy of Religion* 64 (1996): 61–88.

Kavka, Martin. "The Meaning of That Hour: Prophecy, Phenomenology and the Public Sphere in the Early Heschel." Pp. 108–136 in *Religion and Violence in a Secular World: Toward a New Political Theology,* edited by Clayton Crockett. Charlottesville: University of Virginia Press, 2006.

Keane, Webb. "Religious Language." *Annual Review of Anthropology* 26 (1997): 47–71.

Kengor, Paul. *God and Ronald Reagan.* New York: Regan Books, 2004.

Kirshenblatt-Gimblett, Barbara, and Joel Sherzer. *Speech Play: Research and Resources for the Study of Linguistic Creativity.* Philadelphia: University of Pennsylvania Press, 1976.

Kosslyn, Stephen M. *Psychology: The Brain, the Person, the World.* Boston: Allyn & Bacon, 2000.

Labov, William. "Intensity." Pp. 43–70 in *Meaning, Form and Use in Context: Linguistic Applications,* edited by Deborah Schiffrin. Washington, DC: Georgetown University Press, 1985.

Lamont, Michele. *The Dignity of Working Men: Morality and the Boundaries of Race, Class, and Immigration.* Cambridge, MA: Harvard University Press, 2000.

Landau, Mark J., Michael Johns, Jeff Greenberg, Tom Pyszczynski, Andy Martens, Jamie L. Goldenberg, and Sheldon Solomon. "A Function of Form: Terror Management and Structuring the Social World." *Journal of Personality and Social Psychology* 87 (2004): 190–210.

Latour, Bruno, and Steve Woolgar. *Laboratory Life: The Construction of Scientific Facts.* Princeton, NJ: Princeton University Press, 1986.

Lawson, Erma J., and Cecelia Thomas. "Wading in the Waters: Spirituality and Older Black Katrina Survivors." *Journal of Health Care for the Poor and Underserved* 18 (2007): 341–353.

Levi-Strauss, Claude. *Structural Anthropology.* New York: Basic Books, 1963.

Lewis, C. S. *Through the Shadowlands.* Nashville, TN: Fleming H. Revell, 1994.

Lord, Charles G. "Was Cognitive Dissonance Theory a Mistake?" *Psychological Inquiry* 3 (1992): 339–342.

Malinowski, Bronislaw. *Magic, Science, and Religion.* Glencoe, IL: Free Press, 1948.

Martin, John J. "The Nature of the Atonement." *American Journal of Theology* 14 (1910): 382–405.

Martindale, Wayne. *Beyond the Shadowlands: C. S. Lewis on Heaven and Hell.* Wheaton, IL: Crossway Books, 2005.

Masuzawa, Tomoko. *The Invention of World Religions.* Chicago: University of Chicago Press, 2005.

McCutcheon, Russell T. *Manufacturing Religion: The Discourse on Sui Generis Religion and the Politics of Nostalgia.* New York: Oxford University Press, 1997.

McMinn, Lisa. "Y2k, the Apocalypse, and Evangelical Christianity: The Role of Eschatological Belief in Church Responses." *Sociology of Religion* 62 (2001): 205–220.

Miller, Donald E. *Reinventing American Protestantism: Christianity in the New Millennium.* Berkeley and Los Angeles: University of California Press, 1997.

Mills, C. Wright. "Situated Actions and Vocabularies of Motive." *American Sociological Review* 5 (1940): 904–913.

Milroy, Lesley, and Pieter Muysken, eds. *One Speaker, Two Languages.* New York: Cambridge University Press, 1996.

Morgan, David, and Iain Wildinson. "The Problem of Suffering and the Sociological Task of Theodicy." *European Journal of Social Theory* 4 (2001): 199–214.

Morison, Gary Saul, and Caryl Emerson. *Mikhail Bakhtin: Creation of a Prosaics.* Stanford, CA: Stanford University Press, 1990.

Mueller, Gustav E. "Calvin's Institutes of the Christian Religion as an Illustration of Christian Thinking." *Journal of the History of Ideas* 4 (1943): 287–300.

Mulkay, Michael. *The Embryo Research Debate: Science and the Politics of Reproduction.* New York: Cambridge University Press, 1997.

Mullen, Patrick B. "The Function of Magic Folk Belief among Texas Coastal Fisherman." *Journal of American Folklore* 82 (1969): 214–225.

Myers-Shirk, Susan E. "'To Be Fully Human': U.S. Protestant Psychotherapeutic Culture and the Subversion of the Domestic Ideal, 1945–1965." *Journal of Women's History* 12 (2000): 12–36.

National Science Foundation. *Science and Technology: Public Attitudes and Public Understanding.* Washington, DC: Government Printing Office, 2004.

Noll, Mark A. *The Scandal of the Evangelical Mind.* Grand Rapids, MI: Eerdmans, 1994.

Orbuch, Terri L. "People's Accounts Count: The Sociology of Accounts." *Annual Review of Sociology* 23 (1997): 455–478.

Orsi, Robert. *Between Heaven and Earth.* Princeton, NJ: Princeton University Press, 2005.

Osborn, Robert T. "Bultmann on Freedom." *Journal of Religion* 42 (1962): 22–33.

Parsons, Talcott. *Societies: Evolutionary and Comparative Perspectives.* Englewood Cliffs, NJ: Prentice-Hall, 1966.

Poloma, Margaret M., and George H. Gallup Jr. *Varieties of Prayer: A Survey Report*. Philadelphia: Trinity Press International, 1991.

Price, Don K. *The Scientific Estate*. Cambridge, MA: Harvard University Press, 1965.

Prothero, Stephen. *Religious Literacy: What Every American Needs to Know—and Doesn't*. New York: Harper, 2007.

Pyszczynski, Tom, Sheldon Soloman, and Jeff Greenberg. *In the Wake of 9/11: The Psychology of Terror*. Washington, DC: American Psychological Association, 2003.

Rawls, John. *Political Liberalism*. New York: Columbia University Press, 1993.

Redman, Ben Ray. *The Portable Voltaire*. New York: Viking, 1949.

Ricoeur, Paul. *Freud and Philosophy*. Boston: Beacon, 1970.

Rodgers, Joseph Lee, Craig A. St. John, and Ronnie Coleman. "Did Fertility Go Up after the Oklahoma City Bombing? An Analysis of Births in Metropolitan Counties in Oklahoma, 1990–1999." *Demography* 42 (2005): 675–692.

Rogers, Richard L. "The Role of Elites in Setting Agendas for Public Debate: A Historical Case." Pp. 234–247 in *Vocabularies of Public Life: Empirical Essays in Symbolic Structure*, edited by Robert Wuthnow. London and New York: Routledge, 1992.

Rorty, Richard. *Philosophy and Social Hope*. New York: Penguin, 1999.

———. "Religion as a Conversation Stopper." *Common Knowledge* 3 (1994): 1–6.

Roth, Andrew L. "Social Epistemology in Broadcast News Interviews." *Language in Society* 31 (2002): 355–381.

Sadovnik, A. R., ed. *Knowledge and Pedagogy: The Sociology of Basil Bernstein*. Norwood, NJ: Ablex, 1995.

Schilbrack, Kevin. "Religion, Models of, and Reality: Are We Through with Geertz?" *Journal of the American Academy of Religion* 73 (2005): 429–452.

Schirmer, Daniel, and Stephen Rosskamm Shalon, eds. *The Philippines Reader*. Boston: South End Press, 1987.

Schmidt, Leigh. *Hearing Things: Religion, Illusion, and the American Enlightenment*. Cambridge, MA: Harvard University Press, 2000.

———. *Restless Souls: The Making of American Spirituality from Emerson to Oprah*. San Francisco: Harper Collins, 2005.

Schrijvers, Joep P. M. *The Way of the Rat: A Survival Guide to Office Politics*. London: Cyan Communications, 2004.

Sharlet, Jeff, and Peter Manseau. *Killing the Buddha: A Heretic's Bible*. New York: Free Press, 2004.

Shevtsova, Maria. "Dialogism in the Novel and Bakhtin's Theory of Culture." *New Literary History* 23 (1992): 747–763.

Sibley, Brian. *Through the Shadowlands: The Love Story of C. S. Lewis and Joy Davidman*. Nashville, TN: Revell, 2005.

Silverman, Kenneth. *The Life and Times of Cotton Mather*. New York: Columbia University Press, 1985.

Singleton, Andrew. "'Your Faith Has Made You Well': The Role of Storytelling in the Experience of Miraculous Healing." *Review of Religious Research* 43 (2001): 121–138.

Smith, Christian. *Soul Searching: The Religious and Spiritual Lives of American Teenagers*. New York: Oxford University Press, 2005.

Snow, C. P. "The Two Cultures." *New Statesman* 52 (1956): 413–414.

Stark, Laura. *Morality in Science: Evaluating Research in the Age of Human Subjects Regulation*. Ph.D. dissertation, Princeton University, Department of Sociology, Princeton, NJ, 2006.

Stenger, Victor J. *God: The Failed Hypothesis, How Science Shows That God Does Not Exist*. New York: Prometheus, 2007.

Stepan, Alfred. "Religion, Democracy, and the 'Twin Tolerations.'" *Journal of Democracy* 11 (2000): 37–57.

Stout, Jeffrey. *Democracy and Tradition*. Princeton, NJ: Princeton University Press, 2003.

Strober, Gerald, and Ruth Tomczak. *Jerry Falwell: Aflame for God*. Nashville, TN: Thomas Nelson, 1979.

Suckiel, Ellen Kappy. *Heaven's Champion: William James's Philosophy of Religion*. Notre Dame, IN: University of Notre Dame Press, 1996.

Sue, Christina A., and Edward E. Telles. "Assimilation and Gender in Naming." *American Journal of Sociology* 112 (2007): 1383–1415.

Swatos, William H., Jr. "Weber or Troeltsch? Methodology, Syndrome, and the Development of Church-Sect Theory." *Journal for the Scientific Study of Religion* 15 (1976): 129–144.

Swidler, Ann. *Talk of Love: How Culture Matters*. Chicago: University of Chicago Press, 2003.

Taves, Ann. *Fits, Trances, and Visions*. Princeton, NJ: Princeton University Press, 1999.

Thumma, Scott, and Dave Travis. *Beyond Megachurch Myths: What We Can Learn from America's Largest Churches*. San Francisco: Jossey-Bass, 2007.

Tillich, Paul. *The Courage to Be*. New Haven, CT: Yale University Press, 2000.

Tooby, John, and Leda Cosmides. "The Psychological Foundations of Culture." Pp. 19–136 in *The Adapted Mind: Evolutionary Psychology and the Generation of Culture*, edited by Jerome H. Barkow, Leda Cosmides and John Tooby. New York: Oxford University Press, 1992.

Trigg, Roger. *Rationality and Religion*. Oxford: Basil Blackwell, 1998.

Troeltsch, Ernst. *The Social Teaching of the Christian Churches.* New York: Macmillan, 1931.

Turner, Victor. *The Ritual Process: Structure and Anti-Structure.* New York: Aldine, 1969.

Tweed, Thomas A. "Marking Religion's Boundaries: Constitutive Terms, Orienting Tropes, and Exegetical Fussiness." *History of Religions* 44 (2005): 252–276.

Tylor, Edward B. *Primitive Culture,* 2nd ed. New York: Holt, 1889.

Ure, Jean. "Approaches to the Study of Register Range." *International Journal of the Sociology of Language* 35 (1982): 5–23.

van den Bos, K., and J. Miedema. "Toward Understanding Why Fairness Matters: The Influence of Mortality Salience on Reactions to Procedural Fairness." *Journal of Personality and Social Psychology* 79 (2000): 355–366.

Voltaire. *Candide or Optimism.* Translated by Robert M. Adams. New York: Norton, 1966.

Weber, Max. *Economy and Society.* Berkeley and Los Angeles: University of California Press, 1978.

———. *The Protestant Ethic and the Spirit of Capitalism.* New York: Charles Scribner, 1948.

———. *Sociology of Religion.* Boston: Beacon, 1963.

Wesley, Charles. *Hymns Occasioned by the Earthquake, March 8, 1750, to Which Is Added an Hymn Upon the Pouring Out of the Seventh Vial, Rev. Xvi.Xvii Occasioned by the Destruction of Lisbon.* Bristol: E. Farley, 1756.

Wolfe, Alan. *One Nation, after All: What Americans Really Think about God, Country, Family, Racism, Welfare, Immigration, Homosexuality, Work, the Right, the Left, and Each Other.* Baltimore: Penguin, 1999.

———. *The Transformation of American Religion: How We Actually Practice Our Faith.* New York: Free Press, 2003.

Wuthnow, Robert. *Acts of Compassion: Caring for Others and Helping Ourselves.* Princeton, NJ: Princeton University Press, 1991.

———. *After Heaven: Spirituality in America since the 1950s.* Berkeley and Los Angeles: University of California Press, 1998.

———. *After the Baby Boomers: How Twenty- and Thirty-Somethings Are Shaping the Future of American Religion.* Princeton, NJ: Princeton University Press, 2007.

———. *All in Sync: How Music and Art Are Revitalizing American Religion.* Berkeley and Los Angeles: University of California Press, 2003.

———. *America and the Challenges of Religious Diversity.* Princeton, NJ: Princeton University Press, 2005.

———. *Meaning and Moral Order: Explorations in Cultural Analysis.* Berkeley and Los Angeles: University of California Press, 1987.

———. "Trust as an Aspect of Social Structure." Pp. 145–167 in *Self, Social Structure, and Beliefs: Explorations in Sociology,* edited by Jeffrey Alexander, Gary T. Marx, and Christine L. Williams. Berkeley and Los Angeles: University of California Press, 2004.

———, James Davison Hunter, Albert Bergesen, and Edith Kurzweil. *Cultural Analysis: The Work of Peter L. Berger, Mary Douglas, Michel Foucault, and Jürgen Habermas.* London: Routledge and Kegan Paul, 1984.

Zaleski, Philip, and Carol Zaleski. *Prayer: A History.* New York: Houghton Mifflin, 2005.

Index

ABC News survey, 120
ability, Christian freedom and, 227–29, 231
accounts: anticipatory, 293; reasons and, 293–94
action: catastrophic danger and motivation for human, 142; prayers asking for God's, 59–60, 62–65, 67–68, 88–89; schemas and, 59
addiction, Christian freedom and recovery from, 231–36, 245
afterlife, belief in, 155. *See also* heaven
Against All Gods (Grayling), 1
aging, belief in life after death and, 158, 208*n*16
agnostics, professors as, 21
Alcorn, Randy, 181
All Dogs Go to Heaven (film), 178
altruism, individualism and, 265
ambiguity, code switching and, 81
ambivalence, over who will be in heaven, 190–97
American culture: corrosive effect on religion, 32–33; freedom in Christ and, 238–41

American higher education, failure to educate students on religion, 27–28
American public opinion: belief in God, 2–3, 20, 21–22, 26–29; belief in heaven, 155, 158, 161, 206*n*3, 208*n*16; belief in miracles, 20, 47, 114–15; on comfort offered by religion, 102; effect of scientific advances on religious belief, 20–21, 26; on God's role in Hurricane Katrina, 120–21; prayer, 22–24; on science, 260, 269; on science and religion, 252–54
angels, 195
answered prayer blogs, 48
anthropomorphizing God, schema alignment and, 61–62, 62–63, 87
anticipatory accounts, 293
antidemocratic nature of belief in God, 13–15
anti-slavery movement, Christian freedom and, 220
atheists: Dawkins and, 11; dogmatic, 17; free inquiry and, 13; professors as, 21; scientists as, 262–63
Atkinson, Richard C., 261–62
atonement, 247*n*13